RETELLINGS

Lauer Series in Rhetoric and Composition
Editors: Thomas Rickert and Jennifer Bay

The Lauer Series in Rhetoric and Composition honors the contributions Janice Lauer has made to the emergence of Rhetoric and Composition as a disciplinary study. It publishes scholarship that carries on Professor Lauer's varied work in the history of written rhetoric, disciplinarity in composition studies, contemporary pedagogical theory, and written literacy theory and research.

Books in the Series

Creole Composition: Academic Writing and Rhetoric in the Anglophone Caribbean (Milson-Whyte, Oenbring, & Jaquette, 2019)
Retellings: Opportunities for Feminist Research in Rhetoric and Composition Studies (Enoch & Jack, 2019)
Facing the Sky: Composing through Trauma in Word and Image (Fox, 2016)
Expel the Pretender: Rhetoric Renounced and the Politics of Style (Wiederhold, 2015)
First-Year Composition: From Theory to Practice (Coxwell-Teague & Lunsford, 2014)
Contingency, Immanence, and the Subject of Rhetoric (Richardson, 2013)
Rewriting Success in Rhetoric & Composition Careers (Goodburn, LeCourt, Leverenz, 2012)
Writing a Progressive Past: Women Teaching and Writing in the Progressive Era (Mastrangelo, 2012)
Greek Rhetoric Before Aristotle, 2e, Rev. and Exp. Ed. (Enos, 2012)
Rhetoric's Earthly Realm: Heidegger, Sophistry, and the Gorgian Kairos (Miller) *Winner of the Olson Award for Best Book in Rhetorical Theory 2011
Techne, from Neoclassicism to Postmodernism: Understanding Writing as a Useful, Teachable Art (Pender, 2011)
Walking and Talking Feminist Rhetorics: Landmark Essays and Controversies (Buchanan & Ryan, 2010)
Transforming English Studies: New Voices in an Emerging Genre (Ostergaard, Ludwig, & Nugent, 2009)
Ancient Non-Greek Rhetorics (Lipson and Binkley, 2009)
Roman Rhetoric: Revolution and the Greek Influence, Rev. and Exp Ed. (Enos, 2008)
Stories of Mentoring: Theory and Praxis (Eble and Gaillet, 2008)
Writers Without Borders: Writing and Teaching in Troubled Times (Bloom, 2008)
1977: A Cultural Moment in Composition (Henze, Selzer, and Sharer, 2008)
*The Promise and Perils of Writing Program Administration (*Enos & Borrowman, 2008)
Untenured Faculty as Writing Program Administrators: Institutional Practices and Politics, (Dew and Horning, 2007)
Networked Process: Dissolving Boundaries of Process and Post-Process (Foster, 2007)
Composing a Community: A History of Writing Across the Curriculum (McLeod and Soven, 2006)
Historical Studies of Writing Program Administration: Individuals, Communities, and the Formation of a Discipline (L'Eplattenier and Mastrangelo, 2004). Winner of the WPA Best Book Award for 2004–2005
Rhetorics, Poetics, and Cultures: Refiguring College English Studies Exp. Ed. (Berlin, 2003)

RETELLINGS

Opportunities for Feminist Research in Rhetoric and Composition Studies

Edited by Jessica Enoch and Jordynn Jack

Parlor Press
Anderson, South Carolina
www.parlorpress.com

Parlor Press LLC, Anderson, South Carolina, USA

© 2019 by Parlor Press
All rights reserved.

Printed in the United States of America
S A N: 2 5 4 - 8 8 7 9

Library of Congress Cataloging-in-Publication Data on File

1 2 3 4 5

Lauer Series in Rhetoric and Composition
Editors: Thomas Rickert and Jennifer Bay

Cover design by David Blakesley.
Cover image: "Starry Night and the Astronauts" by Alma Thomas. © 1972. Art Insitute of Chicago. Restricted gift of Mary P. Hines in memory of her mother, Frances W. Pick

Printed on acid-free paper.

Parlor Press, LLC is an independent publisher of scholarly and trade titles in print and multimedia formats. This book is available in paper, cloth and eBook formats from Parlor Press on the World Wide Web at http://www.parlorpress.com or through online and brick-and-mortar bookstores. For submission information or to find out about Parlor Press publications, write to Parlor Press, 3015 Brackenberry Drive, Anderson, South Carolina, 29621, or email editor@parlorpress.com.

Contents

Acknowledgments   *vii*

1 Introduction: The Endless Opportunities for Feminist Research   *3*
   Jessica Enoch, Jordynn Jack, and Cheryl Glenn

Part I: Feminist Rhetoric in Contemporary Global Politics   *17*

2 Bending Toward Justice: Women's Rhetorical Performances—Local and Transnational, Then and Now   *19*
   Shirley Wilson Logan

3 Silence and Listening: The War On/Over Women's Bodies in the 2012 US Election Cycle   *34*
   Krista Ratcliffe

4 "Beyond-Gender" Analysis of Power Relations in Language: The Case of Net Hate in the Nordic Countries   *54*
   Brigitte Mral
   Translated by Judith Rinker Öhman

5 Philanthropic War Narratives and Spectacular Protection Scenarios   *68*
   Berit von der Lippe

Part II: Feminist Rhetoric and Identity Studies   *93*

6 "As Sisters in Zion": Constructing Mormon Women's Identity through the Spatial Topos of Zion   *95*
   Rosalyn Collings Eves

7 Closets and Classification: The Archive as an Epistemic Resource for Identity   *117*
   Jean Bessette

Part III: Feminist Methods and Methodologies 137

8 Institutional "Protections," Assumptions of Research, and the Challenges of Compliance: Opening a Conversation Space for Feminist Scholars Working with Participants *139*
   Heather Brook Adams

9 *Abuela, si estas aquí*: Writing Our Histories as Liberatory Praxis *163*
   Cristina D. Ramírez

10 Opening the Scholarly Conversation *183*
   Wendy B. Sharer

11 Fragile Archives: Questions of Survival, Rhetorical Listening, and Breast Cancer Narrative *202*
   Anita Helle

Part IV: Feminist Teaching and Mentoring 223

12 "I Don't Read Such Small Stuff as Letters, I Read Men and Nations": Reading the World with Black Middle School Girls *225*
   Elaine Richardson

13 In Theory and Practice: Constructing an Embodied Feminist Rhetorical Pedagogy *246*
   A. Abby Knoblauch

14 Teaching Interpretive Agency: Introducing Constructed Potentiality into Rhetorical Training *262*
   Sonja K. Foss and Karen A. Foss

15 Re-inscribing Mentoring *283*
   Michelle Eble and Lynée Lewis Gaillet

Contributors *305*

Index *313*

Acknowledgments

Retellings would not be possible without the rigorous scholarship, steadfast mentorship, and enduring friendship of Cheryl Glenn. She has touched and supported each person in the collection in deep and important ways, and we want this book to mark her contribution to the field and to our lives. Our appreciation goes to our contributors for their thoughtful arguments, engaging writing, and enduring patience. We're thrilled that this conversation has made it into print. We are especially grateful to Parlor Press editor David Blakesley for his stewardship, encouragement, and speed. It has been an absolute pleasure working with the Parlor Press team. We thank the anonymous reviewers to this collection for their critical feedback; the book is better due to their comments. Funding from the University of Maryland and the University of North Carolina, Chapel Hill (particularly the Chi Omega Term Distinguished Professorship) helped bring this book to production. And finally, we thank our personal support teams: For Jess, *Retellings* would not have moved from beginning to end without the encouragement from Scott, Jack, Nancy, and Teddy. For Jordynn, this project could not have succeeded without support from Ryon, Penelope, and Frankie.

Retellings

1 Introduction: The Endless Opportunities for Feminist Research

Jessica Enoch, Jordynn Jack, and Cheryl Glenn

> [W]e do not have to compete for bits of female rhetoric, nor do we have to scramble after a few pages of women's letters. . . . [T]he opportunities for feminist work are endless.
>
> —Cheryl Glenn, *Rhetoric Retold*, 177–78

As collaborators, we, Jess, Jordynn, and Cheryl, write this introduction together to mark an anniversary and to set the course for this collection—a collection that takes stock of and imagines new opportunities for feminist rhetorical studies. In 1997, Cheryl published *Rhetoric Retold: Regendering the Rhetorical Tradition from Antiquity to the Renaissance*, the first continuous history of rhetoric inclusive of women. As two scholars coming of age in the wake of *Rhetoric Retold*'s publication, Jess and Jordynn understood and witnessed the wide-ranging influence of this book. Moving into its third edition, taught frequently at the undergraduate and graduate level, and found on students' comprehensive lists across the country, the book has sustained a significant place in our field's conversations. Scholars have found *Rhetoric Retold* useful in studies of African American, Chinese, and Native American women; of rhetorics of the body; and of women politicians, scientists, and journalists. Beyond that, it has been cited by scholars in history, education, literature, and religious studies. But more personal, anecdotal stories also attest to the importance of this text.

The first piece of feminist historiography Jess read in graduate school, this book is now dog-eared and has loose pages, but on page seven is a passage that she continues to come back to and that has propelled her scholarship forward: "histories *do* (or *should do*) something, . . . they fulfill our needs at particular times and places" (Glenn 7). Her work in rhetorical education, historiographic methods, spatial rhetorics, and memory studies has been driven by Cheryl's invitation to think about what histories should do for us and our students. Jordynn first read *Rhetoric Retold* in a graduate history of rhetoric seminar while also taking a course on Feminist Science Studies. *Rhetoric Retold* inspired her dissertation project on women in the history of science. These women, she found, paralleled the women rhetors Glenn studies in that understanding their rhetorics required more than a regendering of the male-dominated history. It necessitated a recognition that history (of rhetoric, of science) should not merely be "compensatory or additive" (Glenn 10), but performative, requiring a rethinking of the conceptual foundations of that field. This insight prompted Jordynn's dissertation project and first book, *Science on the Home Front*, where she considers how scientific rhetorics (as part of the institution of science as a whole) continued to disavow women's contributions and unique perspectives, even during a time when women's participation in science was actively encouraged.

Of course, we are not alone in acknowledging how *Rhetoric Retold* has catalyzed our work. A contributor to this volume, Cristina Ramírez, found inspiration in *Rhetoric Retold* for her recovery of *mestiza* rhetors. She reflects on her relationship with the book in this way:

> As a graduate student, I read chapter one of *Rhetoric Retold*, "Mapping the Silences, or Remapping Rhetorical Territory" countless times. I carefully deciphered its feminist theoretical frame, as well as the call for future research. Sensing that [Cheryl] was speaking to me when she wrote, "[T]he feminist challenge is vital to locating invisible and silenced women and restoring them and their voices to rhetorical history" (2), I picked up my own pen and journal and visited the archives in Mexico. I searched the discursive histories of Mexico, looking for women who had been forgotten and left behind.

Ramírez's words echo the comments of Jess and Jordynn: it is not so much what *Rhetoric Retold taught* many budding feminist scholars, but what this book *did* for them and how passages and ideas from the book enabled them to imagine ways they might contribute to this conversation and do their own work.

Another contributor, Shirley Wilson Logan, underscores the importance of *Rhetoric Retold*, explaining that this book is the "the go-to text for teachers and researchers who want to break the silence around the question of women's always already participation in the development of rhetoric and rhetorical theory" (email). Paging through her copy filled with "marginalia and post-it notes," she finds one "heavily underlined passage" that continues to "prod [her] to attend to all that is yet to be done: 'Exploration into silence, silences, and silencing works to remind us of how very much more about women's silence we have to learn' (177)." Here, Logan highlights two key feminist investments: restless inquiry into and relentless reflection on silences and erasures of all kinds. In response to these investments, feminist scholars ask different questions, challenge received scholarship, test the efficacy of staid research methods, and chart new scholarly agendas. And they must do so with the full knowledge that their answers may only be provisional, may serve best as a stepping stone or even revision point for the next researcher.

This kind of inquiry and reflection is the project for *Retellings: Opportunities for Feminist Research in Rhetorical Studies*. In this collection, the contributors see the anniversary of *Rhetoric Retold*'s publication as a kairotic moment to assess feminist rhetorical research and test out new possibilities. As editors of the collection, Jess and Jordynn asked contributors to explore what it means to do feminist rhetorical research after twenty years and more of prolific scholarly productivity. They ask and answer together, what does it or should it mean to engage rhetoric from a feminist perspective? In response, contributors zeroed in on four particular trajectories of research and intellectual inquiry:

1. The place of feminist rhetoric in contemporary (real-world and transnational) politics;
2. The relationship between feminist rhetorical studies and identity studies;
3. Feminist research methods and methodologies;
4. The feminist rhetorical commitment to "paying it forward" through teaching and mentoring.

In what follows, we describe each of these points in further detail, demonstrating how and why they are crucial for feminist rhetorical researchers to pursue and explaining the ways the contributors in each section approach them from their own scholarly perspectives. Important to note, though, is that as these scholars pursue these four research trajectories, they do so by keeping key feminist principles in play. Borrowing from Jacqueline Jones Royster and Gesa Kirsch, the scholars here make use of feminist practices of critical imagination and strategic contemplation. Leveraging critical imagination, contributors deploy a heuristic "mechanism" that "brings attention to the challenge of expanding knowledge and re-forming not only what constitutes knowledge but also whether and how we value and accredit it" (Royster and Kirsch 20). And embracing strategic contemplation, the scholars "tak[e] the time, space, and resources to think about, through, and around [their] work as an important meditative dimension of scholarly productivity" (Royster and Kirsch 21).

A last point before we move on: we want to make clear that the four concerns contributors developed are meant to be inventional, invitational, and organizational. That is, they are not meant to circumscribe all that feminist scholarship should be or what scholars should do. Certainly, there are many arguments left unsaid. Indeed, we are cognizant that *Retellings* does not investigate the full spectrum of raced, gendered, and cultured groups; it does not exercise all relevant methods and methodologies or theorize all possibilities for rhetorical production—the digital being a significant one. Yet, as Cheryl writes in the opening epigraph, we must always remember the "endless opportunities" before us. Complimenting this understanding is the reminder that there is no need to "compete" for research and against one another; rather the goal is for scholars to collaborate, build on one another's findings, and even wrestle in productive agonism with the intention of carving out a complex, complicated, expansive, and ever-expanding understanding of feminist rhetorical studies. Indeed, Cheryl's words should shift (and have shifted!) the relationship of scholars to their work and to one another. Instead of self-interestingly guarding one's findings and research subjects or pinpointing a lack or what's *not* been done, we should be working together; we should be in conversation with one another (as feminist rhetorician Jane Donawerth admonishes us to do) to explore how much more we can do together. Only by coalescing across our differences and despite our self-interests can we begin to realize the infinite opportunities to invigorate our field and to think anew about our work. Simply put, we must work together if we are going to transform the study of rhetoric and retell its history.

THE PLACE OF FEMINIST RHETORIC IN CONTEMPORARY (REAL-WORLD AND TRANSNATIONAL) POLITICS.

Today, more women than ever serve as political leaders, from Namibian President Saara Kuugongelwa to Taiwanese President Tsai Ing-wen to Germany's Chancellor Angela Merkel. Yet, overall, and as the 2016 presidential election in the United States came to prove, women's participation in politics continues to lag behind, especially in the US, where in 2019 only 20 percent of the House of Representatives and 23 percent of the Senate are women. At present, then, the United States ranks 78th in the world in terms of the number of women in government.[1] More broadly, issues associated with women (wages, job opportunities, and reproductive rights) continue to be used as wedge issues in political races, with these same issues remaining under attack across the globe (along with those of LGBTQ, non-white, indigenous, and poor people). Politics continue to be driven by masculinist privilege, power, and domination over others, where women candidates are maligned and attacked by their opponents, and where candidates such as Donald Trump are even elected after admitting to sexual assault and excusing it as "locker room" talk. The 2016 election is a critical reminder that feminist rhetorical analysis and intervention is absolutely necessary to navigate the world in which we live. Angela Davis's words have become a clarion call for post-election feminist political action: "I am no longer accepting the things I cannot change. I am changing the things I cannot accept." Thus, the role of feminist rhetoric in contemporary and global politics is, now more than ever, to *do something*. Feminist rhetors and rhetoricians use their discursive power to confront the continued silencing and marginalization of women and other vulnerable groups. They also use it to demonstrate how discursive power (feminist rhetorical agency, no less) can bring people together to imagine new modes of being, or even to understand the ways our linguistic and embodied practices keep us apart.

Engaging these concerns, the contributors in Section 1 show how feminist rhetorical research can grapple with contemporary politics as well as international and transnational political concerns. In chapter 2, "Bending Towards Justice: Women's Rhetorical Performances—Local

---

1. In comparison, Sweden ranks fifth, with forty-seven percent of its Parliament composed of women. Rwanda ranks first, where women comprise sixty-one percent of the government, and Rwandan women gained suffrage in 1961, in comparison to Swedish and American women, who gained suffrage in 1921 and 1920, respectively. See http://archive.ipu.org/wmn-e/classif.htm.

and Transnational, Then and Now," Shirley Wilson Logan examines the ways twenty-first century women develop moral authority out of the experience of injustice through the rhetorical strategy she terms *righteous discontent*. Here, Logan traces this rhetorical strategy not only transnationally, noting its use by Leymah Gbowee (Liberia), Tawakkol Karman (Yemen), Aung San Suu Kyi (Burma), Nikky Finney (US), and Angela Davis (US), but also transhistorically. Locating righteous discontent in speeches by nineteenth-century African American rhetors Caroline Healy Dall, Maria Stewart, and Francis Harper, Logan demonstrates how common rhetorical tactics develop out of similar rhetorical situations women have faced across space and time.

In a turn to the recent history of US politics, Krista Ratcliffe examines in chapter 3 how the "war on women" trope circulated during the 2012 presidential election and investigates her own response using the methods of rhetorical listening. In this way, she reimagines her own stunned silence around the reemergence of antiquated arguments about women's rights to their own bodies, finding in these debates a site for invention as well as intervention. In the wake of the 2016 election, Ratcliffe's examination becomes even more poignant and prescient.

Chapters 4 and 5 continue to explore the rhetorical significance of silence. Brigitte Mral investigates a contemporary example of silencing in a different international context: the phenomenon of "net hate" in Nordic countries. Like Ratcliffe, she finds strategies of resistance in women's refusal to be silenced by online intimidation and threats. In the final chapter in this section, Berit von der Lippe examines the silencing that first-world women sometimes impose on third-world women. She takes as her case study the political discourse of two women Norwegian defense ministers, both of whom drew upon feminist discourses of gender equality to further their own political careers at the expense of Afghan women, whose voices were silenced.

THE RELATIONSHIP BETWEEN FEMINIST RHETORICAL STUDIES AND IDENTITY STUDIES

Given that feminist rhetorical studies, like feminist studies, has too often been criticized for being the domain of mostly white middle-class heterosexual women, feminist rhetoricians must now make generative connections between feminist rhetorical studies and identity studies. Such a connection means that feminist scholars do not treat gender alone.

Instead, the imperative is clear that our own identities and the identities of the figures we study are *intersectional*—a term coined by Kimberlé Crenshaw and one that Leslie McCall writes is "the most important contribution that women's studies has made so far" (1771). Embracing, acknowledging, and interrogating intersectionality means that we move to understand how one mode of identity—gender—is shaped, complicated, and enriched by race, culture, class, sexuality, religion, disability, and nationality, among a legion of other factors. Indeed, the work by all of the scholars in this volume underscores the fact that women are not just women but are African American, Afghan, Nigerian, Nordic, Chicana, working class, middle class, upper class, (dis)enfranchised, heterosexual, lesbian, single women, mothers, and of course more. Adrienne Rich aptly captures this intersectional stance—one she identifies as a politics of location—when she writes, "I need to understand how a place on the map is also a place in history within which as a woman, a Jew, a lesbian, a feminist I am created and trying to create" (212). We are thus each unique amalgams of a range of differences, and we should make sure this basic truth sits at the foundation of our feminist research agendas and scholarly projects.

Feminist rhetoricians, though, must go further than acknowledging the animating power of difference. First and most obviously, there is critical work in expanding our scholarly vision beyond the white, able-bodied, middle-class, heterosexual woman to include in our studies the work of *Other* women. But a key part of this expansion is to realize how intersectional identities shape both rhetorical production and rhetorical analysis. The identities we inhabit are indeed epistemic, knowledge generating resources (see Appiah, Lloyd, Moya, Mohanty, Rich), but they are also heuristic, enabling, shaping, and inspiring rhetorical production and hermeneutics. Rich herself gestures to this point in the quotatio above when she separates locational politics into two parts (1) understanding who we are and how *we are created* and (2) interrogating how the identities we inhabit inflect *our creations*, our rhetorics. For feminist rhetorical scholars, point two is critical: who we are shapes what we say and how we interpret. But, of course, we can push this point further. Feminist rhetorical approaches to politics of location and intersectional identities should also include engagements with cross-identity conversations that result in what Krista Ratcliffe has defined as rhetorical listening as well as rhetorical mis-steps and even rhetorical failures. Looking especially to the work of Elizabeth Miller and Stacey Sheriff, feminist scholars should also leverage an intersectional analytical lens to understand better what impedes coalition building in the face of difference.

The scholars in section 2 take up this work, as these contributors circle back to Rich's focus on how place inflects both identity construction and rhetorical production. In chapter 6, Rosalyn Collings Eves demonstrates the ways geographical places serve as a resource for identity, taking as her case the nineteenth-century Mormon rhetor Eliza P. Snow. For Snow, the landscape of the American West, particularly Utah, represents a place of separation and uniqueness that shored up the separate and unique identity of Mormon women. In chapter 7, Jean Bessette turns to a different physical site where identities can be invented and rhetorically constituted: the Lesbian Herstory Archives in New York City. Bessette argues that the physical layout of the archives and the ways they juxtapose different kinds of artifacts open up alternatives to the dominant, often pathologized narratives of lesbian identity. Both Eves and Bessette, then, contend that identity can be understood by feminist rhetoricians as rooted in place, yet this construction of identity is inflected by how individuals embody and shape those places themselves.

The Rethinking of Research Methods and Methodologies

Traditionally, research methods in rhetoric (as in other fields) have been grounded in the concept of *objectivity*. Feminist scholars have argued, however, that the very concept of objectivity is a research stance available only to people who already have power and cultural capital. In science, for instance, Evelyn Fox Keller has argued that an emphasis on objectivity elides the many personal choices that make up a scientific research program: "Judgments about which phenomena are worth studying, which kinds of data are significant—as well as which descriptions (or theories) of those phenomena are most adequate, satisfying, useful, and even reliable—depend critically on the social, linguistic, and scientific practices of those making the judgments in question" (11). Historically, those who have been in the position to make such subjective choices—but label them as objective—have been white empowered men.

Carol Gilligan's work is a case in point. When she investigated the moral development of girls and compared that moral development with the allegedly universal moral development theories that Lawrence Kolberg had established with his study of boys, Gilligan—not Kolberg—

was charged with conducting *subjective* research. Gilligan is just one of a number of feminist researchers who unveiled the subjectivity lurking behind any so-called objective study, showing us that doing research does not mean denying our subjectivity, but rather taking responsibility for it, openly acknowledging what it is we are trying to find out—and why we are trying to find it out. In terms of feminist rhetorical study, Jacqueline Jones Royster offers such an acknowledgement of her stance. Echoing Rich's understanding of a politics of location, Royster writes in *Traces of a Stream*: "Occasionally I find I cannot, nor do I want to, set aside the fact that the story of African American women and literacy is my story too" (13). This personal connection, she argues further, is in fact a strength: a personal stance has advantages "in acknowledging connections, in considering the ethical implications of these connections, and in admitting the biases that must inevitably inform any scholarship that might be produced as a result of an acknowledgment of ethical space" (13).

Feminist rhetorical methodologies center on and wrestle with the fact that *all* research contains elements of subjectivity. Our methodologies especially contend with the understanding that too often, we "see" and search for what we already know, as in Kenneth Burke's concept of *trained incapacity*: the more we train ourselves to know, to recognize, to understand phenomena, the more we are neglecting development in other areas, which become our trained incapacities (3). The work for feminist scholars then is to acknowledge, make use of, and challenge our trained ways of seeing. For instance, writing histories that attend to the rhetorical contributions of women and other marginalized groups often entails "rethinking what constitutes primary and archival materials" (Glenn and Enoch 325). Our trained incapacities also have prompted us to ignore the epistemic potential of "unimportant" artifacts, research sites, data sets, interview subjects, and archives. And our trained incapacities lead us, frequently, to overlook materials published in languages other than the ones that are dominant in a disciplinary and national context (for US scholars, English).

Our third section includes four essays in which the authors extend feminist research methods and methodologies by reflecting on their own research practices. In chapter 8, Heather Adams takes up the ethical challenges feminist researchers face when they conduct "human subjects research" that requires approval from an Institutional Review Board. While ostensibly aiming to uphold the highest ethical standards for such research, IRBs, Adams argues, actually have the potential to impose ethical standards grounded in assumptions that do not always square with those of feminist researchers, such as collaboration. Adams calls for feminist researchers to develop "critical access" to IRB procedures that would allow us to intervene in practices that do not fit with our feminist alignments.

In chapter 9, Cristina Ramírez similarly considers the ethical implications of her research practices, especially her own personal situatedness with relation to her research subjects—women journalists in Mexico who lived and wrote through the late nineteenth through the mid-twentieth century. Ramírez argues that narrating her own connection to these women—by virtue of her own family history and identity as a Chicana scholar—is a *proyecto* (Dussel 77), a deeply political act, since this "personal history has the potential to intervene and shift the dominant narrative" that has excluded Chicanas from the history of rhetoric.

In chapter 10, Wendy Sharer takes up the ethics embedded in the very genres through which we share our research. She argues that traditional research genres, such as the scholarly article or monograph, silence researchers whose personal and professional situations do not support a single-minded focus on research (such as the large percentage of rhetoric and composition PhDs who work in teaching-focused institutions). Instead, she suggests, feminist scholars should embrace new genres that would allow for greater collaboration, privilege research process and not just research products, and enable experimentation with alternative formats. In the final chapter of this section, chapter 10, Anita Helle centers methodological attention on the archive. Here, she reflects on the "fragile archive" of postmillennial breast cancer narratives that a number of feminist scholars constituted in a special, double issue of *Tulsa Studies in Women's Literature* titled "Theorizing Breast Cancer: Narrative, Politics, Memory"—an issue that Helle edited with colleague Mary DeShazer. Helle explores the editorial decisions she and DeShazer made that helped create and circulate this archive about breast cancer and its narratives.

THE FEMINIST RHETORICAL COMMITMENT TO "PAYING IT FORWARD" THROUGH TEACHING AND MENTORING

The collective goal of feminist teaching and mentoring is to articulate a vision of high scholarly expectations and rigorous scholarly preparation tempered by care, collaboration, dialogue, ethics, mutual respect, and hope. Teaching and mentoring are put in the service of ethical action, social responsibility, and the shaping of the next generation of teachers and scholars. And, teaching and mentoring are closely related, sometimes overlapping, and always capable of being separated. With feminist mentoring, the goal is to help the scholar develop into the best scholar they can possibly be, offering the support and critique that will fuel that development. The trick, though, is to always remember that mentoring is a two-way (or more) street, as the less experienced scholar may well have better insights into a situation than the more experienced one. And *feminist* mentorship might—and even should—shift and reshape rhetorically and amoeba-like given the exigencies of the situation and the needs and desires of both the mentor and mentee. With teaching, a feminist teacher is collaborative, attentive to power dynamics, and inclusive of diverse backgrounds, ideas, and ways of being in the classroom. But given the disruption of traditional (read masculinist) teaching practices, the feminist teacher can be at a disadvantage, given the fact that still—in the twenty-first century—so many students are suspicious if not dismissive of feminism. A feminist teacher, then, can be vulnerable, and we need to think through what is at stake and at what cost this vulnerability has on the feminist teacher and her teaching.

The final section of this collection suggests feminist rhetorical approaches to teaching and mentoring. The chapters in this section share an interest in developing mentoring and pedagogical practices that make a difference in the lives of our colleagues and students. In chapter 12, Elaine Richardson outlines a theory of African American Female Literacy as a critical, cultural literacy that enables young black women to develop awareness of the unique ways of knowing and being in the world so that they can negotiate a society hostile to them. Richardson demonstrates how this pedagogical approach works in an afterschool program she developed, BlackGirlsUnite. In chapter 13, Abby Knoblauch outlines a pedagogical approach founded upon feminist rhetorical theory, one that focuses specifically on embodied rhetoric as a means of helping students to negotiate difference. In chapter 14, Sonia K. Foss and Karen Foss outline their "paradigm of constructed potentiality," which focuses on how symbols can be exploited as resources for change, and they set out a pedagogical program (replete with exercises and assignments for students) that enables students to develop an awareness of how changes in language can foster changes in reality. Finally, in chapter 15 Michelle Eble and Lynée Lewis Gaillet outline a theory of *mentoring networks* that challenges traditional, top-down models of mentoring. As they argue, in a networked model, mentoring can occur across scholarly rank, institutional affiliation, and disciplinary expertise, with the ultimate goal of empowering members of the network as scholars, teachers, and agents of change.

Twenty years after the publication of *Rhetoric Retold*, our contributors *retell* rhetoric—yet again. They make clear that national, international, and transnational leadership and political practice; identity productions; research methods; and teaching and mentorship are complex and compelling points of discussion that should continue to garner our scholarly attention. In their chapters, these scholars circle back to and elaborate on many of the themes Cheryl initiated in *Rhetoric Retold*, such as rhetorics of silence as well as historiographic research and methodological revision—themes she has pursued further in subsequent publications. The work of our contributors deepens these conversations and invites others to participate in them because there are indeed "endless opportunities" for contribution within and beyond the four inventional nodes that structure this book. As we look to the next twenty years we are confident that rhetoric will indeed be retold by feminist scholars doing innovative and exciting work beyond what our imaginations can anticipate. As Cheryl writes in the conclusion to *Rhetoric Retold*, "Just think of the possibilities that lie before us. . . . [T]he opportunities for exploration are rich and plentiful for anyone who wants to do the necessary work" (178).

Works Cited

Appiah, Kwame Anthony. *The Ethics of Identity*. Princeton UP, 2005.

Burke, Kenneth. *Permanence and Change*. 1934. U of California P, 1954.

Donawerth, Jane. *Conversational Rhetoric: The Rise and Fall of a Women's Tradition, 1600–1900*. Southern Illinois UP, 2011.

Dussel, Enrique. *Philosophy of Liberation*. Translated by Aquilina Martinez and Christine Morkovsky, Wipf & Stock, 1985.

Glenn, Cheryl. *Rhetoric Retold: Regendering the Tradition from Antiquity Through the Renaissance*. Southern Illinois UP, 1997.

Glenn, Cheryl, and Jessica Enoch. "Drama in the Archives: Rereading Methods, Rewriting History." *College Composition and Communication*, vol. 61, no. 2, 2009, pp. 321–41.

Keller, Evelyn Fox. *Reflections on Gender and Science*. Yale UP, 1985.

Lloyd, Moya. *Beyond Identity Politics*. Sage, 2005.

Logan, Shirley. "Quick Question." Received by Jess Enoch and Jordynn Jack, 21 May 2015.
McCall, Leslie. "The Complexity of Intersectionality." *Signs*, vol. 30, no. 3, 2005, pp. 1771–800.
Miller, Elizabeth Ellis. "Reframing Rhetorical Failure: Confession and Conversion in Sarah Patton Boyle's Desegregated Heart." *Rhetoric Review*, vol. 35, no. 4, 2016, pp. 294–307.
Mohanty, Satya P. "The Epistemic Status of Cultural Identity." *Reclaiming Identity: Realist Theory and the Predicament of Postmodernism*, edited by Paula M. Moya and Michael R. Hames-García, U of California P, 2000, pp. 29–66.
Ratcliffe, Krista. *Rhetorical Listening: Identification, Gender, and Whiteness*. Southern Illinois UP, 2005.
Ramírez, Cristina. "Quick Question." Received by Jess Enoch and Jordynn Jack, 21 May 2015.
Rich, Adrienne. "Notes toward a Politics of Location." *Blood, Bread, and Poetry: Selected Prose 1979–1985*, Norton, 1994, pp. 210–31.
Royster, Jacqueline Jones and Gesa Kirsch. *Feminist Rhetorical Practices: New Horizons for Rhetoric, Composition, and Literacy Studies*. Southern Illinois UP, 2012.
Royster, Jacqueline Jones. *Traces of a Stream: Literacy and Social Change among African American Women*. U of Pittsburgh P, 2000.
Sheriff, Stacey Ellen. *Rhetoric and Revision: Women's Arguments for Social Justice in the Progressive Era*. 2009. Pennsylvania State University, PhD dissertation.

Part I: Feminist Rhetoric in Contemporary Global Politics

2 Bending Toward Justice: Women's Rhetorical Performances—Local and Transnational, Then and Now

Shirley Wilson Logan

> Dear brothers and sisters, we want schools and education for every child's bright future. We will continue our journey to our destination of peace and education for everyone. No one can stop us. We will speak for our rights and we will bring change through our voice. We must believe in the power and the strength of our words. Our words can change the world.

These words come from Malala Yousafzai, the sixteen-year old girl from the Swat Valley region of Pakistan, who, at the age of eleven, drew international attention to the Taliban's oppressive tactics, especially its opposition to the education of Pakistani women and girls. In October of 2012, she was shot in a Taliban assassination attempt. As a result of her heroic political activism, she made the short list of nominees for the 2013 Nobel Peace Prize and was invited in July of 2013 to address the United Nations Youth Assembly, where she gave the address from which the above quotation is taken. Continuing her campaign in a March 2014 speech at the annual celebration of the Commonwealth of Nations, Yousafzai challenged the Westminster Abbey audience to support education for women and girls. Such twenty-first-century rhetorical activity serves to remind us that transnational feminist rhetoric is increasingly inserting itself into contemporary public discourse.

All too often, feminist rhetorical scholars fail to recognize effective rhetoric in our own time. It is true that historians of rhetoric have recovered the rhetorical performances of our foremothers and sisters—Aspasia, Margery Kempe, Maria Stewart, Abby Kelly, Elizabeth Cady Stanton, Anna Dickinson, Sojourner Truth, Ida Wells, Frances Willard and many others—and they have given them the scholarly attention they deserve. It is often more difficult to appreciate the effectiveness of present-day transnational feminist rhetoricians, primarily because we are only beginning to adopt a global as well as national perspective in identifying effective persuasive strategies of justice-seeking women.

In this chapter, I consider the persuasive work of several politically active twenty-first century women who have argued to improve the material conditions under which women around the world live: three Nobel Peace Prize winners, Leymah Gbowee (Liberia), Tawakkol Karman (Yemen), and Aung San Suu Kyi (Burma); a poet, Nikky Finney (US); and political activist/scholar, Angela Davis (US). I close by returning to the words of teen activist Malala Yousafzai (Pakistan), who gives assurance that the tradition of outspoken women will continue. In spite of differences in occasion and audience expectations, these women have expressed what historian Evelyn Brooks Higginbotham called their *righteous discontent*. While Higginbotham used the term as the title of her history of the women's movement in the black Baptist church at the turn of the nineteenth century, these women have done so in the context of larger national, international, and global issues.

Although I consider specific contemporary events, I observe throughout this chapter the extent to which today's women build upon a long tradition of women in public discourse by comparing their arguments to those advanced by some of their nineteenth-century rhetorical foremothers, including Caroline Healey Dall (1822–1912), Maria Stewart (1803–79), and Frances Harper (1825–1911). The purpose here in looking back is not to recover women from the past, not to say, "Look what these nineteenth-century women were doing and saying." The purpose is to attend to the means of persuasion they employed that appear to be timeless in their impact. The focus is less on the women than their strategies. By looking back, we recognize how women continue to use these strategies effectively in discursive work today. Elsewhere, I describe the recurring rhetorical practices among nineteenth-century African American women, borne out of common experiences of discrimination, oppression, racism, and sexism (Logan xiv, 145). The rhetorical situations of earlier women were not so different from those women face now, and I see in these current situations many of the same rhetorical strategies recurring once again. Since we have new technologies of communication that inform us, often in real time, about what women are experiencing, doing, and saying in other parts of the world, we have more opportunities to understand the extent of our global connectedness. Still this is not a new quest. Even ancient rhetorical theorists believed that while the art of persuasion came naturally to some, there were others for whom it was a developed skill worthy of careful study.[1] Today, we have the advantage of a larger, more diverse archive of texts. We can compare and contrast the performances of men and women from around the world, at different moments in history and in new rhetorical situations.

The term *righteous discontent* seems particularly applicable to the rhetorical situations these women (past and present) found themselves in because they spoke and speak with a moral authority borne out of the strong belief that they were correcting injustices, not just advancing ideas. Righteous discontent describes their attitude, their ethos, and their demeanor, rather than a specific rhetorical strategy. I consider here three manifestations of discontent, which I label (1) Telling the Stories of People, (2) Invoking the Past, and (3) Establishing a Common Identification. These rhetorical moves overlap and reinforce one another in much the same way that the three rhetorical appeals (ethos, logos, pathos), while doing separate work, are nonetheless interdependent.

TELLING THE STORIES OF PEOPLE

Leymah Gbowee won the 2011 Nobel Peace Prize, along with two other human rights activist women—Ellen Johnson Sirleaf, President of Liberia, and Tawakkol Karman, a Yemeni journalist and politician—in recognition of their "non-violent struggle for the safety of women and for women's rights to full participation in peace-building work" (Nobel Peace Prize). Gbowee led the women's peace movement that helped

---

1. Aristotle observes in *Rhetoric* I, 1, 1354a: "Accordingly all men [sic] make use, more or less, of both; for to a certain extent all men attempt to discuss statements and to maintain them, to defend themselves and to attack others. Ordinary people do this either at random or through practice and from acquired habit. Both ways being possible, the subject can plainly be handled systematically, for it is possible to inquire the reason why some speakers succeed through practice and others spontaneously; and every one will at once agree that such an inquiry is the function of an art."

bring an end to the Second Liberian Civil War in 2003. On March 14, 2010, the final day of the Women in the World Summit, Gbowee talked about the power of images in telling the stories of what was happening to women in the world. She describes what she considers to be the most effective persuasive strategy for calling people to action. She observes, "Issues don't cut it but stories do. Tell the stories of people—the actual horrifying [stories]." Gbowee goes on to relate one story of a Liberian girl who was gang raped, had feces placed in her mouth, and was killed. The local authorities tried to cover it up by burying her hurriedly, but someone took a photo, which was sent to Liberian president Ellen Sirleaf Johnson. President Sirleaf Johnson was so moved by the image of the atrocity that she had a pathologist investigate the cause of death and the suspects were charged. Gbowee offers this as one example of how "stories cut it," as well as visual images, when abstract discussions of issues fail. She practices this principle in her Nobel Lecture, if perhaps with more restraint, due to the formality of the occasion. Here is a passage in which she relates a portion of the history of struggle: "Women had become the 'toy of war' for over-drugged young militias. Sexual abuse and exploitation spared no woman; we were raped and abused regardless of our age, religious or social status. A common scene daily was a mother watching her young one being forcibly recruited or her daughter being taken away as the wife of another drug emboldened fighter" ("Nobel Lecture"). Contemporary scholars of rhetoric will recognize this practice as *enargia*, which Richard Lanham defines as "vigorous ocular demonstration," bringing the "stories of people" before the audience's very eyes (65).[2] Thus, this is not a new tactic.

In 1849, abolitionist and woman's rights activist Caroline Healey Dall not only offers story as argument but also explains why she supports her claims about slavery through narrative. In "Amy: A Tale," a short story written for the annual publication in *The Liberty Bell*, Dall tells the story of Amy, who is owned by Edith, her white half-sister. As young girls, the two were best friends. This already problematic relationship changes when a friend of Edith's husband expresses an interest in purchasing Amy, and Edith, after some resistance, agrees to the sale. Amy subsequently commits suicide. After this narrative, Dall explains why she supports her claims about slavery through narrative, which she refers to here as "facts," rather than through direct argument. Dall writes:

---

2. See also the *Rhetorica Ad Herennium*, Book IV.

> [D]uring the last three years I have presented to your notice annually one of those terrible facts, which are the most available weapons of the friends of Freedom. None are so much dreaded by the slave master. He knows as well as anybody, that a fact will reach and touch a dozen hearts, long before an argument or an abstract truth has conquered a single mind . . . unthinking men are oftentimes capable of comprehending an evil consequence, when they do not see the whole extent of moral obliquity involved in the institution which is its cause. (17)

In Dall's story, we have both a demonstration of the persuasive strategy and commentary on its use. In the same closing section, Dall restates her belief in the value of specifics over argument: "I ought perhaps, to apologize for the form of narrative in which I have presented my facts. I know myself to be little skilled in it; but confining myself to a limited space, I had determined to have nothing to do with argument, and I could not but believe that however clumsily I might arrange them, the facts themselves would find a voice" (18).

Providing examples is, of course, one of the most reliable and effective methods for supporting or demonstrating a claim. It was the second elementary exercise in the classical *progymnasmata*, dating back at least to the fourth century BCE. This second element requires the student of rhetoric to relate historical or fictional stories, which play an important role in persuasive discourse. "Give me an example" is likely to be the request of an interlocutor who does not follow a rhetor's argument. What is significant in the discourse of both Dall and Gbowee is not so much that they provide examples—fictional and historical—as that they do so in full awareness of their rhetorical effect. These speakers remind us of the rhetorical tactics they employ. This self-conscious inclusion of examples suggests that disempowered or marginalized women do not expect that their assertions will be believed without support. They understand the inevitable resistance that often mutes their assertions. Examples provide a form of narrative counter-resistance.

Invoking the Past

Closely tied to historical and fictional narratives is the practice of invoking past people and past actions as sources of inspiration and motivation. Nikky Finney's powerful statement upon acceptance of the 2011 National Book Award in Poetry provides a moving example of how a speaker draws on cultural memory to create a desired effect. Finney, a poet and English professor at the University of Kentucky, won the award for a collection of poems, *Head Off & Split*, that comment on public and private aspects of African American life. In her acceptance speech, she calls forth her ancestors, inviting them to join the celebration they helped make possible. This epideictic moment highlights the extraordinary significance of her achievement in the context of a troubled past:

> We begin with history. The Slave Codes of South Carolina, 1739: a fine of one hundred dollars and six months in prison will be imposed for anyone found teaching a slave to read, or write, and death is the penalty for circulating any incendiary literature.
>
> The ones who longed to read and write, but were forbidden, who lost hands and feet, were killed, by laws written by men who believed they owned other men.
>
> Their words devoted to quelling freedom and insurgency, imagination, all hope; what about the possibility of one day making a poem? (Finney)

Finney's argument, embedded in the description of the arrival of her ancestors to the party, reminds her audience of the struggles of African Americans: the history of their arrival in the American colonies, the physical abuse, black codes, anti-literacy laws, and other prohibitions against innumerable forms of freedom. Finney's rhetorical act might be thought of as a form of *rememory*, a term coined by author Toni Morrison and often defined as a way of invoking past people and events as if alive in the present. I understand it as an act of calling up events from the past that many may have forgotten, for the purpose of re-presenting them to support a claim. While the original event may have been degrading or painful, its rememory can often be empowering. Finney calls up her ancestors, whose presence on this occasion is itself a form of protest, a call for twenty-first century justice:

> The king's mouth and the queen's tongue arranged, perfectly, on the most beautiful paper, sealed with wax and palmetto tree sap, determined to control what can never be controlled: the will of the human heart to speak its own mind. Tonight, these forbidden ones move all around the room as they please. They sit at whatever table they want. They wear camel-colored field hats and tomato-red kerchiefs. They are bold in their Sunday-

go-to-meeting best. Their cotton croker-sack shirts are black washpot clean and irreverently not tucked in. Some have even come in white Victorian collars and bustiers. Some have just climbed out of the cold wet Atlantic, just to be here. We shiver together. (Finney)

Much like Dall and Gbowee, Finney's use of vividly descriptive language here places before the eyes an event that never happened. Her use of enargia, however, does the work of rememory by invoking her ancestors to make the argument that these uninvited guests have earned the right to be there and to witness this award for her poetry.

Close to two centuries earlier, Maria Stewart delivered her 1833 "Farewell Address," calling forth women of the past to inspire Boston's "Daughters of Africa." Stewart, a young self-supporting woman, moved from Hartford, Connecticut, to Boston, married and became a widow before the age of thirty. In Boston, she was also a close friend of the firebrand David Walker, who may have inspired her to political activism. After only one controversial year of public speaking, she decided to leave Boston but not before delivering a fiery farewell address. She needed to motivate the black women of the city to rise up and take control of their families and communities in order to achieve the goals of racial uplift, since, in her view, the men were not adhering to the traditions of their forefathers. Speaking publicly was a bold move for a widowed black woman living in antebellum Boston:

> What if I am a woman; is not the God of ancient times the God of these modern days? Did he not raise up Deborah, to be a mother, and a judge in Israel? Did not queen Esther save the lives of the Jews? And Mary Magdalene first declare the resurrection of Christ from the dead? Come, said the woman of Samaria, and see a man that hath told me all things that ever I did; is not this the Christ? St. Paul declared that it was a shame for a woman to speak in public, yet our great High Priest and Advocate did not condemn the woman for a more notorious offence than this; neither will he condemn this worthless worm. (68)

Here Stewart draws examples from women whose lives are recorded in the Old and New Testament. These were historical women to the members of her audience, their religious ancestors. She invokes them not only for what they did but also for what they said, arguing for their right to say it. She continues in the next paragraph to offer further evidence of women's abilities from ancient times. In fact, at the foundation of all four of the addresses she delivered during her year of rhetorical activism sits an appeal to the past accomplishments of their African ancestors. She characterizes those in her audience as "daughters of Africa," "sons and daughters of Ethiopia," and "sons of Afric." Nonetheless, in this final address, she abandons her rhetorical efforts, believing that her attempts to make a difference in her Boston community through oratory had failed. Of course, we now know that many others would mount the podium and continue her crusade for racial uplift and justice.

Both Finney and Stewart reach back to recover a past that can inspire their auditors to action. Although Finney is responding to an epideictic occasion, she uses the opportunity to remind those gathered of just what an amazing accomplishment this award represents by invoking the past. Of course, we can identify other women warrior poets, like Audre Lorde, who have employed this tactic of invoking the past to inspire future action.[3] But I think it is especially significant to observe this practice in Maria Stewart's 1833 "Farewell Address" to the black women of Boston, who felt disempowered in the context of early nineteenth-century prohibitions against participating in civic discourse. It is as if the accomplishments of these women had taken on a life of their own, separate from those who achieved them. We might understand them as memories "out there in the world," to borrow the words of *Beloved*'s Sethe, when she describes rememories to her daughter Denver (Morrison 36). These words called Stewart's audiences to action.

IDENTIFYING WITH THE AUDIENCE

Today women around the world address audiences that are much more diverse than those of nineteenth-century US women arguing for their own rights and the rights of the enslaved. They find themselves on international stages, capable, as a result of communication technology, of being seen and heard by people who speak different languages and represent different cultures and religions. Thus, the challenge of establishing common ground becomes particularly salient. In this section I consider how both contemporary women and historical women have worked to establish a common bond. Rhetoric scholar Kenneth Burke's discussion of identification is helpful here. He observed that "a speaker persuades an audience by the use of stylistic identifications," adding that "the

---

3. See, for example, Audre Lorde, *Our Dead Behind Us: Poems*, Norton, 1986.

speaker draws on identification of interests to establish rapport" (Burke 46). How have women of the past and present established this rapport?

We find one such example in Angela Davis's acceptance speech for the 2011 Ethecon Blue Planet Award before an audience in Dusseldorf, Germany. Ethecon is a German environmental organization that recognizes those who have demonstrated "outstanding commitment to the conservation and preservation of our Blue Planet" (Ethecon). A well-known warrior for social justice, Davis first reminds the audience of her previous civil rights activism and establishes common ground in recalling that many of the people of Germany supported her when she was defending herself against fraudulent charges leveled against her. By paying "tribute to the role that international solidarities played in that movement to free me," Davis makes clear that she and they are not strangers. After reviewing her current involvement in prisoners' rights legislation, she links those concerns with Ethecon's world concerns about the environment and the people in it, moving back and forth between the local and the global:

> We need a world without the death penalty; we need a world without prisons; we need a world in which human problems are taken seriously, a world whose human inhabitants care about the oceans, the soil, the plants and the other animals with whom we share the planet. We need a world populated by people who are dedicated to eradicating violence, not perpetuating it through the persistence of the prison. (Davis)

Davis had the advantage on this occasion of already being an international figure for over forty years, and she wisely built on that long-standing relationship to establish identification with her audience by articulating the shared concerns regarding what "we need."

This was not the case with Yemeni 2011 Nobel Peace Prize winner Tawakkol Karman, one of the women, as Cheryl Glenn observed, who "should be attracting our sustained scholarly attention" ("Interview"). Introduced on the world stage in Norway with her acceptance speech, Karman was recognized for her revolutionary work during the Arab Spring uprisings. In her acceptance speech, Karman established a link between the uprisings in which she was involved and general international unrest by invoking, in her remarks, the name of one of the Western world's chief proponents of peace and justice:

> What Martin Luther King called "the art of living in harmony" is the most important art we need to master today. In order to contribute to that human art, the Arab states should make reconciliation with their own people an essential requirement. This is not merely an internal interest, but also an international one required for the whole human community. The dictator who kills his own people doesn't only represent a case of violation of his people's values and their national security, but is also a case of violation of human values, its conventions and its international commitments. Such a case represents a real threat to world peace. (Karman)

As this quotation reveals, Karman not only identifies with her audience by invoking the familiar and revered King but also by claiming that the problems in the Arab states are not isolated and particular. Rather, she makes her shift from the local to the global in stating "[t]his is not merely an internal interest, but also an international one required for the whole human community." On this international occasion, she is aware of the importance of universal appeal and develops this line of argument as a way of establishing identity. By invoking the name of Dr. Martin Luther King, himself a former Nobel Peace Prize winner, Karman instantly unites her cause with the worldwide cause for peace and justice.

On June 16, 2012, another Nobel Laureate, Burmese activist Aung San Suu Kyi, delivered her Nobel lecture after having been awarded the Nobel Peace Prize in 1991, twenty-one years earlier, while under house arrest for her role in opposing the Burmese anti-democratic regime. The 2012 Nobel lecture was an especially significant event due to these circumstances, and, no doubt, she was keenly aware that the world was listening. This was a moment to remind auditors that Burma's plight was a universal one:

> [T]he Nobel Prize had drawn the attention of the world to the struggle for democracy and human rights in Burma. We were not going to be forgotten.
>
> To be forgotten. The French say that to part is to die a little. To be forgotten too is to die a little. It is to lose some of the links that anchor us to the rest of humanity. When I met Burmese migrant workers and refugees during my recent visit to Thailand, many cried out: "Don't forget us!" They meant: "don't forget our plight, don't forget to do what you can to help us, don't

forget we also belong to your world." When the Nobel Committee awarded the Peace Prize to me they were recognizing that the oppressed and the isolated in Burma were also a part of the world, they were recognizing the oneness of humanity. So for me receiving the Nobel Peace Prize means personally extending my concerns for democracy and human rights beyond national borders. (Aung San Suu Kyi)

Like Karman, Suu Kyi transitions from the local to the national and the transnational: the oppressed of Burma are "part of the world" and by recognizing her work, the Nobel committee was seeing the "oneness of humanity." This rhetorical move, so apparent in these three addresses, met a different response in the nineteenth-century when the move to identify and the call for common humanity were met with great resistance.

The need to establish identification was more complicated and arguably more critical for nineteenth-century black women like Frances Harper and Fannie Barrier Williams (1855–1944). They were both educated, respectable society women, who were defending the rights of formerly enslaved black women and their descendants to the same privileges and opportunities as the white women they addressed. Williams grew up in Brockport, New York, a member of the town's only black family. She attended the New England Conservatory of Music and the School of Fine Arts in Washington, D.C. She was probably better educated than most of the white women often in her audience, but she was also aware that she viewed as the exception. The same was the case for Frances Harper, who, after an early education in Baltimore, went on to become a teacher, a lecturer for the abolitionist cause, an author, and a well-traveled public intellectual; many in her audience members found it difficult to believe that such a poised and polished woman could be a member of what many considered to be a despised race. The challenge, then, for both Harper and Williams, was to argue that black, formerly enslaved, marginalized and disenfranchised women were entitled to equal justice. They both recognized that as long as their auditors did not identify with black people, did not see them as equally human, they would not feel that African Americans were entitled to equal rights.

Harper, in 1866, proclaimed a direct unity with her audience, warning that women "are all bound up together in one great bundle of humanity, and society cannot trample on the weakest and feeblest of its members without receiving the curse in its own soul" (217). Some thirty years later, Williams explained to the women assembled at the 1893 World's Congress of Representative Women in Chicago that "[a]s American women generally are fighting against the nineteenth-century narrowness that still keeps women out of the highest institutions of learning, so our women are eagerly demanding the best of education open to their race" (109). Williams proclaimed unity by pointing out ways she, the black women she represented, and the women attending the Congress of Representative Women were, after all, the same. The calls here from both Williams and Harper are for identification at a basic level of acceptance of common humanity. This was an identification many of their auditors were slow to accept. In truth, the best argument for Williams and Harper may have been the visual rhetoric of their nonthreatening, carefully coifed, and modestly dressed selves rather than their words. But theirs was a two-pronged appeal to identification, identification with a common humanity as well as a common cause.

Conclusion

I close by returning to Malala Yousafzai's United Nations Youth Assembly speech. In recognition of her advocacy for education and rights for girls, July 12, 2013, her sixteenth birthday, was declared Malala day. It was also the day on which she gave her first public speech at the United Nations Headquarters since she was shot, and it provides examples of all three of the tactics considered here. Vivid description is apparent in her reference to Taliban violence: "Dear Friends, on the 9th of October 2012, the Taliban shot me on the left side of my forehead. They shot my friends too. They thought that the bullets would silence us. But they failed." In this instance, few questioned whether the crime occurred; thus, there was little need for an argument from the stasis of fact, less need for the kind of specific details Leymah Gbowee employs to demonstrate the violence perpetrated against the women of Liberia. Yet this brief reference to what transpired is powerful, even in the absence of copious details.

Yousafzai invokes the past, proclaiming,

> I do not even hate the Talib who shot me. Even if there is a gun in my hand and he stands in front of me. I would not shoot him. This is the compassion that I have learnt from Muhammad-the prophet of mercy, Jesus Christ and Lord Buddha. This is the legacy of change that I have inherited from Martin Lu-

> ther King, Nelson Mandela and Muhammad Ali Jinnah. This is the philosophy of non-violence that I have learnt from Gandhi, Bacha Khan and Mother Teresa. And this is the forgiveness that I have learnt from my mother and father. This is what my soul is telling me, be peaceful and love everyone.

Here she invokes a historic, transnational list of nonviolent activists to support her claims.

She also calls for common identification. In fact, it is this appeal to what Frances Harper called a "bound up" humanity that is most salient in the speech. She refers to her auditors as "brothers and sisters" and places herself among the masses of people who have suffered the consequences of terrorism.

> Dear brothers and sisters, do remember one thing. Malala day is not my day. Today is the day of every woman, every boy and every girl who have raised their voice for their rights. There are hundreds of human rights activists and social workers who are not only speaking for human rights, but who are struggling to achieve their goals of education, peace and equality. Thousands of people have been killed by the terrorists and millions have been injured. I am just one of them.

Yousafzai ends with a forceful recognition of the power of the word, the power of language and literacy: "So let us wage a global struggle against illiteracy, poverty and terrorism and let us pick up our books and pens. They are our most powerful weapons" (Yousafzai).

For centuries, speakers have called upon a range of rhetorical strategies to bend the long arc of the moral universe toward justice—an image called forth by nineteenth-century abolitionist Theodore Parker, civil rights activist Martin Luther King Jr., US President Barack Obama, and many others. The women considered here have engaged these strategies to focus especially on justice for women and other marginalized groups. The use and recurrence of these strategies is a by-product of their responses to an unjust world. For the sake of discussion, I have categorized a few of them—telling the stories of people, invoking the past, and establishing a common identification—but these women were not concerned with rhetorical strategies; they were concerned with bringing justice to bear on conditions around the world fraught with injustice. They were drawing on the resources of language, the power of the word. We recognize that this is a longstanding tradition. I reached as far back as the rhetoric of Maria Stewart in 1833, but as we know from texts such as Glenn's *Rhetoric Retold* women like Sappho, Aspasia, Diotima, Julian of Norwich, Margery Kempe, Anne Askew, and Elizabeth I were performing rhetoric and employing similar tactics many centuries before. In *Rhetoric Retold*, Glenn points out the irony that Plato, in spite of his restrictive views on women, is a chief source of references to rhetorical activities of both Aspasia and Diotima, women associated with the Greek classical period. Glenn also identifies ways Julian of Norwich and Margery Kempe, Christian women of the medieval period, developed rhetorical power through advocacy of their religious faith and describes the dire consequences of the outspokenness of Anne Askew (*Rhetoric Retold*). Such scholarship reminds us that women have long been involved in rhetorical activism. Malala Yousafzai and other contemporary rhetors have come forward in this century to continue the tradition and to call upon others to speak out for a more just universe.

Works Cited

Aung San Suu Kyi. "Nobel Lecture." *Nobelprize.org*. Nobel Media AB 2012. www.nobelprize.org/prizes/peace/1991/kyi/26192-aung-san-suu-kyi-speech/. Accessed 28 Oct. 2013.

Burke, Kenneth. *A Rhetoric of Motives*. U of California P, 1969.

Dall, Caroline Healy. "Amy A Tale." *The Liberty Bell. By Friends of Freedom*. National Anti-Slavery Bazaar, 1849, pp. 4–21.

Davis, Angela. "Prof. Angela Davis: Acceptance Speech." *Ethecon*, www.ethecon.org/en/1410. Accessed 31 Oct. 2013.

Leymah Gbowee. "Leymah Gbowee—Nobel Lecture." *Nobelprize.org*. Nobel Media AB 2013, www.nobelprize.org/prizes/peace/2011/gbowee/lecture. Accessed 28 Oct 2013.

"Leymah Gbowee talks about the Power of Images." *YouTube*, uploaded by The Daily Beast, 14 March 2010, www.youtube.com/watch?v=D-e2Qlcgu2GM. Accessed 28 Oct. 2013.

Glenn, Cheryl. Interview with Jessica Enoch: "Feminist Rhetorical Studies: Past, Present, Future." *Composition Forum*, vol. 29, Spring, 2014, compositionforum.com/issue/29/cheryl-glenn-interview.php. Accessed 28 Oct. 2013.

—. *Rhetoric Retold: Regendering the Tradition from Antiquity Through the Renaissance*. Southern Illinois UP, 1997.

Harper, Frances W. "We Are All Bound up Together." *A Brighter Coming Day: A Frances Ellen Watkins Harper Reader*, edited by Frances Smith Foster, The Feminist Press, 1990.

Lanham, Richard. *Handlist of Rhetorical Terms*. 2nd ed., U of California P, 2012.

Logan, Shirley Wilson. *"We are Coming": The Persuasive Discourse of Nineteenth-Century Black Women*. Southern Illinois UP, 1999.

Morrison, Toni. *Beloved*. Signet Classic, 1987.

"The Nobel Peace Prize for 2011 to Ellen Johnson Sirleaf, Leymah Gbowee and Tawakkol Karman—Press Release." *Nobelprize.org*. Nobel Media AB 2013, www.nobelprize.org/prizes/peace/2011/press-release/. Accessed 28 Oct 2011.

Stewart, Maria W. "Mrs. Stewart's Farewell Address to Her Friends in the City of Boston," September 21, 1833. *Maria W. Stewart, America's First Black Woman Political Writer: Essays and Speeches*, edited by Marilyn Richardson. Indiana UP, 1987, pp. 65–74.

Williams, Fannie Barrier. "The Intellectual Progress of the Colored Women of the United States since the Emancipation Proclamation." *With Pen and Voice: A Critical Anthology of Nineteenth-Century African-American Women*, edited by Shirley Wilson Logan, Southern Illinois UP, 1995, pp. 106-19.

Yousafzai, Malala. "Malala Yousafzai delivers defiant riposte to Taliban militants with speech to the UN General Assembly." *The Independent.com*. 12 July 2013, www.independent.co.uk/news/world/asia/the-full-text-malala-yousafzai-delivers-defiant-riposte-to-taliban-militants-with-speech-to-the-un-8706606.html. Accessed 29 Oct. 2013.

3 Silence and Listening: The War On/Over Women's Bodies in the 2012 US Election Cycle

Krista Ratcliffe

This chapter originated in anger, disbelief, and despair, triggered by the war-on-women debates during the 2012 election cycle. I first articulated these emotions as a rhetorical problem in May of 2012 while writing a proposal for a Conference on College Composition and Communication (CCCC) panel that included Cheryl Glenn, Shirley Logan, and Joyce Middleton. At the time the Tea Party was making a bid to become the dominant voice in the Republican Party, and my anger, disbelief, and despair surfaced because the Tea Party's political rhetoric about women strongly echoed repressive pre-1970s gender discourses. Were Democrats and Republicans really invoking the term *war on women* to describe one another's assumptions and proposed policies? All I kept thinking as I listened to campaign chat after campaign chat was: I cannot believe we are once again asking, "Who controls women's bodies?" and "Who controls laws about women's bodies?"

I am chagrined to admit that my anger, disbelief, and despair about the war-on-women debates was so intense that I had difficulty talking in public, either with friends during dinner or with students in the classroom. During such discussions, I would get so exasperated that I simply could not speak rationally or otherwise. Consequently, I retreated into two unproductive rhetorical stances: I either howled at the moon when alone or retreated into a dysfunctional silence when in public. In telling friends about my problematic silence, I discovered that some of them were reacting similarly, and suddenly I realized that the silences haunting the war-on-women debates constituted a rhetorical problem that needed to be addressed because although howling at the moon may soothe the howler (admittedly in a self-righteous way) and embracing a dysfunctional silence may seem a fine solution in the short term (when one is in a huff and, frankly, privileged enough to afford silence), rarely does either stance allow for productive debate and/or action. To counteract these two unproductive stances, I determined to define the rhetorical problem of the war-on-women debates and then discover "all the available means" of composing a better response.

To begin, I defined what I felt to be *the* key question about the war-on-women debates: "Why did they make me (and others) so angry, so disbelieving, so despairing . . . to the point of silence and inaction?" Because silence was my immediate rhetorical problem, my first available means was Glenn's *Unspoken: A Rhetoric of Silence*, which reminded me that "[t]here is not one but rather many silences," both functional and dysfunctional (160), that "[a]ll silence has a meaning" (11), and that silence may be "an invitation into the future, a space that draws us forth (160). Armed with Glenn's insights, I chose in May of 2012 to be determined not to let my silence fester dysfunctionally but, rather, to invite a rhetorical analysis of the war-on-women debates. My goal was to reimagine the silences haunting the war-on-women debates more productively as well as to generate more productive responses to existing debates, those responses being first a conference paper and later this chapter. In the spirit of invitation, I framed my silence as a site for contemplating what my (and others') silences could teach me. Thus, my second available means became my own text *Rhetorical Listening*, which encouraged me to listen to the war-on-women debates and their surrounding silences by studying the dominant tropes in the debates, the cultural logics haunting the usage of these tropes, and the stakes of their significations.

While thinking through this method, I gained two important insights. First, I realized that I had fallen prey to anger, disbelief, and despair because of the resonances surrounding a dominant trope in the 2012 election cycle: that trope, of course, being *war on women*. Second, I had fallen prey to the seductive lure of a dominant US cultural logic, that of evolutionary historical progress, or the idea that each generation marches ever onward and upward. This method and resulting insights, in turn, clarified three important questions:

1. How exactly does the trope *war on women* signify?
2. How are the significations of this trope influenced by cultural logics?

3. What is at stake in the silences generated by this trope and its cultural logics?

In the following sections, I address each question to demonstrate that a dysfunctional silence and any resulting inaction may be countered by laying Glenn's ideas about silence as a rhetorical art alongside my own ideas about rhetorical listening as a rhetorical art.[1]

THE WAR-ON-WOMEN TROPE

The war-on-women debates are not a series of sponsored events; rather, the term *war on women* is a media label that was employed to name an on-going, escalating series of political claims about women during the 2012 election cycle. This label serves as an umbrella term to classify a host of issues, such as reproductive rights, pay equity, women's sexuality, women's health, women's roles within religion, etc. The question that I want to address in this section is: How exactly does the trope *war on women* signify?

First, though, the term *trope* needs to be defined. In classical rhetorical theories, *trope* refers to the use of a word in a way that changes the word's meaning, with the master tropes being metaphor, metonymy, synecdoche, and irony. In more recent semiotic and poststructuralist theories, *trope* assumes an extended definition: that is, if language is assumed to be inherently metaphorical (i.e., if a word represents a thing and if the distance between word and thing always already exists), then all "words" or terms function as tropes, signifying different "things" across different spaces and times (Ratcliffe 111–12). Although physics now tells us that space-time is one entity and impossible to separate, the following examples demonstrate how tropes work differently over space and time. In terms of space, the trope *woman* signifies differently in the US than in Saudi Arabia in terms of, say, the right to drive in 2019; likewise, in terms of time, the trope *woman* signifies differently in 1814 than in 2019 in the US in terms of, say, marital property rights. Because all words function as tropes, another trope pertinent to this study is *war*.

The trope *war* has frequently been invoked in US political discourse. President Lyndon Johnson declared a war on poverty and an associated war on hunger. President Ronald Reagan and Nancy Reagan declared a

---

1. For discussions about the intersections of silence and listening as rhetorical arts, see Glenn and Ratcliffe's *Silence and Listening as Rhetorical Arts*.

war on drugs. There have also been wars on cancer and on terror. During the 2012 election cycle, *war* once again became a dominant trope in election discourses, but it took a decidedly silly turn. There was a war on dogs (referring to Mitt Romney's carting a dog on top of his car), a war on Christmas (promoted by liberals, according to Fox News), a war on obesity (referring to Michelle Obama's healthy eating initiative), a war on pornography (led by Rick Santorum), and a war on religion (led by President Obama, according to Rick Perry) (Robbins-Early et al). Though the impulse to martial metaphors in politics is a topic worthy of an entire study, I focus here on the decidedly un-silly extension of this metaphor in 2012 political discourses, that is, the use of the *war-on-women* trope in the war-on-women debates.

As mentioned in the introduction, my first insight about the war-on-women debates was that I had primarily emotional reactions to the trope itself. To me, *war on women* felt regressive and violent, so I initially resisted engaging the trope and fell into silence. To resist my resistance and its resulting silence, I decided to reframe my silence more productively as an invitation to research. I focused my research on when the media began using the trope *war on women* in 2012 to describe political claims about women. Below are just some of my findings. I lay these claims alongside one another not just to provide an interesting timeline of media events but also, and perhaps more importantly, to offer a history of the escalation of the war-on-women debates and to map a nexus of discourses associated with these debates and its umbrella trope, *war on women*.

FEBRUARY 2012

If women keep their legs together, holding a Bayer aspirin between their knees, then they won't get pregnant. This claim was made by Rick Santorum's supporter Foster Friess in an interview with Andrea Mitchell: "Back in my days, they used Bayer aspirin for contraceptives. The gals put it between their knees, and it wasn't that costly" (Haberman). To his credit, Friess later apologized on his personal blog for his ill-conceived "joke": "To those who applauded my comments and remembered the joke, thanks for your encouragement. To those who thought I was callously encouraging that as a prescription for today, I kindly ask your forgiveness. God Bless, Foster" (Friess). And for good measure, he noted that his wife didn't like the joke, either. Nevertheless, the salvo against women's reproductive rights was fired, and a cultural script plotting renewed propriety in women's sexual behavior was in play. The war on women was on.

If women use birth control, they are "sluts" and "prostitutes." This claim was offered by Rush Limbaugh on his February 27 show. He likened thirty-year-old Georgetown law student Sandra Fluke to a "slut" and a "prostitute" when she advocated that, regardless of religious affiliation, an institution such as Georgetown University should include birth control in its benefit packages for students. Limbaugh likened receiving a birth control benefit to being paid to have sex, hence his prostitute claim (Tapper). After at least ten sponsors pulled their ads from his show, Limbaugh apologized, saying, "And I again sincerely apologize to Ms. Fluke for using those two words to describe her" (Harris). Limbaugh's initial claim echoed Friess's claim by linking reproductive rights with cultural scripts for women's proper and improper sexual behavior, but Limbaugh upped the ante by demonizing women's sexuality both in terms of his own moral code and his own pocketbook, thus his argument that he did not want to subsidize via his insurance premiums women (or in his terms, *sluts*) having sex.

MARCH 2012

Virginia passes law requiring abdominal ultrasounds before abortions are performed. This claim emerged in media reports about Governor Bob McDonnell's signing this state bill into law. An earlier version of the bill had required transvaginal ultrasounds, which many critics denounced as "medically unnecessary and physically invasive" (Madison) and even as "state-mandated rape" (Russo), so Governor McDonnell requested the change from transvaginal ultrasound to abdominal ultrasound, which is to be undergone twenty-four hours before any abortion procedure. This change, though an improvement, remains a state invasion into a citizen's body. This political debate continued to define the war-on-women debates in terms of women's reproductive rights, but it offered a new cultural script, that is, women submitting to state-mandated medical procedures' being performed on their bodies.

May 2012

Arizona bans public funding for Planned Parenthood. This claim emerged from the Arizona state legislature's debate about public funding of abortions. When Governor Jan Brewer signed the "Whole Woman's Health Funding Priority Act," she stated that it "closes loopholes in order to ensure that taxpayer dollars are not used to fund abortions, whether directly or indirectly" (qtd. in Castellanos). In this instance the war-on-women debates remained grounded in women's reproductive rights, but it linked those rights to government fiscal policy. No longer was it simply Limbaugh talking about his own pocketbook; the entire tax base was involved. And, of course, little discussion was had about Planned Parenthood's myriad other services

US House Republicans seriously weaken the Violence Against Women Act. This claim appeared in a *New York Times* editorial that describes how the House's revised version of the Violence Against Women Act omitted "protections for gay, Indian, student and immigrant abuse victims that are contained in the bipartisan Senate bill." The consequences of this omission diminished protections for women within these categories; for example, an immigrant woman dependent upon a citizen husband has fewer rights/options, which makes leaving an abuser more difficult. Suddenly in the war-on-women debates, the discourses of reproductive rights, women's proper sexual behavior, personal fiscal responsibility for insurance, and government tax policy were overtly intersected with legal discourses and haunted by discourses of "minority" rights and stereotypes.

June 2012

US Senate Republicans block pay equity bill. This claim was reported in the *New York Times* after the Senate debated a bill that would have rendered pay discrimination easier to litigate; the bill was prevented from moving forward on procedural grounds by Senate Republicans. The bill's purpose was to "bar companies from retaliating against workers who inquire about pay disparities and open pathways for female employees to sue for punitive damages in cases of paycheck discrimination" (Steinhauer). Stopping this bill echoed earlier Republican legislation supported by Wisconsin Governor Scott Walker, legislation that repealed Wisconsin workers' ability to sue for discrimination in state courts ("Recall"). Here the war-on-women debates were extended to include discourses on women's financial agency, the results being that women's access to financial success and, perhaps, to political influence was constrained.

AUGUST 2012

Legitimate rape rarely leads to pregnancy. This claim was announced by Todd Akin, a GOP senate candidate in Missouri, who claimed his understanding was as follows: "If it is a legitimate rape, the female body has ways to try and shut that whole thing down" (Williams). Akin apologized by saying that he "misspoke" and by noting that his spontaneous comments did not "reflect the deep empathy I hold for the thousands of women who are raped and abused every year" (Williams). He lost his bid for a Senate seat. And well he should have. This irresponsible recitation of a false legal category (i.e., "legitimate rape") and false medical knowledge (i.e., such rape "rarely leads to pregnancy") creates a cultural script that links pregnant rape victims as somehow responsible for their own situations.

OCTOBER 2012

Mitt Romney requested binders full of women. Governor Romney's claim, which emerged during a presidential debate, referred to his tenure as governor of Massachusetts when he supposedly asked for binders full of women's resumes so that he could hire more women. In fact, the binders were prepared before his gubernatorial election by the "Massachusetts Government Appointments Project, a coalition of nonpartisan women's groups" (Cardona). And sadly, the percentage of women working for the Massachusetts state government went from 30% before Governor Romney's election to 27% after his election and then up to 33% after the next governor took office (Cardona). Aside from the political cartoon image of a binder literally full of women, this claim continued the use of inaccurate information in war-on-women debates, this time in terms of state government hiring policies.

Abortion is never medically necessary to save a woman's life. This claim by Joe Walsh, a GOP congressman from Illinois, was supplemented by his corollary claim that "[w]ith modern technology and science, you can't find one instance [of a medically necessary abortion]." He lost his race to

Tammy Duckworth. Again, here is more evidence in the war-on-women debates of inaccurate medical information haunting discourses of reproductive rights.

Finally, the *coup de grace*: *God intends even horrible situations like rape to happen*. This claim by Richard Mourdock, an Indiana GOP senate candidate, split the national Republican Party in terms of whether or not he needed to apologize. Mourdock claimed this comment garnered him votes, and although he did apologize for people's misunderstanding him, he did not apologize for the comment (Gabbatt). Mourdock lost his bid for a Senate seat. And this claim brought to the forefront the conservative religious discourses that often ground the aforementioned claims, particularly in relation to reproductive rights and medical procedures.

As evidenced by the above media stories, the trope *war on women* became a staple in how media framed US political discourses during the 2012 election cycle (Lowen). Of course, not all media employed this term; *New York Times* reporters regularly wrote about the *campaign against women*. Nevertheless, the catchiness of the trope *war on women* caught on, and its use extended beyond the media's use of it to classify the above stories. Simultaneously, debates abounded about the accuracy and efficacy of the trope. Non-Republican political operatives used it to name Republican attitudes and actions, as represented in the news stories above. The Republican National Committee chairperson denied this naming, claiming that it was as much a "fiction" as if Republicans had been charged with conducting a "war on caterpillars" (Blake). Indeed, Republicans argued the "real War on Women is coming from Democrats against conservative women and unborn women" (Alexander). Thus, from all political locations, the trope *war on women* entered public discourse, earning its own Wikipedia entry and offering cultural scripts not just for how women should think and behave but also for how two sides in this political debate should perform their evaluations of and discussions about women. Thus, as it gained traction, the trope *war on women* came to signify attacks on women's rights and on women's bodies as well as the intersections of said rights and bodies.

Cultural Logics: From Evolutionary Historical Progress to Circling Historiography

Rhetorical listening encourages listeners to listen not just to tropes and claims but also to cultural logics within which tropes and claims function (Ratcliffe 33). Quite simply, a cultural logic is a way of reasoning common to a group of people, a way of reasoning that changes over time and place. For example, the Republican Party of Lincoln embraced a cultural logic that championed a strong national government; the Republican Party of Tea Partiers does not. The importance of cultural logics is that they influence significations of words functioning as tropes. Indeed, the claim "gender matters" signifies one way when articulated or heard within a feminist cultural logic and a very different way when articulated or heard within a patriarchal cultural logic. Same words, same claim, very different meanings. So, to understand how the *war-on-women* trope and its associated claims function, it is important to listen not just to the trope and the aforementioned media claims but also to the cultural logics from within which this trope and its associated claims are both produced and received.

My reception of the *war-on-women* trope culminated in a dysfunctional silence because I was, as mentioned in my introduction, functioning within a cultural logic of evolutionary historical progress. This cultural logic undergirds the American Dream by presuming that each generation marches ever onward and upward toward a better future. In terms of gender politics, this cultural logic unfolds as follows:

- *If* we assume that each generation evolves ever upward by becoming healthier, wealthier, and wiser,
- *then* we believe that women's political and economic gains (that have resulted from hard-fought cultural debates) emerge as a stable base . . ., and
- *therefore,* we conclude that the stable base ensures current rights and future gains for women.

While I was functioning within this cultural logic, my silence seemed reasonable. After all, US citizens had engaged in political negotiations over women's bodies before. The negotiations were conflict-ridden and, at best, unpleasant. I did not want to have to engage them again, and it did not seem fair to be asked to do so.

But once I became conscious of the fact that this cultural logic of evolutionary historical progress was generating my public silence, I realized that the seductive power of this cultural logic lies not only in its claim of ever-upward progress but also in its corollary: the idea that a problem once solved remains solved. This corollary echoes claims that gender and race issues have been solved and, thus, are no longer with us. Clearly, my prior research attests that I do not believe such claims, but I found myself unconsciously seduced by this same pattern of thinking in relation to the 2012 debates classified via the *war-on-women* trope. There I was during the 2012 election cycle, enmeshed in this cultural logic: in my mind women were marching onward and upward on an evolutionary path toward gender nirvana . . . while the world around me was circling back to tropes about women that seemed outmoded and dangerous.

But why would I have ever assumed that, once cultural debates have been waged, they need never be waged again? As a feminist and rhetoric scholar/teacher, I should have known better. After all, I have read Jean-Francois Lyotard's *The Postmodern Condition*, which tells us that we live *within* an "agonistics of language" and function within rhetorical situations that demand our continual, active engagement in "language games" (10). The war-on-women debates should be imagined, then, as another language game, with the expectation that these debates need continual monitoring. Moreover, I have read Rita Felski's *Doing Time*, which argues that "[i]f we want to persuade others of the value of feminist claims, [then] we need to engage . . . questions rather than simply retrenching and insisting on a self-evident identity or reality" (195). If women's rights are not "self-evident" to everyone, then feminists need to engage others about issues associated with the war-on-women debates to protect and perpetuate these rights. In sum, I should have recognized that a cultural logic of feminism is a social construct, not "the Truth." I should have known that the cultural logic of evolutionary historical progress takes a very short-sighted view of history. (Just ask the Trojans, the Romans, the Soviet Union, the women in Iran). So why was I seduced by this cultural logic into silence?

I don't know . . .
A desire for a stable identity and a stable reality?
A desire not to be inscribed in the postmodern dilemma?
A desire for problems once solved to remain solved?
Maybe I was just tired.

Regardless of the cause, as soon as I dismissed dysfunctional silence as a valid rhetorical response to the war-on-women debates and acknowledged a desire for more productive silences and responses, I knew that I was going to have to articulate a better cultural logic from within which to receive this debate. So, I turned to eavesdropping as a rhetorical tactic to expose problems with the cultural logic of evolutionary historical progress.

Harkening back to my eavesdropping chapter in *Rhetorical Listening* or its earlier iteration as an article in *JAC*, I reminded myself that a cultural logic of circling historiography focuses on usage (not origins) and assumes that we "circl[e] through time in order to expose the circling of time in our daily attitudes and actions" (108–9). Such circling enables the following three moves: (1) identifying moments when trope, body, and culture converge, as during the writing of my CCCC paper proposal when the *war-on-women* trope, my silence, and the 2012 election cycle converged; (2) articulating how such moments trigger our troubled identifications, as when I articulated in my CCCC's paper how I could not identify with political parties that attacked women's rights and associated women with the violence of war; and (3) articulating how such trope/body/culture moments expose the "*then-that-is-now*" (or the past that informs the present) in ways that make visible our own accountability for action, as when the use of outmoded language about women motivated me to figure out the cultural logic that fostered my dysfunctional silence as well as to discover an alternative one to foster my speaking out (111).

Thus, firmly entrenched in a cultural logic of circling historiography, I turned my analytical focus from cultural logics of reception to cultural logics of production, recognizing of course that reception and production are two interwoven parts of the same process. More specifically, I identified, analyzed, and evaluated the cultural logics from within which the *war-on-women* trope and its attendant discourses were reemployed, recognizing of course that cultural logics sometimes intersect or overlap. Simultaneously, I identified my troubled identifications with these cultural logics so as to provide a place from which to speak.

The most obvious cultural logics haunting the production of the *war-on-women* trope are political ones: Republican and Democrat. As a rhetoric scholar, I find the current Republican Party far more rhetorically interesting because, in trying to be a "big-tent" party, it has fractured into multiple cultural logics whose advocates do not really play well together and who do not really agree on how to define or address debates about women's issues. What follows, then, is an analysis of four contemporary Republican political cultural logics[2] and one Democratic cultural logic, highlighting both their influences on the meanings generated by the media's usage of the *war-on-women* trope and my own troubled identifications with the cultural logics.

One Republican cultural logic is traditional conservatism, the Republican Party of President William Taft, Senator Barry Goldwater, and President Ronald Reagan. This cultural logic is grounded in the assumption that government should play a limited role in all aspects of an individual's life so that the market can stabilize a nation and provide opportunities for individuals to pull themselves up by their bootstraps;[3] thus, people functioning within this cultural logic resist laws that regulate our financial, social, and personal lives. In terms of women's issues, traditional conservatives will not necessarily advocate for pay equity bills to engender women's rights because they assume that women may rise and be paid on their individual merits. On the other hand, traditional conservatives will not readily write laws that require vaginally invasive ultrasounds either, preferring to let cultural norms, not government bills, discipline women. For people functioning within this traditional conservatism, the media's use of the trope *war on women* to name Republican policies signifies as nonsensical because individualism allows women to rise if they are talented enough. My troubled identification with this cultural logic lies in my belief that the trope *individualism* is coded to celebrate the individual, to ignore the structural, and to gender the term *individual* as male. Consequently, the status quo is privileged.

A second Republican cultural logic is neo-conservatism, the Republican Party of President George W. Bush, Vice President Richard Cheney, and Secretary Donald Rumsfeld. This cultural logic is grounded in the competing assumptions that people should pull themselves up by their bootstraps but that a powerful government (i.e., the US) should assert its power around the world to enforce what it deems good and true and possible. Thus, people functioning within this neo-conservative cultural logic reward individualism domestically yet impose social engineering

---

2. Cultural logics within a system, such as the Republican Party, are bound to overlap somewhat because people function within overlapping discourses. But distinguishing one cultural logic from another is important for defining the different "wings" of the party.

3. For discussions about the bootstraps cultural logic, see Victor Villanueva's book by the same name.

in foreign policy, promoting democratic government and "enlightened" social practices for all nations, even if the people in other nations do not have cultural principles or values that can yet sustain such impositions. Because many neo-cons assume their beliefs to be universal Truths (capital T), rather than cultural constructs, they often do not bother to build consensus for their "Truths" and, thus, inadvertently by imposition encourage opponents to fight back rather than to negotiate and collaborate. In terms of women's issues, neo-cons may reward individual women in the US for their accomplishments but deny support for Planned Parenthood because its values conflict with the neo-cons' logic; conversely, they may advocate for other countries to promote laws that ensure women's right to vote or to receive an education. For people functioning within this cultural logic, the media's use of the trope *war on women* to name Republican policies is nonsensical because women can rise by their own merits and proper values are self-evident. Instead, within a neo-conservative cultural logic, this trope signifies mostly as what Democrats do (by promoting reproductive rights abroad) or as what people from other cultures perpetuate on *their* women and girls (by denying them education). My troubled identification with this cultural logic lies in its overestimation of the power of individualism domestically, its hubris or cultural blinders abroad, and its bully pulpit mentality.

A third Republican cultural logic is religious conservatism. Grounded in a fundamentalist Christian assumption that government should involve itself in people's social and personal lives so as to generate a more godly society, this cultural logic champions God's Truth (capital T) as interpreted by fundamentalists. In terms of women's issues, this cultural logic celebrates "traditional" women's roles such as wife and mother and denounces "modern" women's roles such as head of household or decision-maker about her own body. Because this cultural logic also champions laws to enforce the approved roles, vaginal ultrasounds before abortions emerge as a reasonable possibility. For people functioning within this cultural logic, the media's use of the trope *war on women* signifies as nonsensical when applied to their beliefs and policies because they see themselves as desiring to protect women; however, within this cultural logic, the *war-on-women* trope signifies as logical if applied to Democrats who, social conservatives believe, wage a war on women by promoting a radical feminism that defames women's traditional cultural and moral standing. One of my troubled identifications with this cultural logic lies in my belief that government should advocate for a more perfect union in terms of legal and economic rights for men and women but not in terms of only one specific religion; certainly, claims such as Richard Mourdock's that God intends rape to happen should not be the first principle for designing government policies about women.

A fourth Republican cultural logic is the grassroots Tea Party conservatism. Generally grounded in the assumption of limited government in terms of finance (no debt, few taxes) and in terms of personal responsibility (no affirmative action needed), this cultural logic advocates a nostalgic bootstrap individualism reminiscent of traditional conservatives. But Tea Partiers are less likely to negotiate (e.g., to avoid government shutdowns) or stick to the facts (Obama's birth certificate), and they invoke cultural scripts coded with sexism (personal attacks on Pelosi) and racism (personal attacks on Obama). In terms of women's issues, this cultural logic explains the emergence of claims during Senate races that "legitimate rape" is a real category (Williams) and during presidential races that legitimate birth certificates are not real (Karlamangla). For people functioning within this cultural logic, the trope *war on women* signifies, as it does for religious conservatives, as nonsensical if applied to themselves but pertinent if applied to Democrats who, Tea Party proponents believe, wage war on women via a politically correct feminism. My troubled identification with this cultural logic lies in my perception that many of its claims are haunted by racism and sexism and are either patently exaggerated or untrue (e.g., that "legitimate rape" cannot end in pregnancy).

Of course, there are also Democratic cultural logics: progressive, liberal, moderate, and conservative. Because of space constraints and because Democrats' competing cultural logics are not as interestingly diverse as the Republican ones, I focus only on the moderate Democratic cultural logic made popular by President Bill Clinton. This moderate cultural logic is grounded in the pragmatic assumption that a candidate should appeal to the middle of the political spectrum to get elected and, thus, to get things done. In terms of women's issues, this cultural logic (as well as other Democratic ones) proceeds by invoking the trope *war on women* to generate resistance among voters (particularly women) for Republican policies and politicians. For people functioning within this cultural logic, the media's use of the trope *war on women* functions as a politically explosive election tactic because it signifies a cultural backlash that must be stopped, most notably by electing Democratic candidates. My troubled identification with this cultural logic lies in my worry about the rhetorical and material consequences of yoking the tropes *women* and *war*.

By articulating the above cultural logics and my troubled identifications with them, I created a rhetorical situation wherein I was no longer unconsciously functioning within a cultural logic of evolutionary historical progress, which afforded me only the nonproductive rhetorical stances of howling at the moon or being dysfunctionally silent. Rather, deciding to reframe my silence more productively led me to choose to function within the cultural logic of circling historiography; in turn, this choice enabled me to discover language within which to analyze the political cultural logics surrounding the war-on-women debates. Consequently, I became able to initiate public conversations with friends and students and you the reader about how the trope *war on women* signifies differently within different cultural logics as well as how each of us might interpret political cultural logics differently depending upon the cultural logics we value. By analyzing these cultural logics, I was able not only to ascertain motivations for the litany of war-on-women news reports listed earlier but also, and perhaps more importantly, to identify the stakes of this debate.

Stakes of the War-on-Women Debates

The stakes of the war-on-women debate were, and are, high in that they have implications for people's lives both individually and collectively. One stake is a stake that is always a stake: power. When women's issues are thrown into the political arena for vote-getting, who wins such elections has a direct effect on laws that are passed, on court decisions that are rendered, and on real women's material bodies in terms of the ways they can live both in the US and, given foreign aid stipulations, in other parts of the world as well. To be effective in such public debates, feminists would do well to heed the combined power of silence and listening as rhetorical arts as a means of displacing any dysfunctional silences that may arise.

A second stake is the cultural definition of *women's bodies* and the attendant gender scripts that are presented as norms for these bodies to perform and by which to be evaluated. These scripts affect real women's bodies in terms of how the scripts socialize both women's and men's expectations about the way women should behave and be treated. Listening to these scripts both for what is silent and for what is said may serve as a productive rhetorical tactic for displacing any dysfunctional silences that may arise. Perhaps it is not coincidental, or maybe it is just ironic, that the hit song contemporaneous with this moment is "Let It Go" from the Disney movie *Frozen,* which encourages young women to let go of constraining cultural scripts.

A third stake is the possibility of pedagogy and its implications both within and outside the classroom. Teachers need to find ways to invite students from all political parties to enter political conversations with one another; after all, one of the first principles of rhetoric is that reasonable people may disagree (with the caveat, of course, that one should always keep in mind who is empowered to define *reasonable*). Studying how to listen to silences as well as to the tropes and the cultural logics that foster these silences can facilitate conversations across multiple political parties, not just across Republican and Democrat. If teachers "preach" only one cultural logic in class, they tend to get nods from those who agree and, at best, sighs or, at worst, complaints from those who disagree. Analyzing cultural logics side by side puts myriad ideas and assumptions in play in ways that enable students to see the constructed nature of cultural logics and to reflect on their consequences. Moreover, students and teachers suddenly find themselves delaying the question of whether one is right or wrong and, rather, analyzing how one's logics are constructed and how they inform one's attitudes and actions, which, in turn, leads to a deeper understanding for grounding claims about whether one is right or wrong. An effective pedagogical tool for demonstrating this point could very well be the *war-on-women* trope with its attendant cultural logics.

A fourth stake is political coalition-building. As Lyotard teaches us, in communication there always exists a differend (or a gap, whether large or small, between a speaker's *intent* and a discourse's actual *effect* on audiences). Because we cannot totally control reception, we cannot escape the differend. To negotiate differends, coalitions often generate compromise by focusing on common ground and downplaying differences, which enacts Kenneth Burke's definition of *identification* as the bridging of necessary differences (*Rhetoric* 55). But the best coalitions are aware and respectful of the differences that are being downplayed. Today, the differend that haunts contemporary US politics is tremendous; thus, a strategic common ground needs to be constructed among people across political parties and also among second- and third-wave feminisms. First, in terms of political parties, Republicans who might vote for fiscal conservatives may turn to Democratic alternatives when social conservatives offer "legitimate rape" as an accepted norm within political discourse; likewise, Democrats who disagree with social conservatives on invasive ultrasounds might align themselves with fiscal conservatives to help promote the latter's influence. Second, in terms of competing feminisms, although second- and third-wave feminists may disagree about whether asserting one's sexuality is an opportunity for objectification or an assertion of power, they need to discuss together whether the trope *war on women* is a dangerous commonplace to reinforce before they use it. They also need to articulate ways to talk back to political cultural logics, both Republican or Democrat, wherein the trope *war* and the trope *women* are uttered in the same breath and wherein the cultural logic of evolutionary historical progress hovers, just waiting to seduce us not just with the ideas of "stable progress" and "solved problems" but more insidiously, with an anger, disbelief, and despair that engenders a dysfunctional silence and inaction. Such silences and inaction are dangerous, for by engendering an absence of feminist voices, they empower the "other sides" to dismantle the very progress on women's issues that has been so dearly won.

To prevent such dismantling but also to construct a vision for future action, feminists and others committed to maintaining and enhancing women's rights would do well to attend to the possibilities of their silences. For as Glenn notes, "We live inside the act of discourse, to be sure, but we cannot assume that a *verbal* matrix is the only one in which the articulations and conduct of the mind take place" (153). While some silences may be dysfunctional, they may also be reimagined, as Glenn suggests, as functional sites that invite further inquiry (160). When silence is coupled with rhetorical listening, then a rhetorical situation emerges where silence and listening may function as sites for recursive intersections of delivery (Glenn 150) and invention (Ratcliffe 33). Thus imagined, silence and listening as rhetorical arts may function as powerful tools for participating in public debates, even ones labeled "war on women."

Addendum

As this chapter was moving through the publication process, the presidential election of 2016 occurred. Although the term *war on women* was not invoked in 2016 as frequently as in 2012, this trope haunted the rhetorical moves of the 2016 election, from Hillary Clinton's being expected to perform "the reasonable woman" role on debate stages to

Donald Trump's being held harmless for his "locker room talk." As such, the 2016 election deserves its own analysis, and this addendum is included here to invite such important work.

Works Cited

Alexander, Rachel. "The Democrats' War on Women." *Townhall.com*. Town Hall, 2 May 2012, townhall.com/columnists/mikelachance/2018/07/14/the-democrats-phony-war-on-women-has-come-home-to-roost-n2499692. Accessed 30 Dec. 2013.

Blake, Aaron. "The 'War on Caterpillars,' and What Reince Priebus Meant." *The Washington Post*, 5 Apr. 2012, www.washingtonpost.com/blogs/the-fix/post/the-war-on-caterpillars-and-what-reince-priebus-meant/2012/04/05/gIQABU9ixS_blog.html?noredirect=on&utm_term=.d5d7510adb7e *washingtonpost.com/blogs/*. Accessed 30 Dec. 2013.

Burke, Kenneth. *A Rhetoric of Motives*. U of California P, 1969.

Cardona, Maria. "Romney's Empty 'Binders Full of Women.'" *CNN.com*, 18 Oct. 2012, www.cnn.com/2012/10/17/opinion/cardona-binders-women/index.html, Accessed 25 Jan. 2014.

Castellanos, Dalina. "Arizona Gov. Jan Brewer Bans Public Funding of Planned Parenthood." *Los Angeles Times*, 5 May 2012, http://www.latimes.com/news/nation/nationnow/la-na-nn-arizona-planned-parenthood-20120505,0,4712705.story. Accessed 30 Dec. 2013.

"The Campaign Against Women." *New York Times*, 19 May 2012, www.nytimes.com/2012/05/20/opinion/sunday/the-attack-on-women-is-real.html. Accessed 30 Dec. 2013.

Felski, Rita. *Doing Time: Feminist Theory and Postmodern Culture*. New York UP, 2000.

Friess, Foster. "For Those Who Misunderstood My Joke Today, Here's My Quest for Forgiveness." *Fosterfriess.com*, 17 Feb. 2012. Accessed 30 Dec. 2013.

Gabbatt, Adam. "Republican Richard Mourdock: I Gained Votes After Rape Remarks." *The Guardian*, 25 Oct. 2012, www.theguardian.com/world/2012/oct/25/republican-richard-mourdock-rape-remark. Accessed 25 Jan. 2014.

Glenn, Cheryl. *Unspoken: A Rhetoric of Silence*. Southern Illinois UP, 2004.

Glenn, Cheryl and Krista Ratcliffe, editors. *Silence and Listening as Rhetorical Arts*. Southern Illinois UP, 2011.

Haberman, Maggie. "Foster Friess: In My Day, 'Gals' Put Aspirin 'Between their Knees' for Contraception." *Politico.com*, 2 Feb 2012, www.politico.com/blogs/burns-haberman/2012/02/foster-friess-in-my-day-gals-put-aspirin-between-their-knees-for-contraception-114730. Accessed 30 Dec. 2013.

Harris, Dan. "Rush Limbaugh Apologizes: Too Little, Too Late?" *ABC News*, 5 Mar. 2012, abcnews.go.com/Politics/OTUS/rush-limbaugh-apologizes-calling-sandra-fluke-slut/story?id=15841687. Accessed 30 Dec. 2013.

Karlamanga, Soumya. "Hawaii Plane Crash Fuels Obama 'Birther' Theories." *Los Angeles Times*, 13 Dec. 2013, www.latimes.com/nation/la-na-hawaii-plane-crash-20131213-story.html. Accessed 26 Jan. 2014.

Lowen, Linda. "What is 'The Republican War on Women' and When Did It Start?: A Look at the History of the Term, Elements of and Meaning Behind the Phrase." *About.com*, 12 Nov. 2012. Accessed 30 Dec. 2013.

Lyotard, Jean-Francois. *The Postmodern Condition: A Report on Knowledge*. Translated by Geoff Bennington and Brian Massumi, U of Minnesota P, 1984.

Madison, Lucy. "Virginia Gov. Bob McDonnell Signs Virginia Ultrasound Bill." *CBS News.com*, 7 Mar. 2012, www.cbsnews.com/news/virginia-gov-bob-mcdonnell-signs-virginia-ultrasound-bill/. Accessed 30 Dec. 2013.

Ratcliffe, Krista. *Rhetorical Listening: Identification, Gender, Whiteness*. Southern Illinois UP, 2006.

"Recall Target Wisconsin Gov. Scott Walker Says Worker Discrimination Law Was 'Gravy Train' for Lawyers." *Politifact.com*, 27 Apr. 2012, https://www.politifact.com/wisconsin/statements/2012/apr/27/scott-walker/recall-target-wisconsin-gov-scott-walker-says-work/. Accessed 30 Dec. 2013.

Robillard, Kevin. "Walsh: Abortion Never Saves Mom's Life." *Politico.com*, 19 Oct. 2012, www.politico.com/story/2012/10/rep-walsh-no-life-exception-needed-082620. Accessed 25 Jan. 2014.

Robbins-Early, Nick, Perry Stein, and Eric Wren. "The War on [Insert Noun]: The Uses and Misuses of Martial Rhetoric." *The New Republic*, 19 April 2012, newrepublic.com/article/102751/romney-obama-war-dogs-nouns-drugs-fehrnstrom. Accessed 24 Jan. 2014.

Russo, Eva. "Virginia Governor Signs Pre-Abortion Ultrasound Bill." *USA Today*, 7 Mar. 2012. Accessed 30 Dec. 2013.

Steinhauer, Jennifer. "Senate Republicans Again Block Pay Equity Bill." *New York Times*, 5 June 2012, www.nytimes.com/2012/06/06/us/politics/senate-republicans-block-pay-equity-bill.html. Accessed 30 Dec. 2013.

Tapper, Jake. "Rush Limbaugh Calls a Woman a 'Slut.'" *ABC News*, 2 Mar. 2012, abcnews.go.com/GMA/video/rush-limbaugh-calls-woman-slut-15831822. Accessed 30 Dec. 2013.

Villanueva, Victor. *Bootstraps: From an American Academic of Color*. NCTE, 1993.

"War on Women." *Wikipedia.com*, 25 Jan. 2014, en.wikipedia.org/wiki/War_on_Women. Accessed 26 Jan. 2014.

Williams, Matt. "'Legitimate Rape' Rarely Leads to Pregnancy, Claims US Senate Candidate." *The Guardian*, 19 August 2012, www.theguardian.com/world/2012/aug/19/republican-todd-akin-rape-pregnancy. Accessed 24 Jan. 2014.

4 "Beyond-Gender" Analysis of Power Relations in Language: The Case of Net Hate in the Nordic Countries

Brigitte Mral
Translated by Judith Rinker Öhman

As gender researchers began to shed light on women rhetors and rhetoricians throughout history, it became increasingly clear that the question of who had access to rhetorical arenas, of who had the *possibility and the right* to speak, was completely tied to the question of what status the speaker held in society. Over the centuries, women—and other groups in underprivileged positions—have developed sophisticated strategies for making their voices heard in the patriarchal rhetorical field. These strategies, which could be called "alternative rhetorics" or "rhetorics of resistance," often do not fit the traditional patterns of rhetorical practice. They have begun attracting the attention of researchers only in recent decades (Gray-Rosendale and Gruber; Mral, "Motståndets retorik").

The aim of this chapter is to present methodological frames for the analysis of power relations and the role of rhetoric in maintaining or challenging them. The chapter begins with a brief exposé of feminist rhetorical criticism and the recent development of gender research in the Nordic countries, especially Norway and Sweden, and then looks more closely at issues of status and resistance. The chapter concludes with a sample analysis of the phenomenon of "net hatred" in this region and how women encountering it seek to respond to the attacks and find effective rhetorical strategies of resistance, refusing to be silenced.

Nordic Feminist Rhetorical Scholarship

Since the 1970s, gender research in the US has focused on two kinds of work. First, feminist scholars have attempted to "save" women orators from the oblivion of history. This work is far from complete and many examples of women rhetors, both historic and current, remain to be analyzed. But just as gender does not only refer to women, gender research has not settled with highlighting only women in the history of rhetoric. The historical studies have generated new theoretical insights into the terms of communication in society from a power perspective. Feminist rhetorical theory has expanded the field, which now comprises other marginalized groups. This second kind of scholarship, which I would like to call "beyond-gender research," has—along with other critical and diversity-minded groupings within rhetoric study—opened up analyses of uneven power relations, discrimination and privileging based on ethnicity, class, age, ability status, sexual preference, etc. (Glenn; Glenn and Ratcliffe). Cheryl Glenn's concept of a *rhetoric of silence* has been pivotal in this process, with its focus on the rhetorical strategies used to silence others, to purposefully adopt silence, and to break silence. The turning of the perspective from the rhetoric of the dominant to the rhetorical strategies of the dominated also exposes the breadth of rhetoric. Another important aspect in this context concerns which audiences are included, not to mention excluded: the issue of a *third persona*, that is the groups excluded from a dominant discourse, those who are silenced, ignored or objectified (Wander).

In the Nordic countries and the rest of Europe, as late as the 1990s, gender issues within rhetoric research were virtually a non-theme. Only recently has gender research within rhetoric developed. In 1999, for example, the first book on women's rhetoric and female rhetoricians throughout history was published: *Talande kvinnor. Kvinnliga retoriker från Aspasia till Ellen Key* (Eng. *Speaking Women. Female Rhetoricians from Aspasia to Ellen Key*) (Mral). In 2003, a themed issue of the journal *Rhetorica Scandinavica*, "Retorik och genus" focused on rhetoric and gender and offered both a Swedish translation of Karlyn Kohrs Campbell's "The Rhetoric of Women's Liberation: An Oxymoron" and a number of studies of both theoretical and empirical character by Nordic researchers. One of the articles focuses on Swedish women writers in the eighteenth century, and the possibilities and obstacles they faced to participate in the public sphere (Öhrberg, "At då jag qwinna är"). Another text addresses the classical Swedish nurse uniform's visual rhetoric and how its colors, attributes, and the movements it allowed for accentuate the nurses' ethos (Öberg). In yet another article that centers on gender and the body in war, the author conducts an analysis of the use of metaphor in George W. Bush's rhetoric (Lippe, "Kjønn og kropp i krig og (u) fred"). Finally an article on women's historical and contemporary argumentative strategies provides examples of rhetorics of resistance (Mral, "Motståndets retorik").

Since 2003, scholarship on gender and rhetoric has steadily developed based on rhetorical approaches concerning, for instance, war and gender, women's authorship in history, religion and sex, women politicians' rhetorics, and issues of gender and argumentation (Lippe, "Images"; Öhrberg "The Strömfelt Sisters"; Mral, Borg & Salazar; Mral, "Some Gender Aspects"; Mral, "A Womanization of Public Discourse?"). This research is usually done through single case studies, but there are also attempts to develop feminist theories concerning, for instance, argumentation and the use of metaphor, often in relation and response to American research and, recently and more specifically, to Glenn's groundbreaking work. Early in 2014 an anthology was published containing studies of rhetoric within the women's suffrage movement, with contributions from Norwegian and Swedish researchers as well as Glenn (von der Lippe and Tønnesson). This scholarship reinforces the idea that, in recent years, gender research has encompassed more than issues of gender to move instead toward expanding the concept of rhetoric as it applies to historical and contemporary issues.

One such issue that has captured both popular and scholarly attention in the Nordic region is net hate. Net hate can be defined as prejudiced and unreasonable assertions about people or groups made online that are mixed with invective and at times direct threat. It involves expressions of malice, formulated in a bantering, degrading way. At its core lies a wish to indict or expose a person one dislikes or a group one hates. When it comes to attacks on individuals via email or short messaging service (SMS), the goal is often to frighten them; and in public forums like blogs or social networking and discussion sites such as Facebook or Flashback[1] the aim is to reduce trust, lower status, and crush the person or group in front of others. In rhetorical terms, this phenomenon can most accurately be regarded as an epideictic genre, as it entails insulting people and views, often with the aim of strengthening one's own group's cohesiveness and identity. Net hate is mostly based on sexism

---

1. A Swedish online discussion forum: https://www.flashback.org.

and racism. It especially targets women and the mostly anonymous contributions focus their attacks on women who express a feminist agenda or otherwise act in a strong and self-confident way. Men are much more rarely affected, except men with immigrant backgrounds or dark skin who speak out in public.

In this chapter, I explore acts of and responses to net hate within the Nordic countries, especially Sweden. Relying on Glenn's rhetorical theory, I argue that the rhetorical situation surrounding acts of net hate reveals the specific ways actors attempt to silence women rhetoricians who are opinion-makers in the region. The analysis shows, on the one hand, strategies entailing attempts to silence women in the public eye through forms of verbal threat in more or less anonymous posts in social media. And on the other hand, it shows the resistance strategies the victims of these attacks choose in their refusal to be silenced. Before taking up my exploration, though, I offer a brief summary of Glenn's theory regarding silence as a rhetorical tactic, in relation to theories of social status and rhetorical resistance.

From Feminist Research to Power Analysis

The idea of a rhetoric of silence as it has been developed by Glenn entails, as is well known, that silence can be just as powerful as speech. Silence can be used as a domination strategy, to silence and thereby exclude others or to refrain from responding, to express superiority. Silence can also be a low-status strategy; one might be silent because silence is what is expected, or because it carries advantages. As Glenn writes, "After all, people use silence and silencing every day to fulfill their rhetorical purpose, whether it is to maintain their position of power, resist the domination of others, or submit to subordination—regardless of their gendered positions" (153).

The language of power, seen historically, has always included elements of silence. Allowing oneself long pauses, for example, is a sign of self-confidence. Sayings like "Silence is golden" show that silence is more than simply the absence of communication but rather in some contexts is a virtue. The art of saying nothing is important, not least in the Nordic culture, where one should "speak well or not at all." A quiet person is a wise person; in the old Nordic mindset, silence is an expression of the speaker having control over both themselves and the surroundings. Too much talking without contemplation is a sign of stupidity, as pointed out in the medieval poem Hávamàl:

> Wise is he not who is never silent,
> Mouthing meaningless words.
> A glib tongue that goes on chattering
> Sings to its own harm. (Hávamál 29)[2]

Peter Burke has discussed silence as a tool for showing respect and deference, one that is closely connected to society's social structures. Historically, women were to be quiet in the company of men, and children in the company of adults (136fn). Thus, silence can have many different rhetorical functions, from being a means of dominance to being an expression of subordination. It goes without saying that an analysis of silence strategies should take its starting point at the specific rhetorical situation and consider the place of the silent subject in the social hierarchy. What is made clear when one turns the focus of the analysis to strategies of silence are issues of superiority and subordination, status and power.

Rhetorical practice and the possibilities to express oneself are always directly dependent on the speaker's initial ethos, primarily when it comes to whether they are in a high or low position, in a position of power, or in a dependent relationship. Therefore, here I introduce a category that is closely related to a speaker's initial ethos: rhetorical status; that is the speaker's position in the social and cultural power hierarchy.[3] Status is not something set in stone once and for all but is instead assigned by society at large or by one's audience or opponent. At the same time, rhetorical status can be raised or lowered depending on how successful one is in adapting to an opponent's prejudices and expectations. Behaving in a way traditionally expected by society—for instance, when a minister, politician, lawyer, or professor acts with authority, a strong voice, thoughtfulness, and stature—can enable one to strengthen an already high status and thereby argue effectively. Low-status groups have often been forced to develop other strategies to be able to meet expectations

---

2. http://www.ragweedforge.com/havamal.html.

3. The concept of status, introduced by Max Weber in the field of sociology as a relativization of the concept of class, is used but not theoretically developed in the field of rhetoric in Keith Johnstone's *Impro: Improvisation and the Theatre*. See also Viveka Adelswärd, *Kvinnospråk och fruntimmersprat: forskning och fördomar under 100 år*, and Vivianne Wester, "Bör kvinnor sära på benen?"

and be heard. In an analysis of marginalized rhetorics, it quickly becomes clear that they have to a great degree developed more sophisticated and varied rhetorical strategies than have speakers who are accepted within the dominating public.

Marginalized groups' resistance strategies comprise a broad and engrossing field. There are different approaches that have been used to create space in the face of rhetorical power: for example, a humorous attitude that can encompass brutal satire and burlesque has the potential to call into question the prevailing order, as well as subtle cunning and mild irony. Strategies also include nonviolent actions, demonstrations, and other symbolic rhetorical actions. Here, silence can have a central function of refusing aggressiveness and violence. There is also a certain argumentative strategy called *antistrephon*, which involves using the same proof one's opponent uses or turning the opponent's argument and proof to one's own advantage.[4] Finally, one can call to mind the silent demonstrations in East Germany before the Wall fell, or "Madres de la Plaza de Mayo"—also known as "the madwomen"— a group of Argentinian mothers whose children "disappeared" during the military dictatorship (1976–1983) and who held weekly silent manifestations for decades.

"Beyond-Gender" Analysis of Discursive Power Relations

How then is one to analyze power relations, superiority and subordination, and marginalization in discourses? An analysis of discursive power relations to a great degree concerns the choice of perspective and object, much more than a formalized method. An analysis of power can be done using any critical method, depending on the questions asked, the form of the material, and the focus of the research. However, when it comes to a rhetorical analysis of the rhetoric of resistance—or of dominance—one can ask the following specific questions:

- Who is allowed to speak in a certain situation; who is allowed to demonstrate rhetorical drive—and who is not?
- Who is the audience being addressed and which audiences are excluded?
- Is the recipient assigned subordinate or superior roles?

---

4. See, for example, Ritchie and Ronald, 61-70.

- Are there stereotypes regarding how certain groups "should" be?
- What factors are presented as "normal"?
- Are there perceptions of diversity, or are people presented as homogenous?
- What themes are not discussed, even though it is obvious they are relevant?
- Are obvious domination strategies used, and if so, how are they responded to?

All these questions concern developing a sensibility for what is not said—for more or less subtle mechanisms of silencing and exclusion. But, as mentioned, an analysis of rhetorical power relations can also concern discovering or mapping situations, genres, and groups that do not follow rhetoric in the classical sense by turning one's gaze to groups and actions that offer resistance to a dominant discourse.

In the following section, I analyze the phenomenon of "net hate" and the attempts to respond to these attacks seeing this as a current example of the rhetoric of dominance as well as resistance. Net hatred entails attempts to silence opinion-makers, especially women. Therefore, Glenn's concept of *rhetorical silence* and silencing is especially relevant in an analysis of hate strategies and resistance strategies.

Sample Analysis: "Men Who Net-Hate Women" and Women's Counter-Movements

Net hate affects both men and women in the Nordic countries and is primarily of a sexist and racist character. In a survey conducted by the Swedish communications bureau Cision, in a total of 515 journalists' responses, four out of ten claim to have been exposed to net hate. According to this survey, women encounter it somewhat more often than men (46% as opposed to 42%) (Thambert). The clear difference though is that the hate expressed toward the women is often extremely sexualized, entailing everything from derogatory comments about their appearance and lack of attractiveness to threats of various grotesque forms of sexual assault. Men are virtually never attacked on the basis of their gender.

This analysis focuses on the phenomenon of more or less anonymous (men) actors attacking public women media personalities in a sexist manner, and how the latter attempt to respond to these attacks. These are attempts to silence and dominate, not muted groups but, strong individuals. In Glenn's words, the rhetorical work is to exclude them "from the formulation, validation, and circulation of meaning" (25).

The material examined is an episode of the investigative television program *Uppdrag granskning* (Eng. *Mission: Investigation*) in which a number of women journalists and public opinion-makers are profiled due to their experiences with net hate, and seven of these exposed women are interviewed. The aim is to highlight possible resistance strategies in a situation in which the attacker is anonymous and a dialog is neither possible nor desired.

The rhetorical situation of the program is complex. The circumstances—"exigencies," to use Llyod Bitzer's word—are clear. To bring the verbal, and in some cases physical, threats out into the public eye, it is necessary to act rhetorically. The audience is to a certain degree comprised of the attackers themselves, but is mostly made up of the general public and decision-makers who are to be made aware of the problems and be encouraged to repudiate the threats. Regarding constraints to the rhetorical situation, actions are limited since the attackers are mostly anonymous, and the situation can be made worse when those attacked air the problem publicly. On the other hand, the space for rhetorical action is significant as the women have access to media, among other things, via this current program.

On 6 February, 2013, the episode "Män som näthatar kvinnor" ("Men Who Net-hate women") was broadcast. The title of the program alludes to Stig Larsson's famous novel from 2005 *Män som hatar kvinnor* (*Men who hate women*, English title: *The Girl with the Dragon Tattoo*). The program addresses the phenomenon of net hate from different perspectives. On the one hand, it confronts some of the aggressors, the so called "net trolls" directly. They are identified and interviewed, responding to questions such as, "Why does a man wish a young girl to be raped because of a post on Facebook?" Most of the program, however, features women who are exposed to net hate. Ten women media personalities are given the opportunity to read excerpts from hateful emails and posts on (Swedish) discussion sites. The women are all relatively young and have different functions in the media. They are, as stated in the program, "program hosts, editorial writers, news journalists, bloggers and social commentators. They have completely different backgrounds and images, but are seen and heard and this apparently carries a price."

Common to all is that these women are visible and outspoken. These are examples of bloggers with feminist profiles, such as a leftist culture journalist and a militant feminist writer. Some are "angry young women," but there are also some professional, politically nonprofiled news anchors and TV debate leaders. Suffice it to say, they are anything but "muted," which obviously provokes those men trying to silence them through verbal nasty attacks, but also through direct death threats or threats of rape. The women are "seen and heard," and as such, they are subject to threats that seek to silence them.

To illustrate the type of attacks involved, a number of quotes are included below, ranging from short, hateful outbursts to elaborate, violent fantasies:

- "You are so hideously ugly that it is inconceivable that you've got a job on TV. You are by far Sweden's ugliest woman."
- "I hope you and your children are raped sometime soon."
- "What you need is to get fucked down with a baseball bat. Die, can't you just die?"
- "You get an ultimatum: Either resign from the newspaper and live out your pathetic life anonymously in some suburb, or be prepared for war to be declared and to never be able to feel safe. One day I'm personally going to slit your throat and leave you there with the knife stuck in your cunt."
- "It's time now— now it's time for us to meet up and have sex. I'm going to wait for you outside the TV building. If you say no you'll be butchered, and then I'll hang all the pieces from meat hooks. After that I'm going to fry up your breasts in butter— that's going to taste good."

The attacks are obviously frightening, and they consistently combine sexist and racist attacks ("You Muslim-loving whore"). The women reacted differently to the attacks. Some tried to answer them with rational arguments, but gave up as the attacks got worse. Most tried not to bother to answer, but reported the threats to the police, usually without results.

In the program, the women are filmed one by one on a dark stage, sitting on a barstool. They are shown on screen with their names, and they recall their net-hate attacks in calm voices. The mood is suggestive, and the amassing of horrid statements as evidence creates strong identification. The women are also interviewed about how they experienced the situation, with brief comments during the program and longer quotations on the program's website. The overarching theme in the interviews is silence—particularly not allowing oneself to get silenced. Virtually all the women admit to censoring themselves sometimes, choosing not to address topics and opinions they expect will draw protest and retaliation, such as explicitly feminist or anti-racist statements. Columnist Frida Jönsson states, "I have lots of things I'd like to bring up but I'm silenced by a bunch of men." Columnist Sanna Lundell similarly notes, "I don't always have the energy to write about things I know are going to generate these types of comments." Even with these claims of self-censorship, though, these women enter into a rhetorical situation in which they expose themselves to the audience watching the program and put words to their experiences.

Not only do the net haters try to frighten the women into silence but the police also try to silence them, or rather to silence the problem, presumably with good intentions to protect the women from continued attacks. As cultural journalist Åsa Linderborg says in her interview, "We journalists always hear from the police that 'you shouldn't talk about this.' And then I wonder: who does that help? The people threatening us or the police . . . at any rate, it doesn't help democracy." Program host Jenny Alversjö comments: "It's easy to be quiet, partly because you're advised to be quiet because there's a security risk . . . The security people say it's individual people who are going to put the threat into action and that we shouldn't talk about it. Even people in the business say I should be quiet but I don't think so. It's a threat to democracy." That net hate is a democratic problem is something many of the women mention; the threats lead to certain opinions not coming to light and to freedom of speech being restricted.

It is difficult to offer an unequivocal explanation for net hatred toward women. Some of the program's debaters assert that it is a case of frustrated men who are unable to cope with seeing a steadily growing number of strong women in the public eye. In Sweden, feminism holds a strong position in both theory and social practice, and women continue to occupy more and more space. The debate sites and other channels that allow anonymous comments can, for many men, function as an unrestricted space that lets their hate and frustration hiss out. The reason for the male aggressiveness can be found in a sense of inferiority that many men seem to feel due to economic reasons, especially in this time of high unemployment and social insecurity. Perhaps it is also a sign of inferiority related to the fact that proportionally more young women than men today have a high education degree and are visible in the public sphere.

Some of the net haters are interviewed on the program, and they assert that it is mostly a case of jargon; that it is not meant to be taken literally, and that even death threats are merely verbal. "It's just Facebook, who cares? I mean I don't want her to be raped for real." But the fact is that in most cases the women journalists do feel like it's real: they have had to hide themselves and their families and receive constant security protection.

The women's behavior in the program is not actually a defense strategy; they do not feel they have anything to defend since they have every right to speak. But even though these women are not entirely muted, they are under verbal attack, and they demonstrate verbal resistance to verbal domination by speaking out and "talking back" (Glenn 26). The women in the program also offer resistance by using the attackers' weapons against them, reading their messages in public. At times an ironic smile can be discerned, for example in the following quote that was read: "In contrast to you, I have the gift of intelligence—I'm going to murder you when you least expect it. Unfriendly greetings, the Breivik Fan Club."[5] These public readings can be seen as a form of *antistrephon*, the strategy of turning one's opponent's "argument" to one's own advantage. It is a demonstrative strategy aiming to strengthen the identity and cohesiveness of one's own group—in this case, women journalists and public opinion-makers.

And thus, to the question of how the situation can be interpreted in terms of rhetorical status: Net hate should be considered an offensive and aggressive low-status rhetorical strategy. The nearly always anonymous actors express anger and frustration through unbridled insults. The women, on the other hand, are in a position of high status as journalists and public opinion-makers with access to the public stage. Linderborg describes this context in the following way: "We're living in hard times with an incredible number of people who can't influence anything. Compared to them I'm a person with great power. It's my job to point out injustices in society and of course that's going to provoke people." The women also move on the offensive by bringing the insults and threats into the public light. Editorial writer Maria Sveland says: "You want me to be silenced, then I'll turn up the volume even more and write a book about it." They thereby express a clear high-status strategy, as these women can access and make use of media like the publishing houses.

---

5. Anders Behring Breivik is a Norwegian right-wing convicted terrorist who killed seventy-seven persons 11 July 2011.

The program was received and debated well, and it is constantly referred to when the theme of net hate arises. It also has certainly had significant meaning for the cohesiveness within this group of women, as it has raised the problem from the individual to the societal level. However, it has hardly changed the phenomenon itself. The trolls who wish to air their aggression under the Internet's relative anonymity continue to do so. But this theme is now discussed in the public sphere on a recurring basis. There is now a site called *nohate.se* (the No Hate Speech Movement, a European initiative), which offers advice, discussion, and inspiration for a better Internet culture. Additionally, in the spring of 2014 a Swedish commercial TV channel aired the program "Trolljägarna" (Eng. Troll Hunters), in which individual net haters were approached and confronted in situations in which they could not hide behind their computers. Even in this program the victims of net hate could speak out. This time however not all the victims were women and not all the trolls were men, although the problem persists as one of masculine aggressiveness that is both sexist and racist. And the jargon is still grotesque. In later debates about the phenomenon, the conclusion was made that the problem must not only be handled in a legal way, if possible, as a hate crime but also that such attacks must be publicized and not be silenced.

In conclusion, how can this example be discussed in terms of discursive power relations and rhetorics of silence? When it comes to net haters, they apparently seek to exercise power by attempting to frighten the women into silence. Many of the women interpret net hate as an expression of men's frustration and experienced lack of power. Acting through aggressive attacks is then seen as an attempt to assert oneself and gain the upper hand in this discourse by limiting the women's free speech. As showcased in the program, the women, for their part, possessed a certain amount of actual power over the word as they have access to the public sphere and use this possibility to offer resistance and refuse to be subordinate. They respond to the threatening and anonymous aggression with an outspoken but calm personal deportment. Just the rhetorical action of reading the frightening but also somewhat ridiculous excerpts then becomes a way to discredit the opponent and regain the driver's seat so they are able to express themselves on any issue that may arise. In this case, then, the theoretical concepts of a rhetoric of silence and status relations function the other way around. The women refuse to be silenced, and they use their high status and access to public channels to speak out loudly and calmly about the problems caused by aggressive men with low status. Feminist thoughts regarding equality, the liberating potential of rhetoric, and rhetoric as a means of countering acts of violence have great relevance here. The women rise above their slanderers by turning the verbal weapons back on them, offering resistance—without aggression but with pride and authority.

Works Cited

Adelswärd, Viveka. *Kvinnospråk och fruntimmersprat: forskning och fördomar under 100 år*. Bromberg 1999.
Burke, Peter. *The Art of Conversation*. Polity, 1993.
Glenn, Cheryl. *Unspoken: A Rhetoric of Silence*. Southern Illinois UP, 2004.
Glenn, Cheryl, and Krista Ratcliffe, editors. *Silence and Listening as Rhetorical Arts*, Southern Illinois UP, 2011.
Gray-Rosendale, Laura, and Sibylle Gruber, editors. *Alternative Rhetorics: Challenges to the Rhetorical Tradition*. SUNY Press, 2001.
Johnstone, Keith. *Impro: Improvisation and the Theatre*. Corr. ed. Methuen, 1981.
Lippe, Berit von der. "Kjønn og kropp i krig og (u)fred." *Rhetorica Scandinavica*, vol. 27, 2003, pp. 83–97.
—. "Images of Victory, Images of Masculinity." *Nordicom*, vol. 27, no. 1, 2006, pp. 63–80.
Lippe, Berit von der and Johan L. Tønnesson. *Retorikken i kampen om kvinnestemmeretten*. Vidarforlaget, 2013.
Mral, Brigitte. "Motståndets retorik. Om kvinnors argumentativa strategier." *Rhetorica Scandinavica*, vol. 27, 2003, pp. 34–50.
—. "Some Gender Aspects Concerning the Concept of 'Strategic Maneuvering.'" *Considering Pragma-Dialectics*. Edited by Peter Houtlosser and Agnès van Rees, Lawrence Erlbaum, 2006, pp. 223-34.
—. *Talande kvinnor: kvinnliga retoriker från Aspasia till Ellen Key*. 2. utg. Retorikförlaget 2011.
—. "A Womanization of Public Discourse?" *Scandinavian Studies in Rhetoric. Rhetorica Scandinavica 1997–2010*, edited by Jens E. Kjeldsen and Jan Grue, Retorikförlaget, pp. 350–66.
Mral, Brigitte, Nicole Borg, and Philippe Salazar. *Women's Rhetoric. Argumentative Strategies of Women in Public Life*. Åstorp, Retorikförlaget, 2009.

Öberg, Lisa. "Den som ej äger en lätt gång måste öva sig'—Om kroppens och dräktens retorik i sjuksköterskyrket 1850–1950." *Rhetorica Scandinavica*, vol. 27, 2003, pp. 68–82.

Öhrberg, Ann, "At då jag qwinna är, jag skrifwa vill som kar' Kön och retorik under svenskt 1700-tal." *Rhetorica Scandinavica*, vol. 27, 2003, pp. 51–67.

—. "The Strömfelt Sisters: Gender and Power Within The Swedish Moravian Movement During the Eighteenth Century." *Pietism, Revivalism and Modernity, 1650–1850*, edited by Daniel Lindmark and Fred van Lieburg, Cambridge Scholars P, 2008, pp. 185-208.

Ritchie, Joy, and Kate Ronald, editors. *Available Means: An Anthology of Women's Rhetoric(s)*. U of Pittsburgh P, 2001.

Thambert, Frederik. "Undersökning: 4 av 10 journalister utsatta för näthat." Resume. 26 Feb 2013. Accessed 5 May 2013.

Uppdrag granskning. "Män som näthatar kvinnor." 6 Feb 2013. Accessed 5 May 2013.

Wander, Philip, "The Third Persona: An Ideological Turn in Rhetorical Theory." *Contemporary Rhetorical Theory: A Reader*, edited by John Louis Lucaites, Celeste Michelle Condit, and Sally Caudill, Guilford Press, 1999, 357-79.

Wester, Vivianne, "Bör kvinnor sära på benen?" *RetorikMagasinet*, vol. 10, 2001, pp. 7–11.

5 Philanthropic War Narratives and Spectacular Protection Scenarios

Berit von der Lippe

Narratives of war, victory, and glory have sprung from (some) men's memory, hopes, and ambitions and have done so since all time (Yuval-Davis, Abu-Lughod, Enloe, Tickner). Today, Western women are present not only on battlefields, as generals, officers, or soldiers, but also as high-ranking politicians dealing with security issues. In what way women's and young girls' presence as agents will change these male-dominated war narratives is difficult to say, but their presence is often portrayed as peaceful—one of "feminist" protection, especially for seemingly less fortunate women such as those living in Islamic countries. Yet, I propose, paraphrasing Gayatri Spivak's well-known expression that "white men protec[t] brown women from brown men" (Spivak), that we describe this new war narrative as "Western women protecting brown women from brown men." In other words, within these narratives Western women end up speaking for Islamic women, thereby silencing them, denying them agency and subjectivity. This modern "feminist" protection scenario became particularly manifest as part of the (so-called) war on terror after September 11, 2001.

"Feminist" rhetoric is here understood as the use of feminist ideas by Western liberal and/or social democratic administrations that differs from the gendered war rhetoric of the past. A "post-feminist achievement," equated with the full realization of gender equality in opposition to an illiberal and gender oppressive generalized Islam, has served as a postcolonial framing in Western protection scenarios of Afghan women (Abu-Laghod; Cloud). What kind of rhetoric is used to advance these "feminist" protection scenarios and whose work does it do? Such issues are complicated. Failing, though, to ask such questions may mean that feminism ends up simply facilitating the existing projects and priorities of militarized globalization in the name of protecting and promoting the interests of (some) women (Cockburn, "Gender"; Cockburn, "Snagged"; Eduards).

The rhetoric analyzed here is Norwegian "feminist" rhetoric used in some speeches by two defense ministers, Anne-Grete Strøm-Erichsen and Grete Faremo. Representing the social democrat Labor party, and as representatives of a country praised for its egalitarian society, gender equality included, these women and their rhetorical activities may, hopefully, be of some interest concerning not only "feminist" war rhetoric, but also feminist rhetoric as such. The ministers' speeches furthermore serve as context for a spectacular publication from an Afghan women's prison, which illustrates better than any speech what is at stake within postcolonial protection of "the other women." One of the ministers, namely Strøm-Erichsen, visited the Afghan prison in 2009 with several reporters and photographers. Due to her visit, the women prisoners' testimonies or very personal stories and traumas could thus be retold. But during the visit, the women and their children were photographed and, as such, they risked the security of anonymity. Various questions arise about the kinds of listening that might have occurred between the minister and the prisoners, as well as the accompanying Norwegian journalists and the public, as spectators, witnessing the identified victims' testimonies.

As the silence imposed on most Afghan women today does not differ much from the silence imposed on them before September 11, 2001 (Amnesty International; Joya, "Afghan People"), it is all the more important to be mindful of the plight of these women. The analysis is limited to the period from 2006 to 2010. The aim is to challenge the rhetorical transformation of war narratives into peaceful "feminist" protection scenarios. This will also be manifested when I outline the theoretical steps taken to approach such "modern" and spectacular Western war narratives.

FEMINIST RHETORIC: SILENCE, LISTENING, AND 'THE OTHER' WOMEN

The feminist rhetorical studies that turn to the rhetoric of silence and listening are essential to start grasping the complex issues indicated above.

Cheryl Glenn's studies on the rhetoric of silence(s) in collaboration with Krista Ratcliffe's work on listening offer important insights regarding what is meant by speaking on behalf of and in place of somebody whose protection, liberation, and security one claims to represent (Glenn, "Silence"; Glenn, *Unspoken*; Glenn and Ratcliffe, *Silence and Listening*). Rather than the different voices of Afghan women, the burqa became hypervisualized some months before and a short time after the war on terror began (post 9–11). Burqas were present as icons of oppression, and the women wearing them became absent because they were muted.

When or if their voices are heard, the question is how the rhetoric of listening might reflect a generalizing of otherness. The question is not only whether speech or silence is more productive, effective, or appropriate, but rather, as Glenn argues, when speech or silence is self-selected and when it is imposed:

> When silence is our rhetorical choice, we can use it purposefully and productively—but when it is not our choice, but someone else's for us, it can be insidious, particularly when someone else's choice for us comes in the shape of institutional structure. To wit, a person can choose silence, but the choice isn't really hers because speaking out will be professional suicide. In short, she's been disciplined—and silenced. ("Silence" 263–64)

Here, Glenn discusses rhetoric and silence within North American culture. Silence may be a means of survival or a conscious method of resistance. When silence is broken but there is nobody to listen, one's value as a human being seems to be nil (*Unspoken*). As Jacqueline Jones Royster puts it: "What I am compelled to ask, when veils seem more like walls, is who has the privilege of speaking?" (36). Who has the privilege of speaking for Afghan women?

The veiling of Afghan women is about much more than the burqa; more important for most Afghan women are those veils that "seem more like walls." The rhetoric of the veil—or the rhetoric of silence—occurs when the speaking subjects speak on behalf of and in place of Afghan women, more or less erasing their subjectivity and denying them agency, so that they then become helpless objects to be rescued and protected by Western women. Both the rhetoric of silence and rhetorical listening will need, however, some theoretical supplements.

The use of feminist ideas for instrumental purposes, is, according to Michaele Ferguson, based on a rhetorical and representational model of framing. Transporting pre-existing feminist ideas into new contexts, feminist rhetoric is introduced into a discursive context in which other frames are already operative. Ferguson uses the term "feminized" rhetoric (14) when analyzing the US rhetoric of liberating Afghan women, focusing on the right to education. This rhetoric is, as already indicated, based on a concern with women's oppression abroad, real or perceived, as well as the presumption that the women's movement in Western countries successfully achieved its goals long ago (see also Flanders; Lippe, von der and Väyrinen).

Co-optation is similar to the framing model but does more than reframing feminist ideas. According to social theorist Maria Stratigaki, co-optation is a common discursive, rhetorical, and linguistic practice that both absorbs and neutralizes the meanings of the original concepts to fit into hegemonic political discourses. Co-optation can take place when the hegemonic ideology on war is not questioned and alternative war stories are silenced or marginalized. Co-optation of women's rights issues, such as gender equality, is more likely when there is a high level of normative legitimacy for the general principle underlying the original policy goal.

The main vehicle for Norwegian "feminist" rhetoric during the war on terror in Afghanistan has first and foremost been the UN Resolution 1325, a resolution on women and security (see UN Resolution 1325). This resolution challenged the "women and children as helpless victims" construct. Women, in this case Afghan women, should now *pace* the resolution, be seen as agents taking part at all levels in conflict situations. By using the original as well as the transformed concept, or as in this case a UN resolution, as an alibi, co-optation often works against mobilization and pressure by interested parties and individuals (Cohn).

These perspectives are in many ways similar to the postcolonial criticism expressed by Spivak some decades ago. Warning that we cannot usefully respond to the silencing of the "subaltern" woman by "representing" that figure or by constructing her as a speaking subject, Spivak reminds us of a colonial past. Even when undertaken with "good intentions," no perspective can turn this other into a self. Lila Abu-Lughod takes us some steps further and focuses on how imperial logic genders and separates subject peoples so that men are the Other and the women are civilizable: "To defend our universal civilization we must rescue the women. To rescue these women we must attack these men. These women are to be rescued not because they are more 'ours' than 'theirs' but rather because they will have become more 'ours' through rescue mission" (469).

The tendency to act according to these ideas will to some extent challenge Glenn's texts on rhetoric of silence as well as Glenn's and Ratcliffe's analysis of rhetorical listening—a listening as a means of negotiation and openness. A rhetorical listening helping us continually negotiate our always evolving standpoints, our identities, with the always evolving standpoints of others, is a listening difficult in the globalized world—and globalized wars—of today. Asking us to identify "the various discourses embodied within each of us and then listening to hear and imagine how these discourses might affect not only ourselves but others," Ratcliffe points to important aspects of rhetorical listening (28). The complexities of rhetorical listening within the protection/liberation scenarios call, though, for an understanding of silence, listening, and identification that recognizes both the colonial histories and the material-rhetorical context of listening and silencing.

When Raka Shome, nearly two decades ago, explicitly criticized the discipline of rhetoric on the whole because of its silence in relation to neocolonialism, few within the field listened. "The silence I have in mind," Shome writes, "has to do with not rereading (and problematizing) our dominant rhetorical paradigms, our theories, our critical tools, and our research agendas, against a larger backdrop of racial and neocolonial politics" (49). Wendy Hesford too proposes that we consider not only gender, race, and class, but also the social location of the speaker or writer as well as the material-rhetorical context into which the utterance or text is projected. The publication of spectacular witnessing of Afghan women prisoners' traumas in question here makes it all the more important to include post-colonial perspectives as well as the importance of materiality brought forth by Hesford.

Before approaching the Norwegian "feminist" rhetoric of benevolent philanthropy, a "what can we do for Afghan women?" rhetoric, I bring forth aspects of Norwegian feminism(s) as well as Norwegian foreign policy tradition to shed some kairotic light on the rhetoric used by the ministers.

Norwegian Gender Equality and Peace Narrative(s)

The official feminist ideology in Norway is strongly geared toward gender equality, based on what is called state feminism. The welfare state is to a large extent responsible to its citizens' needs. This implies rather ample support for working parents and their children but has, on the other hand, nurtured ideas of equality as sameness between men and women as the main strategy. This blurring of equality and sameness contributed to the election of Gro Harlem Brundtland as Norwegian Prime Minister in 1986 with a cabinet known worldwide for its high proportion of women ministers: nearly half, or eight of the total eighteen ministers, were women. Arguments about differences have today more or less disappeared from the discourses of gender equality (Holst, 2009, Bjørnholt et al.).

Women's everyday experiences are, however, assumed to drive them toward care that is a rationally developed standpoint rather than an emotional reaction. They have a tendency to identify with those in need of care, and thereby, develop responsible rationality. Responsible rationality is very much a relational rationality that fits well with the values of Nordic/Norwegian welfare states. Another feature is the emphasis put on maximizing labor force participation by promoting gender equality as well as wealth redistribution, the latter indicative of a different logic than the market logic. In the last decade, the Nordic welfare states have come under neoliberal pressure, less so, though, in Norway because of low unemployment and extraordinary economic strength. This economic strength makes it possible to assist in various philanthropic activities, thereby strengthening the country's philanthropic ethos as a peaceful nation.

The Norwegian responsible rationality is also used instrumentally—as a heritage to be exported, that is, something similar to the marketing of a product, as will be seen in the rhetoric used abroad by the defense ministers. It often takes the form of "patronizing rationality"—a rationality influencing public rhetoric, security rhetoric included (Lippe and Väyrinen). What characterizes Norwegian foreign policy as well as security rhetoric is the story of a remote geographical position that, according to the hegemonic narratives, has historically permitted the state to remain aloof from international engagement. The decision to enter into military alliances was taken after World War II, especially with Norway's NATO membership in 1949. Once a controversial political issue, membership in NATO has been seen in the last decades as an important part of most Norwegians' identity. Solidarity, internationalism, and peacekeeping operations have been the values around which the Norwegian foreign policy rhetoric has been established and in whose name actions are performed.

According to this rhetoric, Norway never takes part in war or warfare; it happens, though, that the country takes part in military engagements or operations. The narrative cultivates the idea that Norway has a long-standing tradition of participation in UN-led peacekeeping activities, conflict prevention through political dialogue, mediation, and overseas development aid on a large scale (Leira, 2005/2014). This understanding seems to fit well in a context where women and women's rights are increasingly gaining credence as issues of national and international security. The marketing of Norway as a beacon of gender equality—a country that is both peace-loving and charitable—is of utmost importance and seems to have been successful.

In the last two decades, most Norwegian defense ministers have been women. Strøm-Erichsen (2005–2009/2011–2013) is the minister who has been the most energetic spokesperson when it comes to rhetorical activities within the "feminist" protection-liberation scenario by applying the UN Resolution 1325 on women, peace, and security. The resolution urges all actors to increase the participation of women and incorporate gender perspectives in United Nations peace and security efforts, but the resolution does not mention the importance of women's participation as soldiers. After this brief summary of Norwegian gender equality and foreign policy, I analyze the ministers' rhetorical practices.

Benevolent Rhetorical Practices

Strøm-Erichsen's unpopular predecessor, Kristin Krohn Devold, representing the right-wing party and a politician who manifestly demonstrated her enthusiasm toward George W. Bush. and US policies, made it more important for Strøm-Erichsen to choose a different and softer rhetoric, while simultaneously respecting Norway's historic loyalty toward the US. The fact that Norway, contrary to the will of most high-ranking politicians and as a result of referendum, is not a member of the European Union (EU) and is associated only through an economic alliance, makes it more important for Norwegian politicians to be visible exactly where the European political power elites are situated and gathered.

In 2006, a year after Strøm-Erichsen was elected defense minister, she spoke in Brussels before representatives of EU members on security issues. The speech serves as an illustration of promoting abroad self-evident truths when it comes to Norwegian gender equality engagement—within an apparently harmonious security discourse (Strøm-Erichsen). She begins the speech with rhetoric resonant of a brave and trustworthy pupil addressing a group of highly respected teachers: "First of all, let me thank the Presidency for inviting me to this Troika-meeting.[1] The opportunity to discuss current security issues with our close European friends and Allies is very much appreciated."

Underscoring the need to improve NATO-EU relations, Strøm-Erichsen approaches security challenges and the complexities of peace-building, paying specific attention to the war in Afghanistan: "First, the international community must coordinate civilian efforts in a better way. Today the civilian aspects of our engagements, in Afghanistan and elsewhere, are often fragmented and uncoordinated. This means that the overall results are less effective." For Strøm-Erichsen, catastrophes for Afghan civilians are presented as a simple coordination problem and the problem is seemingly "gender-neutral."

After panegyrically embracing all Western-dominated institutions, EU, NATO, NGO's, the International Monetary Fund, and The World Bank, Strøm-Erichsen finally turns to the UN resolution that urges all member states to pay attention to women's role in new peace support operations:

> I would also like to welcome the EU conclusion on promoting gender equality and gender mainstreaming in crisis management, in line with the UN Resolution 1325. This is an important progress. Norway puts great emphasis on the UN resolution and has adopted a national action plan to promote gender issues.

Norway, represented by Strøm-Erichsen, seems at this moment to be the head of the European body. The Western security scenario, too, seems rhetorically secured, as the agency of Afghan women is manifestly absent. Strøm-Erichsen's rhetoric is a subtle way of speaking on behalf of Afghan women—the women whose lack of agency was the main reason for the resolution to be born.

The silencing of Afghan women's voices, like that of Malalai Joya, Afghanistan's youngest and most outspoken parliamentarian, was necessary for the use of the resolution as the main rhetorical device. Joya warned in December 2003 against some of the Western allies, calling

---

1. The "Troïka" represents the European Union in external relations that fall within the scope of the common foreign and security policy (CFSP).

them criminals, bandits, and "the most anti-women people in the society" (Joya, "Malalai Joya's Historical Speech"). She had the courage to speak out and has since then lived in danger of being killed. Four years later she states:

> The US government removed the ultra-reactionary and brutal regime of Taliban, but instead of relying on the Afghan people, pushed us from the frying pan into the fire and selected its friends from among the most dirty and infamous criminals of the "Northern Alliance," which is made up of the sworn enemies of democracy and human rights, and are as dark-minded, evil, and cruel as the Taliban. The Western media talks about democracy and the liberation of Afghanistan, but the US and its allies are engaged in the warlordization, criminalization and drug-lordization of our wounded land. (Joya, "The US Has Returned")

Silencing—or choosing to not listen—to such dangerous female voices, Strøm-Erichsen's rhetorical use of the UN resolution may be seen as a subtle form of feminist co-optation as the resolution is hijacked, that is, absorbed and neutralized, to fit harmoniously into hegemonic political discourses. The agency of Afghan women is out of reach. The distance from the material-rhetorical context of the speaker and the European audience to the material context where Afghan women (men and children) live, suffer, or die, could hardly have been greater.

Taking for granted, it seems, that "we," by military means and in collaboration with brutal warlords, can bring civilization to Afghanistan and thus to Afghan women, the disciplined minister delivered a speech for the insiders. As the national narrative cherishes the idea of Norway's long-standing tradition of participation in UN-led peacekeeping activities, this idea has impact on Norwegians in general, including many academics, both women and men, within the fields of international relations and peace researchers. Identifying their common ground as being citizens of an egalitarian society and peace-loving country, Strøm-Erichsen becomes a woman "of good will" and a liberal feminist. An illustration of this enactment is manifested in the speech below.

When addressing Norwegian (mainly women) peace researchers in Oslo 2007, Strøm-Erichsen gives an extraordinary illustration of benevolent philanthropy within a protection-liberation scenario. Having told the audience about her multiple visits to Afghanistan, she takes an extraordinary rhetorical step for a minister of defense:

> I am sure I am not the only person here to have been moved by the stories about the hardships and faiths of the two female characters, Mariam and Laila, in Khaled Hosseini's book *A Thousand Splendid Suns*. Unfortunately, their tragic stories, which include domestic, social and even state violence, are only too realistic and representative.

Referring to splendid and touching literature about Afghan women—and men—she invites her audience to enter a fictional world, a story probably more realistic than the stories she and her colleagues are telling in public. Strøm-Erichsen prefers to silence the agency and heroic bravery of Afghan men as well as women characters. She chooses to render the men characters, who in the fiction risked their lives by supporting, protecting, and empowering their women friends and family members, invisible and nonexistent. She thus omits the collaboration and mutual trust between some men and women characters—thus facilitating feminized rhetoric of silence to succeed, at least for some time. And Abu-Laghod's comments that men are the not civilizable, the women are, is here, at least to some extent, illustrated (Abu-Laghod).

Highlighting several improvements for Afghan women (and children), such as hospitals and education for women and girls, Strøm-Erichsen gradually prepares the ground from which she can explicitly refer to the resolution:

> It is an imperative that we reach out to also the female part of the population in Afghanistan. There are several elements to this. First, we need to see this from a justice perspective. If we are in Afghanistan to improve the lives of the Afghan population, we cannot succeed if it is only the male part of the population that benefits from improvements.

Her imperative promotion of benevolent philanthropy is simultaneously a rhetoric of praise—to Norway and Norwegian "engagement" in Afghanistan. It is a "we" who "see" who must reach out to them, that is, the "female part of the population." This female part, nearly fifteen million women belonging to various tribal communities segregated along ethnicity lines, is—rather than "are"—those to whom "we" will relate. This benevolent philanthropy indicates that it is often easier to identify with oppressed women than with strong and potent women—women who also might need support, based, however, on solidarity as equals. Powerful Afghan women speaking for themselves about needs and aspirations based on their own experiences might have raised problems for the humanitarian rhetoric to be successful.

Strøm-Erichsen continues, stating that "in 'old fashioned' operations . . . the aim was to remove or replace the leadership of a country. In today's operations, the aim is to transform and assist a society and an elected government." Old wars, that is, "old fashioned operations," are thus opposed to "modern operations," because the latter are transforming and assisting a society. Having assured the audience about Norway's philanthropic engagement, the resolution is explicitly brought to the forefront: "The mantra in this is the UN Resolution 1325, which stresses the important role of female personnel in international security operations. We do not have enough women in our armed forces. This is a challenge at the top of my agenda as defence minister." This challenge of increasing women in the armed forces is her own interpretation of the resolution as its focus is on women mainly within civilian police, human rights, and humanitarian personnel. By seeing the Norwegian participation in Afghanistan first and foremost as a peace operation, the soldiers easily become human rights and humanitarian personnel (Lippe).

Legitimating her rhetoric, Strøm-Erichsen then uses the most common vehicle for both persuasion and identification to take place by adding: "I believe that being a woman in itself is a quality and competence that will improve a male dominated military organisation." Women are both equal and different according to the minister, they may contribute to diversity in the military because of a specific resource they are assumed to have as women. Speaking for or speaking on behalf of Afghan women has within the protection scenario become a common practice. Perhaps more interesting and troublesome: The audience eagerly applauded the minister's speech. The few critical questions raised, were not commented upon.

Such a rhetorical strategy is ultimately a reflection of the ideological and political practices of "developed" nations; for it is only when two-thirds of the world can be silenced that it becomes possible for "first-world" subjects to adopt this attitude toward "third-world" countries and people living there—in this case first and foremost Afghan women. Such strategy is, though, hardly perceived as a strategy. Instead, it comes to represent the truth—a taken for granted evidence of a nation's good will. This is manifested vividly—or deadly—in the publication of the minister's visit to the women's prison in Maimana.

Visual Presence, Witnessing Testimony, and Rhetorical Listening

When witnessing testimonies of trauma, the visual absence of the victim is assumed to provide an opportunity for any rhetorical presence. The primary motive for the testifier's anonymity is often that of protection (Hesford, "Documenting"; Hesford, *Spectacular Rhetorics*). The absence often places the viewer, spectator, or listener in a very specific rhetorical relation to this protective absence. Sometimes, though, we may be witnesses to a different kind of testimony—and a different kind of witnessing. Sometimes the victims are present and identified, but absent because someone might be speaking on behalf of the identified victims. By transforming some victims' testimonies into narratives fit for the Norwegian public, a spectacular protection scenario of testimony witnessing is materialized. This kind of protection scenario may illustrate some (un-)expected rhetorical complexities.

What happens when traditional understandings of rhetorical identification and presence reach, or rather transcend, their limit? Let me illustrate. It is September 2009. Strøm-Erichsen has visited Afghan female prisoners in Maimana, a town in North-Afghanistan. The Norwegian public some days later becomes spectators to her deep felt compassion—and I dare add, genuine compassionate listening. The minister is photographed crying in the prison yard. She has returned to this prison she had visited two years earlier. Reports of the visit detail her words in this way: "Then, I found eleven women stewed in an underground basement cellar . . . . It was simply too awful and horrific. I can hardly describe how gruesome it was." So why is she crying now as the prisoners are much better off? Why has she permitted to be photographed crying?

The caption of one of the press releases reads, "When love is kidnapping." Beneath the caption are several photos, the one of the minister wiping her tears, the others of the imprisoned Afghan women with their children—all very much present as they are photographed staring at the camera, thus directly at us as spectators. The fear their faces communicate is striking. The testimonies—or traumatic stories—in the reportage are multiple and so are the photographs of the prisoners, women with and without children. Only two of the testimonies will here be retold, sufficiently, I hope though, to undertake a rhetorical approach to the complexities involved in acts similar to testimony witnessing and rhetorical listening that are linked to multiple aspects of identification and mis- or dis-identification. The first testimony is that of one of the Afghan women, looking anxiously at the spectators, as she somewhat helplessly caresses her three daughters.

Nahla is the name of the woman in this testimony. She is twenty years old, the text tells. Spectators are told that the mother and her children are dressed up, prepared for the visit of the minister. The report does not explain that Nahla and her children were not prepared for a group of Norwegian embedded journalists following her. Nahla, the story goes, has been sentenced to twelve years in prison. She has assisted her cousin to meet a beloved man in secrecy. The report reads, "Her three small daughters are struggling to find a place on the mother's lap. Now they are too small to understand why mum is not living at home." Another woman's traumatic story relates how—and how often—she has been raped by a cousin, who one day told the family and members of the local community about the woman's participation in these criminal activities—as in those of being raped.

Similar traumatic stories or testimonies by the other prisoners are published, similar tragedies and traumas are told. The difference between the Afghan misogynist society and the Norwegian gender equality society is underlined throughout the text and serves as a frame for Norwegian readers and spectators. The bold agency of Nahla, risking her life for her cousin, is not brought forth as any heroic act common to many women in Afghanistan. They are all objectified as victims. In the real world they are victimized three times, first by their relatives, then as prisoners, and finally as represented for spectators to be seen—terrified.

It later emerged that this was a rehearsed scenario, a PR stunt, by the Norwegian defense ministry (Sømme Hammer, *Drømmekrigen*). What is foregrounded, is that the prisoners are all better off now. Thanks to Norwegian philanthropy this prison is a modern prison, recently built by Norwegian means. The report makes clear the living standard for the women and their children has improved. The protection scenarios apparently have many faces because, as in this case, the representational strategies are limited and so are the journalistic conventions. This is, thus, not what makes this reportage specific.

The cultural stigma of the imprisoned women, photographed and identified speaking with foreigners, seen as potential or real enemies, is not considered (Sømme Hammer, *Drømmekrigen*). Because of the misogynist and oppressive culture, the women are all criminals—and after the publication of the testimonies, they may also become traitors. Photographed and identified by foreigners, they have broken one more and one extra important code of behavior: communicating with and thereby permitting foreigners to witness their "crime stories." By unveiling the victims, the news story brings Afghan women into "our" civilization within a protection scenario—risking once more their lives.

For these women the stigma could hardly have been worse. Most of them are not—and never—allowed to communicate with foreigners at all. Only on a few exceptional occasions are they permitted to communicate in public with Afghan men—veiled. The visual absence of the female body will usually remind viewers of the vulnerability of victim in speaking out. Her testimony is usually a testimony standing alongside the thousands of women who cannot speak out: those who are killed or those who choose to keep silent out of fear for their lives and the social stigma in patriarchal cultures.

When pseudonymous testimonials by Afghan women flooded the literary market soon after the war on terror began, Gillian Whitlock took a closer look at the ghoulish burka covers, inviting the readers—as spectators and consumers—to enter into the realm of unknown women's lives. According to Whitlock, the "mass marketing of these images of absolute difference in times of resurgent fundamentalisms" was politically instrumental and a trap that the wary reader needs to avoid (47). She underlines an awareness of life narratives from subalterns who have no cultural capital to the public intellectuals who do. This is an awareness of which politicians, publishers, or journalists seem unaware. The ignorance of Afghan culture is tragically manifested in multiple ways and at various levels.

The Norwegian minister herself had listened. Her tears were hardly an effect of any strategic rhetorical activity. What kind of listening might then best describe the minister's way of listening? Borrowing from Ratcliffe, is she listening to the stories *for* intent—promotion of Norwegian benevolence—as well as *with* intent—with the intent to understand (28)? Rhetorical listening as a "stance of openness that a person may choose to assume in relation to any person, text, or culture" might signify some aspects of a stance of Strøm-Erichsen's openness. "Choosing" or "choice" with regard to rhetorical listening is indeed difficult to define. Spivak's warning that no perspective can turn "the other" into a self, because the project of imperialism has always already historically refracted what might have been an incommensurable other into a domesticated other—in consolidating, the imperialist self will often come to the surface. The domestication and self-consolidation manifestly expressed in the kind of spectacular witnessing discussed here have some commonalities with an imperialist self.

Strøm-Erichsen might have needed time for meditation and critical thinking after being exposed to unimaginable traumatic stories. If her tears were an effect of regret, if she suddenly was regretting the PR stunt and thus the future publishing and identification of the testifiers, the minister could easily have prevented any and all publicity. This is, though, a theoretical possibility only. Her choice was another. The publishing of Norwegian benevolent activities in Afghanistan, in general, and philanthropy for Afghan women (and children), in particular, seemed too important. Still, though, her intentions might have been "good." The "criminals" were "better off" in the newly built prison. Ignoring—or ignorant of—prevailing cultural or symbolic systems, not least when it comes to gender relations and how Afghan men and women interact, she permitted her feminine empathy to be made public. The publication, or better, the PR stunt, was simultaneously a story telling the Western spectators why "our" presence in Afghanistan is needed and necessary.

The internalization of benevolence, of protective attitude and behavior brought forth here, is, at least at some level, an illustration of a postcolonial perspective of protecting "the other women," in this case women prisoners, now brutally stigmatized and scared to death (Sømme Hammer). Strøm-Erichsen was, at some shallow level, aware of the social location of the speakers, that is, the prisoners, as well as the material-rhetorical context into which the testimonies were projected. Whichever way, the minister's—and Norway's—compassionate cosmopolitan stance of good will was published. At a deeper level of awareness Strøm-Erichsen would probably have prohibited Norwegian male reporters to join her and to publish the prisoners and their horrific stories.

Marginal knowledge, selective memory, and selective representation of the "other" are vital to the "saving brown women" mentality and scenario. Unable to see how "the other" women use rhetoric to negotiate with men within patriarchal and even misogynist tribal structures, the "protectors" and "liberators" are listening mainly to their own conviction of benevolence, an internal echo. To illustrate how a similar kind of internal echo may be expressed, I examine the rhetorics of Grete Faremo, manifested in a speech to representatives of UN.

Faremo's Address to UN Security Council in New York

Grete Faremo, Strøm-Erichsen's successor as defense minister 2011, has held a range of political positions for the Norwegian Labour Party. She has, however, performed different kinds of rhetorical activities than those of her predecessor. Faremo's rhetorical performance is somewhat bolder. She has also held leading positions in Security Corporations and has been the head of the legal and public relations function of Microsoft, and later director at Microsoft Norway.

Faremo is a kind of woman who hardly would have appeared wiping her tears in public. She is very much representative of a gender equality perspective that takes "equality" for "sameness"—a perspective focusing mainly on a gender balance, as outlined above. What the two women seem to have in common is the taking for granted of their own perspectives as universalist. Similar to her predecessor, Faremo reserves agency for "us," not "the other" women. Her rhetorical strategy is mainly expressed by references to her own successful biography, an effective vehicle to establish identification with the audience. Analogous to her own civil career as a woman in the civil society, she has argued for a more modern armed force, that is, more women in the army—according to the gender balance perspective (see Faremo, "Vi Må Få En Sterkere Debatt"). The borderlines between civil society and armed forces are thereby blurred. Her qualities as leader might enable her to frame gender equality within the armed forces. Equality to what and equal with whom seems hardly to be of any interest.

When Faremo promoted gender equality and peace in an address to members of the UN Security Council 2010 (Faremo, "Speech by Minister of Defence"), her ethos was probably granted. Norway's economic contribution to the UN in general and the Security Council in particular, are high, and the relation between Norway and the UN is warm, as has been underlined also in the rhetoric analyzed above. The speech might well have been a marketing of herself for future positions in that system.

Faremo begins with the following questions: "What do women want? What do women need? How can women contribute?" She is thus speaking on behalf of all women, Westerners and non-Westerners. Immediately she also makes manifest the explicitly rhetorical aspect of her questions by putting forward a polemic voice: "Thus came Resolution 1325. At least on paper, this resolution gives women a voice, and better protection." The minister wants action, something more than mere words written on a paper. Not only does Faremo regret the small number of Norwegian women soldiers, she also regrets—and nearly blames—the audience for not seeing the importance of the resolution: "Ten years after the adoption of 1325—at the NATO Ministerial Council meeting earlier this month—I called for including 1325 in NATO's concept of operation. We obviously have a job to do, to make the military men take this seriously."

Ten years after the adoption of the resolution, she is, or she must be, well aware of the alarming situation in Afghanistan and the situation of most Afghan women. Her position in this speech is reminiscent of the one Spivak so often has warned of: the voice that silences the "subaltern" woman by "representing" that figure, or by constructing her as a speaking subject. Highlighting the Norwegian engagement for a gender sensitive war, she proclaims: "We will contribute experts on gender and gender-based violence to international peacekeeping operations." The "we" is here "we Norwegians," and the war is here, as elsewhere, not a war, but peacekeeping operations. The taking for granted of one own's philanthropy and gender awareness is intact. White women too, are able to protect "brown women from brown men."

What should then be done? What is her advice to the audience? "As Minister of defense, I note that all of the UN force commanders are men. It is high time to rectify this," she announces, before she calls "on the UN to start searching for women commanders while we continue to improve the gender ratio of our forces." Her own voice, representing the Norwegian voice, is a voice of global dimensions. Reassuring the audience that the number of women Norwegian soldiers and officers is increasing, she finally makes clear "that Norway will strengthen gender education of our armed forces and our police. And we will introduce a new system of reporting on gender and the role of women in field missions." Her identification strategy may be seen with reference to UN as an organization. It is a rhetorical situation where the individual "member" comes to see her reflection in the social mirror of the collective. The interests of the individual and the organization will usually overlap and coincide.

Furthermore, Faremo's gender was presumable a proof not only of Norwegian "modernity," but of the common interest within the UN as an organization, promoting gender equality in "modern" warfare and equally "modern" armed forces. The subtle and complex aspects of identification or disidentification and rhetorical listening are—at least to some degree—often based on utopic dreams when cross-cultural interactions are at stake and global power structures are seen as natural, not political, economic, or cultural.

The rhetorical agency is "ours," not "theirs." Potential oxymoronic dimensions of the non-identification Afghans might perceive with foreign soldiers are made invisible. No attempt to construct Afghan women as speaking subjects with an agency of their own is suggested. Leaving the Afghan "other" totally left out, she thus does not have to turn any other into a self. Her "feminist" rhetoric remains lost in the hegemonic Western tradition, breaking with tradition only by including the importance of agential Western women and the shortage of these in Norwegian armed forces.

Faremo's speaking out here and elsewhere is part of her professional success. Speaking out for most Afghan women living in Afghanistan, is, on the other hand, similar to suicide. If Faremo is disciplined into Western liberal feminist ways, some few Afghan women refuse to be disciplined to silence—they are instead silenced because they are seldom listened to or presented as agential individuals. The "white woman" prefers to talk on behalf of "the other woman." Faremo's impressive career as director in various corporations might well have strengthened her ethos: Women can. And by military means "we" can liberate "the other women" in a fashion similar to former colonialists' projects of liberating "the other"—with military means and in the name of civilization. By turning "war" into "peace operation," Faremo uses Orwellian language that may help her rhetoric to be successful. As of 2019, she holds the position as Executive Director of the United Nations Office for Project Services. Similar to her predecessor, Strøm-Erichsen, Faremo will probably contribute to increased representation of women in power positions by leveraging the kinds of "feminist" rhetoric brought forth above. And like her predecessor, Faremo will probably prefer to swim with the mainstream—his stream. On May 7, 2014 Faremo won a high ranking position within the UN: United Nations Secretary-General Ban Ki-moon made her the Executive Director of the United Nations Office for Project Services.

Compassionate Listening and Feminist Rhetoric

Strategies of silence, as Glenn has told us, enable superiority and subordination, status, and power. In this chapter, I have brought forth some specific kinds of silence—or rather silencing and speaking on behalf of others. The stance of openness that a person may choose to assume in relation to foreigners in times of war is more often than not a difficult stance to assume. Within Norwegian protection scenarios involving the superiority and status of power *vis à vis* "the other women," the rhetoric of silence and listening takes particular forms. Both Strøm-Erichsen and Faremo present themselves as authorized to know what the "other woman" wants. Their rhetorical performances fit well with Western protection scenarios. Strøm-Erichsen welcomes "the EU conclusion on promoting gender equality and gender mainstreaming in crisis management, in line with the UN Resolution 1325"—a resolution she herself has interpreted and used to construct a protection scenario. Faremo often refers to the same resolution, but she sometimes uses a more patronizing rhetoric. When she explicitly is speaking on behalf of all women, she asks, "What do women want? What do women need? How can women contribute?" These questions illustrate an extraordinary self-confidence that, to some extent, is symptomatic for Westerners and an extension of Western gendered behavior.

It goes without saying that both women leaders used rhetorical strategies fitting ministers of defense in times of war. Acknowledging the changing nature of warfare, in which civilians are increasingly targeted, women should now, *pace* the Resolution 1325, not be seen as passive victims but rather as participators in peace processes. As Strategaki notes, it is difficult to oppose something you may agree to, and a resolution seeing women in war zones as agents, not as passive victims, may be difficult to oppose. When the power of agency mainly is "ours" not "theirs," though, the resolution turns on its head; it is co-opted and used for strategic reasons. It becomes a part of the rhetorical legitimation of US-initiated war, dressed in "feminist" clothes. The publication and identification of Afghan female prisoners during Strøm-Erichsen's visit in Maimana might serve as an illustration of Norwegian—or Western—life-threatening philanthropic activities. Compassionate listening is seldom sufficient to obtain trust or confidence between "the care giver(s)" and "the care taker(s)." Lack of knowledge or even ignorance about the material conditions of "the other" makes it more difficult to practice any invitational forms of communication.

In the aftermath of the September 11, 2001 attacks, the politics and rhetoric of the "war on terror," partially justified as promoting "democracy" and "women's rights," have dented both international human rights and feminist ideals. We need to start by asking some basic questions: Whose democracy? Whose liberation? Whose feminism? Who is speaking for Islam? Who is speaking for Afghan women? Who is speaking for feminism? These questions are seldom addressed in academia, media, or activist forums—be it in the US or in Norway. Within the discipline of rhetoric, and among those of us writing feminist rhetorical texts, addressing these questions are among the most important challenges of today.

Among the rhetorical complexities regarding race, culture, gender, and power, it is not just a question of our refusal to recognize differences and thus a refusal of openness. Royster's question—"when veils seem more like walls, . . . who has the privilege of speaking?"—ought indeed to be considered over and over again. The protection scenario is described by Abirafeh and others (Dupree; Giliani; RAWA) as a crucial mistake and a symptom of Western "othering." The failure to recognize that many Afghan women's identities stem from their relationships with family and community rather than a potential relation(ship) with foreign soldiers reveals the Western domestication of "the other" (see also Orford; Shepherd).

To listen when the subaltern speaks requires openness to the message, especially because it may be unsettling, something we may not want to hear. When the subaltern speaks, "we," the Westerners, more often than not are confirmed by listening to their—our?—own echo and our fantasies rather than being able to listen to "the others." The reassuring rhetoric of confirmation and the unsettling rhetoric of dissent should invite us to consider how to transform global meanings and materialize them in local practices. So, too, do we need to understand how identities and identification practices are enabled and constrained by kairos— that is, by material and rhetorical circumstances, as Hesford reminds us. Lacking any experience with tribal local communities, Strøm-Erichsen's listening to the Afghan female prisoners prevented an "openness" necessary for any protection/liberation scenario to be acted out. Whether ignoring or ignorant of prevailing cultural or symbolic systems, she permitted her feminine empathy to be published and manifested—unaware that this philanthropic publication might be life-threatening for the women prisoners.

Glenn is right when she underlines that rhetoric inscribes language and power at a particular point in time by deciding who can speak and what gets said ("Silence" 262). "Western women protecting brown women from brown men"—a tactic especially seen in the rhetorical activities of both the women Norwegian ministers studied here—illustrates that there is more at stake than the rhetorical silencing and listening discussed by Glenn. Her theories regarding silence's rhetoricity have opened rhetorical territories too-long hidden within the discipline. Rhetoric, once a self-interested enterprise of investing white males with the power to speak for and over others, while at the same time denying all others this right, has been revised. Rhetorical complexities and disagreements among feminists about feminist rhetoric ought to be considered and reconsidered over and over, especially when it comes to issues of war and peace.

WORKS CITED

Abirafeh, Lina. *Gender and International Aid in Afghanistan: The Politics and Effects of Intervention*. Taylor & Francis, 2009.

Abu-Lughod, Lila. "Do Muslim Women Really Need Saving? Anthropological Reflections On Cultural Relativism And Its Others." *American Anthropologist*, vol. 104, no. 3, 2002, pp. 783–90.

Amnesty International. "Amnesty International Hosts 'Shadow Summit' With Afghan." *Amnesty International*, 1 Jan. 2012. Accessed 2 Sept. 2012.

Bjørnholt, Margunn. Retfærd. Nordisk juridisk tidsskrift. 36. årgang 2013. no. 3/142.

Cloud, Dana L. "'To Veil the Threat of Terror': Afghan Women and the 'Clash of Civilizations' in the Imagery of the U.S. War on Terrorism." *Quarterly Journal of Speech*, vol. 90, no. 3, 2004, pp. 285–306.

Cockburn, Cynthia. "Gender as Causal in Militarization and War: A Feminist Standpoint." *International Feminist Journal of Politics*, vol. 12, no. 2, 2010, pp. 139–57.

—. "Snagged On the Contradiction: NATO, UNSC Resolution 1325, and Feminist Responses." Contribution to the Working Group on Feminist Critiques of Militarization, 1 Jan. 2011. Accessed 13 Oct. 2013.

Cohn, Carol. "Mainstreaming Gender in UN Security Policy: A Path to Political Transformation?" Boston Consortium on Gender, Security and Human Rights Working Paper 204. 2004.

—. "Mainstreaming Gender in UN Security Policy: A Path to Political Transformation?" Boston Consortium on Gender, Security, and Human Rights 201. 2008.

Dupree, Nancy Hatch. "Cultural Heritage and National Identity in Afghanistan." *Third World Quarterly*, vol. 23, no. 5, 2002, pp. 977–89.

Eduards, Maud. "Jämställdhetens Militarisering" ("The Militarization of Swedish Equality Policy"). Paper Presented at the Swedish Political Science Association Annual Meeting. 2013.

Enloe, Cynthia H. *The Curious Feminist Searching for Women in a New Age of Empire*. U of California P, 2004.

Faremo, Grete. "Vi Må Få En Sterkere Debatt Om Likestilling Og Maktfordeling I Forsvaret." 1 Jan. 2010. Accessed 13 Oct. 2013.

—. Speech by Minister of Defense, Grete Faremo, at the UN Security Council, 26. Oct. 2010b. Accessed 24 Oct. 2014.

Ferguson, Michaele L. "'W' Stands for Women: Feminism and Security Rhetoric in the Post-9/11 Bush Administration." *Politics & Gender*, vol. 1, no. 1, 2005, pp. 9–38.

Flanders, Laura. *The W Effect: Bush's War on Women*. New York UP, 2004.

Gilani, Sabrina. "Reconstituting Manhood: Examining Post-Conflict Its Effects on Women and Women's Rights in Afghanistan." *In-Spire: Journal of Law, Politics and Societies*, vol. 3, no. 2, 2008, pp. 53–71.

Glenn, Cheryl. "Silence: A Rhetoric Art for Resisting Discipline(s)." *JAC*, vol. 22, no. 2, 2002, pp. 261–92.

—. *Unspoken: A Rhetoric of Silence*. Southern Illinois UP, 2004.

Glenn, Cheryl and Krista Ratcliffe, editors. *Silence and Listening as Rhetorical Arts*. Southern Illinois UP, 2011.

Hesford, Wendy S. "Documenting Violations: Rhetorical Witnessing and the Spectacle of Distant Suffering as Pedagogy." *Biography*, vol. 27, no. 1, 2004, pp. 104–44.

—. *Spectacular Rhetorics: Human Rights Visions, Recognitions, Feminisms*. Duke UP, 2011.

Holst, Cathrine. *Hva Er Feminisme*. Universitetsforlaget, 2009.

Joya, Malalai. Malalai Joya's Historical Speech in the Loya Jirga, Loya Jirga Meeting, Kabul, Afghanistan, December 17, 2003/2006, http://www.malalaijoya.com/remarks.htm. Accessed 13 Oct. 2013.

—. "The US has Returned Fundamentalism to Afghanistan," 12 April 2007, http://www.dominionpaper.ca/articles/1148. Accessed 5 Jan. 2012.

—. "The Afghan People Are Fed Up": An Interview with Malalai Joya, http://www.malalaijoya.com/dcmj/joya-in-media/758-the-afghan-people-are-fed-up-an-interview-with-malalai-joya.html. Accessed 20 Mar. 2014.

Leira, Halvard. "Folket Og Freden" ("The People and the Peace")." *Internasjonal Politikk*, vol. 2, no. 3, 2005, pp. 135–60.

Lippe, Berit, von der, and Tarja Väyrynen. "Laura Bush Meets Nordic Feminism." *European Journal of Women's Studies*, vol. 18, no. 1, 2011, pp. 19–33.

Lippe, Berit, von der, and Kirsti Stuvøy. "Kvinnefrigjøring Og Krig – En Selvmotsigelse. FNs Sikkerhetsrådsresolusjon 1325 Og Kvinners Rettigheter I Afghanistan»." *Nytt Norsk Tidsskrift*, vol. 30, no. 1, 2013, pp. 41–52.

Orford, Ann. "Feminism, Imperialism and the Mission of International Law." *Nordic Journal of International Law*, vol. 71, no. 2, 2002, pp. 275–96.

Ratcliffe, Krista. *Rhetorical Listening: Identification, Gender, Whiteness*. Southern Illinois UP, 2005.

Royster, Jacqueline Jones. "When the First Voice You Hear Is Not Your Own." *College Composition and Communication*, vol. 47, 1996, pp. 29–40.

Shepherd, Laura J. "Loud Voices Behind the Wall: Gender Violence and the Violent Reproduction of the International." *Millennium—Journal of International Studies*, vol. 34, no. 2, 2005, pp. 377–401.

Shome, Raka. "Postcolonial Interventions in the Rhetorical Canon: An 'Other' View." *Communication Theory*, vol. 6, no. 1, 1996, pp. 40–59.

Spivak, Gayatri Chakravorty. *Can the Subaltern Speak?* Houndmills, Macmillan, 1988.

Stratigaki, Maria. "Gender Mainstreaming vs Positive Action: An Ongoing Conflict in EU Gender Equality Policy." *European Journal of Women's Studies*, vol. 12, no. 2, 2005, pp. 165–86.

Strøm- Erichsen, Anne Grete. "Peacebuilding, Justice and Security-Security for Women in Afghanistan." https://www.regjeringen.no/no/aktuelt/security-for-the-women-of-afghanistan-/id490255/. Accessed 13 Oct. 2013.

Sømme Hammer, Anders. *Drømmekrigen*. Aschehoug, 2011.

—. *Dette Skulle Ikke Ha Hendt*. Aschehoug, 2014.

Tickner, J. Ann. *Gendering World Politics.* New York: Columbia, 2001.
—. *A Feminist Voyage through International Relations.* Oxford UP, 2004.
UN Resolution 1325. 30 Oct. 2000. http://www.un.org/womenwatch/osagi/wps/. Accessed 20 Oct.2014.
Whitlock, Gillian. *Autographic.* U of Hawaii P, 2008.
Yuval-Davis, Nira. *Gender and Nation.* Sage, 1997.

Part II: Feminist Rhetoric and Identity Studies

6 "As Sisters in Zion": Constructing Mormon Women's Identity through the Spatial Topos of Zion

Rosalyn Collings Eves

> *[E]ach time we face the rhetorical woman, we still see terra nova, barely perceptible on our horizon.*
>
> —Cheryl Glenn, *Rhetoric Retold*, 10

> *While race, class, and gender have long been viewed as the most significant markers of identity, geographic identity is often ignored or taken for granted. However, identities take root from particular sociogeographical intersections, reflecting where a person comes from and, to some extent, directing where she is allowed to go. Geographical locations influence our habits, speech patterns, style, and values—all of which make it a rhetorical concept or important to rhetoric.*
>
> —Nedra Reynolds, *Geographies of Writing*, 11

The study and practice of rhetoric has been linked with identity[1] almost from its inception (Aristotle), yet as Cheryl Glenn and other feminist rhetoricians have noted, this link has been

---

1. Here, I understand identity as the ways in which an individual identifies with and differentiates herself from a variety of collectives. As Rosaura Sánchez explains, identities can be understood as "constellations" that are "all grounded in historically specific social spaces but always open and in flux" (41). Because identities emerge via social interaction (Grabill and Pigg) and through

problematic, particularly for women and other minorities who exist outside the predominantly masculine rhetorical tradition (*Rhetoric Retold* 12). For women, writing themselves into the history of rhetoric has required assuming a strategic array of identities to authorize their voices, from Julian of Norwich's acknowledgement of her gendered body and borrowing of divine authority (*Rhetoric Retold* 96–97) to Elizabeth I's presentation of herself as an androgyne, both a masculine and feminine ruler (167).[2] Scholars such as Glenn, who hope to write these women into the still unfolding territory—the *"terra nova"*—of women's rhetorical history, must then attend to the link between rhetoric and identity and study how women strategically use identity to authorize their speaking.

But as the epigraph from Nedra Reynolds makes clear, this rhetorical mapping project needs to focus not only on the *figurative* territory that women occupy, but also the literal places from which women speak. Both Reynolds and Roxanne Mountford have argued that rhetorical studies more strongly grounds its work in material place.[3] Not only are women's identities rooted in a particular place, but their very speech choices—what to say, how to say it, and to what audience—are shaped in part by their geographical location. Gregory Clark argues that "[r]hetoric involves assertions of identity that develop symbolically" (254), and these symbols are often rooted in *location*. Feminist rhetorician Risa Applegarth defines location as "a richly layered term that includes one's material environment as well as the social and symbolic processes that imbue

---

discourse (Sánchez), they are inherently rhetorical—hence identity remains a concept that is not only useful to rhetoric, but vital.

2. This construction of self in response to a particular rhetorical situation becomes a woman's ethos. And though identity, as the ways in which an individual identifies with and differentiates herself from a variety of collectives, cannot be simply conflated with ethos, ethos as an identity "chosen for presentation" is "shaped by powerful societal influences such as class, gender, and ethnicity" (Desser 317).

3. For an overview of recent work in rhetorics of space, see Jordynn Jack's review article, "Space, Place, and the Public Face of Composition," where she discusses the use of space by feminist rhetoricians, ecocompositionists, memory studies, and electronic spaces; additionally, in my chapter "That We Might Become 'A Peculiar People,'" I overview four common rhetorical approaches to space: historical analysis of the way individuals have been denied access to spaces, discursive studies of the way language shapes our experience of place, symbolic operation of space in discourse, and the influence of physical sites on rhetorical performance.

environments with meaning, shap[ing] who one becomes and how one communicates with others" (43). Hence, as women construct appeals to particular landscapes or explore location-based narratives, they implicitly (and sometimes explicitly) use place to advance particular arguments about identity.

Recent scholarship in rhetoric has pushed our understanding of the way ethos changes when linked with material and metaphorical locations. Julie Nelson Christoph argues that ethos is locationally dependent: identities are more properly understood as "geographies of identity" that vary according to situation and audience and can be strategically deployed (665). Thus, to understand the strategies women speakers develop to authorize their voices, rhetoric scholars must look "not only at *texts* but also at material, social, and political *con*texts" (668). Building on Christoph's idea that identities are situational and strategic, Applegarth demonstrates the way the naturalist genre (a place in and of itself) shaped Mary Austin's efforts to create a persuasive public ethos through her depictions of the American Southwest. But identity strategies include more than just authorial ethos. Such identity strategies might also rely on place-based narratives that help constitute a particular geographic identity, or manipulating configurations of place in ways that allow for different author-rhetor relationships. (See, for instance, Mountford's landmark study on women preachers.)

This chapter excavates a marginalized, gendered, and religious voice from the nineteenth-century American West, Mormon speaker, writer, and poet, Eliza R. Snow. But beyond simply illuminating a shadowy figure, I explore some of the ways place can be used as a resource for identity. As Reynold's epigraph suggests, any rhetoric attempting to account for the ways identity is deployed must also account for the role of place in those identity strategies. In a 2012 special issue on *Regional Rhetorics*, guest editor Jenny Rice argues that regional rhetoric is important because it "disrupts given narratives of belonging that are framed on a national level and between individuals and provide[s] alternate ways of framing our relationships and modes of belonging" (202). Crucially, she suggests that the emerging field of regional rhetoric asks, "what do people actually do in region, as well as through rhetorical appeals to region?" (202). Examining how individual women, such as Snow, use place to reframe identity narratives can help us answer that question.

In this chapter, I demonstrate the way Snow wields geographical identity (inflected by both her gendered and religious identity) as a rhetorical tool. Snow uses identity both as a means and an end by leveraging the place-based topos of Zion (as well as its attendant identity), and she invokes a particular version of Mormon womanhood in her primary audience of Mormon women. Attending to the ways women use place as a rhetorical resource for identity can help us not only map the literal location of women speakers, but it can also help us better understand the following intersections of place, rhetoric, and identity: the ways women weave narratives to locate themselves in places and communities; the ways identity can be locationally dependent; and the ways narratives of place shape both the experience of place and the concomitant identity.

IDENTITY IN CONTEXT

Eliza R. Snow provides an ideal subject for exploring these intersections of rhetoric, place, and identity, because, as a Mormon woman living in the nineteenth-century American West, she was positioned in the midst of shifting discourses about nationhood, womanhood, and religious, racial, and even geographic identities.[4] Because so little is known about nineteenth-century Mormon women in rhetorical circles, this section begins with some background to the Mormon Church[5] and Snow herself, paying particular attention to place. Snow's religious, gendered, geo-

---

4. Krista Comer's study of Western women writers posits that space, like gender, sexuality, and other markers of identity, often functions along a power differential. In America, the northeast (New England in particular) has been and continues to be a normalized site for identity, particularly for Anglo-Americans; a cultural critic speaking from New England has no need to justify his authority or academic lineage in the same ways a Western writer might (Comer). Historian Melody Graulich calls this phenomenon "Eastern cultural hegemony" and points to an 1898 literary map of the US that concentrated most of the literary work in the east and marked some of the western states as "unclaimed" (47). Because "space goes about its cultural work by calling relatively little attention to itself as power broker" (Comer 26), the role of place in Eastern American identity is often unmarked. By contrast, in the West, the impact of place on identity was often more transparent because the cultural value of place was constantly shifting—for some the West represented the endless possibilities of the United States nation (Turner), for others it represented an untamed space that threatened civilization and needed to be domesticated (Kaplan).

5. The Mormon Church is formally known as The Church of Jesus Christ of Latter-day Saints, but I will be using the colloquial term here as it is most familiar to a majority of readers.

graphical, and even racial identity was contingent upon her physical and social location.

Eliza Roxcy Snow was born in Ohio and converted to the still new Mormon church in 1835,[6] after meeting the founder, Joseph Smith (Snow, "Sketch"). As a consequence of her conversion with Smith, Snow embraced her new community, moving to join members in Kirtland, Ohio, and then to Missouri. The early years of the Mormon Church were often unsettled, as local communities viewed them as economic and political threats: Mormons tended to buy and sell primarily from each other and voted as a block, giving them extra influence in local counties (Arrington and Bitton 49–51). In 1839, in response to increasing mob violence and the governor's extermination order,[7] Snow and other Mormons moved to Illinois (Arrington and Bitton 51). In 1844, Joseph Smith was lynched by an angry mob, and Brigham Young assumed leadership of the growing church. Two years later, increasing tension with their frontier neighbors led the Mormons to abandon Illinois for the Far West, settling in Utah in 1847 (Arrington and Bitton). Typical of her persistence in her faith, Snow was among the earliest pioneer companies to reach the Salt Lake valley, arriving in the fall of 1847.

Like other Eastern transplants in the West, Snow found her identity in flux in these new environments. This identity flux was compounded by the fact that Snow, like virtually all Mormon women, was a convert to a new church, and her conversion required her to refigure her identity outside of mainstream Christianity, as part of a radical offshoot (opponents claimed cult) espousing modern-day prophets.[8] The physical isolation from other Anglo-American settlers allowed Snow and other Mormon women to practice, and fully identify with, their new religion in relative peace. Yet, unlike other Western women, conditions particular to Mormon communities made their experience of the Western frontier different. For one, Mormon communities were highly structured

---

6. The Church was founded in 1830.

7. After an election day riot, Governor Lilburn Boggs of Missouri issued the following order: "The Mormons must be treated as enemies, and must be exterminated or driven from the state if necessary, for the public peace" (Arrington and Bitton 44).

8. Jill Derr's essay "The Significance of 'O My Father' in the Personal Journey of Eliza R. Snow" explores some of Snow's identity crisis, particularly related to her position as a woman within the growing church and within Mormon theology.

from the outset (Arrington and Bitton), and most Mormon women were integrated into the Mormon women's Relief Society, an organization that "achieved for Mormon women a power base and a degree of public influence unequalled by 'gentile' women on the frontier" and provided an outlet for creative and charitable abilities (Beecher, "Priestess," 153). In addition, because Mormon men were often absent due to church responsibilities, particularly foreign missions, women were often called on to perform men's labor as well as their own (Arrington and Bitton). The Mormon practice of polygamy meant that polygamous wives were also likely to have more independence, act as head of households, and share financial responsibility, particularly in cases where the family was wealthy enough to afford a separate house for each wife and the husband rotated residency (Jeffrey).

Snow achieved a high level of independence and influence among Mormon women in Utah as one of Brigham Young's plural wives after their marriage in 1844, though their marriage seems to have been primarily a political and economic union (Beecher, *Personal Writings*, 2; Derr, "The Lion and the Lioness"). As prophet, Young patronized Snow's poetry; as a poet, she upheld his role as prophet. And as president of the Mormon Church, Young's work was complimented by Snow's work as presidentess (her preferred title) of the Relief Society. As presidentess, Snow oversaw various home industries (such as raising silk worms and growing grain), charity work, women's health education, and the organization of a hospital for women (Beecher, "The Eliza Enigma"). Reflective of Snow's social position, most of her public speeches were recorded in the *Woman's Exponent*, a bi-monthly periodical by Mormon women, and one of the first enduring newspapers for women published west of the Mississippi (Scott xx).

Snow used this forum, along with public speeches, to exhort her Mormon listeners to adopt specific behaviors and to affirm a particular identity for both herself and her audience. She draws on epideictic rhetoric, with its focus on praise and blame, to recommit women to a particular vision of Mormon community. Unsurprisingly, in the wake of her displacements, Snow invested her physical place with spiritual significance and used it as a resource for symbolic invention.[9] For Snow, the

9. Because land, like other markers of dominant culture identity, often becomes an invisible marker of privilege, land is often only noticed or valued in its absence. Thus, Euro-Americans have historically ignored issues of space, while the narratives of displaced people often write with urgent attention to place, frequently offering alternative conceptions of those places (Brady). In the wake

identity she sought to claim for herself and for other Mormon women was not simply a matter of rhetorical convenience: it was a matter of communal survival, even salvation. Snow believed that without a strong commitment to their religious faith, Mormon women were in danger of succumbing to worldly conventions and practices that might risk their immortal souls ("An Address").

Study of Snow's published speeches in the *Woman's Exponent* demonstrates the role of place in individual identity construction. Not only does Snow leverage her physical location to craft her own spiritual and cultural identity, but she also uses common topoi about Utah as Zion to encourage Mormon women to identify with a particular version of Mormon womanhood.

Identity Emerges Through Discourse and In Place

Historian Jill Derr has argued that no single Mormon woman was more effective in arguing for Mormon women's identity than Eliza R. Snow ("Significance"). One of Snow's primary rhetorical aims is identification, which works to constitute individuals as part of a social whole (Sánchez 40). Snow wants her audience to assume the identity of women in Zion—an identity that is simultaneously theological, social, and geographic.

Snow presents this identity in a variety of ways: through modeling her own ethos as a role model for others, through direct exhortation (even chastisement), and through narratives, as I explain below. In an 1873 speech to the Mormon women's Relief Society, later published in the *Woman's Exponent,* Snow offers her own experience as a model to her listeners:

> When you are filled with the spirit, do you have any trials? I do not think you do. . . . When I am filled with that spirit my soul is satisfied; and I can say in good earnest that the trifling things of the day do not seem to stand in my way at all. But just let me loose [sic] my hold of that spirit . . . and trouble comes. ("An Address" 62)

---

of their own displacements and dislocations, Mormons (like the Israelites they took as their spiritual predecessors), increasingly invested their physical place with spiritual significance.

Here, Snow both establishes her ethos as a spiritual woman and offers her behavior as a model for listeners, promising them freedom from trials if they do so.

Like many preachers, Snow also relies on explicit exhortation to create an identity for her audience: "It is the duty of each one of us to be a holy woman. . . . There is no sister so isolated, and her sphere so narrow but what she can do a great deal towards establishing the Kingdom of God upon the earth" (An Address 63). After detailing possible self-improvements for her audience, Snow humorously acknowledges that her exhortation may come across strongly: "'Well, but now, Sister Eliza, are you not scolding folks?' I have to talk so loud, as I want you all to hear, and it may seem like scolding" (An Address 63). The informal tone suggested by the humor reflects religious historian Catherine Brekus's observation that nineteenth-century women were more likely to exhort in social settings than in formal preaching (128). The humor, along with the self-referential "Sister Eliza," help close any perceived gap between Snow and her audience and soften the potential sting of the correction.

For Snow, creating a clear communal identity for Mormon women was crucial, as their identity was hotly contested inside and outside of Utah. Though Snow might hail her audience as "holy wom[e]n," the Mormon practice of polygamy, publicly acknowledged as part of doctrine in 1852, provoked a very different interpretation from outsiders. By the late 1850s, the eradication of polygamy had emerged as a major moral crusade in the US, forming one of the Republican presidential platforms in the 1856 election (Hafen). Opponents decried the effects of a polygamous system on women: Harriet Beecher Stowe's claim that polygamy was "a slavery which debases and degrades womanhood, motherhood, and family" was fairly typical (qtd. in Embry and Kelley 1). More vehement opponents took the line of John Coyer, a Salt Lake City journalist, who argued in 1878, "if something is not done soon to stop the development of this law-breaking, law-defying fanaticism, either our free institutions must go down beneath its power, or, as with slavery, it must be wiped out in blood" (qtd. in Mulder and Mortenson 407–8).[10] Mor-

---

10. This heated debate illustrates the ways identity often emerges through discourse: much of the rhetoric surrounding polygamy was epideictic in nature—aimed at strengthening the existing values and identity of a group (whether attackers or defenders), rather than converting the opposing side (Scribner, Arrington and Bitton 178). Robbyn Thompson Scribner points out that "much of the justification and praise [of polygamy] worked primarily to recommit people to their support of the practice" (4), and Julie Roy Jeffrey explains that

mon women were seen as ignorant dupes and victims or as being willfully promiscuous—an identity that Mormon women, including Snow, vociferously resisted.[11]

This debate over identity became increasingly linked to place. As Paula M. L. Moya points out, "As social constructs that draw upon available social categories, identities are indexed to a historical time, place, and situation. A consequence of this is that the same identity evokes very different associations in different places" (99). This spatially contingent identity can be seen, at least in part, in the differing interpretation Eastern critics and Utah Mormons placed on the Mormons' relative isolation in Utah. Kate Field, a popular nineteenth-century orator, believed the group's "western isolation was a transparent attempt to obscure the threat such abuse posed to the entire nation" (Gordon 819). In contrast, early Mormon settlers believed their isolation provided the perfect opportunity to craft a utopian community (Hafen 356). Thus, the same social (and religious) isolation that made Snow and other Mormons suspect in the eyes of most Americans became for Mormons a rhetorical source and symbol of a holy, separate identity.

The debate over polygamy challenged not only Mormon women's moral identity, but also their racial and national identity. By the mid-nineteenth century, most Anglo-Americans saw Mormons as non-white, though the majority of Mormons were "displaced Yankees or converts from Northern Europe" (Oman 681). As legal scholar Nathan Oman explains, according to the typical logic of racial identity, behavior was determined by race. But for Mormons, whose practice of polygamy violated the "natural" instincts of whites, their "unnatural" behavior was a form of "race treason" resulting in a new racial identity (684). Thus by virtue of their "non-white" behavior (i.e., polygamy), Mormons were no

---

nineteenth-century anti-polygamy novels reveal more about "the concerns of middle-class Americans than they do about life on the Mormon frontier" (181). Though at its height, only fifteen percent of Mormons practiced polygamy (Mitchell), Mormons as a whole identified strongly with the practice, hence its vigorous defense. They pointed to Biblical precedent (Scribner); contested legislature as the source of the law (claiming divine legislation instead); used their considerable political power in the territory to construct favorable laws; and argued (at least before the Civil War) that polygamy should be entitled to the same governmental protection as the South's "peculiar domestic institution" of slavery (Gordon 821).

11. See Robbyn Thompson Scribner's thesis for a detailed overview of Mormon women's defense of polygamy.

longer viewed as "white" by many other settlers.[12] Like most Mormon women, Snow believed herself to be an ardent US patriot and a moral Anglo-American woman, even as outsiders saw her as part of a "treasonable government" ("What Shall be Done") and a member of an immoral, "non-white" religious sect.

As debates over polygamy raged, both Mormon defenders and their attackers began to conflate Mormons' newly claimed physical location with their spiritual position. In an editorial for the *Independent* in August 1886, an anonymous writer described Utah to a national audience of Americans as "[a]n alien host, a hostile church, a treasonable government set up in the very midst of the Republic." This description—along with the question posed by the article's title, "What shall be done with Utah?"—conflates the physical desert territory with the religious practices of the Mormons located there ("What Shall Be Done"). Some sixteen years earlier, in a speech aimed at Mormon women, Eliza R. Snow presented a diametrically opposed view of the territory as a location of sanctuary and respect for Mormon women: "if to be loved, honored, and respected as wives, mothers, sisters, and daughters by good men is degrading them, then the women of Utah are degraded" ("Degradation"). Both of these views, by conflating physical location and spiritual and political position, point to the inextricable link between place and identity. This link became one that both Mormons and their opponents hoped to exploit: by intervening in the physical and political arrangements of the territory, anti-Mormon and anti-polygamy advocates hoped to dismantle the spiritual identity assumed by Mormons. Conversely, by linking their physical location with their spiritual roles, Snow sought to solidify Mormon women's group identity and strengthen their religious community.

USING NARRATIVES OF ZION TO ESTABLISH WOMEN'S ROLES IN THE KINGDOM

Beyond ethos and direct exhortation, Snow uses a spatial narrative—the topos of Zion—to invite her "sisters" to identify with a material and spiritual community and accept the identity her narrative presumes for

---

12. Even some current historical scholarship reflects this racial re-categorization: historian Glenda Riley classes Mormons with the non-Anglo groups settlers encountered (and in fact seems vaguely surprised that Anglo women were so hostile to encounters with Mormon women, many of whom came from remarkably similar backgrounds and locations).

them, rather than the unflattering identities offered by outside critics. Like many of the more radical Christian sects of the nineteenth-century, Mormon converts saw their baptism as a rejection of worldly values, particularly increasing materialism and secularism (Brekus). This sense of separation from the world intensified in the wake of the religious persecution that drove them to seek a separate physical location in Utah. For Snow, conversion to Mormonism required three important spiritual movements: separating oneself from the world, gathering together with the saints, and building up Zion.

Significantly, each of these inward spiritual movements could be symbolized by outward movement in the material world. As Dana Anderson explains in his rhetorical study of conversion narratives, "A starting point for the rhetorical analysis of identity constitution, then, is to consider how authors define themselves 'in terms of' the various scenes in which they place themselves" (46). Thus, by drawing on spatial narratives of separation and exodus to Utah (and the associated metaphor of Utah's isolation), gathering, and literally establishing a community in "Zion" (Utah), Snow reinforces an orientation narrative for her audience that helps them understand their own place and identity in Mormon society. Ideally, this redefinition provides her listeners with an identity resilient enough to withstand external challenge.

SEPARATION AND GATHERING

Utah's isolation provided a symbolic parallel to the spiritual separation and gathering required by the conversion to Mormonism. This particular aspect of Utah's geography was remarked upon by both Mormons and non-Mormons. One traveler through Salt Lake City commented, "What a strange religion or fanaticism has led this people to seek out this wild and secluded spot, surrounded by savages and wild beasts" (qtd. Mitchell 338). Mormons, however, found this isolation an advantage because it made Utah a refuge from the world (Arrington and Bitton 113).

Snow draws on a shared understanding of Utah's isolation to symbolize the rarefied identity she wants each woman to assume. In a speech given in early 1875 and reprinted in the April 1 edition of the *Woman's Exponent*, Snow reminds her audience that they symbolically withdrew from the world at their baptism and connects this symbolic withdrawal to their physical withdrawal to Utah Territory: "We obeyed the call 'Come out of her (Babylon), that ye partake not of her sins, and receive not of her plagues'—gathered to the places appointed" ("To Every

Branch" 164). This spiritual and physical separation was reinforced as church leaders repeatedly encouraged Mormon converts to "gather" to Utah during the mid- to late-nineteenth-century: some 85,000 converts (many of them European) came West between 1846 and 1887 (Arrington and Bitton 98). Snow defines the purpose of this separation and gathering in opposition to the outside world. The "Saints" gathered spiritually and physically *not* "to build ourselves up after the manner of the Gentiles, by assimilating ourselves into their likeness" but to "become 'a peculiar people—zealous of good works,' and build up the Zion of God" ("To Every Branch" 164). As is typical in conversion, individuals are asked to both identify with a new identity and to disidentify with an old one—what Kenneth Burke calls a radical movement from one dominant orientation (and identification) to another (*Permanence and Change* 125-29); in this case, Snow exhorts Mormon women to discard their worldly identity (and location) and assume a spiritual one.

The identity Snow establishes for her audience is thus enacted in terms of exclusion, both of Mormons by non-Mormons and of non-Mormons by Mormons. As Burke explains in *A Rhetoric of Motives*, identification is often predicated upon disidentification and division—we can identify *with* something (or someone) only to the extent that we identify *against* something (or someone) else (22). Snow figures Mormon women's exclusion in terms of their exile from mainstream America (both physically and culturally) and their status as a "peculiar people." Such renunciations of outside values were reflected in other Mormon speeches of the era emphasizing the importance of gathering, the building of Zion, the need for distinctiveness from the world, and self-sufficiency. By drawing on rhetorics of exclusion, Snow helps her audience of Mormon women to understand themselves as spiritually distinct from outside groups, an important step in embracing their identity as Mormon women.

This rhetoric of spatial and ideological exclusion is by no means unique. Brekus explains that several radical sects growing out of the Second Great Awakening in America wanted to create "islands of holiness"—physically and spiritually separate communities that allowed them to practice the Pauline dictum to be in the world but not of it (155; Romans 12.2). What makes Snow's argument different from these other radical sects is the way she links the narrative of physical separation to her goal of spiritual and economic separation. By drawing on the narrative of gathering, Snow reminds her audience that they have already obeyed the call to physically separate from the world and are thus obligated to maintain the spiritual portion of that call. But this, she emphasizes, is not enough: she extends the idea of gathering to include renunciation of worldly values—and even the purchase of Eastern-manufactured goods, as described in the next section. Snow reshapes a narrative Mormon women were already familiar with (that of their initial separation and gathering) to create a new narrative blueprint for constructing new identities even as they build their communities in Utah.

Building Up Zion

For Snow, physical and spiritual gathering was an essential precursor to the important and all-consuming labor of building Zion. The Mormon concept of Zion was a complex one, not only referring to a spiritually unified community and the cooperative physical community they hoped to build, but also invoking the desert landscape of Utah. Like their Puritan ancestors, Mormons infused the idea of the Holy Land in their new settlement to help accelerate the process of settlement and realize their vision of a glorious future (Greenberg). But Mormons did more than simply draw spiritual parallels between themselves and biblical Israelites: they literally mapped Palestine onto the landscape of Utah, emphasizing the similarities between the Great Salt Lake and the Dead Sea, both of which were highly saline bodies of water fed by a river from a freshwater lake (Hafen, Mitchell). Not coincidentally, Mormon settlers named this river the Jordan River. Settlement narratives, including Snow's, also reflected this Biblical parallel. In an 1885 "Psalm," published in the *Woman's Exponent*, Snow wrote, "Thou who didst command Abraham to leave his native land, and to separate himself from his father's house, Thou art my God . . . In Thine own wisdom, and with outstretched hand, Thou hast brought thy people to these mountain vales" (57). This rooting of her religious identity in the Bible, as a spiritual heir of the Biblical chosen people, allows Snow to endow herself and her audience with a sense of a much longer, established religious tradition. As historian Jan Shipps notes, this perception of Utah as an American Israel profoundly influenced the way Mormons thought about themselves. Although Snow seldom refers explicitly to the physical landscape parallels between Utah and the Holy Land, she does draw on this spiritual parallel to help her listeners understand their own spiritual identity as Mormon women.

In Snow's rhetorical discourse, the building of Zion in the newly sacred Utah territory becomes a vehicle through which she can elaborate the specific roles she expects Mormon women to assume. As she explains to the women of the Relief Society in 1875, "God has called us to an important and highly responsible position; and, let me ask, for what purpose? Is it not that we may efficiently assist in the establishing and building up of His kingdom?" ("To Every Brach," 164). Because the topos of Zion could function as a powerful orientation device for Mormon women—a symbol that explained not only their physical location, but also their place in a spiritual community, including their relationships with one another and to God—Snow invokes the concept frequently. But for this particular spatial topos to fulfill its identifying function, Snow has to first remind her audience of its significance. A little later in the speech, Snow raises a significant question: "What has woman to do in bringing about these grand results?" For Snow, the answer lies in woman's material and spiritual responsibilities.

As the kingdom Snow envisions is material as well as spiritual, she often spends considerable time enumerating the material contributions women could make—and the material consumption they should avoid. During the 1870s, following the completion of the transcontinental railroad, Brigham Young and other church leaders became concerned about the dependence of Mormons on outside good and resources (Arrington and Bitton). In response, Snow organized Retrenchment societies that encouraged women to refrain from extravagance in dress and domestic economy and to establish various home industries (such as wheat growing and silk manufacture). Such economic retrenchment and self-sufficiency were precursors to spiritual retrenchment; as women limited their consumption of material goods, they were also to eschew spiritual pitfalls: "ignorance, the spirit of the world, and everything else that is opposed to noble womanhood, and progress in the path to perfection" (Snow, "To the Young Sisters in Provo" 170). The material work of Retrenchment was meant to provide what Utah's decreasing physical isolation no longer could, following the completion of the intercontinental railroad in 1869: separation from the outside world.

At the same time Snow asks her audience to limit their financial interaction with the outside world, she attempts to physically cordon off the material shape of their world by asking women not to reach beyond their Utah community. Snow exhorts her audience: "Let us assist with all the energies of our souls, in breaking the chains with which we, as a people, are bound; for just as long as we are in debt to, or dependent upon our enemies for the necessaries and comforts of life, we are virtually their slaves" ("To Every Branch" 165). The retrenchment rhetoric

Snow employs furthers the work of building Zion materially and spiritually by encouraging local economic development and discouraging excessive materialism. Such rhetoric also reconstitutes the unique identity of Utah as a place (and, by extension, of the Mormons within it) by reinforcing the close spiritual and economic ties binding the inhabitants to the community.

Although material and economic separation from the world are important to Snow's conception of Mormon womanhood, she is also keenly interested in expanding woman's domestic duties to form a communal place for women to inhabit. While she frequently reiterates that woman's first business was "to perform [her] duties at home," she believed that women's roles were much more expansive than this. She advises women to develop socially and intellectually: "inasmuch as you are wise stewards, you will find time for social duties, because these are incumbent upon us as daughters and mothers in Zion" ("An Address" 63). She also encourages them to become educated, even asking the sisters if anyone was willing to study medicine and indicating that the Relief Society would help defray their expenses ("An Address"). For Snow, this extra-domestic work was an extension of a Mormon woman's spiritual work:

> Outside the boundary of her domestic routine, woman has many sacred, important duties to perform, and a holy, purifying influence to wield—an influence which, although imperfectly exercised, is potent in its effects. How necessary, then, that the Latter-day Saint women—being called to act in a wider sphere, and with higher and more responsible duties devolving upon them, than all others—should be well informed on all subjects affecting the interests of humanity—should possess all the expansion of mind that can be acquired and the attainment of all useful intelligence and true knowledge. ("Position and Duties")

Because Snow believed that woman's sphere was continually expanding beyond her domestic sphere, she was able to repeatedly affirm that "[n]owhere on the earth has woman so broad a sphere of labor and duty, of responsibility and action, as in Utah" ("An Address" 62). Snow herself never felt constrained in her identity as a Mormon woman, and she believed no other Mormon woman should feel so (Derr).

Snow authorizes this extended role for women by linking it explicitly to the spatial topos of Zion: the women are "daughters and mothers in Zion" and they are encouraged to study medicine "for Zion's sake." Thus, in the narrative of Zion, Mormon women are themselves agents, meant to establish God's kingdom prior to His second coming through their own spiritual and physical labor. Snow gestures to this narrative by invoking the place itself (Zion), underscoring Mormon women's self-identity as agents in a divine plan. Through connecting the physical environment (growing communities in isolated Utah) to a narrative of spiritual isolation and kingdom building, Snow infuses women's daily existence in a frontier environment with spiritual meaning. The spatial topos of Zion works as a rhetorical device for identification in part because of the symbolic power of the metonymic trope. In Burke's "Four Master Tropes," metonymy works to reduce "some higher or more complex realm of being to the terms of a lower or less complex realm of being . . . to convey some incorporeal or intangible state in terms of the corporeal or tangible" (*Grammar* 506). In Snow's rhetoric, the complex idea of Zion (the tangible Kingdom of God, the blueprint for idealized spiritual behavior, and the spiritual narrative behind the settlement of Utah) becomes reduced to the simpler, tangible concept of Utah. Accordingly, in her "Salutation to the Women of Utah," Snow can write, "Whatever others, in their ignorance might imagine, we 'know,' that in Utah, are associated the best and noblest spirits that are tabernacled in the flesh—that here, the highest order of intelligence is obtained, and society organized in a purer and more perfect form than anywhere else on earth" (36). Because of the ubiquity of the "Zion" trope, Snow's audience understands that Utah, in this instance, refers to Mormon society—specifically, to its divinely appointed role as the harbinger of God's kingdom. The territory thus becomes a shorthand/metonym for their spiritual identity.

Once Zion-as-symbol becomes conflated with Zion-as-place, Utah takes on symbolic resonance as a kind of shorthand for identity. As Clark argues in *Rhetorical Landscapes*, once public discourses about a place establish a particular frame through which individuals experience that landscape, the landscape itself rhetorically constitutes a particular identity in that individual. For Snow, this means that her repeated narratives of gathering and kingdom building establish a particular lens through which her listeners view the landscape of Utah. Though Snow's use of the Zion topos was not unique, she grounded narratives of kingdom building in Utah to create specific roles for the women in her audience. Her version of the Zion topos outlines for Mormon women a rhetorical vision that places even their most mundane actions (child-rearing, housekeeping, etc.) as part and parcel of a vast spiritual enterprise of kingdom building. Zion as a spatial trope not only reminds listeners of their shared past (separation and gathering), it orients listeners toward their future identity and behavior.

Subsequent to exposure to the "Zion" trope, Mormon women (and Mormons in general) experienced the landscape in ways that also reinforced their shared identity. As Clark explains, "The experience of place—particularly a place that has been made a public symbol—is saturated with prompts to identify the self with a group" (34). Just as "words signify shared concepts to those who use them, places signify shared situations, aspirations, and identities to those who inhabit them" (34). For the women in Snow's audience, "Zion" came to represent not an abstract concept, but a semi-arid region where they relied on irrigation to grow wheat that they then stored in granaries; a place where they grew their own silk (or attempted to), made their own clothes, ran their own stores, and founded the Deseret Hospital (Arrington and Bitton 227). And the landscape around them, thanks in part to Snow's rhetoric, served as a continual reminder of their unique identity: the crests of their "mountain home" brought to mind the hand of God in leading them to a secure, isolated region. The Jordan River fueling the Salt Lake was a constant echo of the Biblical Holy Land.

In Snow's rhetoric, Utah becomes ultimately what Clark terms a "representative place": a place "where people experience themselves as identified with the particular characteristics of the community that the place has come to symbolize" (39). For Snow, Utah represented "the gathering place of the honest of heart . . . the best and noblest spirits" ("Salutation" 36)—or in other words, Zion. By repurposing narratives of separation (exodus), gathering, and building up Zion, Snow creates a vision of Mormon womanhood that makes place for them within the broader Mormon community while simultaneously demarcating a clear boundary from outside communities.

Conclusion

Snow's rhetoric constitutes her largely female audience of the *Woman's Exponent* as a "peculiar people" both through the nature of her address, which assumes their shared identity, and the particular spatial tropes she invokes, which provide her audience with shared symbols for identity. Snow's rhetorical texts address her Mormon sisters as spiritual beings with extraordinary potential, presuming for women the identity she expects them to assume. To the extent that women in her audience accept the identity assigned to them through Snow's discourse, they become a constitutive part of the Mormon community (Charland). This identity exposes some of the interconnections between rhetoric, identity, and place. In this particular instance, Snow's experience of place—her repeated dislocation and her sense of Utah as a spiritual refuge—had significant impact on how she understood her religion and her own role within it, which was to use her spiritual gifts to bring women together.

Perhaps more significantly, Snow used this shared experience of place to offer a spatially-rooted identity to Mormon women. Thus, place provided Snow with a rich source of invention. As an ideologically laden symbol, place functioned as a powerful vehicle for group identification. Not only did this symbol help Mormon women understand their place within the broader Mormon culture, but it, in turn, endowed the physical space from which it was derived with significance. Once Snow (and others) established these place-based identifying myths, women had only to experience the landscape around them to be reminded of those myths. In a mutually constitutive turn, Snow's use of the Zion topos allows Mormon faith and landscape to ground one another: while the faith endows the landscape with particular significance, the landscape, in turn, becomes a site for the enactment of faith and an identifying symbol for that faith. Although in some instances geographical place can serve as an impediment for rhetors, limiting the audience that they are able to reach and creating potentially debilitating stereotypes, for Snow, place, in tandem with identity, ultimately *enabled* her rhetorical practices.

This chapter demonstrates that efforts to understand rhetorical identity need to also attend to the way place (both real and imagined) shapes such identity. As rhetorical scholars, we need more exploration into the ways material place shapes the constitutive identity offered to audiences. We need to understand how narratives endow places with meaning—and how those places in turn create identities for audiences (along the lines of Clark's *Rhetorical Landscapes in America* or Richard Marback's analysis of Robben Island). We might ask, how do individual and community identities become embedded in place *through* discourse? How do we interpret material spaces (natural and built) in ways that reinforce or challenge local identities? How do localized—or regionalized—identities intervene in or support national narratives? How might place (as both a physical location and the discourses surrounding it) provide resources for a rhetor's choice of identity strategies? And, if different places carry with them unspoken expectations for behavior (and by extension, identity) how are speakers and audiences alike constrained or enabled by those expectations? It seems to me that if, with Glenn, we want to resist basic disciplinary beliefs about "who speaks, who is silent, who is allowed (or not allowed) to speak, who is listening (or not), and what those listeners might do," ("Silence" 262), we ought to raise these questions in the context of *place*.

Works Cited

Alcoff, Linda Martín, Michael Hames-García, Satya P. Mohanty, and Paula M. L. Moya, editors. *Identity Politics Reconsidered*. Future of Minority Studies. Palgrave, 2006.

Applegarth, Risa. "Genre, Location, and Mary Austin's *Ethos*." *Rhetoric Society Quarterly*, vol. 41, no. 1, 2011, pp. 41–63.

Aristotle, *Rhetoric*. *The Internet Classics Archive*. Massachusetts Institute of Technology, 2009. Accessed 7 May 2014.

Arrington, Leonard J. and Davis Bitton. *The Mormon Experience: A History of the Latter-day Saints*. Knopf, 1979.

Beecher, Maureen Ursenbach. "The Eliza Enigma: The Life and Legend of Eliza R. Snow." *Essays in the American West 1974–1975*, edited by Thomas G. Alexander. Charles Redd Monographs in Western History. No. 6. Brigham Young UP, 1976, pp. 29–46.

—. "Priestess Among the Patriarchs: Eliza R. Snow and the Mormon Female Relief Society, 1842–1887." *Religion and Society in the American West: Historical Essays*, edited by Carl Guarneri and David Alvarez, UP of America, pp. 153–170.

—, editor. *The Personal Writings of Eliza Roxcy Snow*. Utah State UP, 2000.

Brekus, Catherine A. *Strangers and Pilgrims: Female Preaching in America, 1740–1845*. U of North Carolina P, 1998.

Charland, Maurice. "Constitutive Rhetoric: The Case of the *Peuple Québécois*." *Quarterly Journal of Speech*, vol. 17, no. 2, 1987, pp. 133–150.

Christoph, Julie Nelson. "Reconceiving *Ethos* in Relation to the Personal: Strategies of Placement in Pioneer Women's Writing." *College English*, vol. 64, no. 6, 2002, pp. 660–679.

Clark, Gregory. "'A Child Born of the Land': The Rhetorical Aesthetic of Hawaiian Song." *Rhetoric Society Quarterly*, vol. 42, no. 3, 2012, pp. 251–270.

—. *Rhetorical Landscapes in America: Variations on a Theme from Kenneth Burke.* U of South Carolina P, 2004.

Comer, Krista. *Landscapes of the New West: Gender and Geography in Contemporary Women's Writing.* U of North Carolina P, 1999.

Derr, Jill Mulvay. "Eliza R. Snow and The Woman Question." *BYU Studies*, vol. 16, no. 2, 1976, pp. 250–264.

—. "The Lion and the Lioness: Brigham Young and Eliza R. Snow." *BYU Studies*, vol. 40, 2001, pp. 55–100.

—. "The Significance of 'O My Father' in the Personal Journey of Eliza R. Snow." *BYU Studies*, vol. 36, no. 1, 1996–7, pp. 85–126.

Desser, Daphne. "Reading and Writing the Family: Ethos, Identification, and Identity in My Great-Grandfather's Letters." *Rhetoric Review*, vol. 20, 2001, pp. 314–28.

Embry, Jessie, and Lois Kelley. "A Comparison of Utah Mormon Polygamous and Monogamous Women." *Women in Utah History: Paradigm or Paradox?* edited by Patricia Lyn Scott and Linda Thatcher. Utah State UP, 2005, pp. 1–35.

Eves, Rosalyn Collings. "That We Might Become 'A Peculiar People': Spatial Rhetoric as a Resource for Identification." *Rhetoric: Concord and Controversy*, edited by Antonio de Velasco and Melody Lehn. Waveland, 2012.

Glenn, Cheryl. "Author, Audiences, and Autobiography: Rhetorical Technique in the Book of Margery Kempe." *College English*, vol. 54, no. 5, 1992, pp. 540–553. *JSTOR*. Accessed 5 Mar. 2014.

—. *Rhetoric Retold: Regendering the Tradition from Antiquity Through the Renaissance.* Southern Illinois UP, 1997.

—. "Silence: A Rhetorical Art for Resisting Discipline(s)." *JAC*, vol. 22, no. 2, 2002, pp. 261–291.

Gordon, Sarah Barringer. "'The Liberty of Self-Degradation: Polygamy, Woman Suffrage, and Consent in Nineteenth-Century America." *The Journal of American History*, vol. 83, no. 3, 1996, pp. 815–47.

Grabill, Jeffrey T., and Stacey Pigg. "Messy Rhetoric: Identity Performance as Rhetorical Agency in Online Public Forums." *Rhetoric Society Quarterly*, vol. 42 no. 2, 2012, pp. 99–119.

Graulich, Melody. "Western Biodiversity: Rereading Nineteenth-Century American Women's Writing." *Nineteenth-Century American Wom-*

en Writers: A Critical Reader, edited by Karen L. Kilcup, Blackwell, 1998, pp. 47–61.

Greenberg, Gershon. *The Holy Land in American Religious Thought, 1620–1948: The Symbiosis of American Religious Approaches to Scripture's Sacred Territory*. UP of America, 1994.

Hafen, Thomas K. "City of Saints, City of Sinners: The Development of Salt Lake City as a Tourist Attraction 1869–1900." *The Western Historical Quarterly*, vol. 28 no. 3, 1997, pp. 342–77.

Jack, Jordynn. "Review: Space, Place, and the Public Face of Composition." *College English*, vol. 72, no. 2, 2009, pp. 188–198.

Jeffrey, Julie Roy. *Frontier Women: "Civilizing" the West? 1840–1880*. Hill and Wang, 1998.

Kaplan, Amy. "Manifest Domesticity." *American Literature*, vol. 70, no. 3, 1998, pp. 581–606. JSTOR, www.jstor.org/stable/2902710.

Marback, Richard. "The Rhetorical Space of Robben Island." *Rhetorical Society Quarterly*, vol. 34, no. 2, 2004, pp. 7–27.

Mitchell, Martin. "Gentile Impressions of Salt Lake City, Utah, 1849–1870." *Geographical Review*, vol. 87, no. 3, 1997, pp. 334–352.

Moya, Paula M. L., "What's Identity Got to Do With It? Mobilizing Identities in the Multicultural Classroom." Alcoff et al, pp. 96–117.

Mountford, Roxanne. *The Gendered Pulpit: Preaching in American Protestant Spaces*. Southern Illinois UP, 2003.

Mulder, William and A. Russell Mortensen, editors. *Among the Mormons: Historic Accounts by Contemporary Observers*. Alfred A. Knopf, 1958.

Oman, Nathan B. "Natural Law and the Rhetoric of Empire: *Reynolds v. United States*, Polygamy, and Imperialism." *Faculty Publications*, William and Mary School of Law. Paper 1134. 2011. scholarship.law.wmn.edu/facpubs/1134.

Reynolds, Nedra. *Geographies of Writing: Inhabiting Places and Encountering Difference*. Southern Illinois UP, 2004.

Riley, Glenda. *Confronting Race: Women and Indians on the Frontier, 1815–1915*. U of New Mexico P, 2004.

Rice, Jenny. "From Architectonic to Tectonics: Introducing Regional Rhetorics." *Rhetoric Society Quarterly*, vol. 42, no. 3, 2012, pp. 201-13.

Sánchez, Rosaura. "On a Critical Realist Theory of Identity" Alcoff et al., pp. 31–52.

Firor, Anne Scott. Introduction. *Mormon Sisters: Women in Early Utah*. New Edition. Ed. Claudia L. Bushman. Utah State UP, 1997, pp. xv-xxiii.

Snow, Eliza R. "An Address." *Woman's Exponent*, 15 Sep. 1873, pp. 62–63.
—. "Degradation of Women in Utah," *Deseret News*, April 1870.
—. "Position and Duties." *Woman's Exponent*, 15 July 1874, p. 28.
—. "Psalm." *Woman's Exponent*, 15 Sep. 1885, p. 57.
—. "Salutation to the Ladies of Utah." *Woman's Exponent*, 1 Aug. 1873, pp. 36–37.
—. "Sketch of My Life." *The Personal Writings of Eliza Roxcy Snow*, edited by Maureen Ursenbach Beecher. Utah State UP, 2000, pp. 6–45.
—. "To Every Branch of the Relief Society in Zion." *Woman's Exponent*, 1 Apr. 1875, pp. 164–65.
—. "To the Young Sisters in Provo." *Woman's Exponent*, 15 Apr. 1874, p. 170.
Turner, Frederick Jackson. *The Frontier in American History*. New York: Dover, 1996.
"What Shall be Done with Utah?" *Independent*. 12 Aug 1886: 38. *American Periodical Series Online, 1740–1900*. ProQuest. Accessed 4 Apr. 2007.

7 Closets and Classification: The Archive as an Epistemic Resource for Identity

Jean Bessette

> *Our archives belongs to no one group of lesbians and to no one selected image or formula for liberation; it will eventually pass into the hands of a new generation of rememberers who we hope will keep the door open to the multiplicities of lesbian identity. Our will to remember is our will to change the world, to continually reconstruct the words 'woman,' 'lesbian,' and 'gender' so they reflect the complex creations which we call our lives.*
>
> —Joan Nestle, "A Will to Remember"

> *It is also important to acknowledge the archivists themselves as vital agents in the archival scene. Archivists catalogue the materials, decide what to preserve, and determine how to catalogue it, thereby controlling the materials we can access and the processes we take to get to them.*
>
> —Cheryl Glenn and Jessica Enoch, "Drama in the Archives"

Founded in 1974 in New York City, the Lesbian Herstory Archives (LHA) collective set out to make history on its own terms: to produce and preserve accounts of lesbian pasts that were being forgotten, misrepresented, or elided in official histories, libraries, and archives.[1] The collections LHA amassed are now housed in a three-story Brooklyn brownstone, with their contents spilling out of rooms, closets, and boxes into off-site storage. Still thriving today, LHA is an activist archive, run by volunteer "archivettes" who work to revise the historical narratives that have erased, criminalized, and pathologized lesbians. To change these historical narratives, the collective endeavors to challenge and augment the available sources—the archives and libraries—from which damaging histories are written. As founder Joan Nestle proclaims in the epigraph, "our will to remember is our will to change the world"; by composing a different queer past through a different kind of archiving, the LHA collective hopes to "will" change in the present.

The collective's activism operates through an explicit link between the archive's classificatory principles and a multivalent, fluid lesbian identity. Open to both lay and academic visitors from all over the world, the archive "belongs," as Nestle asserts, to a vast and complex group of women with same-sex desire that exceeds any "one group of lesbians" (233) and even puts pressure on the category of woman itself. LHA's archivettes resist constructing a "role-model" archive by "actively sort[ing] out documentation of the lives of lesbian factory workers, butch-femme communities of the forties and fifties, lesbian prostitutes and sex performers" (Nestle 233). The collection reflects this diversity in the range and juxtaposition of its material objects: "hard hats and hobnail boots sit next to pasties and glossy prints of a famous lesbian stripper of the fifties. They, in turn are joined by the lesbian-feminist artifacts of the seventies" (Nestle 233). For Nestle and the LHA collective, diverse representation mixed up in the archive is a significant instrument of their queer activism, and the term *queer* here echoes the longstanding definition in queer studies as an oppositional force against the norming and stability of identity categories, including homonormative or otherwise static gay and lesbian identity (Warner). By contributing to and absorbing the eclectic collection of material artifacts, women with same-sex desire expand and "continually reconstruct" the terms that define their identities: "woman," "lesbian," and "gender" (Nestle 233). The archive becomes a *resource* for its donors' and visitors' sexual identity formation, encouraging them to create ever-more-inclusive queer communities.

In this chapter, I argue that that LHA composes its archive as a site for complex identificatory (re)formulation, and I explore how the LHA

---

1. Portions of this chapter appear in *Retroactivism in the Lesbian Archives: Composing Pasts and Futures*, published by Southern Illinois University Press, 2017.

becomes a rhetorical and epistemic resource for users' identity formation and reformulation. This investigation builds on recent rhetorical scholarship focusing on LHA. In 2013, for instance, Madhu Narayan published a thoughtful essay narrating her experience in LHA's Brooklyn residence and identifying the trope of "home" employed by the archive to communicate its mission to local and global lesbian communities. Like Narayan, Kate Davy reflects on her research experience inside LHA, where she sought evidence of a queer women's theater group. Expanding upon these scholars' reflections on the experience of researching in LHA, this chapter contributes a granular focus on *classification*. Rather than speaking generally about the role of this archive in lesbian communities or narrating my experience as a researcher, I contend that LHA's resistant system of archival classification encourages a queerer, multiplicitous lesbian identity through the strategic arrangement of its diverse materials. In particular, I pinpoint three rhetorical strategies of material arrangement—fractured research, analogical association, and synecdoche. These devices function to blur the boundaries between archival categories and create connections between seemingly disparate factions of lesbian identity. Through the associations drawn between distinct categories and artifacts—all contained within the purview of "lesbian herstory"—visitors are encouraged to expand their understanding of and relationship to lesbian identity.

To develop this project, I first lay out its theoretical grounding: the fundamental rhetoricity of the archive and the role of classification in the process of identification and the shaping of identity. I then contextualize LHA's classificatory intervention by demonstrating the effect of traditional classification schemas on the lived identities of individuals seeking to learn more about their same-sex desire. Lastly, I turn to the specifics of LHA's resistant system of classification, examining how the rhetorical devices of fractured research, analogical association, and synecdoche work to muddle the boundaries between archival— and identificatory—categories.

Classification and the Queer Archive

In thinking through the mechanisms by which archives become epistemic resources for identity, I begin with the understanding that archives are rhetorical constructs, crafted through decisions about which materials to seek out and accept and how those materials are organized in the physical space of the archive (Glenn and Enoch; Sharer; Morris; Biesecker). These rhetorical decisions are fundamentally *classificatory* in nature, for they depend upon a schema that delineates which materials are appropriate for inclusion in the archive and into which folders, boxes, and shelves the materials are categorized. This concern for the rhetoricity of classification has been celebrated from rhetoric's beginnings as a strategy to break down and discern the parts of a claim. Plato's Socrates, for instance, made the ability to divide and classify central in *Phaedrus*, asserting that "he who is to develop an art of rhetoric must first make a methodical division and acquire a clear impression of each class" (263b). More so than Plato, Aristotle relied heavily on the practice of classification, or divisio, to divide and name the parts of his topics from rhetoric to poetics to science.

In contemporary rhetorical theory, the ancient concern for classification became explicitly connected to identification through Kenneth Burke, who found it "clearly apparent in any system of classification" (*Grammar* 417). Through a process of identification, classification functions by *dividing* views and individuals into groups; as Burke explains, identification is "compensatory to division," motivated by "individuals at odds with one another . . . [for] if men were not apart from one another, there would be no need for the rhetorician to proclaim their unity" (*Rhetoric* 22). In drawing archival classification into conversation with Burke's understanding of identification and division, I emphasize the role of identification in the archive's rhetoricity. Systems of classification in archives draw boundaries around materials, *identifying* records together in distinction from other classificatory categories.

The stakes of identification through classification are significant in an archive defined by gender and sexuality. In contrast to the celebration of *divisio* by Plato's Socrates, who described himself as a "lover of these processes of division and bringing together," classification has a more insidious history for queer people. As Michel Foucault argues, classification has itself been persuasive in encouraging the categorization of individuals into sexual identities. Foucault explains that the late nineteenth century marked a pivotal moment in the production of homosexuality as a category constituted by a distinct group of people in Western society. The category of homosexuality was produced through medical classification ("sciencia sexualis") to regulate and treat as illness what had previously been considered discrete acts of transgression. The classification of homosexuality as an enduring disease made an argument for the nature and treatment of queer people. As Foucault suggests, the creation of a category of homosexuality made possible not only the notions of sexual identity we have today but also the strategic targeting of practitioners of non-normative sexuality. The categorization of deviant individuals facilitated the creation of medical and legal apparatuses that functioned to discipline, sequester, and punish non-normative sexuality.

Thus, in the context of the history of non-normative sexuality, Burke's classificatory *identification* becomes the foundation for sexual *identity*: acts of transgression are categorized into an enduring quality attached to and eventually internalized by individuals, identifying them together across other "complex and contradictory identifications" (Davis 127) into a shared "substance" of sexual identity. As Diane Davis argues in her description of Burke, "there can be no identity without identification, and there can be no identification without the suasive force of meaningful figures" (127). The history of sexuality according to Foucault demonstrates how classificatory categories are themselves "suasive," identifying individuals in terms of pathology. That is, as Foucault sets out, classificatory categories have rhetorically shaped sexual identity based on a shared "substance" of disease and malfeasance.

The classification of queer people into pathological and criminal sexual identity categories has historically been mimicked in the classification systems of traditional archives and libraries. Until the activist efforts of the Task Force of Gay Liberation in 1972, the Library of Congress systematically closeted or pathologized queer materials by either omitting them from the collections entirely or classifying them within categories such as disease or sex crimes (Wolf; Thistlewaite; Adler). Texts tagged as "Homosexuality" were cross-referenced with crime, pornography, prostitution, sexual perversion, and psychological disorders. Manifesting Burke's concept of *identification through division*, the system of classification identified materials within the category of homosexuality as a deviation from the norms of heterosexual relations, marriage, and nuclear families. For example, libraries referred researchers of "homosexuality" or "lesbianism" to a general heading, "Sexual Perversion" (Thistlewaite 10). As librarian Steve Wolf demonstrates, similar associations were made through cross-references in classifications of Medicine: under "sexual deviation" is "homosexuality," under which is the obligatory note, "Cf. HQ 71–79, sex crimes." The Dewey system contained comparable biases to the Library of Congress, using a "See . . ." cross-reference procedure: under "homosexuality" were the entries "crime, see offenses; sex, see sexual disorders" (Wolf 40–41). Even after the Task Force's intervention, "Cf." referral notes remained in the Library of Congress system, which linked homosexuality to categories of crime and disease. For example, under "RA 1141: sexual offenses and diseases," was the note "Cf. HQ 71–471, sex crimes." Since "homosexuality" was classed in HQ 76, it fell within the range of the "sex crimes" classification numbers. So, the Cf. note implicitly classified being gay with crime *and* disease, alongside the "related" subjects of prostitution (HQ 101–440) and pornography (HQ 450–471). These Cf. notes linking pathological and criminal subjects back to "homosexuality" (HQ 76) were present in a variety of categories.

The identification of homosexuality within categories of crime and disease were not benign in the lives of queer people in the 1940s to 1970s, who often turned to libraries for information about their emerging sense of their sexuality (Bessette). For researchers, from professional historians to individuals with same-sex desire seeking evidence of themselves, traditional classification systems effectively rendered documentation of queer lives invisible or pathological with significant effects on sexual *identity*. For example, Del Martin, a founder of the Daughters of Bilitis (a mid-century lesbian organization), described her experience digging through the library for information about her desire for women, only to find sources proclaiming her "perversion," her "psychopathology," her feelings a "crime against nature and a sin against God" (30). With her partner, Phyllis Lyon, Martin explains their response to the library's resources in the category of homosexuality:

> All this is what Del learned about herself after hours of agonized reading at the library. They were talking about her, a Lesbian. And they were right. Lesbians do suffer from feelings of rejection, loneliness, isolation, fear, insecurity, hurt pride, lack of self-confidence, loss of self-esteem. Del felt all these things and more. She was indeed sick. (49)

As Martin and Lyon suggest in this passage, the library sources were *persuasive*, shaping Martin's sense of her emerging sexual identity in terms of individual mental illness. Like Martin, Joan Nestle describes how she too "found no references in the surroundings to Lesbian creations" and "did not even search for markings because [she] knew [they] were not a people, just deviant, sad wanderers meeting in dark places" (LHA Newsletter). Martin and Nestle's isolating experiences searching for "markings" in the library underscore the import of the archive in the formation of identification. Persuaded by the absent and pathological available research, they each identified not as "a people" (that is, a collective identity) but as "deviant, sad wanderers"—dispersed and diseased. It is this persuasive "sense of homelessness," of identification with individual disease and criminality rather than queer community, that motivates Nestle's "commitment to the Lesbian Herstory Archives" (Nestle, LHA Newsletter). Within the archive and outside it, classification is rhetorical, and it has functioned historically to identify individuals with same-sex desire together in pathology with a paradoxical consequence of dispersing them from a shared identity. LHA's system of classification intervenes in this context by drawing provisional associations between eclectic materials and categories, shaping a more fluid and multivalent collective identity in the process.

Classifying LHA: Fractured Research, Analogical Association, and Material Synecdoche

LHA's first archival intervention was to classify the materials it deemed worthy of preservation in direct opposition to the kinds of pathologizing materials from "experts" found by Martin and Nestle. From its beginnings, LHA sought out and made available unpublished material from ordinary and unknown women with same-sex desire rather than medical treatises or the papers of eminent people. Frequently soliciting contributions in their newsletters, LHA characterizes donation and preservation as acts of "rejoicing, reclaiming, and renewing" that are imperative to the formation and survival of a lesbian-identified community. Donation is depicted as a way for ordinary individuals to write themselves into the community by contributing written, spoken (tape-recorded), photographic, or sartorial artifacts to the collective history housed in the archive. In particular, the archive values ephemeral donations, such as grassroots publications, unpublished diaries and poems, worn artifacts like T-shirts and buttons, and scraps and clippings from newspapers. The nature of these ordinary, ephemeral acquisitions is quite distinct from official libraries' published matter and traditional archives' papers of important individuals. Women seeking information about their sexuality thus find very different sources in LHA than Martin and Nestle had in their city libraries: instead of finding evidence of their pathology, visitors are encouraged to identify with the thoughts, lives, and desires of ordinary women.

As significant as the divergent nature of LHA's holdings is the classification schema that organizes those holdings. In contrast to schemas like the Library of Congress, LHA opposes classificatory procedures that would prescribe and exclude people, orientations, and practices that do not fit in normative categories, including pathological, criminal—and homonormative—categories. As Joan Nestle declares in LHA's 1984 newsletter: "we create history as much as we discover it. What we call history becomes history and since this is a naming time, we must be on guard against our own class prejudices and discomforts." Nestle's words suggest that LHA's approach to classification in "this naming time" works against schemas that exclude or pigeonhole on the basis of prejudice and discomfort. Connecting "naming" in archival classification with sexual identity, Nestle pledges that the archive will "sacrifice no one to the abstract concept of what a lesbian *should* be" ("A Will to Remember" 233). No one understanding of sexual identity, that is, will be shored up by narrow and discriminative categories in the archive.

Combating "abstract concepts" and "naming" is a significant challenge in an archive, of course, because archives are by nature arranged in categories to facilitate researchers' investigations. Artifacts are defined and filed according to a designation of what is judged to be their primary essence, distinguished from and grouped with other artifacts, so that future researchers can locate the materials they seek. Yet, at first glance, LHA appears to resist naming by doing little in the way of neat classification. Kate Davy's description of her experience researching the WOW theater group in LHA is telling. After she was directed toward relevant boxes, Davy found that:

> Into these boxes had been tossed, in no particular order, press releases, programs, scripts, copies of opening night reviews, videotapes of some productions, and a smattering of photographs. Archival work in my case resembled more of an archaeological dig—mining memories and boxes of stuff, carefully examining disparate bits and pieces of a whole, widely scattered and deeply buried. (130)

In LHA, the collections are cluttered and jumbled, with boxes and photos spilling out of closets, piled in the corners of hallways and in the middle and edges of rooms. Researchers must unearth and draw connections between "widely scattered and deeply buried" scraps.

While the overwhelming array of "tossed" materials could be dismissed as a consequence of an ever-revolving and time-strapped volunteer staff with limited financial resources, I contend that LHA's collections are organized in a manner that *purposively* encourages the bringing together of unlike elements through analogical association. The archive's system of classification encourages what rhetorician Susan Delagrange describes as the "discovery of affinity and meaning among disparate things" by visitors. Through material rhetorical devices of fractured research, analogical association, and synecdoche, LHA draws connections between the artifacts and papers, their donors, and the archive's visitors—blurring the boundaries between classificatory categories and queering the sense of lesbian identity with which visitors experience and possibly identify.

FRACTURED RESEARCH AND QUEER IDENTITY

As Davy suggests, the archive's system of classification actually fractures researchers and visitors' ability to search for the totality of a single subject or individual, prohibiting a direct avenue to the object of research and encouraging the careful examination of dispersed bits and pieces. Despite their seeming disarray, items in the collection are organized through two major categories: by (1) the medium of an artifact or (2) by its content. Within the medium-specific collection, researchers find materials grouped in categories such as "audio/spoken word" (recorded on cassette tapes), "books," "posters," and "T-shirts and Other Multi-Formatted Ephemera." Within these medium-specific categories, materials are organized under sub-categories. ("Posters," for instance, are divided into "Political Events, Marches, Rallies," "Literary Events," and "Pride Events," among others subcategories.) Within the content-specific collection are subcategories such as "Archival" (for information about LHA itself), "Biographical," "Conferences," "Geographical" for international material, "Organizations" for activist collectives, "Special Collections" for unsolicited donations, and "Subjects" like domestic abuse or lesbian motherhood.

The rhetorical effect of this system of classification is an intentionally exploratory, haptic research experience. The classification schema forces visitors to see, read, touch, and draw connections between far more than the narrow category they may be searching for. Taking my own experience as an example, searching for the Daughters of Bilitis in LHA necessitated digging through far more categories than merely *Organizations*.

While this category does contain a large amount of information about the Daughters of Bilitis, so too do the categories of *Conferences* (as they founded, ran, or participated in many), each of which could alternately be filed *Geographically* by the location of the conference. Likewise, an individual Daughter who might be represented in a *Special* collection or *Biographical* file might also be an important proponent of a *Subject* like lesbian motherhood or employment rights, or a prominent advocate for lesbian-feminism or butch/femme cultural history, which they might in turn have published in a *Book*. Researchers and visitors following these traces and trails are encouraged by the schema to engage with, and associate, a broader and more abundant array of tangible lesbian artifacts.

These cross-categorical associations help to break down the *distinctions* between classificatory categories, expanding the definition of "lesbian" beyond prefigured bounds. Again, in my own research of the Daughters of Bilitis—a 1950s organization sometimes critiqued as conservative and "assimilationist"—I found myself tracing founder Del Martin in the *Subject* files, where I stumbled upon adjacent files for transgender men in the media. Martin has no obvious connection to contemporary transmen like Chaz Bono, but the experience of finding these two individuals in the same drawer—even the same archive—demonstrates the queerness of LHA's classificatory approach. It is a bold move—one likely to be challenged by transgender advocates and lesbian activists alike—to include a transman in a lesbian archive at all, for Bono is male-identified and straight (though he came out as a lesbian in 1995 prior to his transition). Yet, I suggest that Bono's inclusion alongside Martin makes an *anti-*classificatory argument for an ever more inclusive and fluid sense of sexual identity. In this cross-categorical, exploratory research process, researchers like me are compelled to find affinity between seemingly incongruous lives and records. The archive's claims to house "lesbian herstory" color each item in the collections with the identity of lesbian, forcing visitors to expand what that means to accommodate serendipitous incongruities.

While researchers find "more than they are looking for" (Davy 130) through this system of classification, they can also find less than what they came for. Digitized archives and catalogues at other archives are designed to facilitate ease and efficiency for the researcher, with the goal of helping her find precisely (or something close to) what she is looking for. But because many of LHA's holdings are not digitally catalogued, the dispersed classification of the massive collection of artifacts and records leaves researchers with the pleasure of discovery but also the inexorable gaps, the "painful erasures . . . from the inevitable, ongoing process of forgetting" (Davy 130). Yet this too is rhetorical. The gaps and fissures in an archive of sexuality are fitting; as Ann Cvetkovich explains, the "intimacy, sexuality, love, and activism" that comprise of lesbian experience are "all areas of experience that are difficult to chronicle through the materials of a traditional archive" ("In the Archive" 110). When researchers come to LHA and fail to find the totality of a lesbian life and instead find traces of many incongruous lives, drawing connections between them as they cross-categorically dig, a sense of community and the unknowable is reinforced, even if at the expense of the certainty of an individual. Through LHA's system of classification, lesbian identity comes to be defined precisely by this fluid, fractured, at times contradictory collectivity.

Analogical Association and Displayed Artifacts

From the moment visitors enter the archive, it becomes clear that LHA is not a traditional archive with the entirety of the collection neatly housed in boxes and folders on shelves and storage units. Instead, while much of its contents do reside in boxes and folders, the house is "part library, part museum, a community gathering space" (lesbianherstoryarchives.org), littered with objects strategically pulled for display. Buttons and jackets hang in the bathrooms, for example, while photos, book covers, and protest signs are set out on tables and shelves in the main rooms.

Like the connections researchers draw between incongruous categories and lives as we dig through the archive, these displayed artifacts similarly invite visitors to seek affinity between them and with them. As Delagrange suggests, material analogy makes claims for similarity between unlike elements through physical proximity—suggesting that knowledge of one element might help one understand the less familiar other nearby. Rather than reinforce distinct boundaries between categories in the archive, then, the physical proximity of eclectically displayed objects breaks them down.

In their adjacent display, these objects become identified with one another, and when the objects are perceived to represent different, even contradictory factions of lesbian sexuality, the effect is a queering of lesbian identity. As one example of how analogical association functions in the archive to queer identity, consider this pair of boots worn by a marshal of several NYC Dyke Marches set adjacent to a bookcase containing pulp fiction from the 1940s and 1950s (Figure 7.1). At the time this photo was taken, the boots and books were prominently displayed in the archive's dining room—a room that often acts as a social hub for visitors and archivettes, as it opens to the main reading room and contains the central work area for collective members. Their proximate juxtaposition suggests that the boots are "like" the pulps in some way—in spite of the difference in gender aesthetics, function, and time period. The material arrangement invites associative analogy, the drawing of similarity across the difference of the painted, feminine white women on the covers of the paperbacks and the masculine, ironically patriotic boots worn by the parade marshal. Through the analogical association between various ways that a "lesbian" might "look" (what she might wear, how she might be illustrated), the category of lesbian expands and diversifies. The juxtaposition of seemingly unlike objects disrupts neat classification of what a "lesbian should be" (Nestle, "A Will to Remember" 233). Instead of *divisio*, the system of classification provokes analogical association between disparate elements, which broadens the definition of lesbian identity.

Figure 7.1: Dyke March Marshall boots and pulp fiction shelves. Lesbian Herstory Archives interior. Photo by Saskia Scheffer.

Beyond diversifying gender aesthetics, the juxtaposition of the boots and books suggests a unified, if incongruous, tale of lesbian history: a tale, in Nestle's words, as "full and varied as our lives have been." While pride parade boots suggest a history of resilience and celebration, the pulps reflect more traumatic experience. In newsletters and LHA's traveling exhibit, "Queer Covers," Nestle has dubbed the pulp fiction collection "survival literature." Because these paperbacks were the only representation of lesbianism available in the 1940s and 1950s, they were cherished in secret by mid-century women with same-sex desire. But the pulps almost universally punished their lesbian characters with death or heterosexual marriage, and exacerbated stereotypes about lesbianism as a disease born of desperation for, isolation from, or escape from men. In such novels, prostitutes find diversion with other women; rich housewives mitigate boredom with their maids; imprisoned women find solace in their cellmates from their isolation from men. The collocation of these secretly read artifacts of "survival" with a pair of publicly worn pride boots suggests a complex history of trauma and resilience, with which the archive invites lesbian visitors to identify.

The arrangement of displayed objects is, of course, impermanent. At any moment, depending on the whims of an archivist or the uses of the space for different events, the objects may be rearranged, removed, or replaced. But the potential for re-arrangement and re-vision creates the opportunity for ever-new identifications between seemingly incongruous objects and the lives they represent. Despite the potential for ad hoc re-arrangement, the eclectic nature of juxtaposed objects suggests that archivettes endeavor to display particularly diverse materials to increase the potential for similarity-in-difference, for "the discovery of affinity and meaning among disparate things" (Delagrange).

While many archives, of course, contain objects that sit alongside to one another, LHA's practice of collecting and displaying visibly *worn* artifacts intensifies visitors' identification with the lives they represent. It is no accident that the archive takes special care to collect clothing and other used or made objects, including:

> Stickers, buttons, banners from marches, military uniforms, a feather boa, a leather jacket from the Dyketones, an assortment of hats, pasties donated by a lesbian stripper, board games like Lesbian Trivia, rainbow flags and Frisbees, fencing equipment, calendars and date books, roller skates, sculptures and collages. (lesbianherstoryarchives.org)

These worn, used, or handmade artifacts suggest *bodies*: active, flesh-and-blood women's bodies that help bring to life a sense of dynamic lesbian history that itself depends on bodies—on the womanness, desire, and emotion that is the stuff of lesbian experience. Possessions, like the pulp paperbacks donated by Mabel Hampton, a dearly beloved (now deceased) member of the LHA collective, and the boots donated by the Dyke March Marshal, contain the traces of their donors and their donors' worlds. Collections of archival objects like these can "connect and include us with others . . . across time and place" (Noble 242), drawing affinity between contemporary visitors, older artifacts, and their previous owners. These objects are meant to be picked up and touched, the tangible evidence of their use felt in the worn creases of the leather boots and the dog-eared pages of marginalia in the pulps. The donors are made real, *felt* to be real, intensifying visitors' identification with the lesbian identities the objects reflect. The sense of community constructed through the material juxtaposition of these worn objects helps sediment the historical reality of the figures who owned and used them for the visitors who see and touch them.

The kinds of "records" in this archive then, are clearly different from the deviant categories in official libraries that encouraged pathological identifications in visitors like Martin and Nestle. Though the pulps' narratives reflect similar accusations of deviance as the library's system of classification, they are reframed by Nestle's frequent description of them as "survival" literature and their placement next to pride boots. The worn materiality of displayed artifacts (the faded pages, the creases in the leather) is as much a "text" to be read by visitors as the content of the pages, and perhaps more so since visitors rarely pick up a paperback and read it in its entirety during their perusal of the house. These artifacts suggest lives, not diagnoses, and through provoking analogical association among those lives and the life of the visitor, the artifacts expand the definition of "lesbian."

Synecdoche and Repetition

Like analogical association, synecdoche operates in the archive to blur the boundaries between classificatory categories. Synecdoche typically refers to a figure of speech where a part is made to stand for the whole, as when a "hired hand" represents a worker. To refigure synecdoche as a material rhetorical device, I use the term to denote a relationship between artifacts wherein one object is made to represent the whole collection. In LHA, an artifact becomes synecdochic when it comes to stand for LHA itself, spanning several subcategories at once in the system of classification. I suggest that synecdoche functions in an archive when one artifact is made significant and prominent by repeating in various forms and classificatory categories throughout the collection.

A particularly meaningful example of synecdoche is a love letter from a collection of papers once belonging to Eleanor Coit, an early twentieth-century labor activist. After Coit passed away, her family had disposed of boxes of letters, wills, leases, and photographs revealing romantic same-sex relationships she had had in her life. A friend of the archive found the boxes on the street and brought them to LHA for safe-keeping and preservation. One particular love letter, dubbed the "Gutter Letter" by the archive collective, is synecdochic for LHA because it represents how so much of lesbian history is tossed away as trash. The letter is a symbol of the archive's exigency and mission to rescue the scraps of lesbian lives from gutters and dumpsters. The Gutter Letter's history of familial shame and disposal also comes to represent something quintessential about the archive's understanding of lesbian experience and identity. Like the "Gutter Letter," lesbian lives were thrown away, expelled from disapproving families before finding a sense of "home" in LHA. In this way, the letter synecdochically comes to represent the whole of lesbian identity defined by the archive, serving as a cohering factor in the face of the incongruity and diversity I've described.

The original letter is not synecdochic on its own. Rather, it becomes so through its duplication and repetition in many places throughout the archive's system of classification. The original letter is kept in Coit's files, which are a Special Collection. But the letter also reappears in other prominent locations: it is featured in a 1981 LHA newsletter, which is housed in the archive in a binder alongside other newsletters. The newsletter reprinted the letter in its entirety, recounting the circumstances of its acquisition and "emphasiz[ing] the reality that the documents testifying to our love are too often considered garbage, destroyed by dismissing or frightened families" (1981 Newsletter). Its reprinting in the newsletter makes the letter both about Coit and about the archive, since the newsletter binder is the first place visitors go to learn about the archive itself, not just its contents. Because the letter spans categories—existing both in Coit's special collection and the newsletters—the synecdochic letter breaks down the separation between archival categories, no longer representative of itself alone but several categories simultaneously.

Further breaking down classificatory categories and contributing to its more universal representation of the archive's mission, the letter repeats again in LHA's long-running slideshow. The traveling slideshow was a multimodal presentation shown to audiences around the country that began in 1975. Nestle explains that the letter was read aloud against a backdrop of "arresting images" of Coit to tell "another national story about lesbian lives" because Coit's historical moment of the 1920s and 1930s saw the "height of pathologizing of homosexual women and yet here we had another voice, from within the lesbian world, claiming the life affirming power of this love" ("Interview"). Here, Nestle poses the letter in explicit opposition to the deviant categories in traditional libraries and archives, standing for the mission of the archive and the lives it represents and providing a counternarrative of sweet love to the national story of homosexual pathology.[2]

Like the letter, LHA suggests, women with same-sex desire have been shamed and discarded before finding community and home in the archive. This history of trauma, represented and reinforced by the Gutter Letter's synecdoche, functions to provide some coherence to the eclectic and fractured lesbian identity housed in the archive; as a newsletter proclaims, "since the destruction of Sappho's poetry, our herstory has issued a warning that we are among the disinherited." The sense of welcome and rescue that LHA has provided the Gutter Letter, all of the archive's donors, and its diverse visitors colors each of the archive's eclectic holdings, offering an open invitation of identification to visitors whose race, class, subculture, nationality, sexual orientation, and gender identity might diverge and even conflict. Donors and visitors are brought together in all of their complexity through a shared history of "disinheritance."

Conclusion

In this chapter, I have argued that classification is itself persuasive. Further, I suggested that the persuasive force of classification in shaping lesbian identity has been particularly traumatic in traditional archives, which historically classified homosexual topics within categories of de-

---

2. LHA contains several other examples of synecdoche through repetition. The pulp paperback's illustrated covers are reproduced for a periodic exhibit called "Queer Covers: Lesbian Survival Literature" and also featured in the slideshows. One particularly important book, Radclyffe Hall's *The Well of Loneliness*, is represented in the slideshow, as well as several newsletters and in surveys querying women for their experiences receiving the book and its importance in their lives.

viance and pathology. With this theoretical grounding and context, I looked closely at the Lesbian Herstory Archives to uncover its subversive, *anti*-categorical approach to classification. Through rhetorical strategies of fractured research, analogical association, and synecdoche, this archive blurs the boundaries between archival categories, encouraging a cross-categorical research experience characterized by both discovery and loss.

If, as this introduction to this volume also contends, identity is an epistemic resource, this chapter demonstrates how the rhetoricity of archival classification systems can serve as an epistemic resource for identity. LHA's system of classification reflects and encourages a queer, multiplicitous, and even contradictory lesbian identity. As Nestle proclaims in the epigraph to this chapter, the archive's "will to remember" is a will to "continually reconstruct the words 'woman,' 'lesbian,' and 'gender' so that they reflect the complex creations which we call our lives" ("A Will to Remember" 233). I have argued that this continual reconstruction occurs through a system of classification that strategically encourages visitors to associate disparate, even incongruous records and lives, cohering all of this fractured diversity through a shared sense of "disinheritance" and rescue.

Though this chapter has focused on one lesbian archive, my attention to material classification as a rhetorical act of identification has larger implications for feminist and queer historiographers in rhetorical studies. How are the systems of classification in the archives we research persuasive? How, in other words, does the construction of the archive shape our research and the sense of feminist, queer, or scholarly identity that research informs? There is a reason, for example, that feminist scholars have gravitated toward community archives and grandmothers' attics as resources for women's rhetorics (Glenn and Enoch). Like the synecdochic "Gutter Letter" in LHA, these small, local archives help shape feminist historiographers' identities as scholars who rescue forgotten women's rhetorics from the dustbins of history, from their erasure in and rejection from traditional archives. As feminist historiographers continue to reflect deeply on our methodologies, it makes sense to pay attention to how the classification of the archive informs our research and ourselves.

Works Cited

Adler, Melissa. "The ALA Task Force on Gay Liberation: Effecting Change in Naming and Classification of GLBTQ Subjects." *Advances in Classification Research Online*, vol. 23, no. 1, 2013, pp. 1–4.

Bessette, Jean. "An Archive of Anecdotes: Raising Lesbian Consciousness after the Daughters of Bilitis." *Rhetoric Society Quarterly*, vol. 43, no. 1, 2013, pp. 22–45.

Biesecker, Barbara A. "Of Historicity, Rhetoric: The Archive as Scene of Invention." *Rhetoric & Public Affairs*, vol. 9, no. 1, 2006, pp. 124–31.

Burke, Kenneth. *A Grammar of Motives*. U of California P, 1969.

—. *A Rhetoric of Motives*. U of California P, 1969.

Cvetkovich, Ann. "In the Archives of Lesbian Feelings: Documentary and Popular Culture." *Camera Obscura*, vol. 17, no. 1, 2002, pp. 107–147.

Davis, Diane. "Identification: Burke and Freud on Who You Are." *Rhetoric Society Quarterly*, vol. 38, no. 2, 2008, pp. 123–47.

Delagrange, Susan. "Wunderkammer, Cornell, and the Visual Canon of Arrangement." *Kairos*, vol. 13, no. 2, 2009.

Foucault, Michel. *A History of Sexuality Vol 1*. Penguin, 1990.

Glenn, Cheryl and Jessica Enoch. "Drama in the Archives: Rereading Methods, Rewriting History." *College Composition and Communication*, vol. 61, no. 2, 2009, pp. 321–42.

Hall, Radclyffe. *The Well of Loneliness*, edited by Havelock Ellis. Covici Friede, 1929.

Kaplan, Elizabeth. "We Are What We Collect, We Collect What We Are: Archives and the Construction of Identity." *The American Archivist*, vol. 63, no. 1, 2000, pp. 126–151.

Lesbian Herstory Archives Newsletters. Held in LHA. 1974.

Martin, Del and Phyllis Lyon. *Lesbian/Woman*. Glide, 1972.

Morris, Charles E. "The Archival Turn in Rhetorical Studies; Or, the Archive's Rhetorical (Re)turn." *Rhetoric & Public Affairs*, vol. 9, no. 1, 2006, pp. 113–15.

Narayan, Madhu. "At Home with the Lesbian Herstory Archives." *Enculturation*, 28 Feb. 2013. http://www.enculturation.net/lesbian-herstory-archives.

Nestle, Joan. "Slide Show." Received by Jean Bessette, 20 Jul. 2011.

—. "The Will to Remember: The Lesbian Herstory Archives of New York." *Feminist Review*, vol. 34, no. 1, 1990, pp. 86–94.

Noble, Greg. "Accumulating Being." *International Journal of Cultural Studies*, vol. 7, no. 2, 2004, pp. 233–56.
Plato. *Phaedrus*, edited by Harvey Yunis. Cambridge: Cambridge UP, 2011.
Sharer, Wendy. "Disintegrating Bodies of Knowledge: Historical Material and Revisionary Histories of Rhetoric." *Rhetorical Bodies*, edited by Jack Selzer and Sharon Crowley. U of Wisconsin P, 1999, pp. 120–42.
Thistlewaite, Polly. "The Lesbian and Gay Past: An Interpretive Battleground." *Gay Community News* [New York] Feb. 1995: 10+.
Warner, Michael. Introduction. *Fear of a Queer Planet: Queer Politics and Social Change*. U of Minnesota P, 1993.
Wolf, Steve. "Sex and the Single Cataloger." *Revolting Librarians*, edited by Celeste West and Elizabeth Katz. Booklegger, 1972.

Part III: Feminist Methods and Methodologies

8 Institutional "Protections," Assumptions of Research, and the Challenges of Compliance: Opening a Conversation Space for Feminist Scholars Working with Participants

Heather Brook Adams

"I hope you get an 'A' on your paper," said Elizabeth as I turned off my recorder. The eighty-year-old had invited me to her house to share with me her experience of once living in a home for unwed mothers and secretly surrendering her child for adoption.[1] One of the estimated hundreds of thousands of women who were silenced into hiding an unwed pregnancy during the middle of the twentieth century, Elizabeth is among a smaller number of mothers who has since chosen to share her story. As I listened to Elizabeth, I grappled with what telling such a story might mean for women who, in many cases, have long held

---

1. According to the parameters of the first iteration of this research, which was reviewed and received IRB approval, I dis-identified "data" and created pseudonyms that I use in this essay. It is important to note that one once-unwed mother requested that I not use a pseudonym because she perceived it to be a nonconsensual renaming practice similar to what she experienced when she was "given" a different name at a maternity home years earlier. The role of anonymity when gathering "data" is yet another opportunity for potential feminist renegotiation of project design.

on to their "shameful" secret. What might be the risk of speaking this secret to me, a stranger with a recorder? And as a feminist researcher, what assurances and protections could I provide her? Speaking oneself out of a position of being silenced, though purposeful, is, after all, an act of resistance and sometimes an act of danger. As Cheryl Glenn reminds, "those who feel silences fear that if they tell, if they speak, if they so much as discuss a bad situation, they will be harmed in some way—if not immediately, then eventually" (*Unspoken* 42). I had done my best to "protect" Elizabeth as she shared her story and punctured this silence: I brought to her attention the risk of discomfort in revisiting these memories, advised her of her rights as a participant in my study, and respected her ability to determine what part of her story to share. Despite these efforts, Elizabeth's coda stung. I appreciated her well wishes, but her statement that opens this chapter made clear how little she understood the scope and the stakes of this project, my doctoral dissertation. How could I be sure that she understood what "harm" or "risk" might mean when disclosing her now semi-secret past to me? How could I be sure that *I* understood what those terms might mean so early in my project, when I was just beginning to hear such stories and learn from mothers about their experiences?

To prepare for my interviews, I proactively met with a compliance officer at my university and prepared a suite of documents meant to secure Institutional Review Board (IRB) approval. I had also completed online Human "Subjects" Research training through the Collaborative Institutional Training Initiative (CITI). Subsequent document review with the compliance office would ensure that I was transferring the principles of CITI training to my study design—namely that I was ethically and fairly recruiting participants, communicating my assessment of the risks and rewards of being involved in the study, enabling them to provide informed consent to participate, and explaining how I would protect their confidentiality. Once I received this approval, I readied myself to follow IRB protocol in the field, such as reviewing the approved consent form with each participant. Despite my efforts to follow institutional "rules" and my interest in availing myself of field-developed best practices,[2] I was simply not prepared for Elizabeth's comment—one that situated my

---

2. I also tried my best to predict and communicate how, in the short and long term, I might use these stories, inviting Elizabeth to also share with me her ideas about their use. Doing so was my attempt to establish a "nonhierarchical, reciprocal relationship" (Powell and Takayoshi, "Accepting" 395) with partic-

project as a course requirement instead of an effort to shed light on a silenced history for future audiences. Over time, I realized that I framed potential collaboration with her *through* compliance documents upholding university-managed governmental regulations. By relying on these documents, I ensured that Elizabeth voluntarily participated in my research, but I also failed to communicate effectively my interest in establishing a collaborative and reciprocal relationship with her and other participants. Clearly, I needed to redouble my thinking about the costs, benefits, and ethically complex processes of my research for my participants and for me.

This anecdote is just one instance in which ethical quandaries that emerged in the process of gathering first-person narratives from mothers left me feeling unprepared and conflicted. It also highlights what became an unfolding research problem: how to interact with participants in an ethical and responsive manner while securing institutional sanction and following compliance standards that—upon reflection—insufficiently prepared me to accomplish this task. As a novice scholar I yearned heartily to do my research "right," and for me, "right research" with human participants meant learning about IRB protocols and gaining a literacy about the genres, textual artifacts, and processes for securing institutional approval.

I can recognize that my stance of rather uncritical compliance in seeking this institutional endorsement might be understood as my own "trained incapacity," Kenneth Burke's notion of lack of awareness that is borne of the "soundness" of "past training," even when "the very soundness of this training may lead [one] to adopt the wrong measures" (7, 10). My lack of awareness resulted in my inability to see my interaction with the IRB as a rich opportunity to reflect on the epistemologies of this institutional entity and its situated assumptions about "good" and "ethical" research—assumptions that might run counter to feminist ways of knowing and doing. And, as I have realized in retrospect, even if I had been aware of this limitation, I lacked a framework for navigating within and through it.

In what follows, I share some of my experiences with qualitative research to advocate for a feminist rhetorical intervention that would help scholars conducting work with participants to "prepare the ground for

---

ipants and avoid performing what Ellen Cushman has termed "missionary activism" (Struggle 29).

critical access" to institutional compliance (Seigel 141).³ Such critical access would enable researchers to actively examine how their epistemologies uphold, extend, or challenge the assumptions of research regulations, particularly in relation to participant "protections." I contend that institutional regulations for working with participants enact assumptions about the desirability of researcher control over the design and components of research. Specifically, the mandate for protection of "subjects," though laudable, favors and figures a paternalistic relationship between compliance office and researcher and, in turn, between researcher and participant.

To provide a rationale for this call, I first identify several concepts that inform feminist research in rhetoric and composition to suggest the basis for a feminist intervention on the paternalistic assumptions of institutional research compliance. I then offer an overview of the development of and recent adaptations to federal regulations for research with human participants to articulate how compliance, through its understanding and application of "protections," has developed to be of increasing concern for nonpositivistic researchers, particularly those embracing feminist methodologies. Finally, I outline three ways that institutional stances toward protections became complicated during my interactions with participants, encouraging me to question my initial stance of uncritical compliance with institutional regulation. Such a feminist intervention champions a deeper responsibility for collaborating with compliance offices—a goal that could help feminist scholars successfully navigate the complex process of conducting institutionally sanctioned, ethical research with participants in a way that is methodologically sound and beneficial to all parties involved.

USING FEMINIST METHODOLOGIES TO IDENTIFY MY TRAINED INCAPACITIES

Feminist scholars working with human participants can glean much from feminist methodological conversations emerging from literacy and writing studies. Among the most well-developed considerations are those

---

3. In *The Rhetoric of Pregnancy*, Marika Seigel argues for the need for women to have "critical access" to the systems of prenatal care that they find themselves part of when they become pregnant. Too often, Seigel argues, women lack critical access due to fear-based discourses of risk that encourage complicity within highly medicalized prenatal care systems.

that deal with the *process* of conducting research and the commonly unequal distribution of power between researcher and participants. The dual goals of *collaboration* through all stages of the research process and *reciprocity* between researcher and participants have been paramount for feminist scholars who emphasize interactive and dialogic exchanges with participants to minimize power disparities (Kirsch, "Multi-Vocal"199; Kirsch, *Ethical Dilemmas* 46).

Collaboration, according to Gesa E. Kirsch, means listening to participants' stories and also creating two-directional channels of communication with participants through which they can voice "disagreements" and varying perspectives on a researcher's interpretation of findings ("Friendship" 2168). Kirsch also advocates potentially renegotiating decisions about consent, a possibility she admits is far from simple given compliance expectations (*Ethical Dilemmas* 40–41; "Friendship" 2168). Ellen Cushman suggests the synergy of these two goals through her assertion that collaboration can enable "activism" through empowerment, the development of "networks of reciprocity," and solidarity between researchers and the communities with which they interact ("Rhetorician as Agent" 7).[4]

Collaboration and reciprocity might be critically hindered, though, if researchers wait to put these values into effect after a project has been designed within the existing framework of compliance. Joanne Addison draws attention to this issue of timing as she encourages feminist scholars to "uncover the questions that need to be asked from the standpoint of others" by interacting with participants at the *front-end* of research (146–47).[5] Such forward thinking, I argue, typically does not involve critically engaging with issues of regulation, since compliance often functions as a requirement standing between research ideas and implementation. Likely, feminist researchers often either do not anticipate how methodological commitments might be compromised by pursuing institutional approval for conducting research or fail to recognize that they have been interpolated into a position of obedience that diminishes opportunities for negotiating nontraditional research design. I now un-

---

4. Despite these goals, an interest in mutually beneficial work with participants can easily be lost, warn Katrina M. Powell and Pamela Takayoshi, because reciprocity often functions as a "methodological construct" that remains elusive and difficult to deploy in the field ("Accepting Roles" 399).

5. Addison uses "experience sampling" to collect empirical data and thus better understand participants' social locations and lived experiences (146).

derstand that my stance of compliance was influenced by my perceived diminished ethos as a scholar early in my career as well as my feelings of unfamiliarity with IRB (at the institution where I was then conducting research of a new scope and type). In hindsight, I question whether my deferral to the IRB actually enacted the sort of hasty consent from which a feminist researcher might try to "protect" their participants.

Collaboration and reciprocity have been discussed primarily as feminist methodological concerns that relate to researchers interacting with participants; identifying my trained incapacities provokes me to question how these terms might be extended to apply to the hierarchical relationship between an institutional compliance office and researchers, given the shared desire between these parties to work toward high quality and ethically sound research. I propose that *reflexivity*—another key concept in feminist methodology—is a third term that can be used to pursue this goal. Reflexivity, as defined by Katrina Powell and Pamela Takayoshi, involves a researcher "writ[ing] herself into the research" in a systematic and methodological manner ("Revealing" 3–5). In this chapter, I critically assess my own trained incapacities in working with an office of research compliance, which eventually led to subsequent ethical *dilemmas* (to borrow a term popular among feminist qualitative researchers). I'm less *reflecting* on my experiences in a way that emphasizes them as individualized or anomalous and instead thinking about them *reflexively* as worthy of consideration within and against institutional systems of review. Doing so performs what Lois Presser terms "strong reflexivity," or that which situates research into wider contexts and within currents of power (2068–69). Feminist methodological interventions into work with participants have provided researchers with useful guidance in research design and implementation, but without more *systematic* and *proactive* efforts to imagine what collaboration and reciprocity might look like in relation to the institutional apparatuses that ultimately sanction feminist research, these goals might be stymied, even undermined. Such an intervention would need to emerge from a place of knowledge. Thus, I next delineate the recent history of institutional research review to demonstrate how the assumptions and practices of regulation might run counter to feminist epistemologies.

A Brief History of IRB Oversight

One difficulty in upholding feminist methodologies while seeking institutional approval for research is a general lack of awareness of the provenance of research oversight despite some effort to share this history (Anderson, McGee).[6] Further, there are scant interdisciplinary discussions of how that oversight has been systematically critiqued and/or enhanced by researchers who have an especial concern for ethics outside of biomedical research contexts. I contend that feminist scholars working with participants can gain an appreciation for the critical affordances of institutional oversight and prepare to make feminist interventions into institutional review by becoming more fully educated about these dynamic histories. By articulating and making a shared commitment to professional statements and standards of practice, disciplines such as oral history offer valuable models for clarifying ethical challenges of human-participant research *based on their own epistemologies*. In short, they pool collective wisdom related to disciplinary ethics and thereby facilitate uptake of this wisdom among other scholars.

The fundamental idea of protecting research participants, first expressed as part of the 1947 Nuremberg Code, is a useful concept from a feminist standpoint. But the history of subsequent regulatory growth demonstrates how protections have embraced some nonfeminist assumptions. As medical research after World War II increased and shifted from being primarily observational to increasingly experimental, the National Institutes of Health determined that an ethical "system of safeguards" for this research was warranted (Schrag "How Talking" 5). The need for additional oversight became apparent in 1972, when the Tuskegee Syphilis Study garnered wide public attention for its glaring breach of ethics.[7] Shortly after news broke about the Tuskegee study, the US Senate held hearings about this and other ethically problematic government-funded research, leading to the 1974 National Research Act, which established the National Commission for the Protection of Human Subjects of Bio-

---

6. I would guess that a great many researchers—especially those in the humanities who might not have taken qualitative methods courses—think most deeply about IRB regulation when they are seeking compliance and otherwise poised to begin a research project.

7. The forty-year medical research program enrolled 399 African American men suffering from syphilis who did not give informed consent to participate in the study and who were not aware that they were purposefully being denied treatment for their infection (Oakes 444).

medical and Behavioral Research. The Commission was charged with establishing basic ethical principles for biomedical and behavioral research involving human participants and creating guidelines for implementing those principles. After meeting for four years, the Commission produced the Belmont Report, which establishes respect for persons, beneficence, and justice as the three fundamental components of ethical research. These principles translate directly to researchers' obligation to obtain participants' informed consent, assess and balance the possible risks and potential benefits of research, and select participants equally and fairly ("45 CFR 46—FAQs"; Meeker 117). The Belmont Report guidelines were codified in 1981 as Title 45 (Public Welfare), Part 46 (Protection of Human Subjects) of the code of Federal Regulations, establishing a standard for assessing what risk researchers' projects might pose to participants who need to be protected from studies that do not uphold the tenets of respect, beneficence, and justice.

This regulatory code, most often referred to as the Common Rule, is implemented by the Office of Human Research Protections (OHRP) of the US Department of Health and Human Service (DHHS) and grants the federal government the ultimate authority to review any human-participant research. Such breadth both explains why the Common Rule applies to institutions of higher education and why its deployment can pose challenges to feminist researchers. In 1991, the regulations were revised specifically to include all federally funded projects, resulting in establishment of IRBs (Meeker 117). Universities that wish to receive federal funding for research are required to ensure that *any* human-participant research at the institution complies with the Common Rule, whether or not that research is receiving government sponsorship. A particular institution's IRB, then, functions as the apparatus for assessing what research should be reviewed, although IRBs vary as to their interpretation of what work needs oversight (Meeker 118). Significantly, the changing "scope" of institutional compliance efforts, as Sharon James McGee summarizes, includes heightened standards for researchers, such as mandatory and uniform training on research ethics; an expansion of the types of projects necessitating review (IRB "mission creep"); and a perceived shift to institutional risk management (over and above risk management on behalf of participants) (146–8).[8] These varied interpretations of the range

---

8. Consider Kirsch's assertion in 1999 that "[s]o far, qualitative research has received neither the close scrutiny nor the careful guidance that IRBs regularly provide for experimental, quantitative research in the behavioral sciences" (*Eth-*

and depth of IRB activity have led to scholarly critique, particularly as institutional notions such as "research," "risk," and "protections" remain overwhelmingly understood in terms of biomedical and behavioral inquiry and as positivistic assumptions about knowledge-making are increasingly applied to projects that follow nonpositivistic paradigms (McGee 146–47).

In 2017, revisions to the Common Rule were published in the *Federal Register*, and subsequent compliance dates for this revision were assigned by DHHS. The modifications are primarily attributed to the changing landscape of research in terms of methods and technological affordances (United States 7149–50). Although the revisions relate to a variety of regulatory changes, the most relevant portion recasts what sorts of scholarly activity might be excluded from IRB oversight. Specifically, some journalistic and scholarly activities—oral history in particular—are now categorized to not be research and thus potentially not under the purview of the IRB. This change has been encouraged by the work of historians who have positioned themselves outside of the scope of institutional review, doing so on the basis that biomedical and behavioral methods and results are fundamentally different than those of humanist inquiry. These limitations were thought to be so serious that leaders of the Oral History Association (OHA) and American Historical Association (AHA) collaborated and, garnering the support of the OHRP, issued a statement in 2003 exempting oral history projects from federal regulatory oversight because such projects do not "cross the definitive threshold of 'research'" as "generalizable knowledge" defined by the Common Rule (Meeker 116).⁹ The statement clarifies tenets about oral historians' scholarship, including its methodological adherence to the pursuit of specificity and depth of knowledge. The most recent Common Rule

---

ical Dilemmas 42) with what some have referred to as IRB "mission creep" as it casts an increasingly wide net of oversight that implicates a great number of disciplines (see Gunsalus).

9. The policy explains that oral historians "do not reach for generalizable principles of historical or social development, nor do they seek underlying principles or laws of nature that have predictive value and can be applied to other circumstances for the purpose of controlling outcomes" (Shopes, "Legal and Ethical" 150). Instead, oral historians define their work as both a "method of recording and preserving oral testimony" and "the product of that process," noting that personal "reflections on the past" are the central component of work that demands respect for "narrators' equal authority" within the interview situation (Oral History Association).

revision is based on this notion that journalistic and oral history efforts rely on accuracy and evidence-based "portrayal" but do not produce generalizable knowledge (Office for Human Research Protections). In terms of my own research, this revision has meant that my ongoing work with once-unwed mothers has recently been deemed "non-research" and thus is exempt from IRB oversight.

As a feminist rhetorician working in collaboration with participants, I find this history and these recent changes significant to the design and conceptualization of my work and to my understanding of the potential contributions of my scholarship. Although my most recent IRB application was exempted from institutional review, it is important to note that this determination was made as a result of my completing a full IRB application, thus prompting me to identify my research design in the ways described in this essay (through an assessment of risk, considerations of protections, etc.). Additionally, I am asked to resubmit an application should my research design change.

Despite the recent Common Rule modifications, the distinction between "research" and "non-research" activity seemingly remains a site of interpretation—another reason for me to think carefully about how I am understanding and communicating my work. For instance, I submitted my IRB application without a strong sense of how the committee would consider my research design in light of revised DHHS regulations. I remain uncomfortable with knowing that because of my methodological choices, my scholarship no longer holds the label "research." In this instance the label relates specifically to institutional oversight, I realize, and so it does not necessary influence the reception of my work within my home department or my discipline. Nevertheless, this institutionally meaningful relabeling gives me pause for what it could mean to other stakeholders at my university and for what it communicates to others within the academy. The vexed label of research in this context confirms that feminist rhetorical scholarship with participants occupies a liminal space in academia. This liminality is all the more reason to consider the assumptions and dynamics at play when considering ethical and compliant interactions with participants.

A feminist intervention on behalf of nonpositivists seeking compliance—or when determining how to pursue a potential oversight exemption—might involve naming these assumptions as inherently paternalistic in their perpetuation of a researcher-participant hierarchy that values the researcher's ability to successfully predict, control, and "safeguard" participation so as to minimize risk for participants. Additionally, the expectation that researchers will design their research without significant (or any) participant collaboration becomes obvious when compliance (or exemption) remains a precursor to recruitment—a step to be taken *before* deeply interacting with participants. Gaining institutional sanction requires completing generalized training and working with an IRB office that has the ultimate say in when—and if—a researcher has a study design and materials that are reasonably safe for participants or if the study does or does not require oversight.

Rhetoric and composition scholar Paul V. Anderson draws attention to some potentially troubling parameters guiding IRB oversight for scholars who, like me, hope to conduct responsive research that might benefit from a more recursive relationship to project design and implementation. While Anderson—then a member of his campus's IRB—supports the mission of the entity, he admits that scholars in our field "might quarrel with the epistemology underlying the policy's distinction between 'research' and 'practice,'" arguing that it is understood "[w]ithin the paradigm of medical research" and thus will "inevitably" lead to variations in interpretation among different IRBs (279).[10] Although Anderson shared these perspectives before the 2017 revision of the Common Rule, his critical approach to considering the assumptions of research remain relevant. Anderson reminds that pedagogy-related research, especially, can materialize gradually through practice, based on the interactive process of teaching—not just through more isolated

---

10. For example, do teacher-scholars studying student writing only need to seek institutional compliance if they wish to publish or otherwise distribute their findings, since dissemination of knowledge suggests "proof" of generalizability? Is the promise of publication the only measure of the need for protection? And, in this instance, when exactly does "research" begin, assuming that a line of inquiry emerges from teacher-student interactions? A 2005 interdisciplinary white paper that addresses the expanding and sometimes ill-fitting scope of IRBs extends these questions:

> What if, after a lifetime of classroom activity and observations as a practicing teacher, an academic decides to write a memoir of recollections, anecdotes, and general lessons learned. When does this become research? Must the academic retroactively obtain permission from every student whose foibles might be anonymously exposed in such an account? . . . While there are regulatory options covering this kind of work, the fact that they are not well understood or implemented underscores the ambiguity in the distinction between practice and research that exists for IRBs." (Gunsalus 9–10)

intellectual work of researchers. Such an insight suggests that the research/practice distinction assumes the *intent* of researchers following the scientific method (e.g., those testing a hypothesis through controlled investigation) rather than types of inquiry that might arise from—and ideally respond to—the evolving relationship and experiences *between* researcher and researched. Because feminist scholars tend to relinquish some level of researcher "control," feminist inquiry too supports these mindful relationships-in-flux and values them as an ultimate benefit to, rather than a risk of, investigation. I must qualify that IRB-prepared materials can and should be revised to reflect changes in project design after approval. This opportunity for updates, however, encourages adjustments *within* the parameters established by the IRB on projects that have already been shaped in response to compliance assumptions.

The potential remains for miscommunication between researchers (or nonresearching "scholars") and offices of research integrity, especially due to the lack of sufficient education about varying research practices, assumptions, and goals—both on the part of IRB members and those submitting projects for review. Historian Martin Meeker contends that negotiation with compliance offices can happen and explains how the University of California Berkeley has used OHA guidelines to rethink regulation needs for oral historians. I have come to appreciate how fields other than oral history have taken proactive steps to outline ethical principles for scholars—guidelines the likes of which are briefly mentioned in CITI training (Hicks).[11] For example, sociolinguists collectively uphold the "principle of error correction," or the scholarly obligation to correct any widespread idea or social practice invalidated by research; the "principle of debt incurred," or the obligation to use knowledge-making to the benefit of those communities from whom related "data" is obtained; and the "principle of linguistic gratuity," or the responsibility to

---

11. A recent iteration of CITI training (training typically required of researchers applying for expedited or full review or even exemption) mentions that the American Anthropological Association, the Oral History Association, the American Psychological Association, and the American Sociological Association "identify protecting privacy and ensuring confidentiality as key components of respecting the safety and dignity of research subjects" (Hicks). This discussion, although helpful for raising researchers' attention to individual fields' best practice guidelines, does not discuss the OHA's consideration of nonconfidential records to be a boon to oral historians' work. Such an omission could be a site of potential confusion for scholars seeking IRB approval (or exemption) while employing oral history methods.

"actively pursue positive ways" for "returning linguistic favors" to a community to whom the researcher is indebted (Wolfram 225–6).[12] Such principles crystalize broad ethical values in a succinct manner, enabling dissemination among scholars and institutional and community stakeholders.[13] I also argue that such principles do not impose an "overarching guideline" that would hinder the *kairotic* responses of researchers in the field—a concern of Powell and Takayoshi ("Accepting" 414)—but might better enable responsiveness and collaboration with compliance offices and participants.

Participant Protections as Challenges to Feminist Inquiry

My research experiences suggest that assumptions related to protections against risk could be productively rethought from a feminist stance in ways promoted by other scholars who critically engage the idea of compliance and research integrity. I use my field experiences along with these perspectives to problematize preferred ways of assessing risk, pursuing confidentiality through anonymity, and protecting participants through data handling and destruction. These considerations are useful even for researchers who are likely eligible for IRB exempted work, given the possible need to communicate a research design that will lead to exemption. More importantly, though, such considerations enable feminist researchers to replace dispositions of obedience, resistance, or indifference—the latter being the desire to quickly jump through the "hoop" of obtaining an institutional stamp in order to get on with one's research—with more critical and thoughtful dispositions that foster working toward positive participant-research experiences and subsequent scholarship.

---

12. For more recent scholarship related to these principles see Wolfram, Reaser, and Vaughn.

13. These sorts of disciplinary discussions and practices could enrich scholars' navigation of the Conference on College Composition and Communication (CCCC) bibliography for ethical conduct of research involving human participants, which currently includes the OHA's statement of best practices. According to the CCCC Guidelines for the Ethical Conduct of Research in Composition Studies, "composition specialists" are urged to "learn about and comply with all policies, regulations, and laws that apply to their studies," and to confirm with the "appropriate committee or authority" if they suspect that a study might be exempt from the review process" ("CCCC Guidelines").

Rethinking Risk

A central concern that has come to light for me during my research is the problem of gauging a project's potential risk to participants at its outset and before significant interaction with participants has taken place. "Risk" in the context of institutional protections refers to a broad range of social, psychological, physical, economic, or legal issues (Arwood and Panicker). This array of potential concerns must be reasonably assessed to gain IRB approval or exemption because risk has to be communicated to possible participants, for example, on consent forms that must be understood and signed by these individuals before they take part in a study. The difficulty of predicting risk, however, makes its assessment "[o]ne of the most important and challenging tasks researchers and institutional review boards" face (Arwood and Panicker).

As my experiences suggest, risk might be best assessed *in dialogic relationship with participants and throughout the research process* rather than on participants' behalf prior to interacting with them as IRB protocols mandate. As mentioned above, collaboration and reciprocity are feminist stances, but in terms of assessing risk, they are ones that are not upheld by compliance procedures that assume research design (including risk assessment) is a *precursor* to interaction with "subjects." Oral historian Zachary Schrag suggests that researchers cannot effectively evaluate risk at the front end of unfolding, humanistic projects. Schrag conducted oral history interviews with tenant activists in New York City, some of whom were members of the Communist Party during the years of McCarthyism. Over multiple interactions with interviewees, Schrag began to realize the potential "risk" involved in asking activists their stories, the hazard of having engaged conversations that raised the specter of deeply held secrets. Questioning the idea that "risk" and "harm" can accurately be measured at the outset of a project, Schrag reminds that "[o]ral history is a venture into uncharted territory, not a controlled laboratory experiment" ("Roberta").

My interview with Gayle brought to light my own inability to confidently assess risk on behalf of participants in my study. I met Gayle at the medical office where she works after hours, when we were free to speak privately. Prior to meeting Gayle in person, I had been in email contact with her, providing general information about my project and coordinating our meeting time and location. But as soon as Gayle greeted me, I could tell that she was nervous and uncomfortable. She admitted that she responded to my call for participants "after having a glass of wine" and questioned whether she made the right decision in doing so. Clearly, Gayle was conflicted about whether to share her story with me. I assured her that she had a right to decline the interview altogether and that I would respect that decision, a statement that I had included on my consent form. Gayle indicated that she wished to continue, so I explained her right to stop the interview at any time or even decide to withdraw it from my study retroactively. In retrospect, I realize that Gayle's response would have been an excellent opportunity to invite her to help me understand the nature of her worry and whether it was related to the experience of revisiting memories, the idea of disclosing a long-held secret, or perhaps another concern altogether.

Although Gayle said that she understood and agreed to the terms of participation in my project, I found myself conflicted as well. I respect Gayle's ability to determine her participation, and I felt confident that I in no way coerced her. At the same time, meeting Gayle also helped me think about the extent to which revisiting and discussing memories of trauma might impose risks that are difficult to measure. Would being interviewed by me impose a risk to Gayle at the time of the interview? Would the risk of emotional pain come later through recollections that linger after I left? However admirable the goal of "protecting" participants from risk, this aim becomes more complex when participation involves revisiting painful, even traumatic events through memory. Further, I wondered if my goal of inviting mothers to review my completed transcripts for accuracy and in order to make changes—an effort meant to promote accuracy and better situate participants as active partners in creating interview "data"—would unintentionally *reactivate* uncomfortable memories.[14] Perhaps most troubling, many researchers like me do not have the professional competencies to know how to respond to a participant in distress, much less anticipate what questions or topics might be most stressful—particularly at the beginning of the field research journey. I had been surprised that the compliance office that reviewed my project responded to emotional risk by (only) requiring that I include information on my consent form about free or low-cost counseling services that might be used by participants. In the larger scheme of revisiting potentially traumatic memories, this mandate seemed to

---

14. And what about the additional risk of sending transcripts via postal mail to a participant, like Joan, who has not shared her story with the daughter who regularly checks in on her?

direct "protections" less to me—and far less to participants—than to the institution itself.

Do these considerations render my qualitative work more or less risky than biomedical or behavioral studies? For many feminist scholars, this question would not be quickly or easily answered. In retrospect, I can appreciate how dialoging with participants about their *responses* and *reactions to* my project ideas and schedule of interview questions might have provided me the opportunity to more fully understand what risk might look like in the context of this particular project.

Deciding on Anonymity

One large component of participant risk relates to issues of confidentiality, or the "ways in which data will be used and made available to others" (Hicks). Some oral historians contend that IRBs view confidentiality through anonymity as a *preferred* strategy for minimizing participants' risk—a universal assumption that aligns with the values of biomedical research (Schrag, "Ethical Training"). The Common Rule seeks to protect "subjects" from "criminal or civil liability" and to avoid identifying them with responses that could "be damaging to the subjects' financial standing, employability, or reputation" (46.101 [b] [2]). Although this part of the regulation should seem reasonable to any researcher mindful of ethical forms of inquiry, it can present issues to feminist scholars. Consider Schrag's argument that anonymity runs counter to "the view of historians, who believe that [oral history participants] have unique lives and tell unique stories, and that completed interviews are valuable documents that may serve future scholars" ("Ethical Training").

Anonymity, a risk-averting strategy that is useful in many research contexts, can raise concerns for feminist scholars by replicating the practices of silencing and marginalization that our scholarship often seeks to address. After several interviews, for example, I reconsidered the promise I made to the IRB that I would omit interviewees' names from interview transcripts. Listening to mothers' stories about being forced to hide an unwed pregnancy, I gradually understood the troubling role that anonymity played in upholding practices of shame directed at these women. Many mothers who went to a maternity home were required to choose a pseudonym upon entering the home or to only use their first name. These requirements were integral to the secret keeping that maternity homes performed. Indeed, it was this need to keep secret a "shameful" pregnancy that necessitated homes for unwed mothers in the first place. As Gayle explained, "They tried *hard* to make [the experience] confidential." I knew about this practice from reading several memoirs and accessing archival materials, but this early research did not provide me with an understanding of mothers' *experience with* and *reactions to* such policies.

Only through my ongoing conversations with mothers were they able to teach me that the expediency of altering one's name can be understood synecdochally, as a symbolic representation of the women's loss of a motherhood identity. I became most aware of this connection between naming and identity when I interviewed Yvonne, who (very reasonably) questioned my plan to keep her name anonymous in my work. Yvonne asked if she could decide whether to use her name or to use a pseudonym, and she explicitly linked this desire to have a say over the decision with her *inability* to control the renaming she experienced at a maternity home nearly fifty years ago. In another interview, Susan helped me understand how mothers surreptitiously claimed agency within the shroud of forced anonymity in the homes. She explained to me that despite the rules, "if you *felt* comfortable with someone, [those in charge at the home] could not police you and tell you, you know, not to give your real name or to give any information about yourself." And as I learned from Gayle, "You weren't supposed to talk specifically about where you came from, but we all did." These comments encouraged me to question whether I had the right to deny mothers the opportunity to claim their stories now, as they retold them after decades of silence. Although some mothers wanted this anonymity, the decision about how to identify participants is one that would have been most ethically made *in consultation with* these women, long after IRB agreements had been made.[15] Just as Powell and Takayoshi advocate that feminist scholars "allow space" for participants to join in "calling the shots" (404) of research in the context of the participant's *role* in the research, so too can we extend this prin-

---

15. Sociologist Rachel L. Einwohner faced similar questions during her research with archived oral histories of Holocaust survivors. Although Einwohner did not conduct her own oral history interviews (and thus was exempted from seeking IRB approval), she realized in the midst of her research that a choice to use pseudonyms to refer to survivors "would seem to be an unethical and particularly disturbing way to treat Holocaust survivors, for whom just one manifestation of their victimization involved the loss of their names" (425). Einhower's reflection draws attention to how researchers can "unintentionally dehumanize research subjects," which, she argues is "especially troubling if those subjects have been the victims of genocide or other traumas" (423).

ciple of discussing the subject of anonymity with participants in order to build with them "humane relationships" instead of "sterile" research interactions (397). In so doing, we can reclaim on behalf of our participants some control over the notion of anonymity outside of the relatively flat interpretation assumed by IRB compliance.

Collecting and Preserving Stories, not Destroying Data

Finally, compliance protocols tend to favor viewing interview materials as data that should not only be rendered anonymous but destroyed after analysis. Current CITI training suggests that researchers and participants should agree on how data will be handled and offers fourteen questions that can guide research design in terms of this decision. Only the last question raises the possibility of archiving data whereas most of the remaining questions address specific concerns related to data security and destroying or making data anonymous (Hicks). Additionally, it is likely that a plan for handing data would need to be decided upon by the researcher as part of an IRB application before recruitment can begin (and thus before discussions with participants can take place).

While I am pleased to see that the idea of archiving materials actually appears in the CITI information, I admit that this option never dawned on me when I was initially planning my project. My previous, limited experience with an IRB led me to believe that I *must* destroy my anonymous data after analyzing it to be compliant, and that I *must* be compliant with the IRB before starting my recruitment. And as a recipient of several research grants from various funding sources, I felt especially responsible for following institutional protocol perfectly. I assumed a stance similar to writing studies scholar Heidi McKee who, as a graduate student seeking compliance with her campus review board, did not want to "challenge [IRB] conventions" or "jeopardize" her research "by not responding in what [she] thought was the expected and, it seemed, the only appropriate way" (489).

My lack of imagination about the potential uses of my interviews foreclosed an opportunity for me to collaborate with participants to, for example, produce archival memory texts that could then be shared publicly. The problem with assuming that I must destroy mothers' stories became most clear to me once I started listening to these women tell their stories. I ended each interview with the question: What would you like to see me do with the information that I gather from these interviews?

Pam's answer is one that made me stop and wonder who would—and who should—eventually read my writing about this project:

> Well I think that when I talk to you or others it is becoming where they say you empower yourself. Because I'm not feeling like a victim. Nowadays they look back and think, "Oh, you got pregnant." But they don't know—they don't know what we went through. I mean, and how it is not talked about. . . . I think some of it goes back to that [idea of] being bad. People think, "how could you give your baby up for adoption?" That makes you a bad person. But you know what . . . some of these girls didn't have a choice. It really bothers me when I hear people judge other people. This is what it was like back then. It isn't like that anymore. I'm much better now when I hear comments like that, because I want to say, "You just don't get it." *I think it is just good for people to know.*

I do not think that Pam had a specific audience in mind when she offered that she thinks "it is just good for people to know," but I doubt that she was thinking of the academics to whom my work on this project, as an untenured assistant professor, will be directed.[16]

Jessica Enoch poses questions about what it would mean to "think beyond offering our completed research to stakeholders outside the ivory tower and to explore instead whether and how we might share archival materials with them" (43). This impulse to make research open echoes and builds upon earlier warnings of "rhetorical elitism" (Kirsch, *Ethical Dilemmas* 73) and encouragement to "imagine new ways of locating the reader in relation to new forms of texts" (Royster and Kirsch 107). As I entertain Enoch's vision of feminist historiographers who might "become public historians and even activists" (43), I look to feminist oral historians who have cultivated methods intended to maintain a methodological commitment to producing texts, offering insights on those texts, and making both available to public audiences (Gluck 64). I did not explore these options when I began my research in large part because I focused on designing a compliant research project. In retrospect, I can see

---

16. Pam was not the only mother who expressed a hope that her story be shared. Many mothers expressed a similar interest, albeit in fairly vague ways. May was more specific in hoping that adopted children could benefit from my work, since, as she explained, they often struggle to grasp mothers' feelings of lack of choice in the "decision" to relinquish their child to an adoption agency.

how the accepted definitions of compliant research that advances non-feminist assumptions about the what, why, and how of scholarly work shaped my project from its very start.

Conclusion

While revising this chapter, I struck up a conversation with a colleague visiting from another institution. She disclosed to me her own discouraging experience in seeking compliance with an IRB office that questioned her proposed scholarship using diaries archived in her university's library (based on a concern over whether the diarists would have intended such use) and her hope to interview these (women) diary writers about their experiences with cooking. Compliance became such a difficult prospect that this researcher ultimately decided against trying to speak with these women. What stories and understandings were lost with that decision? How many other stories and lines of inquiry have been silenced in the name of compliance? And how might ongoing revisions to participant protections and institutional oversight rules provide an impetus for actively shaping conversations about the ongoing diversity of research methods, products, and purposes in our field?

Reflexively considering my relationship to compliance as a researcher has enabled me to see a curious irony: similar to how "protections" of unwed mothers (through practices of erasure) were the rationale used by those who spoke and acted on their behalf, research "protections" have configured my relationship to participants in ways that seem predetermined and, at times, beyond my control. Greater awareness of the assumptions of institutional review that run counter to feminist ways of knowing can help scholars engage in conversations about ethics that reflect their specific research goals. Some scholars, I realize, have long tried to circumvent IRB regulation by claiming that their method or disciplinary affiliation (oral history, journalism) renders them exempt from compliance. Now this exemption is more likely possible, given the most recent adaptations to the Common Rule. As I have tried to demonstrate, however, such an approach still relies on the interpretation of local IRBs as well as the arbitrariness and often increasingly wide oversight of individual committees. But most importantly, this tactic does not assume the difficult but critical work of opening opportunities for collaboration *with* IRBs toward mutually beneficial goals. Perhaps my call for work with offices of compliance sounds idealistic, but I argue that the alternative is to allow scholars—many of whom are in vulnerable positions in the academy—to navigate these ethically complex waters in isolation.[17] Education scholars Christine Halse and Anne Honey argue that the "moral crevices [between] ethics policy and practice" too often remain invisible because "investments, dilemmas, and implications of researchers' ethical decisions and moral choices" are commonly "secreted away, buried, concealed, and hidden from public scrutiny." The resulting "illusion" is that "'good' research is being done by 'good researchers'" (2142).

The goal of this chapter has been to rethink what "good" research is. The feminist intervention I hoped to make was to demonstrate how methodological reflexivity has the potential to incite increasingly specific conversations about the processes and practices of feminist research with participants that can enable scholars to maintain the estimable goals of our institutions while not losing sight of the methodological values we hold so important.

Works Cited

"45 CFR 46—FAQs." *HHS.gov.* US Department of Health and Human Services, n.d., www.hhs.gov/ohrp/regulations-and-policy/guidance/faq/45-cfr-46/index.html. Accessed 15 May 2013.

Addison, Joanne. "Researching Literacy as a Lived Experience." *Rhetorica in Motion: Feminist Rhetorical Methods and Methodologies*, edited by Eileen E. Schell and K. J. Rawson. U of Pittsburgh P, 2010, pp. 136–51.

Anderson, Paul V. "Ethics, Institutional Review Boards, and the Involvement of Human Participants in Composition Research." Mortensen and Kirsch, pp. 260–85.

Arwood, Tracy, and Sangeeta Panicker. "Assessing Risk-SBE." *CITI Program.* Collaborative Institutional Training Initiative at the University of Miami, 10 Feb. 2014, research.wisc.edu/wp-content/uploads/sites/2/2018/09/Assessing-Risk-SBE-ID-503.pdf. Accessed 27 May 2014.

---

17. CITI compliance training suggests a somewhat flexible and responsive approach toward international research projects, such as ethnographies that "must be carried out in a way that honors the autonomy and dignity of all persons" (Hicks and Simmerling). Feminist scholars working with participants might rely on expectations about conducting nondomestic research as a model for a more negotiated approach to compliance.

Burke, Kenneth. *Permanence and Change: An Anatomy of Purpose.* 3rd ed., U of California P, 1965.

"CCCC Ethical Conduct of Research Involving Human Participants: A Bibliography." *Conference on College Composition and Communication.* NCTE, Nov. 2003, cccc.ncte.org/cccc/resources/positions/ethicalconductbiblio. Accessed 15 Oct. 2013.

"CCCC Guidelines for the Ethical Conduct of Research in Composition Studies." *Conference on College Composition and Communication.* NCTE. n.d., cccc.ncte.org/cccc/resources/positions/ethicalconduct. Accessed 15 Oct. 2013.

Cushman, Ellen. "The Rhetorician as Agent of Social Change." *College Composition and Communication*, vol. 47, no. 1, 1996, pp. 7–28. *JSTOR.* 18 Feb. 2014.

—. *The Struggle and the Tools: Oral and Literate Strategies in an Inner City Community.* SUNY UP, 1998.

Einwohner, Rachel L. "Ethical Considerations on the Use of Archived Testimonies in Holocaust Research: Beyond the IRB Exemption." *Qualitative Sociology*, vol. 34, no. 3, 2011, pp. 415–30. *SpringerLink.* Accessed 1 May 2013.

Enoch, Jessica. "Coalition Talk: Feminist Historiography: What's the Digital Humanities Got to Do with It?" *Peitho*, vol. 15, no. 2, 2013, pp. 40–45. Accessed 30 Sept. 2013.

Glenn, Cheryl. *Unspoken: A Rhetoric of Silence.* Southern Illinois UP, 2004.

Gluck, Sherna Berger. "Has Feminist Oral History Lost Its Radical/Subversive Edge?" *Oral History*, vol. 39, no. 2, 2011, pp. 63–72. *JSTOR.* Accessed 29 Sept. 2013.

Gunsalus, C. K. et al., "Improving the System for Protecting Human Subject: Counteracting IRB 'Mission Creep.'" *The Illinois White Paper*, 2005. Accessed 15 Feb. 2014.

Halse, Christine, and Anne Honey. "Unraveling Ethics: Illuminating the Moral Dilemmas of Research Ethics." *Signs*, vol. 30, no. 4, 2005, pp. 2141–62. *JSTOR.* Accessed 19 Jan. 2014.

Hicks, Lorna. "Privacy and Confidentiality." *CITI Program.* Collaborative Institutional Training Initiative at the University of Miami, 9 June 2011. Accessed 27 May 2014.

Hicks, Lorna, and Mary Simmerling. "International Research." *CITI Program.* Collaborative Institutional Training Initiative at the University of Miami, 8 June 2011. Accessed 27 May 2014.

Kirsch, Gesa E. *Ethical Dilemmas in Feminist Research: The Politics of Location, Interpretation, and Publication.* State U of New York P, 1999.

—. "Friendship, Friendliness, and Feminist Fieldwork." *Signs*, vol. 30, no. 4, 2005, pp. 2163–72. *JSTOR.* Accessed 19 Jan. 2014.

—. "Multi-Vocal Texts and Interpretive Responsibility." *College English*, vol. 59, no. 2, 1997, pp. 191–202. *JSTOR.* Accessed 28 Sept. 2013.

McGee, Sharon James. "Practicing Socially Progressive Research: Implications for Research and Practice." Powell and Takayoshi, pp. 143–57.

McKee, Heidi. "Changing the Process of Institutional Review Board Compliance." *College Composition and Communication*, vol. 54, no. 3, 2003, pp. 488–93. *JSTOR.* Accessed 27 Sept. 2013.

Meeker, Martin. "The Berkeley Compromise: Oral History, Human Subjects, and the Meaning of 'Research.'" Potter and Romano, pp. 115–38.

Oakes, J. Michael. "Risks and Wrongs in Social Science Research: An Evaluator's Guide to the IRB." *Evaluation Review*, vol. 26, no. 5, 2002, pp. 443–479. *SAGE Premier 2012.* Accessed 23 Oct. 2013.

Office for Human Research Protections. "Scholarly and Journalistic Activities Deemed Not to be Research: 2018 Requirements." *HHS.gov.* US Department of Health and Human Services. 20 July 2018, www.hhs.gov/ohrp/regulations-and-policy/requests-for-comments/draft-guidance-scholarly-and-journalistic-activities-deemed-not-to-be-research/index.html. Accessed 24 Jan. 2019.

Oral History Association. "Principles and Best Practices." *Oral History Association*, Oct. 2009, www.oralhistory.org/about/principles-and-practices-revised-2009/. Accessed 15 March 2013.

Powell, Katrina M., and Pamela Takayoshi. "Accepting Roles Created for Us: The Ethics of Reciprocity." *College Composition and Communication*, vol. 54, no. 3, 2003, pp. 394–422. *JSTOR.* Accessed 18 June 2013.

—. *Practicing Research in Writing Studies: Reflexive and Ethically Responsible Research*, edited by Katrina M. Powell and Pamela Takayoshi. New York, Hampton, 2012, pp. 1–28.

—. "Revealing Methodology." Powell and Takayoshi, pp. 1–28.

Presser, Lois. "Negotiating Power and Narrative in Research: Implications for Feminist Methodology." *Signs*, vol. 30, no. 4, 2005, pp. 2067–90.

Royster, Jacqueline Jones, and Gesa E. Kirsch. *Feminist Rhetorical Practices: New Horizons for Rhetoric, Composition, and Literacy Studies.* Southern Illinois UP, 2012.

Schrag, Zachary M. "Ethical Training for Oral Historians." *Perspectives on History.* American Historical Association, Mar. 2007, www.historians.org/publications-and-directories/perspectives-on-history/march-2007/ethical-training-for-oral-historians. Accessed 10 Sept. 2013.

—. "How Talking Became Human Subjects Research: The Federal Regulation of the Social Sciences, 1965–1991." *Journal of Policy History*, vol. 21, no. 1, 2009, pp. 3–37. *Project Muse.* Accessed 10 Aug. 2013.

—. "Roberta S. Gold, 'None of Anybody's Goddamned Business'?" *Institutional Review Blog*, 29 Sept. 2007, http://www.institutionalreviewblog.com/2007/09/roberta-s-gold-none-of-anybodys.html. Accessed 10 Sept. 2013.

Seigel, Marika. *The Rhetoric of Pregnancy.* U of Chicago P, 2013.

Shopes, Linda. "Legal and Ethical Issues in Oral History." *Handbook of Oral History*, edited by Thomas L. Charlton, Lois E. Myers, and Rebecca Sharpless. Lanham, MD: AltaMira, 2006, pp. 135–69.

United States, National Archives and Records Administration. *Federal Policy for the Protection of Human Subjects.* Office of the Federal Register, vol. 82, no. 12, 2017, pp. 7149–7274. Accessed 24 Jan. 2019.

Wolfram, Walt. "Ethical Considerations in Language Awareness Programs." *Issues in Applied Linguistics*, vol. 4, no. 2, 1993, pp. 225–55.

Wolfram, Walt, Jeffrey Reaser, and Charlotte Vaughn. "Operationalizing Linguistic Gratuity: From Principle to Practice." *Language and Linguistics Compass*, vol. 2, 2008, pp. 1–26. *Wiley Online.* Accessed 14 Feb. 2014.

9 *Abuela, si estas aquí*: Writing Our Histories as Liberatory Praxis

Cristina D. Ramírez

In our discipline of rhetoric and composition, we have come to recognize and accept the importance of situating ourselves within our historiographic research, and we see it as an essential academic exercise.¹ This practice locates biases that may exist within our work. It expands our understanding of the various recovery methods that researchers use in their writing, which in turn, adds to our repertoire of research approaches. Cheryl Glenn and Jessica Enoch reiterate the importance of the researcher's transparency regarding the historiographic interpretive work that investigators employ. In "Invigorating Historiographic Practices in Rhetoric and Composition Studies," Glenn and Enoch remind us, "accurate interpretation is never enough" (24). They write, "When we engage in research, we need to know what our self-interest is, how that interest might enrich our disciplinary field as it affects others [. . .] and resolve to participate in a reciprocal cross-boundary exchange, in which we talk with and listen to Others, whether they are speaking to us in person or via archival materials" (24). Glenn and Enoch's insistence on locating and revealing ourselves within our research gave me a moment of pause in my own investigations into Mexican women journalists and activists. In my book, *Occupying our Space: The Mestiza Rhetorics of Mexican Women Journalists and Activists, 1875–1942*, I recover the rhetorical practices of women who were looking to change their stations in life through writing and publishing in small, yet pioneering Spanish-language journals and newspapers. Writing during a time

---

1. The first half of the chapter title translates as "Grandmother, yes, you are here."

when women were not to be heard in Mexican society, they wrote and published essays, epideictic poetry, political editorials, and much more. *Occupying our Space* specifically looks to fill the representational gap of women of color found in feminist historiographic work. To bring their voices to the fore, I cross a variety of borders, including linguistic, disciplinary, national, and political borders. But I admit that I had not done the revelatory work to consider my personal approach to these border crossings. I assumed that my own personal and internal recognition of a maternal genealogical connection to a rich Mexican past was enough. In retrospect, it was merely the beginning. Considering Glenn and Enoch's assertion, I now step back to engage in this reflective practice to consider how researchers within our discipline can make connections between their topic of research and their own family heritage.

In "The Biography of a Graveyard," Ronald R. Stockton concludes that scholars "often fail to acknowledge that research is a very personal activity" (64). Our topics "intersect us" in ways that we may not always acknowledge. To reveal my own research process as a model of inquiry in this chapter, I consider questions such as these: What led me to research the subject of *mestiza* rhetorics of Mexican women rhetors? How does the recovery of Mexican women connect to my own personal relationship with my *abuela* (grandmother), who was a published Chicana writer? What can my experience with researching these women and reflecting on my own history teach other researchers and especially graduate students beginning their own investigation into women's rhetorical practices?

Heeding Glenn and Enoch's call for personal situatedness, I searched out the stories of other rhetoric and composition scholars who had done reflective writing as a way to inform and deepen their historiography. In *Beyond the Archives: Research as a Lived Process*, Gesa Kirsch and Liz Rohan present such stories of scholars who expand the concept of the archive, connecting them to family, social, and cultural history. These stories reiterate the necessity of relating our personal experiences within our historical research projects, calling this practice "giving away your game" (3). Many of the contributing scholars such as Victor Villanueva, Wendy Sharer, Liz Rohan, and Kathleen Wider, relate a family story that worked as the impetus for pursuing a larger research project. Kirsch and Rohan state, "[t]heir work teaches the value of attending to how our family, social, and cultural history is intertwined with more traditional notions of history and culture"(3). These scholar's narratives reveal how personal histories are linked to public histories and to the larger context of our world.[2]

For scholars who occupy marginalized positions, including and especially categories of race, gender, queer, and colonized subjects, I see the act of revealing the backstory to one's research as taking on a deeply political character. A telling of where the research is located in terms of geography, its situated intersection (race, gender, class, religion, sexual preference), and personal history has the potential to intervene in and shift the dominant narrative that has silenced and suppressed these accounts. For example, when I reflect on why I was drawn to Mexican women rhetors, the narrative of my abuela surfaces as a new strand of discursive Chicana activism in the communities where she grew up. Considering ourselves as active agents in the telling of our backstories, our own narratives of gendered, racial, or ethnic silencing, marginalization, rejection, or oppression can serve as a bridge between past and present. This bridge ultimately can have a political impact for change.

I assert that this marked identification or personal situatedness in our research takes on a Dusselian praxis of liberation, also known as a *proyecto*. In *Philosophy of Liberation,* Enrique Dussel states that a proyecto is a mediated critical action for an oppressed people to move from the periphery and speak to the center. The Spanish word proyecto translates to "project," but spoken and defined by marginalized groups or individuals, the term takes on a different epistemological slant. A proyecto is the present constitution of being and the coming into being as a people acting and speaking within oppressive systems to claim a self-determined future. A person or group's proyecto can lead to a liberation of being. Dussel states, "When persons work, they do so for a proyecto. That proyecto determines the possibilities or mediations for its realization" (39). The "work" that Dussel references can come in the form of activism, organizing, and coalition building, as evidenced in the rest of his book. However, it also reaches into the realm of discourse, philosophy, and history generated from the periphery, from the oppressed. He writes, "[W]hen we turn to reality as exteriority, by the mere fact that the exteriority we explore is a *new historical reality,* the philosophy that issues from it—if it is authentic—cannot help being equally new" (39). By reflecting on their personal connections to research, those especially from

---

2. Other scholars certainly also advocate for such work see Rich, Kirsch and Ritchie, Burton, and Spigelman.

historically marginalized groups take on a proyecto that becomes the "new historical reality" and further serves as a heuristic for others' work.

As an emerging Chicana scholar in rhetoric and composition studies, I identify in this chapter the method of self-identification to my research as a proyecto. In "giving away my game," I hope to demonstrate how the act of situating oneself can move into the realm of a proyecto, which serves to uncover "new historical realities" from the periphery. First, I connect my parent's roots and my own upbringing to my research into Mexican women rhetors, showing how in the act of positioning ourselves in and through our family histories we claim the potential to locate ourselves in the greater political, ideological, and historical frameworks that constitute a proyecto. Secondly, I identify my grandmother's late-in-life career as a Chicana writer in the early 1970s as a deeper motivation and connection to my interest in the rhetorics of Mexican women. This move serves as a proyecto because it reveals authentic stories that my abuela, Ramona Gonzalez, told about her life growing up in the Segundo Barrio, a Mexican and Mexican American community located within El Paso, Texas along the border of Mexico and the US.

My narrative, I hope, compels us to reassess how as researchers, our personal impulses and investments connect to local, regional, and even global contexts and recognize the political potential within our personal stories. My work in this chapter serves as a heuristic for other scholars to consider how their backgrounds intersect with their intellectual investments. We should, thus, look back and into our histories to make positive movement forward. These stories many times remain unspoken because academic writing calls for an objective stance. Some may see this practice as an invasion of the private self; however, recognizing our material and historical place within our own work, we have the potential to legitimately shift the normative Western gaze toward a more nuanced and varied view of our world. Furthermore, this practice of reflexivity is not an instinctive practice. It is learned. Hence, I ask, do we as educators consistently prompt our young writers, especially our graduate students, to locate the personal in their topics? Helping our students recognize themselves in topics and lines of study they are drawn to can turn our pedagogical approach also into a greater proyecto. If this identification is a powerful tool for researchers, we should also be extending this practice to our classrooms, asking our students to consider the *why* in their choices of research and writing topics, and in doing so, they may also come to understand a greater political and social understanding of themselves.

An Invitation to Consider

For the last eight years, my research has focused on the rhetorical actions of Mexican women journalists from the turn of the nineteenth to the twentieth century. And while I've fielded numbers of responses and questions about this project, including "I wasn't aware that there *were* Mexican women journalists at that time!," one question is particularly exigent for the purposes of this chapter: "Why have you chosen to research these women?" In the many times and ways that this question has been asked, I have come to hear hints of bewilderment or possibly even concern as to why an Anglo-looking scholar like myself would devote her career to researching the history of Mexico ("that's not even *our* country") and how the women played a part in constructing a Mexican national identity. I sense strong nationalistic tendencies emerging with this comment, or it may also be that my racialized and ethnic connection to these women is not immediately obvious. Indeed, in our society preoccupied with skin color and purity of language, my last name of Ramírez (with a maiden name of Devereaux) and my unaccented English do not resonate with many people's idea of what a Mexican American should be. The mixing of races and cultures has blurred the lines and complicated the definition of what it means of be a "scholar of color." No longer is a person of color necessarily phenotypically marked as "other." In this respect, I, and many others, live diversity not necessarily as a marked, but as a lived experience, or as Amardo Rodríguez proposes, as a verb. He states, "Diversity," in whatever way we live it, "forces us to develop new ways of being and experiencing the world" (78). This line of thinking works well in responding to the questions I have been posed. However, one iteration of the question particularly stood out. When I first started the project, an African American fellow graduate student asked, "Are you brown enough to engage in this research?" The question, framed with tones of race, culture, and familial heritage, took me aback. Ultimately, as I look back on this moment it offered me an important entry point into the practice of personal reflective analysis and positioning.

In my mind, it made perfect sense to research these Mexican women writers, but as I started to unravel my connections, I realized the complexity of my racial and ethnic mixture as a contributing factor as to why I chose this topic. I was born and raised in a deeply maternal *mestiza* household. My mother, Sandra González, an educated, second generation Mexican American who was born with an immigrant father, immersed my three brothers and me in the Mexican culture. At the time that I learned to speak, read, and write, the prevailing theories of language acquisition held that if children are given two or more languages to learn at an early age, they would become confused and not reach fluency in either language. My mother, believing differently, ignored these theories. We were brought up in a household learning the Spanish language, listening to and singing Mexican music, cooking and eating Mexican food, celebrating Mexican holidays, and dancing Mexican cultural dances. These habits became deeply imbedded into who I would become as an adult and later would influence the reason why I study the rhetorics of the Mexican women journalists. Through my studies, I have learned about the heritage of my ancestors; yet, this emerges as only part of my connection to the Mexican women I study.

My paternal side is a mixture of French and American. My father, Neil Jay Devereaux, born in California in the 1940s, was drawn to the Mexican language and culture in his early twenties. He served a Mormon mission in Mexico in the early 1960s. At the time, Mexico was at the height of a cultural and social revolution in the arts, poetry, and music, connected to the growing political unrest. Subsequently, during his cultural immersion, my father fell in love with the language, culture, and people. On a later assignment in 1963 during his mission in El Paso, Texas, he met and fell in love with my mother. She was a Chicana activist during the 1960s and 1970s, who held strong roots and connections to the Mexican people on the border. Before and after they married, she encouraged his linguistic aptitude with the Spanish language. He eventually earned his doctorate of philosophy in Spanish linguistics and literature and became a university language professor. Many Mexicans and Chicanos in our Texas communities call him *"el mexicano adoptivo"* (the adopted Mexican) because of his Spanish fluency and his deep understanding of the Mexican culture. He brought an outsider's appreciation and knowledge of the Mexican culture into our home, seeing the beauty in the language, people, music, and history.

Between the Mexican and Chicano heritage and culture I claim from my mother, the French American background from my father, and the love of Mexican music and literature from both my parents, I identify as a Chicana scholar who has claimed her own agency through historiographic research on Mexican women journalist-rhetors. I am a cross-border, cross-cultural product of the Chicano movement of the 1960s and 1970s in El Paso, Texas, and of the influences that the 1960s Mexican cultural movement had on my father in Mexico City. Standing back and considering my family heritage, I see how my upbringing emboldened my interest in Mexican women rhetors. These experiences came to bear on how my siblings and I were raised in the small, dusty town of San Angelo, Texas. However, the light complexion of my skin, the green of my eyes, and the short, boyish-length of my hair do not tell the embodied and material story of my upbringing. Consequently, I have given the questions from listeners, friends, and peers much thought.

Doing the work of connecting our pasts with our present research can serve as a proyecto to bring multiple pasts to bear upon our histories. The connections are sometimes latent because as academics we are trained to look outward to theories and methods instead of inward for our inspiration and knowledge. These uncovered revelations may lead to historical convergences that can serve to answer some questions yet form others. In what follows, I answer the question of *how* I found the women centered in my research and *why* I have chosen to research Mexican women journalists. This strand parallels a greater connection and discussion of my racial, cultural, familial, and gendered positioning through the Chicana literary writing of my grandmother Ramona González. It is in this rich fusion of cultures, languages, and ideas that a proyecto of liberation is enacted. Dussel posits that a proyecto is the work one does in the present to recover a future (38). He states, "The *proyecto* of liberation that a people carries affirmatively in its culture is the future common good" (77). In the recovery work of women rhetors, the potential exists to recover and construct one's own history.

First Encounters: Esta es mi Historia

I initiated my research project on Mexican women journalists (although sometimes I think that they found me) through the beginnings of another writing project, which was never completed. The summer before entering my rhetoric and composition doctoral program, I started outlining a young adult novel exploring Chicana identities. It was to be set during the American cultural revolution of the 1950s at El Paso High School from which my mother, Sandra, my abuela, Ramona, and many other uncles and aunts had graduated. The purpose of the novel was to reflect on how young Chicana teens struggle with their cultural identity not only along the US and Mexican border but also increasingly in everyday communities far removed from our nation's borders. I planned to weave this historical tale about the clashing of cultures with a coming of age story of how the main character, Sandra, learned to negotiate the two worlds. The grandmother figure, which in my story represents the Mexican influence in young Sandra's life, was to have been an *adelita*. The adelitas were the women who fought or served in many different capacities in the Mexican Revolution, such as nurse, solider, wife, messengers, and general war-time support. While searching for a historical representation of the Mexican grandmother character, I found only limited representation of women in mainstream historical accounts of the Mexican Revolution. Deepening my research, I stumbled upon Shirlene Soto's *Emergence of the Modern Mexican Woman: Her Participation in Revolution and Struggle for Equality 1910–1940*. The book presents a re/visioning of Mexican history to include the many women who not only participated in the revolutionary struggle, but who also *wrote* during that time, representing a radical shift in societal roles. Each chapter concludes with brief historical accounts of pioneering women journalists, focusing on their public exploits, publication successes and failures, battle scars, and rhetorical actions.

Several women in Soto's book stood out as trailblazers, revolutionaries, and activists, who, through their writing, worked to shape the realities of their fellow women caught within a government dictatorship and an even more oppressive patriarchal structure. The women who drew my attention and later became central to my book were Laureana Wright de Kleinhans (1842–1896), Juana Belén Gutiérrez de Mendoza (1875–1942), and Hermila Galindo (1896–1954). During a time when women's voices were not to be heard beyond the boundaries of the kitchen or the lines where the clothes were hung to dry, these women activists engaged the relevant civic issues of their time, such as the politics of war, gender rights, labor, and the construction of a national racialized identity. They garnered my attention because their histories resonated with stories my abuela told me about my own *tias* (aunts), who broke their own gendered barriers. Josefa González worked as a public school administrator and maestra normal in Cuidad Juaréz, Mexico in the 1920s; and another Juana Lopez, became a bar owner in Tucson, Arizona in the 1930s. Soto's histories also paralleled my abuela's life. After years of being a mother and caretaker, she became a published Chicana writer in the 1970s in one of the most important Chicano journals of the time, *El Grito*. Certainly, I felt compelled to research and write about the Mexican women journalists because by uncovering their lives, tangentially I was learning about my family's heritage.

I now had this deep desire to know about them, actively search them out, and read their writings. I was excited, energized by the knowledge that there were many Mexican women who had lived true to themselves by writing against the strict patriarchal and confining social structures of Mexican society. I had a single mind to immerse myself in the study of these women's lives and writings. But the semester started, and I was left with little time to read outside of assigned scholarship. However, that assigned scholarship turned out to be pivotal to my work. In the theoretical essays I read—the work of Cheryl Glenn, Jacqueline Jones Royster, Tom Miller, Victor Villanueva, Carol Mattingly, Hui Wu and many others—only validated my search for these women's voices. But in looking for more about these women, I found little information, that is, in English.

Undeterred, I started my search online through the C. L. Sonnichsen Special Collection archives at the library of the University of Texas, El Paso. Once I looked beyond material in English, I uncovered archival treasures. The stories told in *Beyond the Archives: Research as a Lived Process* revolve around the theme of investigative serendipity, or events of fortunate chance that lead researchers to documents, places, or people that would become central to their study. My serendipity began (and would continue) with the first search entry of Laureana Wright de Kleinhans. At the click of a button, I learned that our library housed an almost complete Spanish-language volume (hundreds of pages) of *Las Hijas de Anáhuac*, the first successful woman's literary journal edited in 1887–1889 in Mexico City by Wright de Kleinhans. Several weeks later, I spent two days and two reams of paper printing every page of the collection. Scanning the writings, I read short stories, poetry, biographical sketches of Mexican heroines, and long, complex philosophical and historical essays. I felt overwhelmed. At the time, I did not know how to comprehend their writings from a rhetorical lens. The nineteenth-century Spanish was difficult, full of literary and rhetorical flourish and allusions. I was aware, though, of the rich literary and intellectual history in which Wright de Kleinhans was taking part because of the many conversations I had with my father, the Spanish professor, about the era and through remembering readings and discussions from undergraduate classes in Mexican literature. Yet, it would take years of researching, reading, further talking with my father and other scholars, and translating the Mexican women's works to unravel and articulate the complex rhetorical positions the women constructed.

Glenn and Enoch suggest that as historiographic researchers we "rethink the starting point of primary and archival research" as a means of breaking with traditional sources of English only texts (15). This remains as excellent advice on how to enter new domains and topics of study. However, as a Chicana fluent in Spanish, I did not have to think twice about the validity of proof these Mexican historical documents presented. The nontraditional—the Spanish—for me is normalized. I bring to my research a *mestiza* consciousness, a bilingual perspective of the world, and because my everyday language crosses borders, subverts dominant discourses, and switches codes, my linguistic experience is already rich and complex. I am accustomed to communicating in Spanish, and for me, these primary documents represented these women's authentic arguments during an important era of Mexican history. I did not question my immediate assumption of the women's rhetorical significance. From a bilingual and bi-cultural position, I am aware of my location as a scholar from an underrepresented group speaking from the academic margins and seeking my own voice with which to speak to the center. Adela Licona's conceptualization of *third space work* describes my reality. She writes, "Through a thirdspace consciousness then dualities are transcended to reveal fertile and reproductive spaces where subjects put perspectives, lived experiences, and rhetorical performances into play" (105). I realize that my own family history, bilingualism, and mixed ethnicity simultaneously marginalize and privilege me, and that I stand within an ontological and epistemic space that is activated with rhetorical potential and ripe with revisionary strategies for social and disciplinary change.

Throughout the writing of my book, I consistently crossed linguistic and cultural borders in my mind and on the page from Spanish to English and vice versa. Translation and interpretation of oral or written texts, a process I call situational linguistic transference, became a crucial method of recovery for my project. As Barbara L'Eplattenier suggests, "Methods make the invisible work of historical research visible" (69). Situational linguistic transference is a skill that comes from having an organic understanding of a language and its culture. The skilled user understands both languages and cultures and is able to bring the understanding of one into the other. Ultimately, this skill is part of the marginalized subject's toolbox in the greater *proyecto*—a liberating political act. It challenges the status quo understandings of one system and replaces them with organic interpretations. For example, the sentences of nineteenth-century Spanish written by Wright de Kleinhans are long, florid, and complex. A non-native Spanish speaker would possibly see the style of endless sentences marked with multiple semi-colons and continuous thought as one that is overly verbose or even incorrect. However, as a native speaker, I understood this style as a culturally marked linguistic and literary style used to demonstrate one's intellectual prowess—a critical rhetorical move for a Mexican woman like Wright de Kleinhans trying to make her mark in an elite literary world dominated by men.

A similar process of situational linguistic transference is used at the word and phrase level of any given sentence. In my research process, I would begin by reading entire essays, histories, or volumes of writing and then select the paragraphs, stanzas, or sentences to explain the larger goals of the woman rhetor's discourse conveyed in hundreds of pages. Next, through linguistic, cultural, and historical translation, I needed to transmit to my audience not only the direct meaning of the phrase, but also the underlying rhetorical implications of the message, explaining how this part stood for the whole. For example, in Wright de Kleinhans's *Las Hijas de Anáhuac*, she speaks to power and to her anticipated male audience in this way: "Con el ramo de oliva entre las manos . . . reverentemente dirige su cordial saludo a todas las clases de la Sociedad, a la Prensa de todos los matices políticos, y a los Hombres del Poder y del Estado" (1). I translated these words as "With the olive branch in hand . . . we reverently direct its cordial greeting to all classes of Society, to the Press of all political shadings, and to the Men of Power and of the State." The words I chose to represent Wright de Kleinhans's writing is significant because as a woman in nineteenth century Mexico, she comes to public rhetorical space not to combat the patriarchal system (that was not possible until the revolution), but to be accepted, or at the very least, recognized by it.

Reading the essay in Spanish for the first time, I had a sense that this phrase summed up the rhetorical strategy of her journal: to come in peace—demonstrated by the olive branch—while strategically addressing "all classes of society." My understanding of rhetorical strategies and the language rituals of Mexican society allowed me to reach this conclusion. Analyzing these translated women's writings through a US-centric, Western lens could be seen as a form of intellectual colonization. However, I used a mixed theoretical approach, drawing from both Mexican rhetorical theorists, such as Helena Beristáin and Gerardo Ramírez Vidal, and scholars such as Cheryl Glenn and Jacqueline Jones Royster to provide an equalizing of voices and perspectives. All of these smaller steps made my research more involved and difficult, becoming a much longer, tedious process.

The practice of translation, working within the structures of two languages and cultures, is a familiar activity for me. My upbringing of being immersed in two languages in the everyday practices of casual conversation through radio and television, religious practices, and dinner conversations makes the method of translation, for me, commonplace. Bringing primary texts and historical understandings from one language and culture into another and into the context of rhetoric, though, should be read as a *proyecto* of liberation. Translation makes a strong political statement in our present time, especially with the overt control some education institutions have taken in silencing and further marginalizing the voice of under-represented peoples. In consciously working within a *proyecto* of translation, the stories of communities, which have been hidden, can emerge.

The Work of Validation

In the research process of learning about the women's lives, searching for their writings, translating their words, and connecting their words with theories of rhetoric, I constructed a parallel discursive history of my mother, my grandmother, and the many Mexican and Chicana women who came before them. Anzaldúa calls this process a validation of our identities as Chicanas: "Seeing the Chicana anew in light of her history. . . . I seek our women's face, our true features . . . new images of identity, new beliefs about ourselves, our humanity and worth no longer in question" (87). Anzaldúa's perspective aligns with Dussel's recognition and construction of oneself through and within a *proyecto*, which he sees as a formation of a "new historical reality" (39). While substantiation is an important purpose for many scholars of color, it is a widely cited reason for conducting research in our post-modern turn of perspective. Many scholars of feminist rhetorical history talk about connecting their projects with their own identity and even with their family history. In *Traces of a Stream*, Jacqueline Jones Royster tells of the connection she had with the African American women breaking societal boundaries through their literacy practices. Charlotte Hogg recounts how finding her grandmother's unpublished writings prompted her research into literacy practices of women in Paxton, Nebraska, which led to her book,

From the Garden Club: Rural Women Writing Community. Lastly, Wendy B. Sharer shares that the discovery of her grandmother's materials of social activism connected to her involvement in women's organizations. Sharer forthrightly suggests that it is imperative for researchers to "reveal how research is connected with lived, and often affective experiences . . . and make them known in a spirit of enthusiasm" (54). These important connections provide a space for the construction of a speaker's ethos and broadens the possibilities of finding uncovered rhetors and rhetorics in hidden spaces (Burton).

For my research project into Mexican women journalists, I am not only driven by my familial connections to Mexico and the frontera, but more so by my abuela's love of writing and her literary career. My proyecto of recovering Mexican women journalists has led to the possibility of recovering my abuela's work. It is in this space of period transference, using one history to trace and locate other stories, where the past can become localized and active. My abuela, Ramona Rodriguez González (also known among family and friends as Doña Ramona) was born in 1906 in Chihuahuita, a border community located on the US side of the banks of the Rio Grande and on the fringes of the Mexican border. This district is significant to me and my family because it represents our spatial and cultural roots in the United States, grounded in the mixed cultural representation of two countries. Chihuahuita served as a stepping-stone for many Mexican immigrants, such as my family, looking to move into El Paso as a sign of economic mobility. With the two-hundred dollars that Asención Rodriguez, Doña Ramona's mother, received from the death of her son, Carlos Chafino, during World War I, Doña Ramona, along with her family, moved out of Chihuahuita. However, her heart remained there. Doña Ramona graduated from El Paso High School in 1924, and after graduation, she was forbidden to pursue a college. Like many of the Mexican women journalists I study, young Mexican American women at the time were limited in their choices for higher education. She wanted to continue her studies but was told that respectable single women did not leave home. Post-secondary education was not a priority for her family. She married my abuelo, or grandfather, Manuel González, an immigrant who was born in Zacatecas, Mexico and raised in an upper-middle-class home. Together they had four children and opened González Grocery, which served a large part of the south El Paso community in the 1930s and 1940s. Throughout her life, Doña Ramona kept literacy practices close by teaching Sunday school classes and by reading avidly. However, it was not until her husband died in 1972 that she felt free to pursue her creative writing publicly.

Doña Ramona's writings, of which our family has recently recovered over two-hundred extant pages, represent her own *proyecto*. These essays, plays, poems, and *dichos* (sayings) have helped me identify what Dussel would call a new historical reality. The stories about her childhood in Chihuahuita capture the organic voices, events, and locations from this now historic community. Her stories of the people of Chihuahuita represent both literally and figuratively people on the margins of society, a people who did not have the discourse to tell their stories. In my abuela's stories and in my historical recovery of Mexican women's writings, the proyectos converge. They are both centered on the mixing and blending of cultures, which focus on representing and remembering our culture, history, and people. My interest in and engagement with the Mexican women journalists in my book is grounded in these stories. My grandmother, as a Chicana writer, was also a rhetor writing within the strict traditions of the Mexican patriarchy and the white American culture. She too, like the Mexican women journalists I study, was writing a new identity for herself.

Since the age of nineteen, I knew of my grandmother's stories. In 1972, she answered a special call for papers from *El Grito: Chicanas en la Literature y el Arte*, a leading Chicano journal out of Berkley, California. The 1973 issue of *El Grito*, edited by Estela Portillo, was dedicated to Chicana writings, and five of Doña Ramona's short stories written in Spanish were published there. Early in my life, I read her publications—"El tesoro enterrado," (The Buried Treasure), "El conjuramento" (The Incantation), "Cuando tienes comezón" (When You Have an Itch), "La talaca" (The Skeleton of Death), and "El camotero" (The Sweet Potato Salesman)—but I had never gone beyond just reading them.[3] That issue of *El Grito* sat on my bookshelf for almost two decades, but its influence emerged in my own writing. Years before I had started my book, I published a poem titled "Abuela" in *Border Senses* as an attempt to articulate a connection with Doña Ramona's writings and my present

---

3. In these translations, it is important to note that the titles are not literal translations. There are no English words equivalent to some words, such as "la talaca," for Doña Ramona even states in her story that there is no clear definition for the word. The translator must take the context, the situation, and culture into consideration when communicating the meaning. I call this process situational linguistic transference.

self. The influence her literary practices and love of the Mexican culture had not gone unnoticed.

"Abuela"

The fragile days I spent
With you
Have broken into a million pieces.
No estás aqui.[4]
I can hear your cuentos y dichos[5]
In my mind
Like echoes through a canyon.
The memories mix with the smell
Of guiso y calabazas.[6]
Your wisdom is the first sign of
Spring on a winter afternoon.
It too, resides in me.
 Before, I would not let the wisdom in,
I thought it to be old-fashioned
Like a song that no one sings anymore.
 Abuela, me has dejado un gran plato
Servido con palabras
De tu juventud.[7]
 Abuela, I feel you now,
Como el sol en las espaldas
De una mujer sin blusa,[8]
I embrace you now
Like a child embraces her mother
For the last time.
Abuela, si estas aqui.[9] (9)

---

4. You are not here.

5. Stories and sayings

6. Meat stew and squash (these are traditional Mexican plates)

7. Grandmother, you have left me a grand plate / Served with words / Of your youth.

8. Like the sun on the shoulders / Of a woman without a blouse

9. Grandmother, yes you are here.

I intentionally wrote the poem in a bilingual format, which represented the way we communicated. As a young adult, I recognized the wisdom she had left through her writings, but at the time, I did not appreciate or understand their true significance. The last line of the poem reads, "Abuela, si estas aqui" (Grandmother, yes you are here), which acknowledges her influence as a Chicana writer on my past and current ontological view of the world. In locating my knowledge and understanding of culture with the voice of Doña Ramona, I too am locating myself and my research within the barrio rhetorics she portrays.

Growing up with Doña Ramona changed me in many ways. Living in a racist Central Texas small town of San Angelo, I shied away in public, such as school and church, from the Mexican and Chicano heritage I was taught at home. For me, it was easy. I hid behind my olive skin, green eyes, and light brown hair. But while living with Doña Ramona, I was reminded of the importance of my Mexican genealogy. She talked about my abuelo, Manuel González, immigrating to the US from Zacatecas, Mexico during the Mexican Revolution. He came with his sisters, my great aunts, Adelaida (Lala), Josefa (Pepa), Antonia (Toña), Guadalupe (Lupe), and Carmelita. Pepa was a *maestra normal* (primary school teacher) and principal in Juárez, Mexico in the 1920's, and her ideas regarding education had a profound impact on my mother. My tias, or aunts, represented the education and refinement of our family, and Doña Ramona picked up on the importance of education through them. Doña Ramona also described the daily work in González Grocery, the family store once located at the edge of downtown El Paso, just three miles from the Mexican border. When my aunts and uncles visited us, they recounted the many versions of the family legend of "La bruja de Missouri St." (The Witch of Missouri St.), a story that captures the spirit of the people my grandparents served in their store and reveals just some of the superstitions or ways of knowing of the barrio culture.

My abuela understood the significance of telling stories and documenting the memories of Chihuahuita because of its influence as a counter-narrative to the many Anglo versions of history of her people. She claimed her voice in the emerging ethnic political movements, such as the Chicano Movement of El Paso, Texas. Now, as a Chicana scholar, I can articulate what Doña Ramona was doing in her writings. She was engaged in her own liberatory practice of a barrio proyecto, articulating a grassroots history of her people as she remembered.

My grandmother's writings and the goals of discourse connect, overlap, and validate my research into Mexican women journalists. My grandmother had an innate understanding of feminist rhetorical historiographic theory. Feminist rhetorical approaches, such as Doña Ramona's, resist the cultural and gendered status quo, following instead the authentic lines and fissures of knowledge of her community. Similarly, the Mexican women writers of my study capture the rhetorical and intellectual rupture from tight social expectations. Within the rhetorical approaches of the Mexican women I recover, my grandmother's literary writings, and my own rhetorical recovery work, I see all of these struggles connecting, overlapping, and bridging time and space. Each of these women were writing from a different context, but from within similar patriarchal systems that sought to silence and erase their identities. These rhetorical connections among Chicanas and Mexican women who write from the borderlands are imperative to the work of feminist remapping in that they locate women's voices within cultural spaces, communities, and positions that had once been associated only with men.

A Generational Proyecto

In *Rhetoric Retold*, Glenn captures the way our discipline will move forward with old and new artifacts, hidden in archives and in plain sight. She writes,

> We must risk, then, getting the story crooked. We must look crookedly, a bit out of focus, into the various strands of meaning in a text in such a way as to make the categories, trends, and reliable identities of history a little less inevitable, less familiar. In short, we need to see what is familiar in a different way . . . to see beyond the familiar to the unfamiliar, to the unseen. (7)

In taking this advice, I ask, what is the immediate connection between the archival work I do with Mexican women journalists and my grandmother's Chicana literary writings? Doña Ramona and I engage in the same kind of writing: claiming an identity and re/historicizing an era and a people with whom we closely identify. She entered the male dominated conversation of the Chicano movement to reflect a women's articulation of Mexican American culture and memory. I was drawn to Mexican women writers, who like my abuela, claimed once forbidden public spaces to express their ideas. And like these women, I too am entering a conversation that has seen limited representation of Mexican women and men. The connection is there.

A much greater diversity of voices has emerged in feminist rhetorical scholarship in the last decade, and we need to tell our stories of (dis)connection to explore their potential and activate more and different kinds of theory and research. Glenn eloquently admonishes feminist scholars of the importance of our work. That it's "doing something." She contends, feminist historiographic "contributions are moving us beyond the restoration of women to rhetorical history; they are revitalizing rhetorical theory by shaking the conceptual foundations of rhetorical study itself" (10). Feminist rhetorical scholarship is therefore not static but infused with strong movement forward. These notions of movement, in the act of looking back to understand our present, especially have repercussions for junior scholars in our discipline. If we consider this academic exercise an important part of our scholarship, should we not also ask our graduate students, those who will be doing the revitalizing and shaking, to make the same connections?

This question is one I've considered with graduate students in my seminar Trends and Methods in Rhetoric. After reading a draft of my feminist recovery project of Mexican women journalists, one of my graduate students, Lori Babel, reflected on the value of positioning oneself within the historiographic project. She states in her reading response, "there is power [in] the participatory nature of the method" (Babel 1). Connecting the research to a present context on a deeper and illuminating level, she notes that it has the potential to "redefine the nature of the researcher." As the historical is illuminated, the personal is transformed (and vice versa). She continues,

> [A] participatory identification resonates between individuals in different times because of recognizable ideas that unite and connect [subjects] across time. The participatory influence is bidirectional, transforming both the researched subject and the researcher; through shared identity, a relational process is brought to life. Part of the process of us becoming more 'awake' as scholars is illuminating what previously was decimated by exclusion, [and now] made invisible.

Another student, Eric House, considered the importance of research to recover voices and communities we once thought imperceptible. As an African American graduate student, Eric seeks to recover a history and identity of his communities, while at the same time find an identity for himself. Reading about the recovery of Mexican women's voices and my own positionality within the research, he saw a model for his work. He writes,

> The true beauty I find in Ramírez's research practices goes back to that word recovery, because she's reminding me that with even as violent and disruptive colonial practices might be, there are pieces of resistance that can and must be found. These pieces contain life and wisdom and the voices of cultures and generations that help us remember. And that memory is even more empowering when the motivations of the researchers are considered.

Here, Eric sees the prospect of a richer research project in considering his own impulse toward his work. This is where I believe Glenn's theory of looking at what is "familiar in a different way" turns into praxis and proyecto. In making these concrete connections, our students will have a more grounded understanding of why they are drawn to certain topics and see the larger social implications to their interests in what they are writing. As I hope to have shown, "giving away one's game" and identifying the racial, cultural, spatial, and historical connections with my past and present has deeper rhetorical and political implications.

Works Cited

Anzaldúa, Gloria. *Borderlands/La Frontera: The New Mestiza*. Aunt Lute, 1987.

Lori Babel. "Cristina's Bidirectional Participatory Historiographic Method?" *D2L Discussion Board*, U of Arizona, https://d2l.arizona.edu/d2l/home, 5 Oct. 2014.

Baca, Damián. *Mestiz@ Scripts, Digital Migrations and the Territories of Writing*. Palgrave Macmillan, 2008.

Castellanos, Rosario. "Language as an Instrument of Domination." *A Rosario Castellanos Reader: An Anthology of her Poetry, Short Fiction, Essays, and Drama*, edited and translated by Maureen Ahern, U of Texas P, 1988.

Dussel, Enrique. *Philosophy of Liberation*. Translated by Aquilina Martinez and Christine Morkovsky, Wipf & Stock, 1985.

Glenn, Cheryl. *Rhetoric Retold: Regendering the Tradition from Antiquity through the Renaissance*. Southern Illinois UP, 1997.

Glenn, Cheryl and Jessica Enoch. "Invigorating Historiographic Practices in Rhetoric and Composition Studies." *Working in the Archives: Practical Research Methods for Rhetoric and Composition*, edited by Alexis Ramsey, et al., Southern Illinois UP, 2010, pp. 11-27.

González, Ramona. "El tesoro enterrado." *El Grito: Chicana en la Arte y la Literatura*, vol. 7, 1973, pp. 22–40.

Hogg, Charlotte. *From the Garden Club: Rural Women Writing Community*. U of Nebraska P, 2006. Print.

House, Eric. "Thoughts on Archival Method and Recovery." *D2L Discussion Board*, U of Arizona, https://d2l.arizona.edu/d2l/home, 5 Oct. 2014.

Kirsch, Gesa, and Liz Rohan, editors. *Beyond the Archives: Research as a Lived Process*. Southern Illinois UP, 2008.

Kirsch, Gesa, and Joy Ritchie. "Beyond the Personal: Theorizing a Politics of Location." *College Composition and Communication*, vol. 46, no. 1, 1995, pp. 7–29.

La Redacción. "Saludo." *Las hijas de Anáhuac*, vol. 1, 1887, p. 1.

L'Eplattenier, Barbara. "An Argument for Archival Research Methods: Thinking Beyond Methodology." *College English*, vol. 72, 2009, pp. 67–79.

Licona, Adela. "'Borderlands' Rhetorics and Representations: The Transformative Potential of Feminist Third Space Scholarship and Zines." *National Women's Studies Association Journal*, vol. 17, 2005, pp. 104–129.

Ramírez, Cristina. "Abuela." Border Senses, vol. 3, 2001, p. 9.

Rich, Adrienne. "Notes toward a Politics of Location." *Blood, Bread, and Poetry: Selected Prose 1979–1985*. Norton, 1994.

Royster, Jacqueline J. *Traces of a Stream: Literacy and Social Change Among African American Women*. U of Pittsburgh P, 2000.

Sharer, Wendy B. "Traces of the Familiar: Family Archives as Primary Source Material." *Beyond the Archives: Research as Lived Experience*, edited by Gesa A. Kirsch and Liz Rohan, Southern Illinois UP, 2008, pp. 47–55.

Spigelman, Candace. *Personally Speaking: Experience as Evidence in Academic Discourse*. Southern Illinois UP, 2004.

Soto, Shirlene A. *Emergence of the Modern Mexican Woman: Her Participation in Revolution and Struggle for Equality, 1910–1940*. Arden, 1990.

10 Opening the Scholarly Conversation

Wendy B. Sharer

When I accepted a position at my current institution—my first job out of graduate school—I recall hearing that a position at a regional state university would be a "good starter job." This was said in the same way that the real estate agent who took me on a tour during my campus visit told me that a house in a neighborhood of little brick ranches abutting student apartments near campus would make a nice "starter home." Both the first job and the first home were acceptable, in the short term, but surely I had higher aspirations for the long term. Something flagship, something "R-1" (as the most research-heavy institutions were labeled at the time in the Carnegie classification system), something with sabbatical so that I could focus on research and publishing; something with at least four bedrooms, something in a well-maintained subdivision beyond the student neighborhoods, something with a garage and a large, screened-in porch so that my car and I could remain bug-free for the summer. The implication that certain institutions are stepping stones, at least for the "serious scholar," has made me bristle on several occasions since that time, whether I am the recipient of a question such as "So, when are you planning to move on?" or whether, as was recently the case, I overhear a similar conversation at a conference:

> Speaker 1: I am going to have to go on the market this year. I worry about big spending cuts and the impact they might have on my position at College X.
> Speaker 2: Oh, good! This will be a great opportunity to find a place where you can work with graduate students and get bet-

ter research support. I never understood why you were staying at College X anyway.

I wanted to say "Perhaps Speaker 1 actually enjoys and feels professionally satisfied by the work he/she does at College X?" but I held my tongue.

Although these experiences have been frustrating, they have helped me to see a disciplinary silencing—the kind of silencing that Cheryl Glenn calls us to "open up" (151). The unspoken subtext in such comments is that research trumps teaching and, because of the opportunities they afford for research, bigger schools are preferable to smaller ones. Let me state up front that I know our field respects teaching. That respect, however, has limits because, as I elaborate below, our traditional and (still) most esteemed genres of scholarship have, with few exceptions, been constructed in a way that serves to exclude the voices of a great many faculty who, often by choice, work at teaching-heavy institutions that do not place as much value on or expend as many resources in support of traditional processes and genres of scholarship. In what follows, I argue that embracing, publishing, and circulating scholarly texts that invite collaboration, that forward the research *process* rather than present a research *product*, and that enable broader participation in professional publications is an essential part of paying it forward, of mentoring, of creating inclusive conditions for success among future generations of scholars. Truly inviting conversation, and truly valuing process as much as product, would enable participation in the field for the many scholars whose institutional and personal contexts—including, for example, heavy teaching loads, little opportunity for any kind of research leave, and extensive family responsibilities—preclude them from having the means to produce the forms of scholarship that are currently privileged in the field. I make this argument knowing that I am currently writing in a traditional genre of scholarship, but this is how I can be heard. For now.

Scholars in rhetoric and composition, often influenced by feminist theory, have interrogated and usefully critiqued research methods and methodologies over the past two decades (Royster and Kirsch; Kirsch and Rohan; Schell and Rawson; Nickoson and Sheridan; Powell and Takayoshi; McKee and Porter; Ramsey, Sharer, L'Eplattienier and Mastrangelo, to name but a few). This work has been extremely generative, fostering a more robust approach to research in composition and rhetoric, largely by drawing attention to the location of the researcher with respect to the materials and people she studies. The lines of inquiry pursued in many of these publications were articulated nicely by Gesa Kirsch and Joy Ritchie more than fifteen years ago in their article "Beyond the Personal: Theorizing a Politics of Location in Composition Research":

> a politics of location must engage us in a rigorous ongoing exploration of *how* we do our research: What assumptions underlie our approaches to research and methodologies? And a politics of location must challenge our conception of *who* we are in our work: How are our conflicting positions, histories, and desire for power implicated in our research questions, methodologies, and conclusions?

Furthermore, Kirsch and Ritchie explain, "researchers need to acknowledge the way race (and for most composition scholars this means examining their whiteness), social class, and other circumstances have structured their own thinking and how that, in turn, has shaped their own questions and interpretations" (142).

In the years since Kirsch and Ritchie called researchers to embrace a politics of location, research methods and methodologies have received productive, consistent attention. Less attention, however, has been paid to the languages, genres, and venues of research *publication* and *circulation* in the field. A politics of location, I want to suggest, should also involve scholars in an ongoing exploration of how we present and propagate the knowledge we create through our research. Despite years of calls for scholarly genres and venues that promote collaborative research and interactive reading experiences, the field still struggles to provide such genres and venues. And while progress has certainly been made on this front—thanks largely to the persistence of scholars of digital writing studies such as Daniel Anderson, Kristine Blair, David Blakesley, Susan Delagrange, Douglas Eyman and Cheryl Ball, Justin Hodgson, Cynthia Selfe and Gail Hawisher, Christian Weisser and Kevin Brock, and Anne Wysocki, to name but a few—emerging multimodal genres often do not address the issue of time. While more voices can be heard and more interaction can occur between audience and text through digital publishing, the valued products of digital publishing still require extensive time commitments for research and writing. In fact, the amount of time required to compose in and for digital venues, as anyone who has tried to publish a digital text will likely affirm, frequently exceeds that required to compose traditional, word-processed articles.

To be sure, representations of authorship in traditional forms of scholarly writing have been challenged in the field: Andrea Lunsford and Lisa Ede have long argued in support of collaborative authorship, calling for us to embrace the notion of *Singular Texts/Plural Authors* in our scholarship. Thanks largely to the work of Lunsford and Ede, co-written and co-edited articles and books are fairly common in composition and rhetoric, but much remains to be done. Collaboratively written projects still often meet with skepticism ("How much did each individual author or editor contribute?" is not an uncommon question for tenure and promotion review) and are not valued as highly by many institutions as the more traditional single-authored publication. The continuing power of singular authors can be clearly seen in the models of professionalism in which we train our graduate students: there are not many collaboratively written dissertations in our field.

The paucity of collaborative dissertations reflects the rhetorical education provided to future scholars in the field, an education that serves to perpetuate the privileging of univocal, single-authored scholarly texts. As I argue below, contributions to research conversations can take many different forms and can occur in many different rhetorical situations, yet, as a field, we value primarily one kind of research genre and thus prepare future scholars to recognize only certain rhetorical situations as valid for research and publication. In an oft-cited 1984 article, Carolyn Miller argues that "what we learn when we learn a genre is not just a pattern of forms or even a method of achieving our own ends. We learn, more importantly, what ends we may have" (165). The genre of the dissertation, as it is widely taught today, serves to restrict the kinds of rhetorical actions future scholars pursue in and through their research.

Even as collaboratively written or edited works are more regularly recognized as valuable, the genres of traditional scholarship—including books, book chapters, journal articles, and dissertations—are resilient. Even if attributed to two or more authors, scholarly publications are still almost exclusively presented as a singular textual achievement that speaks "coherently" to make a larger point or set of points. As Kirsch and Ritchie have argued, "Traditional research reports, for example, urge writers to come to conclusions and announce their findings. That process demands that researchers make coherent what might be fragmented, and thus that they might sometimes reduce complex phenomena or erase differences for the sake of developing coherent theories" (155). More recently, Susan Delagrange has argued that the reading and writing experiences promoted through traditional scholarly genres often perpetuate a particular social and cultural hierarchy: "The hold of traditional print-based practices within the field of rhetoric and composition is strong, and is directly connected to the privileging of logos and rational justification in philosophy and science" (12). The genres resulting from this privilege, Delagrange continues, "prize speed and clarity over reflective inquiry and generative ambiguity" (18). The goal of traditional scholarly publications is to prove a point and to bring the reader to a conclusion as efficiently and smoothly as possible, all the while effacing doubts, uncertainty, conflicting or confusing evidence, and alternative voices that the writer or writers may be hearing. Inquiry is intentionally stopped in the traditional publication. Lingering questions might, at best, show up in a concluding section, pointing the way "forward" for future scholars.

Not only are the limited readerly and writerly experiences created by and embodied in traditional scholarly genres important to consider, so too are the material conditions required for readers and writers to participate in those genres to begin with. By prioritizing, even in many of our new electronic venues, the publication of the results of long-term, multi-sourced, lengthy research projects, we limit the voices that can be heard in our scholarly conversations. What we value and circulate in our "leading journals" are primarily products of lengthy research; copious reading; and extended days, weeks, months, or, in the case of dissertations and books, years of writing and revising. Even electronic journals that allow for the publication of more collaborative and interactive forms of scholarship tend to value texts that require extended research and writing time. As noted above, composing a web-based, multimodal text is often more time-intensive than composing a traditional, word-processed document. Thus, if a scholar takes satisfaction in working at an institution where she teaches multiple courses per semester, sometimes while also holding an administrative post, she will struggle to find time to produce the kinds of scholarly genres that participate in and set the research agenda for the field. This situation is familiar to many of our colleagues: consider the placement-of-graduates data from the 2007 *Rhetoric Review* "Survey of Doctoral Programs in Rhetoric and Composition." Data on the types of positions that 255 newly minted PhDs took during the 2005–2006 year were reported from across sixty-seven institutions in the 2007 survey and are included in Table 1.

Table 1: PhD Placements by Job Type (Brown, Enos, Reamer, Thompson 338).

Job Type	Number of Placements in Job Type
Teaching within emphasis (rhetoric and composition)	67
Research with teaching in emphasis (rhetoric and composition)	64
Writing program administration	54
Teaching across emphases (rhetoric, composition, literary studies, etc.)	25
Writing center administration	7
Teaching outside of English studies	3
Consulting	1
Other	3

The remaining 31 graduates accepted positions outside of academia, did not receive job offers, or did not seek employment. According to this data, those who graduate from our doctoral programs are more than twice as likely to go to positions that focus on teaching and/or administration than research, as traditionally defined.

If a faculty member opts to spend significant time mentoring students or pursuing an activist agenda, one that involves them in community engagement or leadership, time for research and writing that leads to traditionally valued publication genres will shrink further. Because community activism is particularly important for underrepresented groups in the academy, our adherence to traditional genres of scholarly publishing may also be limiting the diversity of our scholarly conversations. Drawing on a study of approximately 60,000 faculty surveys gathered by the Education Research Institute at UCLA (Antonio, Astin, and Cress), Luis J. Urrieta and Lina R. Méndez Benavídez point out that "faculty of color spend more hours per week in community service, as well as teaching and advising students, compared to White faculty" (228). Given the heavy teaching and service work that faculty of color often take on, the kinds of research the field considers to be publishable may contribute to the continuing lack of diverse scholars within it.

Our inherited models of scholarship may be particularly detrimental to our women colleagues. The same Educational Research Institute study found that "higher proportions of women perform service or volunteer work, and women are more likely than men to advise student groups doing service, feature community service in their coursework, maintain educational goals focused on service, and strongly favor institutional policies that support community service and involvement" (Antonio, Astin, and Cress 380). The re-visioning and revaluing of scholarly genres, then, seems important if we are to more fully address the concerns that Kirsch raised in her groundbreaking 1993 study, *Women Writing the Academy*. In reflecting on this text nearly two decades later, Kirsch writes,

> My concern was particularly heightened because academic women, like women in the history of rhetoric, have most often been relegated to the margins, ignored, silenced, or viewed as 'museum pieces,' curious objects to be noted but not central actors in shaping and changing academic institutions. . . . Thus, academic women's voices, visions, and experiences have not been fully heard, represented, or taken into account in writing the history of academic institutions or imagining their future. (Royster and Kirsch, 5)

The persistence of traditional genres of publication increases the likelihood that many academic women in the field of composition and rhetoric will remain museum pieces, if they are identified as contributors to the field's endeavors at all. We silence the women (and men) who choose not to dedicate large chunks of time to produce the valorized genres of scholarship, regardless of the significance of their thoughts and contributions to the field.

In sum, our privileged academic genres can serve to reinscribe elitist academic hierarchies that devalue—to the detriment of many in the field—teaching, administration, and activism. This is not to say that extended research and writing projects—the time- and resource-intensive kinds of publications that have traditionally filled our top journals and scholarly books—are not valuable: they most certainly are. But our scholarly conversation is very limited if these are the only kinds of voices that are regularly recognized and highly valued. What if we created, circulated, and highly valued texts that do not privilege a "singular" voice or a "coherent" point? What if we embrace plural texts/plural authors? What if our revered texts take the form of conversations that are informed by various kinds of evidence and research and that incorporate a variety of forms of discourse, including many short contributions from many people?

What I am suggesting is not entirely unprecedented. Alternative publication formats have been attempted in the past. In the mid-1990s, Kirsch and Ritchie identified several scholars who had successfully published alternative genres of research, including Beverly Clark and Sonia Wiedenhaupt's article on writer's block that takes the form of a dialogue between student and teacher as well as the multi-vocal "Symposium on Feminist Experiences in the Composition Classroom" that appeared in *College Composition and Communication* (*CCC*) in 1992 (Eichhorn et al.). This work, and several examples published since Kirsch and Ritchie's article appeared in *CCC* (Zawacki, 1992; Spooner and Yancey, 1999; Bizzell, Schroeder, and Fox, 2002), "challenges journal editors [and book publishers] to develop a greater tolerance for ambiguity and unconventional forms of discourse, and challenges readers to learn new ways of reading and interpreting texts" (155).

Furthermore, electronic, multimodal venues for scholarship have enabled the proliferation of plural texts/plural authors. The time of genre uncertainty that accompanies the exponential growth of digital publishing, Delagrange explains, provides a much-needed re-visioning of academic writing: "At this *punctum* of technological change, the practices and habits of mind associated with old media are called into question as we struggle to devise principles and practices for the new" (v). Indeed, Delagrange's book, *Technologies of Wonder: Rhetorical Practices in a Digital World*, published through the Computers and Composition Digital Press (an imprint of Utah State University Press), articulates and exemplifies the significant challenges to traditional genres of scholarship made possible via digital writing. Traditional genres that rely on a "coherent," printed-page model of scholarship, Delagrange suggests, can be meaningfully challenged through the capabilities of new media:

> What if designers of interactive digital media imagined a more engaged reader . . . If we were designing for that reader, then we would want to create . . . a hypermediated thinking space that would allow us and our reader to explore, to move things about, to seek out curious and unexpected connections, and to defer closure and certainty while we consider the possibilities for rhetorical action that different arrangements of our evidence might suggest. (108)

In this type of publication, writers do not march readers along a pre-determined path. Rather, writers provide access to and construct the limits of a broader scholarly experience that readers co-determine. *Technologies of Wonder*, with its blending of video, audio, and static alphabetic text, calls forth this kind of engaged reader, as do the growing number of what Christopher Basgier calls "scholarly webtexts" (145), including those published in *Kairos: A Journal of Rhetoric, Pedagogy and Technology*, *Computers and Composition Online*, *Across the Disciplines*, and *Enculturation*. Such "scholarly webtexts," Basgier explains, "specifically *call attention* to the collaborative relationship between author and user, a relationship that most print texts, and even some other new media genres, tend to render invisible" (156).

These alternative genres and digital methods of delivering scholarship are also beginning to find a presence in the traditional hierarchy of scholarly publishing through tenure and promotion documents at places such as Ohio State (Delagrange viii). However, publishing in such venues remains a risk for graduate students and untenured faculty, particularly those in more traditional English departments. Meredith Graupner, Lee Nickoson-Massey, and Kristine Blair point out that, while the Modern Language Association has urged English departments to "better acknowledge the role new media plays in knowledge-making and knowledge-disseminating processes . . . very few administrative leaders and tenure committees know how to assess these new scholarly and creative modes," with the ultimate outcome in many cases that "graduate students and new faculty. . . are ultimately encouraged to reinscribe the privileging of alphabetic literacy in their own discursive practices" (20). Senior faculty in composition and rhetoric are positioned to challenge this privileging, but, as Debra Journet explains, despite the fact that they "are powerful participants in high-stakes decisions about promotion, tenure, or hiring," (108) many of them are often still operating in a print-driven, univocal model of scholarly publication.

In response to this situation, Journet encourages senior scholars in composition and rhetoric to take the lead in moving their departments away from the strictures of traditional print scholarship and to "try out multimodality" (108). I want to amplify and extend Journet's suggestion and urge those with the security of tenure to lead the way in re-visioning and re-valuing genres of scholarship, both digital and print. Those of us who have a level of job security should develop publishing opportunities that promote collaboration and interactivity while *also* creating genres of scholarship that allow for broader participation from a greater variety of teacher-scholars. More specifically, I suggest that, while our field moves in the directions Delagrange recommends, we make a concerted push to change our print-based publishing practices. Changing "the old" in this way lessens the risks that we, as a field, will wind up bracketing new genres of research in new publication venues or reinscribing the privilege accorded to the traditional model of research in those new venues. While the capacity for alternative genres and multiple voices may be more limited in print-based venues than it is in digital spaces, print has the capacity to be visually dynamic and spatially diverse.

Given the noted skepticism with which many of our home departments and institutions regard digital publishing and the time needed for scholars to gain facility with software and hardware for digital, multimodal composing, a two-pronged "attack" might be most effective in bringing about real change to the currently limiting and exclusive scholarly genres. Introducing alternative genres to our print-based interfaces at the same time that more scholarly work appears in digital, multimodal formats will have the added benefit of bringing those most accustomed to and comfortable with traditional print genres—scholars who currently hold senior positions and the relative job security that comes with them—into the conversation in a way that producing more and more digital scholarship, which is less likely to be read by these senior scholars, cannot.

As I explained earlier, I am not saying that we should reduce expectations for good research and strong writing. Instead, I am suggesting that we as a field become more accepting of smaller "chunks" of it. What if, for instance, we were to publish "venues" (not "articles") with participants (rather than "authors")? In addition to undermining a model of scholarship that values a thesis-driven argument and a unified voice, such a "venue" might allow for a broader array of scholars—including those that have heavier teaching, administration, mentoring, and activist commitments—to contribute to scholarly conversations, sharing their "a-ha" moments and/or critical questions drawn from focused reading or from teacher inquiry that they carry out in the courses that they teach. For example, a planned new feature of *Peitho*, the journal of the Coalition of Feminist Scholars in the History of Rhetoric and Composition, aims to serve this purpose. "Recoveries and Reconsiderations," a yearly section of the journal, will debut in 2020 and, according to a recent call for submissions, will "include the work of multiple contributors, with each contribution limited to 2,500 words, and will serve as a forum for sharing innovative perspectives on and application of existing feminist work, as well an incubator for new feminist research projects" ("Call for Submissions").

This new section of *Peitho* is energized and emboldened by the work of feminist theorists and researchers in composition and rhetoric that has made the case for such changes. In supplementing the academic article with venues that bring together many voices and present readers not with a scholarly product but with a scholarly process, we respond to Royster and Kirsch's call to embrace "strategic contemplation" in our research. Drawing on Krista Ratcliffe's concept of *rhetorical listening*, Royster and Kirsch explain that "with the term *strategic contemplation*, we want to reclaim a genre of research and scholarship traditionally associated with processes of meditation, introspection, and reflection. . . . [T]his strategy suggests that researchers might linger deliberately inside of their research tasks as they investigate their topics and sources" (84). I agree with Royster and Kirsch that strategic contemplation "has the capacity to yield rich rewards. It allows scholars to observe and notice, to listen to and hear voices often neglected or silenced, and to notice more overtly their own responses to what they are seeing, reading, reflecting on, and encountering during their research process" (84-85). Without a prominent genre of presentation and circulation that reflects and embodies strategic contemplation, however, it is difficult to see how this critical process will not continue to be devalued or largely invisible. Our traditional publications present a final product, and while scholars are increasingly including discussions in those final products of how they engaged in strategic contemplation, readers cannot witness that lingering in ambiguity, nor can they engage with it. Both writers and readers, thus, miss a potentially rich opportunity to broaden and deepen research through collaborative strategic contemplation. I am in agreement with Royster and Kirsch that "these practices [of strategic contemplation] should be brought out of the shadows and highlighted as important and empowering aspects of the research process" (86). Why not have both sides represented and enable these practices in our publishing venues? Our publications, both print and digital, should represent, embody, and encourage—rather than simply including a recounting of—these critical encounters with uncertainty, ambiguity, and multiplicity.

Part of this change entails a rethinking of the standards by which we identify and evaluate scholarly contributions. The questions Delagrange has raised about how new genres of digital scholarship fit with existing understandings of and criteria for evaluating scholarship also apply to the re-visioned print-based genres that I have advocated for here: "How [will] new forms, organizations, and purposes for interactive digital media meet rigorous standards for intellectual work in the academy?" she asks (2). I suggest that, for the sake of opening up conversations, we rethink what we mean by "rigorous standards" so that those standards do not call out only, or primarily, a particular set of genres that are linear, product-based, and the result of a very lengthy research and writing processes. This doesn't mean we should just publish, circulate, and read whatever anyone composes; rather, we should consider the value of a contribution based on how effectively it promotes and forwards our research conversations. Criteria for our intellectual work, in other words, should support invitational genres that are comprised of and conducive to multiple participants from various locations across diverse identity categories and institutional locations.

Much of my point thus far has been informed by a recognition of how particular scholarly genres can work against the participation of many colleagues in the field because of the time demands that accompany those genres. Of course, time is not the only impediment to voice in scholarly conversations. Discomfort (or, perhaps, disgust) with traditional scholarly genres and the cultural lineages from which they have descended also limits who speaks. As Delagrange eloquently argues, "Unadorned text, written in plain style and organized in a way that can readily be outlined, has long been the paradigm for scholarly performances, and it has been presumed to fit all 'legitimate' academic scholarship. Legitimacy, however, is a conservative, hereditary principle that protects the interest of those who claim it" (10). Here, Delagrange's argument echoes one made by other scholars, such as Geneva Smitherman, Victor Villanueva, Elaine Richardson, and Vershawn Ashanti Young, who have attempted to disrupt and, in some cases, to demonstrate alternatives to conventional academic discourse.

In accord with these scholars, I suggest we create alternative genres for scholarly engagement, paralleling in print—as much as is possible given the constraints of the medium—what Delagrange calls for in digital scholarship. I take inspiration from something—I hesitate to call it an "article"—published a few years ago in *Qualitative Inquiry*. In that publication, Lisa William-White makes an argument—in form and substance—for a "Scholarship Revolution." The first page of William-White's contribution looks traditional enough: there is an abstract, a list of keywords, a heading, a correspondence address for the author, and what amounts to a thesis statement, situated in the scholarly literature: "Here, I argue that Spoken Word (Tedlock, 1983, 1991), as a poetic storytelling method, moves critical qualitative research methodologies forward; heightening the potential for undertaking 21st-century, radical, 'literocratic' (Fisher 2005, 2007), and interpretive scholarship with, within, and about Black, ethnic minority, and youth cultures" (534).

The presentation of William-White's research shifts dramatically, however, after four traditional paragraphs. A poem—formatted in a style that indicates Spoken Word—fills the next five pages. By way of preparing her readers, who may be anticipating traditional paragraphs, headings, in-text citations, and other common markers of "logos and rational justification" (Delagrange 12), William-White explains in her final traditional paragraph that "I champion the potential for, and recognition of, a research methodology where content is framed in context; and where discourse, linguistics, and critical theory allow for conceptual, analytic, nuanced, and stylized performative possibility" (535). Next comes a centered, all-caps rallying cry:

I'M CALLIN' FOR A SCHOLARSHIP REM CALLIN'
FOR A SCHOLARSHIP REVOLUTION!

Stanzas that critique traditional forms and genres of scholarship then follow:

>Not to be dramaturgical
>Or theatrical
>Not to be sensational
>Or emotional
>But to take knowledge
>And make it practical
>*[hook]*
>Merge critical theory discourse[6]
>Activism and teachin'[7]
>Consciousness raisin'
>Signifyin'[8], Rappin'[9]
>and
>Preachin'[10]
>with substance

for IMPACT[11]
Currently what we, in the Academy, lack[12]
and NEED to get back
Or at least GET-on-Top-of-dat![13]
WE NEED A SCHOLARSHIP REVOLUTION!

The "hook" repeats throughout the piece, with references to the ongoing scholarly conversation included in endnotes. In the excerpt above, for example, note six directs readers to "see Crenshaw, Gotanda, Peller, and Thomas (1995)," and note eight provides Geneva Smitherman's definition of "signifying" from *Black Talk: Words and Phrases from the Hood to the Amen Corner*.

William-White also uses footnotes to bridge the cultural divide between her "traditional" academic readers, many of whom are likely white, middle-class, and not familiar with Spoken Word or its connections to African American Vernacular English. Note seven in the excerpt above explains, "In this text, I code-switch between standard American English and African American Vernacular English. Within the verse where one would encounter function morphemes or content morphemes with two syllables (ng words), I delete the 'g,' which is in keeping with the oral phonetic sound intended by the author" (540). Throughout, William-White very consciously genre-fies her call for a re-presentation of scholarship and suggests that the form in which we present research is an essential contribution to (or undermining of) its power to liberate:

Libratory dialogue and praxis
spawns the ability to
to REFLECT
then ACT
Hence, if research lacks the promise of radical democratic practice
To create change
Is so esoteric that the common man can't relate
Or react,
We should REJECT that!
...
CAN WE GET A SCHOLARSHIP REVOLUTION! (536)

William-White's mixture of elements typical in what many of us have come to understand as a scholarly article with elements of Spoken Word poetry illustrates that scholarship is possible in a variety of genres—not just typical scholarly journal articles or book chapters. Welcoming, indeed prioritizing, such "alternative" genres in our well-established publication outlets will allow for new voices and new insights, inviting the participation of those whose class, institutional location, ethnicity, and ideological commitments make the genres typical of "academese" inaccessible and/or inadequate.

We might, as a field, consider the approach of a journal such as *Qualitative Inquiry*, which regularly mixes genres. Poetry, skits, creative nonfiction, reports on small-scope research projects and research-in-progress are included in the same journal with "traditional" scholarly articles that draw on an extensive list of references and that are the result of research and writing completed over a lengthy time period. Indeed, this kind of break with traditional academic genres has gained a foothold within the field through the inclusion of "Course Designs," and a "Composing With" section in the journal *Composition Studies*. The "Course Designs" section allows for teacher-scholars to present and briefly contextualize their pedagogical practices, while the "Composing With" section, as explained in the journal's submission guidelines, includes pieces of 800–1,000 words that "provoke questions regarding what those of us who teach, administer, and theorize writing might learn from broader discussions of composing." To achieve this end, the submissions are "largely narrative, aiming to immerse readers in a particular experience rather than making a traditional academic argument" ("Submissions"). Such challenges to language and genre are essential to challenging assumptions about power. For this reason, language and genre "play" has been a hallmark of the work of several feminist theorists and activists (Mary Daly, Gloria Anzaldúa, Luce Irigaray, and Trihn Min-ha, for example) who challenge social hierarchies by disrupting language expectations and, in the process, reveal the gendered silences upon which that traditional discourse relies.

I realize the contradiction of what I am doing: I am writing a chapter in an academic book published by a major press in the field. While I've provided examples, I've not written an alternative genre: I am right in the thick of the practices I want to trouble. But, what I see myself doing here is engaging in productive dissatisfaction. Productive dissatisfaction, as I conceive of it, is a sense that something is limited or limiting, but, rather than simply causing agitation, the sense is accompanied by an urge to explore, elaborate, and ultimately alleviate that sense of limitation.

I want to close with an important caveat, one that I have raised before in this contribution: I am not suggesting that we should not value or that we do away with the extensive, long-term, lengthy, linear, rational texts that have taught us so much. As Delagrange argues, "Of course, linear propositional logic is itself a pattern, an arrangement, with an important intellectual history that has served us well and will continue to do so" (133). I am suggesting, though, that there are many significant reasons to break that pattern's near monopoly on our processes and products of scholarship and to recognize what and who it omits, devalues, and silences. As Cheryl Glenn has pointed out, "rhetoric always inscribes the relation of language and power at a particular moment (including who may speak, who may listen or who will agree to listen, and what can be said)" (1). I hope to encourage broader consideration and discussion about who we—those who are "established" in the field of composition and rhetoric—agree to listen to and what can be said in our scholarly conversations.

Works Cited

Anderson, Daniel. *Screen Rhetoric and the Material World.* U of Michigan P, forthcoming.

Antonio, Anthony, Helen B. Astin, and Christine M. Cress. "Community Service in Higher Education: A Look at the Nation's Faculty." *The Review of Higher Education*, vol. 23, no. 4, Summer 2000, pp. 373–97.

Basgier, Christopher. "The Author-Function, The Genre Function, and The Rhetoric of Scholarly Webtexts." *Computers and Composition*, vol. 28, 2011, pp. 145–59.

Bizzell, Patricia, Chris Schroeder, and Helen Fox, editors. *ALT DIS: Alternative Discourses in the Academy.* Heinemann, 2002.

Blakesley, David. "New Realities for Scholarly Presses in Trying Economic Times." *Composition Studies*, vol. 42, no. 1, Spring 2014, pp. 97–102.

Blair, Kristine L. "Composing Change: The Role of Graduate Education in Sustaining a Digital Scholarly Future." *Composition Studies*, vol. 42, no. 1, Spring 2014, pp. 103–6.

"Call for Submissions: NEW Peitho Feature: Recoveries and Reconsiderations." *Peitho,* Coalition of Feminist Scholars in the History of Rhetoric and Composition, http://peitho.cwshrc.org/news/. Accessed 4 Apr. 2019.

Brown, Stuart, Theresa Enos, David Reamer, and Jason Thompson. "Portrait of the Profession: The 2007 Survey of Doctoral Programs in Rhetoric and Composition" *Rhetoric Review*, vol. 27, no. 4, 2008, pp. 331–40.

Clark, Beverly and Sonia Wiedenhaupt. "On Blocking and Unblocking Sonja: A Case Study in Two Voices." *College Composition and Communication*, vol. 43, 1992, pp. 55–74.

Delagrange, Susan. *Technologies of Wonder: Rhetorical Practices in a Digital World.* Utah State UP/Computers and Composition Digital Press, 2011.

Eichhorn, Jill et al. "A Symposium on Feminist Experiences in the Composition Classroom" *College Composition and Communication*, vol. 43, 1992, pp. 297–322.

Eyman, Douglas and Cheryl E. Ball. "Composing for Digital Publication: Rhetoric, Design, Code." *Composition Studies*, vol. 42, no. 1, Spring 2014, pp. 114–17.

Glenn, Cheryl. *Unspoken: A Rhetoric Silence.* Southern Illinois UP, 2004.

Graupner, Meredith, Lee Nickoson-Massey, and Kristine Blair. "Remediating Knowledge-Making Spaces in the Graduate Curriculum: Developing and Sustaining Multimodal Teaching and Research." *Computers and Composition*, vol. 26, 2009, pp. 13–23.

Hawisher, Gail E. and Cynthia L. Selfe. "Evolving Digital Publishing Opportunities Across Composition Studies." *Composition Studies*, vol. 42, no. 1, Spring 2014, pp. 107–13.

Hodgson, Justin. "Scholars/Digital Representation/Publishing." *Composition Studies*, vol. 42, no. 1, Spring 2014, pp. 118–22.

Journet, Debra. "Inventing Myself in Multimodality: Encouraging Senior Faculty to Use Digital Media." *Computers and Composition*, vol. 24, no. 2, 2007, pp. 107–20.

Kirsch, Gesa, and Joy Ritchie. "Beyond the Personal: Theorizing a Politics of Location in Composition Research." *College Composition and Communication*, vol. 46, 1995, pp. 7–29. Rpt. in *Feminism and Composition: A Critical Sourcebook.* Edited by Kirsch et. al., Bedford/St. Martins, 2003, pp. 140–59.

Kirsch, Gesa, and Liz Rohan, editors. *Beyond the Archives: Research as Lived Process.* Southern Illinois UP, 2008.

Kirsch, Gesa, et al., editors. *Feminism and Composition Studies: A Critical Sourcebook.* Bedford/St. Martins, 2003.

Lunsford, Andrea and Lisa Ede. *Singular Texts/Plural Authors: Perspectives on Collaborative Writing.* Southern Illinois UP, 1992.

Miller, Carolyn. "Genre as Social Action." *Quarterly Journal of Speech*, vol. 70, 1984, pp. 151–67.

McKee, Heidi and Porter, James. *The Ethics of Internet Research: A Rhetorical Case-Based Process.* Peter Lang, 2009.

Nickoson, Lee and Mary P. Sheridan, editors. *Writing Studies Research in Practice: Methods and Methodologies.* Southern Illinois UP, 2012.

Powell, Katrina and Pamela Takayoshi. *Practicing Research in Writing Studies: Reflexive and Ethically Responsible Research.* Hampton, 2012.

Radcliffe, Krista. *Rhetorical Listening: Identification, Gender, Whiteness.* Southern Illinois UP, 2006.

Ramsey, Alexis, Wendy Sharer, Lisa Mastrangelo, and Barbara L'Eplattenier, eds. *Working in the Archives: Practical Research Methods for Rhetoric and Composition.* Southern Illinois UP, 2009.

Richardson, Elaine. *Hiphop Literacies.* Routledge, 2006.

Royster, Jacqueline Jones and Gesa Kirsch. *Feminist Rhetorical Practices: New Horizons for Rhetoric, Composition, and Literacy Studies.* Southern Illinois UP, 2012.

Schell, Eileen and K.J. Rawson, editors. *Rhetorica in Motion: Feminist Rhetorical Methods and Methodologies.* U of Pittsburgh P, 2010.

Smitherman, Geneva. *Black Talk: Words and Phrases from the Hood to the Amen Corner.* Mariner Books, 2000.

—. *Talkin' and Testifyin': The Language of Black America.* Wayne State UP, 1986.

"Submissions." *Composition Studies*, U of Cincinnati, 2014, http://www.uc.edu/journals/composition-studies/submissions/overview.html. Accessed 10 Oct. 2014.

Urrieta, Luis Jr. and Lina R. Méndez Benavídez. "Community Commitment and Activist Scholarship: *Chicana/o* Professors and the Practice of Consciousness." *Journal of Hispanic Higher Education*, vol. 6, no. 3, 2007, pp. 222–36.

Villanueva, Victor. *Bootstraps: From an American Academic of Color.* NCTE, 1993.

Weisser, Christian and Kevin Brock. "Argumentation, Authority, and Accessibility in Digital Publishing: A Retrospective on *Composition Forum.*" *Composition Studies*, vol. 42, no. 1, Spring 2014, pp. 123–27.

William-White, Lisa. "Scholarship Revolution." *Qualitative Inquiry*, vol. 17, no. 6, 2011, pp. 534–42.

Wysocki, Anne Frances. "A Bookling Monument." *Kairos,* vol. 7, no. 3, 2002, kairos.technorhetoric.net. Accessed 11 Nov. 2013.

Yancey, Kathleen Blake. "Made Not Only in Words: Composition in a New Key." *College Composition and Communication,* vol. 56, no. 2, 2004, pp. 297–328.

Yancey, Kathleen Blake and Michael Spooner. "A Single Good Mind: Collaboration, Cooperation, and the Writing Self." *College Composition and Communication,* vol. 49, no. 1, 1998, pp. 45–62.

Young, Vershawn Ashanti. *Your Average Nigga: Performing Race, Literacy, and Masculinity.* Wayne State UP, 2007.

Zawacki, Terry Myers. "Recomposing as a Woman—An Essay in Different Voices." *College Composition and Communication,* vol. 43, 1992, pp. 32–38. Rpt. in *Feminism and Composition: A Critical Sourcebook.* Ed. Kirsch et. al. Bedford/St. Martins, 2003, pp. 314–20.

11 Fragile Archives: Questions of Survival, Rhetorical Listening, and Breast Cancer Narrative

Anita Helle

In 2012, my colleague and co-editor, Mary DeShazer, and I posted a call for critical essays on the topic of theorizing breast cancer narratives for *Tulsa Studies in Women's Literature*.[1] We did so knowing that more than 1.4 million women receive a breast cancer diagnosis each year, and in that same timeframe 500,000 women will die from the disease. In the interest of evolving cross-disciplinary communication and advancing global understanding of women's rhetorical responses to breast cancer, we were prepared initially to consider transnational, queer, environmental, biomedical and bio-political rhetorics and theories, and to welcome contributions that considered a wide range of archival material, including genres and sub-genres of personal narratives and pathographies that had not previously been studied. What we as co-editors could not have anticipated is that we would receive an abundance of essays with a postmillennial focus, propelling us to follow Lisa

---

1. Among many individuals who guided this project and provided opportunities for public discussion, I wish to acknowledge Laura M. Stevens, editor of *Tulsa Studies in Women's Literature*, as well as Mary Foskett, Professor of Religious Studies and Director, Wake Forest Humanities Institute, for her role in organizing a symposium on breast cancer narrative and counter-narrative, co-sponsored by the Wake Forest School of Medicine and the Humanities Institute, spring 2013. Deepest gratitude is owed to my co-editor, Mary K. DeShazer, who accompanied me on long walks in Oregon in the fall of 2014, as I assembled reflections for this chapter.

Ede, Cheryl Glenn, and Andrea Lunsford's injunction to "stand at the border" of rhetoric and feminism, to "gain new perspectives" on a deeply gendered site of embodiment, stigmatization, silence, and cultural production (402). Nor could we have anticipated the productive theoretical and rhetorical linkages that emerged as we reflected on not only Audre Lorde's 1977 impassioned speech to feminist activists and writers to "transform silence into language and action" (a speech which included anecdotal reference to having briefly confronted the "ultimate silence of death" when a breast cancer biopsy tested benign)[2] but also Glenn's *Unspoken: A Rhetoric of Silence* (2004), as well as her co-edited collection with Krista Ratcliffe, *Silence and Listening as Rhetorical Arts* (2011).

Considering spoken and previously unspoken or under-researched arts of breast cancer expression, the ten essays Mary and I selected for development and publication encompass research on primary archival material from a wide variety of genres and sub-genres: from autobiographies, memoirs, auto-thanatographies (memoirs on one's own dying) and auto-performances, to new genres incorporating visual and multi-modal rhetorics, online communities, and digital archives. We titled the special issue "Theorizing Breast Cancer: Narrative, Politics, Memory," and I like to think that the final arrangement that emerged pushes against the traditional parameters of rhetorical canons, especially invention, memory and delivery. My focus for this chapter, however, turns attention to the archives contributors drew from to compose their essays and the archive we created through the process of composing the volume.

To analyze and engage the archival work conducted for and created through the special-issue process, I take up the work that Glenn and Jessica Enoch propose in "Drama in the Archives: Rereading Methods, Rewriting History." Here, I look critically and capaciously at what "counts as a primary resource, as an archive, and especially what counts as contribution to rhetorical theory" (328). My work in this chapter is to meditate on authorial and editorial archival decisions, exploring how these decisions shape our understandings about breast cancer experiences and narratives that work to articulate these experiences. In particular, I show how "strategic contemplation"—the intentional "processes of medita-

---

2. Audre Lorde's MLA address "The Transformation of Silence into Language and Action" was given December 18, 1977, at the first Lesbian and Literature panel of the Modern Language Association; doctors at the time had diagnosed her breast cancer lump as benign. One year later, she was re-diagnosed with breast cancer: the 1980 edition of *The Cancer Journals* re-contextualizes this essay as the first chapter.

tion, introspection, and reflection"—(Royster and Kirsch 84)—can illuminate the fissures, omissions, and agnotologies[3] of the scholarship on breast cancer narratives. Strategic contemplation allows for the rhetorical space to pause and ruminate, reconsider judgment, acknowledge archival complexity, and build awareness of creative and intuitive processes that accompany the researcher's embodied experience (Royster and Kirsch 85). It is the work of listening closely and rhetorically to the scholarly decisions one makes and the moves of others to gain a capacious understanding of what these moves do and how they operate.

As Mary and I retrospectively searched for suitable conceptual categories to organize scholarly articles on breast cancer narrative, the phrase "fragile archives" became part of my inner, working vocabulary for understanding the distinctive (dialectical and material) rhetorics of breast cancer narratives and the challenges this work presents. At one level, the materials are "fragile," of course, because they confront us with awareness of mortality if not horror and dread ("not me, or not me, not yet" too readily comes to the mind of any researcher working with these materials, if she has not been diagnosed). In addition, we recognize the historiographic risk of easily mis-handling the materials: archival materials are "fragile" when they are damaged or fragmentary, or when there is a lack of rhetorical or public positioning—embodied, contextual, theoretical—for display and preservation, so that morphing or translation is required. In what Susan Sontag calls the "kingdom of the sick and the well," fragile archives are also fragile because of the maladies of language, discourse, and situation in which they are embedded (3). This chapter, then, leverages strategic contemplation to better understand the multiple facets of the fragile archives that emerged through the authors' research and writing and through Mary's and my editorial processes as we all contributed to this special issue.

Before moving into my analysis of these fragile archives, a brief overview of the special issue offers a glimpse of the archival work taken up therein. Section I of the special issue, "Postmillennial Theories and Feminist Genealogies," inquiries into contested feminist generational differences in the difficult choices, strategies, and rhetorical challenges faced by women identified with BRCA 1 and BRCA 2 genetic mutations. Section II, "Narrative Genres: Memoir, Fiction, and Theater," teases out public pedagogical and performative dimensions across feminist-inspired

---

3. Agnotoloy, as used here, as a term for trained incapacity, was coined by Robert N. Proctor to describe the "cultural production of ignorance" (8).

resistance to silence and rhetorically empowered speech in popular romances, polemical plays, and journalistic memoirs. Section III, "Visual Culture: Comics, Film, Photography, Painting," expands the academic terrain of breast cancer narrative to visual rhetorics of embodiment, raising new and persistent aesthetic, affective, and political considerations in ways that re-locate and engage both subjectivities and identities of viewers, spectators, readers, and participants in more complex affective and political positionings.

Trends in Scholarship

By 2014, the conversation our special issue entered into regarding breast cancer narratives and memory had become a vociferous one. Since the 1970s, scholars have deeply engaged the study of breast cancer narratives, seeing the genre as a productive realm of feminist and rhetorical inquiry and giving feminist and rhetorical criticism a critical purchase on qualitative archival research. I note below scholarly trends in this area of research.

First, feminist engagements in theories, practices, and histories of archival material research in medicine have shifted the terrain from documenting master narratives of doctors' stories to questioning how scholars might practice more careful, ethical, and responsive rhetorical listening to silences and stigmatization in breast cancer *patient* narratives. New rhetorical methodologies, such as Rita Charon's method of engaging a "physician's witness"—the medical student makes her own witnessing notes while the physician is engaged in communicative exchange with the patient, and then both the physician and witness review their double-edged discourses—highlights the growing importance of listening and telling within the clinic (x). Feminist scholarship in medical anthropology, narrative studies, as well as rhetorical studies have all brought attention to the rhetorically situated politics of the patient as an essential methodological and diagnostic tool.[4]

Second, the academic study of illness narratives as a *genre*—and recognition of emergent sub-genres—has expanded understandings of epideictic possibility. As Judy Z. Segal has argued, rhetorical criticism of the tricky category of auto-pathography requires examination of an "epideictic rhetoric of pathography and an epideictic rhetoric of pathography

---

4. Notable in studies of breast health and women's rhetoric is Susan Wells in *Our Bodies Ourselves and the Work of Writing*.

study" (61). While this doubled hermeneutic needs some unpacking, the proliferation of breast cancer narratives in westernized and nonwesternized nations has caused scholars to pay close attention to the rhetorical patterning and expected values such narratives produce. Rhetorical studies of pathographies have compelled closer scrutiny to the ways expected beginnings and endings of the *genre* of the personal illness narrative (the most narrow definition "pathography") function as a driver of triumphalist rhetorics through expected patterns of plot, conflict, and progress. In rhetorical studies, Segal's scholarship sounds a cautionary note for scholars in this field, alerting us to the possibility that the work of pathography may also be epideictic, when praise and blame are attributed to certain responses to illness (18).

In addition, material critiques of the relationships among multi-national corporate culture, rhetoric, and technoscience have advanced awareness of the role corporations play in "pinkwashing," breast cancer into narrative "rosiness" and infantilizing the woman patient. Complicating our understanding of the differences between pre- and post-millennial breast cancer narrative is the postmillennial proliferation of breast cancer narratives that include critique of corporate and techno-scientific discourse.[5] Barbara Ehrenreich's well-known polemic, "Welcome to Cancerland," epitomizes scholarly critiques of "the cult of pink kitsch" voiced also in such studies as Samantha King's *Pink Robbins, Inc.: Breast Cancer and the Politics of Philanthropy*, Zillah Eistenstein's *Manmade Breast Cancers*, and Jackie Stacey's *Teratologies: A Cultural Study of Cancer*. These works have been broadly influential, inside and outside the academy, enabling scholars and patients to breach a difficult border between examining the relationship of coercive and persuasive mechanisms within breast cancer awareness social movements (including those that deflect analysis of multi-causative and environmental factors), while acknowledging the powerful role such rhetorics have in creating communal solidarities. In so doing, what Segal describes as the "complicating narratives" (62) of women's health rhetorics further authorize personal narratives that combine appeals to pathos with more overtly activist and resistant public discourse.

---

5. I am grateful to J. Blake Scott in "Rhetoric and Technoscience: The Case of Confide" for analysis of HIV-AIDs testing kits manufactured under the brand name Confide, which provides a useful model for rhetorical and literary scholars of breast cancer pathography.

A fourth wellspring of rhetorical interest, originating with Sontag's *Illness as Metaphor*, is the resurgence of tropological analysis of the breast cancer narrative. Given its fetishization in Westernized culture, the female breast has long been a site of lavish metaphorical attribution, rife with opportunities for ideological insight through analysis of sleeping metaphors.[6] Anne Hunsaker Hawkins, in *Reconstructing Illness: Studies in Pathography*, notes that pathographies as a genre tend to repeat the "same metaphorical paradigms": the paradigm of regeneration ("survivorship" in breast cancer narratives), the idea of illness as battle, "the war on cancer," the athletic ideal, the journey into a distant country, and the "mythos of healthy mindedness"(27). Postmillennial scholarship on the sub-genre of breast cancer narratives such as Mary DeShazer's *Fractured Borders: Reading Women's Cancer Literature* points to tropes specific to breast cancer: women's bodies in breast cancer narratives are figured as *medicalized, leaky, amputated, prosthetic,* and *not-dying*. These five tropes, DeShazer, argues, are frameworks for understanding "how stigmatization diminishes ill women's subjectivity and how feminist writing can enhance it" (13). Inquiries into women's pathographies make clear the political implications of such metaphors, and these metaphors must be approached with special acuity, for there is no guarantee that use of these tropes outside a given context indicate whether its claims, beliefs, or even its rhetorics of hope are reactionary or progressive. If feminism's claims are that excavating such metaphors or inventing new ones help us come closer to women's experiences with disease, we need as well to know how they persuade us, how they re-stage what breast cancer disease looks like as an illness phenomenon, and what this illness discourse will look like in the future.

While these scholarly developments have made the rhetorical study of breast cancer narratives exigent, I work in this chapter to re-deploy the rhetorical methodologies of moving what is spoken or unspoken from the margins of defined scholarly practice and archival research. In particular, strategic contemplation on the fragile archives that support contributors' work in our special issue brings to the fore important insight regarding ways to read and understand breast cancer narratives.

---

6. On fetishization and metaphorical attribution, see Marilyn Yalom, *A History of the Breast*.

Identifying the Fragile Archive of Breast Cancer Narratives

The primary archival materials of women's breast cancer narratives are volatile and mutable, affectively charged, and embedded in polysemous relational contexts and discourses. For researchers, tapping an unexpected archival site requires close listening.

To take one example, contributor Melissa Zeiger listens in on the voices of heroines in breast cancer-themed popular romances. She finds that heroines often navigate their relationship to cancer by meditating on their surgical scars:

> Almost always, these meditations have as their starting point her surgical scar, that indelible mark of what she has experience. The heroine finds it extremely ugly but comes to accept and sometimes even to value it as an important marker of her strength and persistence. The hiding of the scar recalls the histories and literatures of racial passing and of the closet: the contest between pride and shame, the damaging psychological and social experiences of the protagonist, and the hope for an ultimate self-acceptance and resilience in the face of further tribulations. The heroine will eventually reveal the scar; the scar, in turn, will act as a catalyst . . . In control of whether and when to reveal her scar, she shows a new consciousness in directing her life. (117)

Surprisingly, romance novels offer one space in which this embodied rhetoric—normally unseen and unspoken—can be contemplated.

Zeiger's ability to locate breast cancer narratives in romances suggests that, unlike the well-defined institutional spaces of the leprosarium and the clinic,[7] postmillennial breast cancer narratives are located nowhere in particular yet everywhere we look, often in tense spaces of interpersonal and public rhetorical transactions. Postmillennial breast cancer memoirs are now published in abundance, but these represent a small fraction of narratives embedded in family lore, in journals and scrapbooks and photo albums, in blogs, internet chat rooms, oral narratives relayed person to person or passed down in family records with telegraphic urgency. Such records are still often stigmatized and muted—many women are

---

7. See Michel Foucault, *The Birth of the Clinic: An Archaeology of Medical Perception.*

reluctant to "go public" with their stories. The narrative authority and rhetorical efficacy of such materials cannot be characterized in terms of singular authorship. For example, one woman's text may be finished by another, or the posthumous publication of a memoir may take on a new life in prompting posthumous memorial tributes and new forms of conversation. For this reason, one of our conclusions as editors was that breast cancer narratives are generating new forms of *partial, continent, sporadic, collective co-authorship*, which might be best described as alternative forms of witnessing and testimony, wherein friends or family members pick up the narrative threads that terminal cancer patients have left off.

Given the diversity, complexity, and fluidity of breast cancer narratives, then, it likely comes as no surprise to find there is no national US archive of breast cancer narratives; there are no mass-memorial projects comparable to the HIV-AIDS (Names) quilt. While some cultural institutions have collected and exhibited or digitized art on breast cancer,[8] we, as editors, observed that scholars of breast cancer narratives seldom undertake time-consuming and expensive travel to distant sites to do their research. In bringing together essays that consider the mass of materials, Mary and I thus recognized the necessary incompleteness of pathographic archives, their rootedness in the *kairos* of time and place and situation, their vexed dependence on rhetorics of science, technology, and biomedicine, and their proximity to what I term *alternative epideictics* of loss and mourning as readers respond to narratives by women who are "living in prognosis" or dying of the disease.

Archival Selection and New Narratives of Genetic Identity

Because Mary and I were conscious that our project "stands on the shoulders" of many feminist scholars, activists, and rhetoricians, and within a burgeoning field of research where many "bodies" are yet to be counted as casualties or survivors, we entered into this project with an awareness that the process of vetting and selecting essays on postmillennial breast cancer narratives would have consequences for hierarchies of exclusion

---

8. See Frank Cordell's *The Century Project* (www.thecenturyproject.comexhibt) and also the postmillennial exhibits of the work of Hollis Sigler, reproductions of which have been hung in hospitals under the sponsorship of the Society for the Arts and Healthcare (Tanner 222).

and inclusion, for research into health care policies, and for categories of feminist identity politics that have yet to be written. In other words, we realized that our special issue would become part of the archive of scholarship on breast cancer narratives, so we were conscious of the archive we were creating as we selected (and rejected) material for inclusion.

One area we found especially troublesome is the disproportionate emphasis our special issue gives to finding new critical frameworks for pre-vivor memoirs—memoirs by or about women who do not yet have cancer but have been identified with BRCA1 and BRCA2, a hereditary mutation that increases risk for developing the disease. Perhaps a leaning in this direction was to be expected, but we, as co-editors, felt uneasy about the potential conflation of rhetorical artifacts by breast cancer survivors with artifacts from pre-vivors, especially since only one in ten women diagnosed with breast cancer is accounted for by hereditary mutations (although these still account for about 25,000 cases each year in the US). Moreover, the process of testing for BRCA, as well as the post-diagnostic remedies such a test might entail, are costly and time-consuming—it is, from one standpoint a privilege to have access to testing and to afford the surgeries.[9]

Despite being a minority among those diagnosed with breast cancer, narratives by those identified with the BRCA gene have been popularized due in part to the fact that several well-known writers and journalists have published them. Genetic testing and contralateral or pre-emptive, "prophylactic" mastectomies and breast reconstructions as a taken-for-granted remedy have become notoriously visible in media and popular press among women who have not been diagnosed with breast cancer illness (Orenstein).

We also wondered: Would our presentation of BRCA-related memoirs ironically reconfirm the fetishization of the hoped-for whole, maternal, hetero-sexualized breast so common in Western representational systems? What message would we be sending by focusing on diseases most common to a narrow sector of the world's population that has already been privileged in feminist theorizing? Would redefinition of "identity politics" and "alternative identities" do enough to clear rhetorical space for intersectional differences rather than, as one contributor noted, "re-emploting women's bodies as established cultural narratives

---

9. For a potent demonstration of missing African-American voices in the breast cancer pre- and post-vivor survival narrative, see NPR's recent interview series, "Under her Skin: Living with the Realities of Breast Cancer."

that seek to erase embodied difference under the aegis of unifying notions of 'survival'" (Waples 64)? Further, a disproportionate amount of attention being given to BRCA narratives forces recognition of a new sub-genre of illness narratives (written by the not-yet-sick), but does it also lead to the unquestioning reinforcement of the belief that we are only "good" citizens when we are better at managing risk? If a woman with a "deleterious mutation" (the diagnostic term for BRCA-positive anomalies) does not, in fact, signify a woman with breast cancer, what is the identity politics of which "pre-vivor" discourse persuades?

In the end, we chose three among ten essays that emphasized the archive of pre-vivor narratives, largely because the "new" archives of BRCA narratives are super-abundant, and we were committed to a postmillennial chronological frame. As editors, we chose to exercise the power of arrangement: the sometimes-hyperbolic rhetorics of BRCA narratives about breast cancer appeared in several essays that examined some of the same texts with a certain acknowledgment that these texts represented a relatively narrow transnational sampling. The intention here was to open up new thinking about feminist identity politics at the intersection of new techno/medical sciences and expose yet unresolvable, relatively unexplored issues.

We do not regret our decisions, but our selection continues to complicate our understanding of what is ethically at stake for women, health policy, and social movements. Carolyn Miller has usefully argued that technical rhetoric in science privileges "advance forecasting" and tends to read the promise/benefits and risks/threats of such forecasting as a "trajectory into the future and a message of appropriate action in the present" (89). We found, however, that attunement to differing modes of rhetorical embodiment, far from affirming a triumphalist rhetoric of clear-cut decision-making, casts the kairos of rhetorical action and forms of narrative closure in a more ambiguous light. One contributor, Amy Boesky, for example, in "'This is How We Live': Witnessing and Testimony in BRCA Memoirs," and in her earlier memoir, *What We Have* (2010), a multi-generational memoir about her family's experience with BRCA1 genetic mutation, argues that written representations of breast cancer genetic mutation depart from conventional modes of illness narrative by providing unexpected temporal variations and a "continuous, helical, twisting together of past, present, and future iterations of loss," repetitively cycling and blurring generational differences and commonalities ("'This Is How We Live'" 89).

This section of our special issue then prompts readers to ask, who then *is* the "I" who finds herself a BRCA-positive subject, a patient even before she becomes ill? Diane Price-Herndl responds to this question provocatively in her essay, "Virtual Cancer: BRCA and Posthuman Narratives of Deleterious Mutation." Price-Herndl's essay probes the contentiousness of a subject constructed at the "convergence between new technologies and bodies" and the paradoxes of apparent kairotic urgency in the biomedical world (the implied imperative of a need to act). The paradox lies in the "conflation of an apparent healthy state and a possible future state" into one "hyper-real definition" (and I would argue, often hyper-feminized) direction (30). One might add that conflating the temporal distance between past, present, and future of BRCA-identified mutations in the absence of actual disease erases both health and illness and confounds any obvious tip of the rhetorically figured scales of kairotic action. The "virtual cancer patient" in the biomedical regime could be said to twist Virginia Woolf's phrase from her essay, "On Being Ill," to approach the condition of being impossibly ill, neither one or the other, but both at the same time. Clearly a BRCA-narrative that begins with this ambiguous temporality defies generic expectations of the auto-pathography; simultaneously, it exposes material, discursive, and social dimensions of kairotic action in stunningly unsettling ways.

When Audre Lorde issued her challenge to "transform silence [about breast cancer] into language and action," she implicitly called feminists to rhetorically re-construct breast cancer embodiment (and its silences) and see this as a feminist project that would mobilize a set of collective values among women themselves to refuse consumer-driven restitution ("Transformation"). But feminisms, too, have changed. In this special issue, Mary and I chose to address the intergenerational differences among feminist narratives of identity by book-ending Herndl's essay with a searing memoir by a twenty-five-year-old self-described "third wave feminist," Emily Waples, who opens her essay with a narrative about sharing a hospital room on the occasion of her mastectomy. In the bed next to her, the transsexual pointed toward her own new prosthetic breasts, and mimed, "*You should get some of these*" (47). Waples's pointed silence in this exchange does not circumvent biology or illness. Rather, her silence is a rhetorical strategy that points beyond women's specularity and reworks the gendered demands of "having" breasts—one need not have "some of these" to be a woman. In her essay, Waples reframes culturally emplotted breast cancer narratives for younger women and issues urgent challenges to resist a subjectivity defined by normative, consumer-inspired survival ethics. G. Thomas Couser's earlier work on breast cancer narrative had argued that the master plots of breast cancer narratives make women "survivors by definition" because they are "well enough to write" (39). Waples redirects the debate by noting how the progression from disease to survival is gendered, not only in subscribing to the master plot of singular identity in general, but by linking "survival values" to what Lauren Berlant argues is a "central fantasy of women's culture"(qtd. In Waples 50), defined as the "constantly emplotted desire of a complex person to rework the details of her history to become a vague or simpler, idea of herself—all too readily in a realm of consumer-inspired, compulsively repetitious femininity" (qtd. in Waples 50). By selecting essays such as these for the special issue, then, Mary and I composed and, we hope, troubled the emergent archive of the pre-vivor memoir, offering scholarship that overtly interrogates and pushes the generic boundaries of BRCA narrative.

Affect and the Archive: Mourning, Witnessing, Post-Memory

While our special issue aims to press the boundaries of postmillennial archival research and expand the research base by including narratives from out-of-the-way places, we cannot ignore that a feminist definition of the research process as "lived experience" (Kirsch and Rohan) presents challenges for ethics and methodologies of rhetorical research. In a culture where breast cancer is still stigmatized, many women do not want their stories told, while many others, pushing graphic descriptions of wounded and vulnerable bodies into public visibility make self-representations that, for some audiences, blur the lines among hopeful activist rhetoric, "obscene" representations, and voyeuristic responses. Here the vexed need to listen to what Glenn describes, as "eloquent silences" becomes relevant to interpretive practices for scholars of pathography who are committed to the study of material in which questions of feminism are not necessarily first-order questions for narrators (18).

Part of understanding our approach as editors to this special issue and the archives our contributors would draw from was to reflect critically upon our own scholarly locations and personal connections to breast cancer and breast cancer narratives. Neither Mary nor I had been diagnosed with breast cancer, yet both of us had been stricken with loss through proximity—and extended stints of caregiving—with friends and colleagues who had died of the disease. Retrospectively, we recognized the extent to which our rhetorical motives and feminist identifications were grounded in the desire to use the material power of research to more deeply understand and more hopefully act upon grief and loss, matters we had not fully expressed until we began to listen beyond the politics of division and argument, to understand rather than persuade. Such grounding motives, acknowledged and unacknowledged, raise deeper questions for feminist rhetorical study's ongoing interest in opening up new spaces for human variability and social difference in rhetorical listening: How do we act on an ethic of hope and caring for others that so often fuels feminist rhetorical (and pathography) studies, while also justly attending to the rhetorical burden of others? How do we act ethically in considering the multiple audiences for our work, the scholarly communities for which the work is written, and the communities we study, of women who have too often succumbed to the disease?

Another version of this special issue might have included women's first-person testaments and texts without interpretive comment, as inter-chapters; yet another representation of archival sources might have foregrounded auto-ethnographic reflection on the nature of our research as a lived process and cultural encounter in handling fragile materials, as I did in an earlier volume of archival research (Helle). And still another kind of essay collection might have materialized reciprocal witnessing of those whose narratives were dissected and re-framed by scholarly research we had undertaken, so that a pathway could be created for subjects of our research to talk back to researchers through less filtered depths.

Mary and I knew from private conversations that at least half of our scholarly contributors were breast cancer "survivors," even if they would not choose to describe themselves in this way. Some chose to include their own narratives as part of broader scholarly textual analysis, but some were steadfastly reluctant to do so, believing (especially those who had been genetically tested) that the "outing" of female relatives who might also be gene-carriers but had not yet been tested should not be done in public. We gently prodded contributors to express their own locational values, but in the end, we let them decide how much of the "personal" to reveal, even as they interpreted auto-pathographies of others. In this decision, we saw the concept of rhetorical listening to silences as an acknowledgment of dissimilar affective registers operating in different times and places, and a gesture toward broader dialogic possibilities as well as potential solidarities (Glenn 15–16).

Much has, and much remains to be said, about the affective-sensate and ethical response to working with texts that confront us with mortality in forceful and primal ways and about the challenge of listening responsively to testimonies of pain and suffering that breast cancer archives present. Here, in multi-sensate listening, we find some especially relevant and unplumbed depths for strategic contemplation of the archival materials authors drew on and the archive we created through the special issue. As co-editors, Mary and I retrospectively shared a few of the common experiences we have had in working with this material:

- Exhaustion with the pain and suffering of others, a numbness accompanied by a desire to deflect pain and suffering into what becomes "intellectually interesting";
- Conversely, exhaustion with the pain of others, accompanied by heightened sensitivity, sleeplessness, self-preoccupation, the wish to become oblivious;
- Anticipatory anxiety and vulnerability, a sense of having been passed over by an affliction so common among women that it seems almost inevitably to arouse fears of impending disaster and awareness of our own mortality;
- Concerns, ethical and intellectual, about the appropriate stance for scholarly witnessing, grief, and mourning in cases where, as in cases of trauma, the ghostly revenant of a photograph or a tribute in a blog might be all that remains of the life of another.

In conferences where we presented our work in progress, we were often caught up short by an awareness of the limited range of affective registers that much scholarly work presupposes and the academic ethos that readily elevates "suspicious interpretation" over an implied naivete of "experience."[10] Organizers of breast cancer narrative symposia have been sensitive to these issues; panels on which we served with women who provided oral narratives of breast cancer treatment have taught us the value of decentering our authority, as well as the necessity of being patient with how the contingencies of a breast cancer narrative (pre-vivor or post-operative, prosthetic or non-prosthetic) reshapes and qual-

---

10. Anne Jurecic elaborates a critique of the hermeneutics of suspicion in mainstream literary criticism, in favor of a more rhetorically-informed, "reparative reading" of pathographies in *Illness as Narrative*, 113-131.

ifies scholarly argumentation in print.[11] For some of our friends and fellow-colleagues, Breast Cancer Awareness month, with its exhortations to "race or shop or walk" pink (Waples 47), has provided communal reassurance and eased the pain of isolation. A medical humanities scholar-physician whose practice is focused on breast cancer offered that he would be reluctant to recommend the kind of scholarly interpretive work we were doing to his patients—the stark black and white photographs of double-mastectomies included in the issue, albeit an intentional and deliberate act of self-exposure on the part of patients, might not be encouraging, he anticipated.

We have considered whether conscious acts of "willful vulnerability" on the part of some breast cancer patients constitute an alternative rhetorical paradigm for postmillennial narrative by qualifying presumed generic expectations that personal narrative gives us access to any perceived interior life. Challenges to our research often took the form of arguments that the threshold between life and death that a reader moves through in beholding a photograph of a post-mastectomy patient is an encounter with the "limits of representation," and therefore counter-discursive in its content. However, we clung to the notion that a rhetorical and material space for exchange and close listening is opened up by what some might call rhetorically intentional and "extreme" acts of public exposure. We persisted in believing that the presence of readers and viewers as implied audiences and witnesses in visual rhetoric, oral, print, and digital narratives give fullest life and meaning to pathographies.

Michelle Peek's essay in the special issue offers a poignant example. Her piece focuses on breast cancer representations in both *The Century Project*, a photographic collection of unconventional nude photographs of women of all ages, health, and ability (including breast cancer images of women who have since died), and a pioneering collaborative autobiographical narrative, *Cancer in Two Voices*, in which Sandra Butler and Barbara Rosenblum relay their shared experiences living with and responding to Rosenblum's breast cancer. Peek's article reveals the possibility of "willful vulnerability" as a paradigm for sharing the humanity of others-in-trauma even in the face of knowable or unknowable limits of mortality (189). Drawing on the legal meanings of "willful" as in a "last

---

11. See conference website for "HerStories: Breast Cancer Narratives and Counter-Narrative," March 1-2, 2013, an interdisciplinary conference sponsored by the Wake Forest University Humanities Institute and the Wake Forest School of Medicine: http://humanitiesinstitute.wfu.edu/events/herstories-breast-cancer-narratives-counter-narratives.

will and testament" that is both an "ethical offering to another," (206) and a backward, self-reflexive glance, Peek brings the dual meanings of a rhetorical performance and a gift-without-obligation into the context of our research. Texts that are temporally oriented toward the future in their willful use of direct address ("you must see this," "this is for you") and simultaneously engaged retrospective self-reflection ("this is my picture of me at that moment") provide one alternative to the romantic notion of co-creation and reciprocity based on sameness because they refuse to foreclose on an awareness of the difference between bodies that present themselves and those who view, read, or write about them. Such visual rhetorics, Peek suggests, are both generous and avowing; they "pay forward" the notion that we belong to a co-constructed world, even if we as scholars, researchers, viewers, or friends, can't claim epistemic authority in relation to such depictions of others' pain.

As Mary and I re-encountered the ethical in a retrospective gaze in the special issue, we were also compelled to re-evaluate the opposition between the sentimental and the rational in feminist-inspired work on breast cancer narratives. While artifacts of Breast Cancer Awareness movements tend to emphasize sentiment over activist critique, postmillennial feminist and activist rhetorics adamantly valorize anti-sentimentalism, often in agonistic terms: for example, Barbara Ehrenrich begging her rampaging cells to "Let me die of anything but suffocation by the pink sticky sentiment embodied in that teddy bear" (45). Sober consideration and respect for the variety of breast cancer narratives written by many women who are not interested in feminist activism per se would warrant us to find many other ways to remember, other than those that loosen (or bury) ties to the dead in stirring polemics. When beholding photographs of women dying from cancer, or witnessing dialogic posthumous responses to women who have died, we were often moved to re-consider and re-theorize the relationship between engagement and empathy, intimacy and distancing, in relation to the communities of scholars we hoped to persuade and the communities we studied and sought to better understand. As Mary notes in *Mammographies*, "those dying of breast cancer deserve our visual and political activism; those dead from cancer deserve not to be forgotten" (171). Our scholarly task as we work in these archives, then, is to engage the question of post-memorial possibility, enlarging the circle of those who witness and remember. If, as Sontag argues, in *Regarding the Pain of Others*, "remembering is an ethical act, has ethical value in and of itself. Memory is, achingly, the only relation we can have with the dead," (115) then the post-memorial task from a rhetorical perspective takes on both public and pedagogical functions: if there is no such thing as collective memory (exactly), then there is, as Sontag notes, such a thing as "collective instruction" (85).

Evaluating the ethics—and the efficacy—of breast cancer memorial "instruction" and public memorialization is in many ways the unfinished rhetorical business of our scholarly work on postmillennial breast cancer archives and narratives. Ironically, it is often frustration with traditional binaries of consolation and critique, and with hermeneutics of empathy and a hermeneutics of suspicion, that has fueled continued interest of scholars from diverse interdisciplinary fields to turn questions of breast cancer narrative embodiments toward the study of postmillennial witnessing, memory, and trauma-theory. As I cycle recursively around our guiding assumptions and editorial decisions for the special issue, it seems that the study of breast cancer narratives position scholars of pathographies to acquire a radical awareness of the ways the frames of rhetorical listening and telling are always mis-hung, askew from the beginning when we look in on the lives of those who live in proximity to that liminal spaces of life and death or die of disease. What I have acknowledged retrospectively is that the numbness or hyper-sensitivity of our own responses is in part a recognition that Burkean terministic screens and trained incapacity intervene in scholarly understanding at any point in the process of paying responsive attention, even as—and perhaps especially as—we confront liminal spaces of unknowing in the deaths of others.[12] Along with S. Lochlann Jain, whose exceptional writing on the urgency of "pushing the private face of cancer cultures—grief, anger, death, and loss into the public cultures of cancer" (89), we find ourselves seeking new ways to engage in an "elegiac politics" even as its contours are not fully known.

Our contributors point to and leverage new public archives that share several common and distinctive features: they rhetorically perform mourning without loosening ties to the dead; they experiment with transferring authority from tellers to listeners, viewers and witnesses; and they work against cultural forgetting by exposing differential forms of embodiment.

---

12. For more detailed discussions of trained incapacities and terministic screens, see Kenneth Burke's *Permanence and Change* and *Language as Symbolic Action*, respectively.

Works Cited

Berlant, Lauren. *The Female Complaint: The Unfinished Business of Sentimentality in American Culture*. Duke UP, 2008.
Boesky, Amy. "'This Is How We Live': Witnessing and Testimony in BRCA Memoirs." *Tulsa Studies Women's Literature*, vol. 32, no. 2, vol. 33, no. 1, 2013–2014, pp. 89–105.
—. *What We Have: One Family's Inspiring Story about Love, Loss, and Survival*. Penguin Books, 2010.
Burke, Kenneth. *Language as Symbolic Action: Essays on Life, Literature, and Method*. U of California P, 1966.
—. *Permanence and Change: An Anatomy of Purpose*. U of California P, 1984.
Charon, Rita. *Narrative Medicine: Honoring the Stories of Illness*. Oxford UP, 2006.
Couser, G. Thomas. *Recovering Bodies: Illness, Disability, and Life Writing*. U of Wisconsin P, 1997.
DeShazer, Mary K. *Fractured Borders: Reading Women's Cancer Literature*. U of Michigan P, 2005.
—. *Mammographies: The Cultural Discourses of Breast Cancer Narratives*. U of Michigan P, 2013.
DeShazer, Mary K. and Anita Helle, eds. Special Issue. "Theorizing Breast Cancer: Narrative, Politics, Memory." *Tulsa Studies in Women's Literature*, vol. 32, no. 2, & vol. 33, no. 1, 2013–2014, pp. 7-23.
Dowling, Colette. *The Frailty Myth: Women Approaching Physical Equality*. Random House, 2000.
Ede, Lisa, Cheryl Glenn, and Andrea Lunsford. "Border Crossings: Intersections of Rhetoric and Feminism." *Rhetorica: A Journal of the History of Rhetoric*, vol. 13, no. 4, Autumn 1995, pp. 401–441.
Eistenstein, Zillah. *Manmade Breast Cancers*. Cornell UP, 2001.
Ehrenreich, Barbara. "Welcome to Cancerland," *Harper's Magazine*, November 2001, pp. 50-53.
Foucault, Michel. *The Birth of the Clinic: An Archaeology of Medical Perception*. Translated by A.M. Sheridan Smith. Pantheon, 1973.
Gessen, Masha. *Blood Matters: From Inherited Illness to Designer Bodies—How the World and I Found Ourselves in the Future of the Gene*. Harcourt, 2008.
Glenn, Cheryl. *Unspoken: A Rhetoric of Silence*. Southern Illinois UP, 2004.

Glenn, Cheryl, and Jessica Enoch. "Rereading Methods, Rewriting History." *College Composition and Communication*, 2009, pp. 321–342.

Glenn, Cheryl, and Krista Ratcliffe, editors. *Silence and Listening as Rhetorical Arts*. Southern Illinois UP, 2011.

Hawkins, Anne Hunsaker. *Reconstructing Illness: Studies in Pathography*. Purdue UP, 1999.

Helle, Anita Plath, editor. *The Unraveling Archive: Essays on Sylvia Plath*. U of Michigan P, 2007.

King, Samantha. *Pink Ribbons, Inc.: Breast Cancer and the Politics of Philanthropy*. U of Minnesota P, 2006.

Kirsch, Gesa, and Liz Rohan. *Beyond the Archives: Research as a Lived Process*. Southern Illlinois UP, 2008.

Jurecic, Ann. *Illness as Narrative*. U of Pittsburgh P, 2012.

Jain, Sarah Lochlann. "Living in Prognosis: Toward an Elegiac Politics." *Representations*, no. 98, vol. 1, 2007, pp. 77–92.

Latour, Bruno. "Why has Critique Run Out of Steam?: From Matters of Fact to Matters of Concern." *Critical Inquiry*, vol. 30, no. 2, 2004, pp. 225–48.

Lorde, Audre. *The Cancer Journals*. Aunt Lute, 1980.

—. "The Transformation of Silence into Language and Action." *Identity Politics and the Women's Movement*. Edited by Barbara Ryan. New York UP, 2001, pp. 81-84.

Miller, Carolyn R. "Opportunity, Opportunism, and Progress: Kairos in the Rhetoric of Technology." *Argumentation*, vol. 8, no. 1, 1994, pp. 81–96.

Orenstein, Peggy. "The Wrong Approach to Breast Cancer." *New York Times*, 26 July 2014, nytimes.com/2014/07/27/opinion/sunday/the-wrong-approach-to-breast-cancer.html. Accessed July 2014.

Price-Herndl, Diane. "Virtual Cancer: BRCA and Posthuman Narratives of Deleterious Mutation." *Tulsa Studies Women's Literature* vol.32, no. 2, & vol. 33, no. 1, 2013–2014, pp. 25–45.

Proctor, Robert N. *Cancer Wars: How Politics Shapes What We Know and Don't Know About Cancer*. Basic Books, 1995.

Queller, Jessica. *Pretty Is What Changes: Impossible Choices, the Breast Cancer Gene, and How I Defied My Destiny*. Spiegel and Grau, 2008.

Rabinovitch, Dina. *Take off Your Party Dress: When Life's Too Busy for Breast Cancer*. Simon and Schuster, 2014.

Rosenblum, Barbara, and Sandra Butler. *Cancer in Two Voices.* Spinsters, 1991.
Royster, Jacqueline Jones, and Gesa E. Kirsch. *Feminist Rhetorical Practices: New Horizons for Rhetoric, Composition, and Literacy Studies.* Southern Illinois UP, 2012.
Rudnick, Joanna, director. *In the Family.* Kartemquin Films, 2008.
Scott, J. Blake. "Rhetoric and Technoscience: The Case of Confide." *Rhetorical Bodies*, edited by Jack Selzer and Sharon Crowley, U of Wisconsin P, 1999, pp. 239–75.
Segal, Judy Z. *Health and the Rhetoric of Medicine.* Southern Illinois UP, 2005.
Sontag, Susan. *Illness as Metaphor.* Farrar, Straus, and Giroux, 1977.
Stacey, Jackie. *Teratologies: A Cultural Study of Cancer.* London: Routledge, 1997.
Tanner, Laura. "Living Breast Cancer: The Art of Hollis Sigler." *Tulsa Studies Women's Literature*, vol. 32, no. 2, & vol. 33, no. 1, 2013–14, pp. 219–39.
"Under her Skin: Living with the Realities of Breast Cancer." *The Takeaway.* National Public Radio, 22 July 2014.
Waples, Emily. "Emplotted Bodies: Breast Cancer, Feminism, and the Future." *Tulsa Studies Women's Literature*, vol. 32, no. 3, & vol. 33, no. 1, 2013–2014, pp. 47–70.
Wells, Susan. *Our Bodies Ourselves and the Work of Writing.* Stanford UP, 2010.
White, Hayden. *Metahistory: The Historical Imagination in Nineteenth Century Europe.* Johns Hopkins UP, 1973.
Woolf, Virginia. *Collected Essays.* Vol. 1. Hogarth P, 1967.
World Health Organization. "Breast Cancer: Prevention and Control." *World Health Organization*, www.who.int/cancer/detection/breast-cancer/en/index1.html. Accessed 28 April 2014.
Yalom, Marilyn *A History of the Breast.* Ballantine, 1997.
Zeiger, Melissa F. "'Less Than Perfect': Negotiating Breast Cancer in Popular Romance Novels." *Tulsa Studies in Women's Literature*, vol. 32, no. 2, & vol. 33, no. 1, 2013–2014, pp. 107–28.

Part IV: Feminist Teaching and Mentoring

12 "I Don't Read Such Small Stuff as Letters, I Read Men and Nations": Reading the World with Black Middle School Girls

Elaine Richardson

> [It] is regendering that unsettles stable gender categories and enacts a promise that rhetorical history will be a continuous process of investigating the works of women and men rather than a final project that can be finally or universally represented.
>
> —Cheryl Glenn, *Rhetoric Retold*

> [A Story told to bell hooks by her grandmother, Saru] . . . This story is about a magic woman who lives inside smoke. She hides in the smoke so no one can capture her. Using the smoke she turns herself into a male. She must be male to be a warrior. There are no women warriors. She fights fiercely against her enemies. They cannot understand when the arrows that pierce her body do not cause her to fall. . . .
> In my sleep I have seen the magic woman fighting battles, shooting her arrow into enemy after enemy. The part of the dream that troubles my sleep, the part I do not like to tell Saru is that the face of the young male warrior looks like my face. I stare into his eyes as if I am looking into a mirror.

> When I tell Saru of my dream, of the young warrior who wears my face in battle, she says that this is the face of my destiny, that I am to be a warrior. . . .
>
> —bell hooks, *Bone Black: Memories of Girlhood*

> I don't read such small stuff as letters, I read men and nations. I can see through a millstone, though I can't see through a spelling-book. What a narrow idea a reading qualification is for a voter! I know and do what is right better than many big men who read.
>
> —Sojourner Truth, "Woman Suffrage"

Cheryl Glenn's work to unsettle traditionally received understandings of rhetorical history from Antiquity to the Renaissance seeks to uproot patriarchal suppression of women and their contributions to the rhetorical arts. In honoring women and uncovering and regendering cultural practices, Glenn's work shares common ground with critical language, literacy, and rhetorical education of African American women and girls—analyzing and producing culture in hopes of creating a freer world.

Similarly, the penultimate epigraph from bell hooks's memoir reveals the embedded structures of place, race, gender, and sexuality in a southern rural Black community that threaten to limit a young girl's vision of her life and the world. bell's grandmother, Saru, tells her stories of her African and Indian cultural heritage that come back to young bell in dreams. Saru's stories encourage bell to imagine herself beyond herself, to shapeshift, "to locate new ways of imagining oneself and of remaking one's surroundings" (Cox 29). bell seeing her face on the male warrior symbolizes her ability to define her own identity, to chart her own life course, that she is magic. Belief in the supernatural, superstition, and magic are ways of knowing, transforming, and envisioning truth in traditional African American culture that have been discredited by dominant society and academia because African Americans are discredited. (Morrison, "Rootedness" 342). Yet, as we see, this belief system offers young bell hooks regendering as a vision for transformative identity development in her journey to build a liberatory self.

The final epigraph comes from the Signifying Mother of Black Critical Literacies Studies—Sojourner Truth. Though it is often underscored in histories of Sojourner Truth's life that she could not read and write by conventional dominant conceptions of literacy, her ability to critically read and act upon discourses of white male supremacist patriarchy, slavery, sexism, racism, and disenfranchisement, or, for short, her ability to read men and nations, did more for empowerment and liberation of women and Black people than many "big men [and women] who read [and write]" (qtd. in Painter, 270). Jacqueline Jones Royster in *Traces of a Stream: Literacy and Social Change among African American Women* aptly discusses Truth's statement as critique of the narrow ways that literacy is conceptualized and used. What Truth demonstrates is

> . . . literacy [as] a sociocultural phenomenon, a use of language, a component of a complex system of understandings and intents from which decoding and encoding texts must inevitably get their shape, direction, and momentum. Truth's comment acknowledges that making meaning with language is at essence a social act and suggests that it is also a political act, in keeping with [and predating] the analysis of [Freire & Macedo] when they talk about reading the word and the world. (Royster, 45)

Sojourner Truth's reading of men and nations illuminates the gendered, raced, classed and otherwise socio-politically situated nature of language and literacy. Sojourner Truth's signifying[1] critique deconstructed the dominant concept of literacy and linked it to oppression. Constructing language and literacy in her own interest reveals people's ability to create new liberatory futures. Similarly, she deconstructed the concepts of *woman* and *femininity* when she called the question: "Ain't I A Woman?" in her 1851 address at a woman's rights convention in Akron, Ohio, Truth testified that she worked as hard as any man, yet she was a mother who birthed thirteen children and suckled white children of her enslavers. Because the system of white supremacy counted Black people as 3/5ths of a human being and exploited our labor as slaves, Sojourner Truth was not accorded whatever courtesies white men bestowed upon white women; however, she was a powerful, brilliant, and brave woman with knowledge of herself and her worth as a beautiful spiritual human being. "Rather than accepting the existing assumptions about

---

1. In *Talkin and Testifyin*, Smitherman defines Signifying as a Black mode of discourse. In *Talkin That Talk*, she continues it is "the art of ceremonial combativeness" (255) that is often intertextual, and that works as a "sociolinguistic corrective" employed to drive home a serious message without preaching or lecturing." (255)

what a woman is and then trying to prove that she fit the standards, Truth challenged the very standards themselves" (Hill Collins, *Black Feminist Thought* 15).

As this brief introduction has broached engendering literacy, it helps us to see literacy as something that we do (Kynard, *Vernacular Insurrections*), that reflects who we are, the world that we live in, and the ones we (might) create. Engendering literacy education for Black girls and women (and boys and men) is a necessary and important endeavor, for it invites us to invest in people's literacies for brave new worlds of critical collective consciousness and movement for social justice, as opposed to schooling people to literacy for compliance with larger systems of patriarchal domination, social stratification, and individualism. These are the ideas that undergirded an afterschool club for Black middle school girls based on what it means to be Black women and girls as literacy education.

Before delving into the nuts and bolts of the work, what follows is a rationale for the significance and need for this work. Second, I discuss theory and research tenets of African American female literacies (AAFL), out of which principles of "Black Girls Unite" (the after-school club) was envisioned. I move on to set out the Black feminist pedagogical approach that generated our ever-evolving curriculum and praxis. I then describe the afterschool club and its context before sharing a class reading and discussion of a text. A description and critical discourse analysis of the class discussion is offered to provide the reader with an example of a Black girl's critical reading and writing of the world in action.

Rationale

A pressing concern in Black literacy education centers on teaching and learning standardized language and literacy. You know the spiel. Reading and writing are keys to gainful careers, businesses, and equality, or at least a tool in one's survival arsenal. Reading and writing are neutral tools unrelated to issues of power, racism, economic impoverishment, and historical and contemporary disenfranchisement. Reading in our schools is built on the traditional cognitivist paradigm, also referred to by some as "real reading" [as opposed to critical reading or critical literacy], is construed as "decoding, word recognition, and comprehension of 'literal meaning,' rather than in terms of language, literacy and learning as they are situated within multiple sociocultural practices in and out of schools." (Gee, "Critical Issues," 358). One way that dominant groups control the oppressed is through discourse access. Discourse access refers to what can be said, written, heard, and read to/from whom, where, when and how (van Dijk). In other words, the dominant group (rewarded for reproducing colonizing and dehumanizing values) gets to define what reading, language, literacy, and knowledge is valid and worthwhile.

This fact alone aligns education with domination, by and large, promoting one type of reading, writing, and learning among historically and continuously disenfranchised groups: the poor, the dis-preferred or undocumented immigrant, Black, Latinx, Chicano, and Native American. Maisha Winn and Nadia Bihizadeh write:

> It is important to note that by being offered only one version of literacy, students are in effect denied literacy because isolated and irrelevant instruction often fails to result in the development of rich literate practices that are necessary for social and political involvement . . . . Literacy as a civil right really translates into "literacies" as a civil right, including children's right to their own creative and cultural literate practices, academic literacy, which is on the test, and critical literacy, which transcends what can be tested, for example, epistemic writing in which writing becomes "a personal search for meaning." (151) [2]

Needless to say, the National Assessment of Educational Progress (NAEP) shows a disparity of anywhere from 25 to 31 points between the eighth grade reading assessment scores of Black and White students from 1992 to 2013.[3] In "From the Achievement Gap to the Education Debt: Understanding Achievement in U. S. Schools," Gloria Ladson-Billings discusses the ways that poor and of color youth have been denied a quality education diachronically. She argues, "the historical economic, sociopolitical and moral decisions and policies that characterize our society have created an education debt" [as analogous to the national debt that has been accruing for centuries] (5).

There is currently a smoldering of the simultaneous movement of educators, social activists, scholars, and community members. This move-

---

2. Winn and Bihizadeh are quoting Bereiter here, p. 88.

3. US Department of Education, Institute of Education Sciences, National Center for Education Statistics, National Assessment of Educational Progress (NAEP), 1992, 1994, 1998, 2000, 2002, 2003, 2005, 2007, 2009, 2011 and 2013 Reading Assessments. Report generated using NAEP Data Explorer. Http://nces.ed.gov/nationsreportcard/naepdata/

ment demands more adequate and relevant social, political, educational, and economic policies that address oppression, poverty, the new jim crow, the prison-industrial complex, educational failure, and their dire and disproportionate effects on Black people. During President Obama's tenure, My Brother's Keeper (MBK) was established as a gender-focused initiative that came out of (white Jewish Latino) George Zimmerman's exoneration for the killing of the young Black unarmed male teenager Trayvon Martin, and the public outcry that ensued, to send a message that boys of color are in crises. President Obama explained:

> Just to be clear, My Brother's Keeper is not some new, big government program . . . . We can help give every child access to quality preschool and help them start learning from an early age, but we can't replace the power of a parent who's reading to that child. We can reform our criminal justice system to ensure that it's not infected with bias, but nothing keeps a young man out of trouble like a father who takes an active role in his son's life. (7)

Besides some problematic yet sophisticated rhetorical maneuvering that President Obama exhibits in this brief excerpt from his speech to downplay the structural racism surrounding the cycle of oppression that threatens the future lives of Black males, the President goes on to explain that support is forthcoming from private entities and foundations to give Black male youth the foundation they need to change their disproportionate dismal life outcomes.

President Obama also discusses poor children not being ready for kindergarten and how this affects their middle school achievement; how children who struggle to read in third grade are less likely to graduate high school; how Black kids are four times more likely than white kids to be suspended from school, while Latinx kids are two times more likely than white kids. President Obama expounds:

> The plain fact is, there are some Americans who, in the aggregate, are consistently doing worse in our society—groups that have had the odds stacked against them in unique ways that require unique solutions, groups who have seen fewer opportunities that have spanned generations. And by almost every measure, the group that is facing some of the most severe challenges in the 21st century in this country are boys and men of color. (6)

Over one thousand women responded to the President's MBK's males-only-focused approach by signing onto a letter titled "Why We Can't Wait" that was developed by the African American Policy Forum[4]. The excerpt below captures some of the rationale for a gender inclusive racial justice approach:

> Our lives are disproportionately at risk, as data on violent victimization make clear. Native American girls are victims of rape or sexual assault at more than double the rate of other racial groups, while Black girls have the highest rates of interpersonal victimization from assault and are more likely to know their assailant than all other groups. Additionally, the homicide rate among Black girls and women ages 10–24 was higher than for any other group of females, and higher than white and Asian men as well.
>
> Our daughters' access to education is disproportionately compromised. Black girls are more than 3 times more likely to be suspended from school than white girls, and are disproportionately funneled through the juvenile justice systems. This is the first step in a process that leads to the over incarceration of Black women, who are 3x more likely to wind up behind bars than white women. Additionally, the four-year graduation rate for Latinas is the lowest among all girls. Dropping out of high school places all youth at risk, but the negative effects on their long term economic security is even greater for girls than it is for boys. (www.aapf.org/recent/2014/06/woc-letter-mbk)

The letter points to gender and race barriers in the job market, the median wealth for Latinas and Black women ($120.00/$100.00 consecutively). The letter also underscores why the White House Council on Women and Girls (WHCWG) insufficiently addresses the needs of women and girls of color:

> [Like] many gender-focused initiatives on women, [WHCWG] lacks an intersectional frame that would address the race-based challenges faced by young women of color in a racially-strat-

---

4. There was also a separate letter with hundreds of men of color advocating for a gender inclusive racial justice approach to The President's MBK. The African American Policy Forum is co-founded by law professors Kimberlé Crenshaw and Luke Charles Harris as an organization that fights for racial justice, gender equality and human rights nationally and internationally. www.aapf.org.

ified society. We note as well that the scale and magnitude of the issues addressed within MBK are specific to the needs of communities of color. The White House Council on Women and Girls should of course, be encouraged and supported to do more; however, girls and women of color suffer, struggle and succeed with the men and boys in their lives. Only together will our collective well-being improve.

The African American Policy Forum has been spearheading a campaign, which includes television and other social media appearances/blitzing, on and offline forums, and workshops highlighting various people, efforts, and strategies around the country fighting for gender and racial justice. This work promotes awareness of the multiple social forces that perpetuate gendered violence against Black women and girls represented by hashtags such as #SayHerName, #BlackGirlsMatter, #BlackWomenMatter, and #WhyWeCantWait. This movement engenders the fight for racial justice, so that the needs of girls and women are fully addressed, and it works to dismantle institutional and systematic racism for collective empowerment of the Black community as represented in #BlackLivesMatter.

There is a growing body of work in Black girlhood studies, new literacies, and communication studies, to name a few, emphasizing the importance of social approaches to education, literacy and overall well-being (Baker-Bell; Brown, *Black Girlhood Celebration*; *Hear Our Truths*; Cumi, Washington, and Daneshzadeh; Durham; Greene; Kynard; Love; Morris; Muhammad; Muhammad and Haddix; Richardson; Stokes; Winn; Wissman, for example). Common threads in these works are the centering of Black girls and women in their own complex experiences by illuminating their humanity, genius, beauty, and survival/thriving strategies and the identification and discontinuance of practices that devalue them in a racist, sexist, classist, gendered, and otherwise un-free world.

Theoretical Framework

In *African American Literacies* I attempted to map the emergent but not fully codified interdisciplinary field. Therein, I wrote:

> For people of African descent, literacy is the ability to accurately read their experiences of being in the world with others and to act on this knowledge in a manner beneficial for self-preserva-

tion, economic, spiritual, and cultural uplift. African American literacies are ways of knowing and being in the world with others. When we think of African American cultural practices as literacy technologies or literacy practices, we see reading, writing, speaking, storytelling, listening, rhyming, rapping, dancing, singing, computing, phoning, mopping, ironing, cooking, cleaning, performing... among other activities as vehicles for deciphering and applying knowledge of public transcripts to one's environment or situation in order to advance and protect the self. (35)

I traced the development of African American-centered rhetorics and literacies through the eras of enslavement, Reconstruction, "separate but equal" racial segregation, the Harlem Renaissance, the Civil Rights Movement, the Black Power Movement, and Hiphop.[5] I argued that African American experience and culture provides rhetorical models and literacies that demonstrate how Black people have negotiated our existence in a hostile society.

One aspect of this work is a gendered approach demonstrating how Black women and girls successfully negotiate this society from their particular vantage points, with their special ways of knowing, and in the development of language and literacy practices that resist White supremacist, patriarchal, and economically motivated stereotypes conveying subhuman or immoral images. I defined African American female literacies (AAFL) as ways of knowing and acting and the development of skills in vernacular expressive arts and crafts that help females to advance and protect themselves and their loved ones in society. African American females' contribution to knowledge creation should be central in their literacy education and at least seriously engaged in that of others to gain a fuller, more humane, and just understanding of the world.

---

5. Different Hiphop scholars and artists/activists use different spellings and representations of the word. When I use it, I spell it Hiphop. People I am quoting may spell it Hip-Hop, Hip Hop, Hip-hop or hip-hop. As an insurgent scholar, I respect the spellings that circulate in the community of scholars and artists and let them stand as they represent them when I quote them. Though mainstream Hiphop is commodified, its commercialization and standardization has not yet killed vernacular spelling ideology—which means it still reflects the vernacular of the people, and they spell it how they want to.

The lives of Black girls and women is important literacy work. That is the heart of AAFL theory and research. AAFL, as I envision it, is heavily informed by Black feminist thought. As Patricia Hill Collins notes:

> ... [The] legacy of struggle among U. S. Black women suggests that a collectively shared, Black women's oppositional knowledge has long existed. This collective wisdom in turn has spurred U. S. Black women to generate a more specialized knowledge, namely, Black feminist thought as critical social theory. Just as fighting injustice lay at the heart of U. S. Black women's experiences, so did analyzing and creating imaginative responses to injustice characterize the core of Black feminist thought. (*Black Feminist Thought*, 12)

Oppositional knowledge refers to outsider-within status that allows a Black woman or girl to draw on her unique being, background, and standpoint and produce a creative response that opposes dominant ideologies, discourses, and definitions while developing alternative Black feminist worldviews. This knowledge "can take the form of poetry, music, essays, and the like . . ." (Hill Collins 9). As such, Black feminism and AAFL are inextricable and constitute "the particular ways Black women have understood, thought about, and written about the problems of racism and sexism across space and time" (Cooper 34). Black feminism is about loving Black women and girls (Cooper 35).

BlackGirlsUnite

In designing an afterschool site for "urban" middle-school-aged Black[6] girls ("BlackGirlsUnite") that focuses on Black women and girls' lived experiences and representations in society, as critical literacy education, a major question that drove our inquiry was: What does it mean to be a healthy Black woman and/or girl?

BlackGirlsUnite for middle school girls aspired to:

1. Provide gender-specific mentoring and critical cultural literacy experiences for African American girls to meld their knowledge of self, critical social awareness, and self-efficacy.

---

6. I use the terms *Black* and *African American* synonymously here to include all individuals of Black sub-saharan African descent and mixed-race individuals with Black African ancestry living in America.

2. Promote an agentive consciousness of solidarity among African American women and girls as it relates to Black woman and girlhood, critical literacy, and overall well-being.
3. Provide a forum outside of the public sphere for girls and women to discuss and explore our everyday lives while illuminating traditions of Black women's movement.

BlackGirlsUnite sought to center Black girls in historical and contemporary issues and experiences faced by Black women and girls in relation to our everyday lives. Popular culture played a major role because of its massive ability to distribute hegemonic ideas, create discourse, and challenge our identities. Our inquiry-based pedagogy was informed by Hill Collins's ideas about past in present racism or the new racism and its reliance on mass media and popular culture to disseminate the semblance of democracy, while promoting consumption and compliance (*Black Sexual Politics*, 17). In other words, our quest is to bring to the surface our struggles against the new racism in our everyday lives. Hill Collins argues that we must pay attention to the ways that the new racism takes gender specific forms, that we must also pay close attention to the politics of gender and sexuality and Black popular culture as a site of struggle and contestation.

Pough's discussion of Hiphop feminism and the connection between past and present Black women's agendas aligns with Hill Collins's ideas of past in present struggles and was a background for our activities:

> The black feminist and womanist agendas are agendas that hiphop feminists, the majority of whom are black women share with their foremothers who saw their struggles with gender oppression as intimately connected to their struggles with race and class oppressions. They were women whose agendas kept firmly in sight the survival of the entire people. A hip-hop state of mind—one that freely samples, mixes, and remixes—influences the theoretical underpinnings of hip-hop feminism as well as the activism of hip-hop feminists. (79)

Pough encourages Hiphop feminist literacy, which actively opposes sexism, misogyny, homophobia, complicity in inequality and oppression. Hiphop feminist literacy promotes dialogue on issues of relationships between Black women and men, health, social justice, and overall well-being.

In continuing to sample, remix, and incorporate Black feminist ideas, BlackGirlsUnite strives for unapologetically Black feminist pedagogy. Black feminist researchers have observed the implicitly and explicitly political character of Black feminist teaching. Themes of Black feminist women teachers include: "Teaching as a Lifestyle and a Public Service, Discipline as Expectations for Excellence, Teaching as Othermothering, Relationship Building, and Race, Class, and Gender Awareness" (Dixson, 225). Further, Black women's pedagogy comprises womanist themes of Activism, Caring as a key force for activism, and Lifelong human development. Womanist approaches value women's individuality, recognize women's central contributions to survival and transcendence of their communities, validate Black women's mother wit, and offer counternarratives to hegemony (Beauboeuf Lafontant).

Following Hiphop and Black feminist pedagogues, as a Black woman with a legacy of Black girlhood, I am simultaneously facilitator, co-learner, and participant with the girls because they have a lot to teach me about their experiences of Black girlhood and womanhood. I am passionate about making the girls conscious of their power and potential. I was traumatized by a fight my parents had when I was around five and then by a rape at age thirteen, which led to me being plagued by low-esteem and then being recruited into teenage sex-trafficking by my first boyfriend. I grew up in a noninsulated, poverty-stricken Black community. I struggled to find myself, nurture my intellect, and love myself. My research and outreach are about me. Through learning with the girls, I learn more about myself and how to be part of the village of Black girl love and the black girl movement. I want to be part of dismantling the sexism, racism, and classism that has cut off so many Black girls' lives. These ideologies undergird BlackGirlsUnite.

Context/Participants

This piece is part of a larger study in a large Midwestern city school district in a predominantly poor working-class Black community. At the time of this study, the school that sponsored our club served 520 students. Ninety-three percent were on free or reduced lunch. The school was 100 percent Title I due to high poverty. The demographic make-up of the school community was 92.5 percent African American, 3.5 percent Hispanic, 2.5 percent Caucasian, and 1.5 percent "Other." For the 2012–2013 school year, the school reported that 55.5 percent of its Black seventh graders read at the proficient level or above. Participants in the study ranged in age from 11 to 14 years old and are in grades 6 thru 8. During year one, I recruited participants on Back to School Night, where I handed out fliers and gave information to girls and their parents. In subsequent years, some of the girls from the previous year returned, as well as new girls whom the school counselor recommended. The core of regular participants is about twelve, but numbers vary from 8–16 girls for our weekly two-hour sessions. I am a participant observer in the club and lead mentor. Numbers of mentors change from year to year, with two community members who are Black women, three undergraduate Black women, and graduate students of varied racial, gender, and class backgrounds participating in years one and two. However, one Black female graduate student became the most dedicated and the two of us were the only two adults in years three and four. I collected as data, field notes, journal entries, poems, essays, drawings composed by the participants, audiotapes of interviews with the girls, and videotapes of our sessions and transcriptions.

CONTENT

A theme in our discussions centered around what we needed to be healthy Black women and girls. Basically, we studied ourselves in everyday life, the ways we are represented to ourselves in popular culture. We studied other Black women and girls' lives, such as Waangari Maathai, Shirley Chisholm, Flo Kennedy, Queen Amina, and Michelle Obama. We also watch documentaries such as the *Life and Times of Sara Baartman*; *The Souls of Black Girls*; *A Girl Like Me*; *How to Be a Pop Star*; *We Need to Talk: A Message to Our Daughters*. We watched music videos, snippets of shows and documentaries on YouTube, and TV commercials. We discussed images of young Black women in magazines, on TV, in film, and online. We talked about our mothers, fathers, sex (kinda), boyfriends, husbands, families, our aspirations and dreams. The girls wrote journal entries and interviewed and debated each other and me. Some of the girls made videos, artwork, and poetry. Most of our discussions took place in a circle, and most of the girls had no problem offering their experiences and ideas. At the beginning of each session, we enjoyed refreshments, mingled, and played a game, before getting into our set agenda of a chosen text, video clip, or discussion item, but we also let our time together flow as the spirit led.

In the following section, I offer a brief critical discourse analysis of one of our year two discussions, which was prompted by our reading about the ancient West African Queen, Amina. The brief reading underscored Amina's exemplary military and economic prowess. She was known as the Queen who ruled like a man because, among other acts, after defeating a people and gaining their spoils she'd have her way with a man of her choice and behead him when she was done. After the reading, the floor opened for comment and discussion. I offer this example to demonstrate how the space can open creative intellectual opportunities for girls to speak back to texts, reflect to ideas of womanhood and girlhood, and to consider what it means to create critical black literacies.

CRITICAL DISCOURSE ANALYSIS

As an applied linguist, I use critical discourse analytical perspectives as they complement new literacies studies' focus on examining the ways people make language (and other acts of identity) work to (re)construct, maintain, negotiate, and/or resist identities/situations, or oppressions. In *An Introduction to Discourse Analysis*, Gee calls this recognition and enactment work. Gee's discussion of discourse and critical literacy in *Social Linguistics and Literacies* aligns with my quest to identify empowering and liberatory acts of literacy and meaning- making, as he states that literacy is powerful when we can use it as a "meta-language or a meta-Discourse . . . for the critique of other literacies and the way they constitute us as persons and situate us in society" (144). Gee explains that this liberating literacy "is a particular use of Discourse (to critique other ones), not [necessarily] a particular Discourse" (177). Gee's theorization also aligns with our focus on engendering literacy education for Black girls and women as investment in their literacies for brave new worlds of critical collective consciousness and movement for social justice, rather than compliance with larger systems of patriarchal domination. The present analysis focuses on agentive creative knowledge making moves for liberating literacy and what I have called critical literacies of Black girlhood. The critical discourse analyst seeks to bridge micro-level language use to macro-level social structure to explain and interpret how social discourses and social relations are maintained, reproduced, or challenged (Van Dijk, "Critical Discourse Analysis"). I am looking for ways that students make meaning, paying particular attention to their problematization of practices. In the excerpt below DE=Dr. E, and Odetta is a sixth-grade Black girl.

Excerpt from Class Reading and Discussion of the Queen Who Ruled Like a Man: Healthy Black Womanhood?

> **DE**: It was accepted at that time for a king to uhm... take the spoils from whatever land or country that they had or... whatever people they conquered and they could have their way with them. She went down in history because she ruled like a man. Men were known for taking whatever women they wanted and having their way with them.
> **Odetta**: (6th grader) How is that healthy Black womanhood? She didn't have to kill them.
> **DE**: No, she didn't have to, but the point is that she ruled like a man.
> **Odetta**: But I don't see how that's healthy Black womanhood.
> **Lorain**: (8th grader) What she did was accepted in that kingdom in that land.
> **Odetta**: I don't think it was right. She didn't have to kill them after she had sex with them.
> **Lorain**: She was the queen. She had the right to have sex with them and chop off they heads because they were her prisoners.
> **DE**: So O maybe we need to talk and define for ourselves what we feel is healthy black womanhood. So what are so*meummmm* things that you think healthy Black women should do? So what do you wanna say about healthy Black womanhood?
> **Odetta**: uhm, when you are an, if you want to live a healthy Black womanhood you should be able to lead people in the right path. You shouldn't do something just because it's ok.
> **DE**: Does everybody agree with that?
> **Community**: yes.

CRITICAL LITERACIES OF BLACK WOMANHOOD

The clause "It was accepted..." is foregrounded in the structure of the facilitator's utterance. As the lead clause of the subject of the utterance, this bit of language gives prominence to the ideas introduced later in the utterance (take spoils from... people... and have... way with them).

The utterance does not foreground the people who are acted upon. The king is the only actor in the utterance. In these ways, the discourse positions the hearers/readers to endorse the idea that kings have the right to conquer and dispossess people of their property, their bodies, their lives. Similarly, the following utterance puts Queen Amina on par with the king because it foregrounds Amina as a revered historical figure: "She went down in history because she ruled like a man." One of my goals for using this reading was to focus the girls on gender norms, to not see them as boundaries to power possibilities. However, in my quest to focus on the social construction of gender (power and violence as maleness), I neglected to focus on the value of human life and rights, thereby reproducing an ideology of dominance rather than contesting it. This perspective is reiterated again in DE2.

This problem is not lost on Odetta, who calls the question (How is that healthy Black womanhood?) that functions more like a declarative statement and is followed by one: "She didn't have to kill them" and again: "But I don't see how that's healthy Black womanhood." Eighth grader, Lorain, takes up the foregrounded line of thought of accepted practice of power and violence as maleness (as my discourse strategies have positioned her to do). Additionally, Lorain shows that she has understood the fullness of my premise—that women can construct themselves as male or de-gender powerful practices such as violence and rape when she states: "She was the queen. She had the right to have sex with them and chop off they heads because they were her prisoners."

By now, I realize that I am not problematizing fully the social construction of gender, and I accept and respect what this sixth grader, Odetta, is putting on the table: that we need to problematize and define healthy Black womanhood for ourselves as I ask O: "So what are *someummmm* things that you think healthy Black women should do?" O's definition is profound and simple: *uhm, when you are an, if you want to live a healthy Black womanhood you should be able to lead people in the right path. You shouldn't do something just because it's ok.*

In putting forth this precept of healthy Black womanhood, Odetta demonstrates a critical reading of not only the literal text, but discourses surrounding the text. Gender ideologies of normativity position elite patriarchal practices in all of the ways they wound and violate as normative. Odetta challenges this. She has created her own healthy Black girl (woman's) discourse that critiques male gendered discourses of power and women's complicity in them. Odetta has kept her eye on the prize so to speak by centering and giving voice to those who were silenced, slaughtered, and conquered in the text, thus demonstrating oppositional knowledge, a core theme in Black feminist thought. Her resistance to patriarchal epistemic hegemony positions her to envision a world in which power is compassion. Odetta's critical reading of the text and context convey her desire for collective humanity, justice, and equity. Indeed, she is taking a stand for healthy Black womanhood.

Final Thoughts

What is interesting about this excerpt from our discussion is that both Lorain (an eighth grader who was a returning participant from the previous year) and I had already read the piece and participated in a discussion the year prior. Lorain asked to read the story of Queen Amina because she enjoyed learning about her. The prior year's discussion focused on Amina's ability to rule like a man and didn't question the hegemonic ideologies and discourses of men's ways of ruling and what that means for Black women. Both Lorain and I at first missed Odetta's critique. Her question: "How is that healthy Black womanhood?" is one that we ask of each other all the time to monitor our thoughts and actions toward each other and life. Odetta uses it to bring wreck, which Pough (2004) defines as a Hiphop discourse practice young women use to open a space for their stance. Lorain continued to try to advance Queen Amina's gender role transgression, while Odetta holds her stance with the statement, "But I don't see how that's healthy Black womanhood." This prompts me to ask Odetta to define healthy Black womanhood. Her phrasing is very important: "if you want to *live* a healthy Black womanhood you should be able to lead people in the right path. You shouldn't do something just because it's ok." Odetta's use of "live" underscores that being a healthy Black woman is not something that you know, it is something that you live, as is critical literacy, as illuminated by Carmen Kynard (*Vernacular Insurrections*). Healthy Black women transcend customs and traditions in search of a collectively higher humanity. Odetta's response brings wreck, and it demonstrates her critical literacy, which includes the ability to use one discourse to critique another. By centering empowering discourses of healthy Black womanhood, Odetta, a sixth grader, analyzes the workings of power and sexual oppression, a theme central to the lives of women and girls.

Our talks and interactions in BlackGirlsUnite are around texts that focus on issues of Black women and girls and are shaped by them. These texts in turn influence how we think about ourselves and subsequently recognize ourselves. In this way, as argued by Fairclough,

> We . . . [can] recognize that texts are involved in processes of meaning making and that texts have causal effects (i.e., they bring about changes) that are mediated by meaning making. Most immediately, texts can bring about changes in our knowledge, beliefs, attitudes, values, experience, and so forth. We learn from our involvement with and in texts, and texturing (the process of making texts as a facet of social action and interaction) is integral to learning. (229)

As I hope to have shown in this brief example, young Black girls are engaged by materials that focus on the lives of Black women and girls. They are able to tease out issues of equity and humanity in a critical womanist manner.

My praxis evolves from a culturally responsive, Black and Hiphop feminist pedagogy. I use qualitative approaches to understand literacies as aspects of social practices developed by individuals who constitute a community of readers. These practices are embedded within teaching/learning spaces and informed by a particular community pedagogy, which focuses upon the social situatedness of Black women and girls, how young Black women are positioned to speak, think and act in particular ways, and to take up or refuse those positions. This tradition, of reading men and nations, laid down by women such as Sojourner Truth, is about creating a just world.

WORKS CITED

African American Policy Forum. "Why We Can't Wait: Women of Color Urge Inclusion in 'My Brother's Keeper,'" *African American Policy Forum*, June 17, 2014, www.aapf.org/recent/2014/06/woc-letter-mbk.

Baker-Bell, April. "For Loretta: A Black Woman Literacy Scholar's Journey to Prioritizing Self-Preservation and Black Feminist-Womanist Storytelling." *Journal of Literacy Research*, vol. 49, no. 4, 2017, pp. 526–43.

Beauboeuf-Lafontant, Tamara. "Womanist Lessons for Reinventing Teaching." *Journal of Teacher Education*, vol. 56, no. 5, 2005, pp. 436–45.
Bereiter, C. "Development in Writing." *Cognitive Processes in Writing*. Edited by L.W. Gregg and E.R. Steinberg. Erlbaum, 1980, pp. 73-93.
Brown, Ruth Nicole. *Black Girlhood Celebration: Toward a Hip-Hop Feminist Pedagogy*, Peter Lang, 2009.
—. *Hear Our Truths: The Creative Potential of Black Girlhood*. U of Illinois P, 2013.
Collins, Patricia Hill. *Black Sexual Politics: African Americans, Gender, and the New Racism*, Routledge, 2004.
—. *Black Feminist Thought: Knowledge, Consciousness and the Politics of Empowerment*. 2nd ed., Routledge, 2000.
Cooper, Brittney. *Eloquent Rage: A Black Feminist Discovers Her Superpower*, St. Martin's Press, 2018.
Cox, Aimee Meredith. *Shapeshifters: Black Girls and the Choreography of Citizenship*. Duke UP, 2015.
Cumi, Kish, Ahmad Washington, and Arash Daneshzadeh. "Standing in Solidarity with Black Girls to Dismantle the School-to-Prison-Pipeline." *Power of Resistance: Culture, Ideology and Social Reproduction in Global Contexts*, edited by Rowhea M. Elmesky, Carol Camp Yeakey, and Olivia Marcucci. Emerald, 2017.
Davis, Kiri, writer and director. *A Girl Like Me*. Reel Works Teen Filmmaking. 2007.
Dixson, Adrienne. "'Let's Do This!': Black Women Teachers' Politics and Pedagogy." *Urban Education*, vol. 38, no. 2, 2003, pp. 217–35.
Durham, Aisha. *Home with Hip Hop Feminism: Performances in Communication and Culture*, Peter Lang. 2014.
Gee, James Paul. *Social Linguistics and Literacies: Ideology in Discourses*. Taylor & Francis, 1996.
—. "Critical Issues: Reading and the New Literacy Studies: Reframing The National Academy of Sciences Report on Reading." *Journal of Literacy Research*, vol. 31, 1999, pp. 355–74.
—. *An Introduction to Discourse Analysis: Theory and Method*. Routledge, 1999b.
Glenn, Cheryl. *Rhetoric Retold: Regendering the Tradition From Antiquity Through the Renaissance*. Southern Illinois UP, 1997.
Greene, Delicia Tiera. "'We Need More 'US' in Schools!!': Centering Black Adolescent Girls' Literacy and Language Practices in Online

School Spaces." *The Journal of Negro Education*, vol. 85, no. 3, 2016, pp. 274–89.

hooks, bell. *Bone Black: Memories of Girlhood*. Henry Holt and Co., 1996.

Kynard, Carmen. "From Candy Girls to Cyber Sista-Cipher: Narrating Black Female Color Consciousness and Counterstories In 'And' Out 'Of School.'" *Harvard Educational Review*, vol. 80, no. 1, 2010, pp. 30–52.

—. *Vernacular Insurrections: Race, Black Protest, and the New Century in Composition-Literacies Studies*. SUNY P, 2013.

Ladson-Billings, Gloria. "From the Achievement Gap to the Education Debt: Understanding Achievement in U. S. Schools." *Educational Researcher*, vol. 35, 2006, pp. 3–12.

Love, Bettina. *Hip Hop's Li'l Sistas Speak: Negotiating Hip Hop Indentities and Politics in the New South*, Peter Lang, 2012.

Maseko, Zola, director. *The Life and Times of Sara Baartman*. Icarus/First Run Films. 1998.

Morris, Monique. *Pushout: The Criminalization of Black Girls in Schools*. New P, 2016.

Morrison, Toni. "Rootedness: The Ancestor as Foundation, An Interview with Mari Evans." *Black Women Writers 1950–1980: A Critical Evaluation*, edited by Mari Evans, Anchor/Doubleday, 1984, pp. 339–45.

Morton, Janks, director. *We Need to Talk: A Message to Our Daughters*. iYAGO Entertainment Group, 2010.

Muhammad, Gholnecsar. "Creating Spaces for Black Adolescent Girls to 'Write It Out!'" *Journal of Adolescent and Adult Literacy*, vol. 56, no. 3, 2012, pp. 203–11.

Muhammad, Gholnecsar, and Haddix, Marcelle. "Centering Black Girls' Literacies: A Review of Literature on the Multiple Ways of Knowing of Black Girls." *English Education*, vol. 48, no. 4, pp. 299–336.

Obama, Barack. "My Brother's Keeper" Reprinted in *Reclaiming Children and Youth*, vol. 23, no. 1, 2014, pp. 5–8.

Painter, Nell Irvin. *Sojourner Truth: A Life, A Symbol*. Norton, 1996.

Pough, Gwendolyn. "What It Do, Shorty?: Women, Hip-Hop, and a Feminist Agenda." *Black Women, Gender, and Families*, vol. 1, no. 2, 2007, pp. 78–99.

Richardson, Elaine. *African American Literacies*, Routledge, 2003.

—. "'She Was Workin' Like Foreal': Critical Literacy and Discourse Practices of African American Females in the Age of Hiphop." *Discourse & Society*, vol. 8, no. 6, 2007, pp. 785–805.

Royster, Jacqueline Jones. *Traces of a Stream: Literacy and Social Change Among African American Women.* U of Pittsburgh P, 2000.

Smitherman, Geneva. *Talkin and Testifyin: The Language of Black America.* Boston, Houghton Mifflin, 1977; reissued, with revisions, Wayne State UP, 1986.

—. *Talkin That Talk: Language, Culture and Education in African America.* Routledge, 2000.

Tokes, Carla. "Representin' in Cyberspace: Sexual Scripts, Self-Definition, and Hip Hop Culture in Black American Adolescent Girls' Home Pages." *Culture, Health & Sexuality*, vol. 9, no. 2, 2007, pp. 169–84.

Truth, Sojourner. "Woman Suffrage." *Black Women in Nineteenth-Century American Life: Their Words, Their Thoughts, Their Feelings*, edited by Bert Loewenberg and Ruth Bogin, Pennsylvania State UP, 1976.

Valerius, Daphne, writer and director. *The Souls of Black Girls.* Femme Noire Productions, 2008, Soulsofblackgirls.com.

van Dijk, Teun. "Principles of Critical Discourse Analysis," *Discourse & Society*, vol. 4, no. 2, 1993, pp. 249–83.

—. "Critical Discourse Analysis." *The Handbook of Discourse Analysis*, edited by D. Schriffrin, D. E. Tannen, and H. Hamilton, Blackwell Publishers. 2001, pp. 352–71.

Winn, Maisha and Nadia Behizadeh. "The Right to Be Literate: Literacy, Education, and the School-to-Prison Pipeline," *Review of Research in Education*, vol. 35, March 2011, pp. 147–73.

Winn, Maisha. "'Betwixt and Between': Literacy, Liminality, and the Celling of Black Girls." *Race, Ethnicity and Education*, vol. 13, no. 4, 2010, pp. 425–47.

Wissman, Kelly. "'Rise Up'!: Literacies, Lived Experiences, and Identities Within an In-School 'Other Space,'" *Research in the Teaching of English*, vol. 45, no. 4, 2011, pp. 405–38.

13 IN THEORY AND PRACTICE: CONSTRUCTING AN EMBODIED FEMINIST RHETORICAL PEDAGOGY

A. Abby Knoblauch

> *What would it mean to read feminists as rhetorical theorists of writing, rather than predominately social theorists? What can this sort of directed reading teach us about writing and rhetoric? And what can we do with what we learn?*
>
> —Laura Micciche

In this chapter, I illustrate how constructing pedagogies rooted in feminist rhetorical theories can provide concrete strategies for feminist pedagogy. In doing so, I revise slightly Laura Micciche's question in the opening epigraph. Moving in a similar vein, I ask, what would it mean to read feminist rhetoricians as theorists of teaching, as guides to pedagogical practice? What can this sort of reading show us about the teaching of writing and rhetoric, especially across difference? And how can we use those theories to make connections—between students, between students and teachers, between students and texts—that count?

Building pedagogical practice from rhetorical theory is not uncomplicated, which might account for the relative dearth of scholarship explicating connections between pedagogical practice and feminist rhetorics or feminist rhetorical theories. As Kate Ronald and Joy Ritchie lament in their collection *Teaching Rhetorica*, "Despite the current energetic conversations about this newly reclaimed body of women's rhetorics and its significant contributions to regendering an understanding of rhetorical history and theory, there's been little documentation or theorizing about its effect on teaching writing and rhetoric" (5). The authors go on to say that we need to recognize how the presence of feminist rhetorics "might affect the kinds of classroom structures, projects, and goals we might create" (5). To that end, in this chapter I offer a strategy for developing what I call *feminist rhetorical pedagogy*: building pedagogical practices rooted specifically in feminist rhetorics and feminist rhetorical traditions.

The construction of pedagogical theory from feminist rhetorics is complicated, but the connection between the two realms is quite clear. While Micciche reminds us that feminist pedagogy itself "is not a discrete set of practices but, much like feminism generally, a flexible basis from which to launch intersectional pedagogical projects," feminist pedagogies do share a number of goals and practices, many of which reflect the foci of feminist rhetorics themselves ("Feminist" 129). Both, for example, work toward social transformation, more equitable distributions of power, and more nuanced approaches to difference. What differentiates feminist *rhetorical* pedagogy from other branches of feminist pedagogy more broadly is a matter of emphasis. What makes such a practice feminist is the emphasis on the connections between the personal and the political, the recognition of unequal power relations and a desire to challenge such structures, as well as an engagement with cultural identities. What makes it *rhetorical* is the explicit attention to often-overlooked discursive and epistemological practices, not only as content (although that might also be true), but also as practice. A pedagogical theory constructed from feminist rhetorics and rhetorical theories makes visible and central ways of meaning-making that are often marginalized within the academy in part because they are often associated with women, with the feminine, and/or with the body. In very practical ways, feminist rhetorics can serve as a theoretical basis for structuring, guiding, and responding to discussions; constructing learning objectives; designing activities and writing projects; and positioning ourselves (and our students) within the classroom. Feminist rhetorical pedagogy, then, might be imagined as one kind of "intersectional pedagogical project" housed under the larger term of feminist pedagogy.

Additionally, practitioners of both realms are concerned with discourse and power, and therefore such theories seem well suited to a college composition classroom. That is not to say, however, that feminist rhetorical pedagogies are suited solely for the college *composition* classroom. In the same way that feminist pedagogies are portable, crossing disciplinary boundaries into fields as seemingly disparate as chemistry, engineering, education, and kinesiology, for example—feminist rhetorical pedagogies might be practiced in any classroom space. However, as many college composition instructors ask students to consider how discursive practices influence social dynamics and systems of power (including how silence functions within the classroom), composition classrooms provide one particularly fruitful arena for illustrating the potential for feminist rhetorical pedagogies.[1]

The development and practice of feminist rhetorical pedagogies also builds on the still-crucial call of Gesa Kirsch and Joy Ritchie to further theorize—and problematize—a politics of location in our work (7). Drawing on the work of Sandra Harding, Kirsch and Ritchie encourage feminist scholars to continuously interrogate our research practices, asking, "What assumptions underlie our approaches to research and methodologies?" (9). I argue that understanding the assumptions that underlie our theories and practices of teaching also helps us work toward a politics of location, reflecting on how "we both affirm the importance of 'location,' and yet understand the limitations of our ability to locate ourselves and others," this time in the classroom (Kirsch and Ritchie 7).

As is true of feminist pedagogies in general, feminist rhetorical pedagogies can take many forms, pulling from a variety of feminist rhetorical theories to structure classroom practice. Because my own goals within the classroom revolve around negotiating difference, I am drawn toward theories that explicitly take that as a focus. In this chapter, I focus on embodied rhetoric as a pedagogical foundation. I take examples from a sophomore-level persuasive writing class that was part of a three-semester teacher-research study on utilizing feminist rhetorical pedagogies. The study was conducted at a mid-sized (just under fifteen thousand students) public university on the East coast with a predominantly white population.[2] Based on the results of this study, I continue to incorporate

---

1. Additionally, as feminist rhetorical pedagogies draw on feminist rhetorics and feminist rhetorical theories, a background in such information is useful for any teacher hoping to practice this approach. The content of the classroom itself is not limited to rhetoric or writing, but some form of communication as a tool for meaning-making would need to be present. I can imagine, however, such practices including discussion, writing, art, dance, and theater, to name a few.

2. This class was an elective writing intensive course within an English department at a mid-sized (approximately 14,800 students) public university on the East coast. IRB #3569. While there are certainly limits to teacher-research, it is well-suited to a self-reflexive project such as this one because of the way it attempts to put theory into practice. John Loughran argues, in fact, that teacher

embodied pedagogy into my classes at all levels. For those teacher-scholars attempting to enact a self-reflexive feminist pedagogy in any class, a pedagogy that interrogates issues of authority, power, and difference in the classroom, I argue that embodied rhetoric offers a productive source from which to develop lived classroom practice.

Embodied Rhetoric

An embodied pedagogy is rooted in theories of embodied rhetoric—a somewhat ambiguous term within composition and rhetoric. While many scholars reference the body, few identify a specifically embodied form of writing or rhetoric. William P. Banks and Jane E. Hindman have provided some of the most concentrated work in this area. In his article "Written Through the Body: Disruptions and 'Personal Writing," Banks attempts to define what he calls "embodied writing"—a form of personal writing that comes *through* the body. Banks argues that we make sense of the world through our bodies, and those bodily impressions are left on the text itself. Embodied writing, for Banks, reflects the movements of the body: "embodied writing hedges because the body hedges, moves in fits and starts, pushes toward puberty and holds back, has days without knee pain and days with. Writing through the body lets writing make the same (often) tentative steps the body does, and as readers, we recognize those movements as metaphors of our own lived experience" (25). Embodied writing, for Banks, reflects the way we understand the world through our own embodied—literally, as creatures in bodies—experience.

Banks uses the term embodied *writing* to talk about the ways our experiences in specific bodies impact our creation and interpretation of knowledge. Jane E. Hindman, on the other hand, uses the term embodied *rhetoric* to refer to writing that "call[s] to the surface at least some of the associations that [our] thinking passes through, associations evoked by [our] gender, race, class, sexual orientation, politics, and so on" ("Writ-

---

research can "begin to address the theory-practice gap that is so often cited as a barrier to progression in teaching and learning" (11). This link between theory and practice is, in part, due to what David Hobson, one of the editors of the collection *Teachers Doing Research,* sees as an attention to "theories-in-use" (8) and "reflection-as-action" (9), both concepts that appeal to me as both a teacher and a researcher, and both concepts that reflect the self-reflexivity that is a core tenet of feminist rhetorical pedagogies more broadly.

ing an Important Body" 104). Building on the work of Banks and Hindman, I have previously defined embodied rhetoric as "the purposeful effort by an author to represent aspects of embodiment within the text he or she is shaping" (Knoblauch 58). Overall, Hindman encourages us to find ways to "mark [the] body's presence" in the text (104). By doing so intentionally and strategically, an embodied rhetor draws attention to the productive epistemological power of the body and makes clearer the situatedness of knowledge itself.

In other words, while most scholars would agree that aspects of one's social identity such as race, class, gender, sexual orientation, ethnicity, and able-bodiedness (among others) influence how a person makes knowledge, embodied rhetoric asks that the author to discuss *in the text itself* how such facets of embodiment impact knowledge production. That is, embodied rhetoric asks that authors reveal the person behind the proverbial curtain, making explicit the construction of knowledge itself. In this way, embodied rhetoric makes impossible the often-unstated assumption that knowledge comes from a mythical neutral perspective, which Susan Bordo has called "a dis-embodied view from nowhere" (4).

But knowledge *does* come from somewhere, and that somewhere is very much situated in the body. As Banks explains, "it is, quite simply, impossible (and irresponsible) to separate the producer of the text from the text itself. Our belief that we could make such a separation has allowed masculinist rhetorics to become 'universal' in modernist discourses because the bodies producing the discourse have been effectively erased, allowing them to become metonymies of experience and knowledge" (33). In other words, because logic has traditionally been coded male (and white) and emotion has traditionally been coded female (and sometimes non-white), and because "theory" has historically been the realm of privileged white males, this attempted (textual) bodily erasure presumes that "any *body* can stand in for another," thereby negating the importance of bodily and experiential difference in the creation of knowledge (Banks 38). Embodied rhetoric, on the other hand, (re)inscribes the body onto the page, textually (re)connecting logic and emotion, mind and body, and making clear the role of social identity factors such as race, class, gender, size, age, able-bodiedness, and sexual orientation in knowledge production. So, what might an embodied pedagogy actually look like?

Embodied Pedagogy

An embodied pedagogy translates this feminist rhetorical theory into teaching practice by foregrounding the epistemological importance of material and embodied difference(s). Yet, while embodied rhetoric itself is situated on the page, pedagogy cannot be limited to the acts of writing and reading. An embodied pedagogy, then, takes the textual inclusion of aspects of embodiment as its foundation but expands beyond the act of writing. By challenging the belief that material bodies are—or should be—outside of the realm of knowledge production, an embodied pedagogy brings material and cultural differences to the forefront in writing, in reading, in discussion, in interpretation of all kinds of texts and materials, asking at every turn that students examine "their experiences as reflections of ideology and culture," and move beyond any statement of embodied experience as if it exists outside of social norms and narratives (Kirsch and Ritchie 8). By reflecting on the interplay of bodies, ideology, epistemology, and language, an embodied pedagogy continually calls into question the disembodied view from nowhere and the notion of knowledge as a value-free commodity one simply acquires or attains. It moves beyond statements of embodied location to examine how that embodiment actually shapes (and hides) knowledge.

To achieve these goals, an instructor practicing an embodied pedagogy draws students' attention to the following:

- to lived experience and embodied social positionalities (education, personal histories, identity markers, etc.) of both teacher and students to better recognize the situatedness of knowledge creation and interpretation.
- to both the power and limits of such situated knowledge by putting different embodied experiences, subjectivities, stories, etc. into conversation with each other. This might take the form of classroom discussion, assigned readings, student writing, or a combination thereof.
- to the embodied *responses*, physical and emotional, of both teacher and student in order to examine how those responses contribute to practices of meaning-making.

While a pedagogy based in embodied rhetoric illustrates that meaning is not something that is "out there," but is instead made through the body, this does not mean that knowledge is *solely* individual. Rather, the idea is that the individual in society is constantly constructing meaning from norms and expectations swirling around embodied social positionalities such as (but not limited to) gender, race, sexuality, able-bodiedness, and size. Yet, meanings are also not housed in "subject matter," an assumption students often make that presumes meaning is transparent and fixed—there to be found. Instead, through an embodied pedagogy an instructor pays particular attention to students, teachers, and authors as people *in bodies* who construct meaning in rhetorical interaction of text, body, and social and discursive expectations. By calling attention to how her response is conditioned by the experience of living in her particular body, feminist teacher-scholar Madeleine Grumet believes that "cultural norms and assumptions . . . [can] be identified, investigated, challenged, and changed" (253). Further, if we claim, interpret, voice, and embody our subjectivities, "we cannot continue to gather together in classrooms behaving as if each of us is there alone" (Grumet 255). Instead, an embodied pedagogy asks that we gather together in recognition of our differences, working to illustrate how meaning is created, not simply found, in an effort to communicate effectively across the spaces between us.

The Instructor's Body

It is important to ask students to recognize how their own embodied experiences contribute to the act of producing meaning, not simply claiming understanding; however, as with all good teaching, it is important that the instructor do this work as well. In fact, in the context of embodied pedagogy, it is crucial that the instructor model this form of embodied thinking, as doing so helps to complicate traditional notions of teacherly authority—a goal of many feminist teachers. Pointing out the process of the teacher also making meaning through the body challenges the perception of the teacher as the-one-who-knows. Instead of imagining that the teacher is the authority, students may begin to see the teacher as sometimes claiming or performing authority, and, at other times, choosing not to do so. This approach makes clearer that authority and power are sometimes earned, sometimes conferred, and often complicated. Drawing attention to the relationship between bodies and authority can also clarify that access to such power is not equally distributed, even in the classroom space. Finally, drawing attention to bodies themselves can highlight how thinking is often (perhaps always) done through the body.

Allow me to clarify with an example. The following is a story I shared with my undergraduate persuasive writing classroom. One morning I was third in a line of four people waiting to get onto a campus shuttle. When I boarded, there was only one seat left (and one more person behind me). So, I made my way to the open space at the back of the bus and stood, allowing the person behind me to take the final open seat. As we were about to depart, the young man in front of me turned around and offered me his seat. I thanked him, but declined.

I tell this brief story to my students when we start talking about the differences bodies can make in meaning-making. This young man was generous, offering his seat to me. It was a polite gesture and, I think, a sincere one. It is one of those moments where I have hope for the future, if nice young men like this are in it.

Except . . .

I start to wonder *why* he offered me his seat. Would he have made the same offer if I were a man? Is it because he thinks I'm his elder? (I am, but at that point I wasn't that much older.) Because he thinks I'm *pregnant*? And this is the part where my students start to get a little uncomfortable, because now we're talking very specifically about the fact that my body is a heavy one. Most of the young women in my undergraduate classes are thin and/or athletic. I do not look like them.

No, my students assure me, he was just being polite. You offer your seat to a woman.

Yes. Right. But why is that, I ask? Why is it polite? They're not sure. Who do we give our seats to, I ask? Women who are pregnant, the elderly, those who struggle to stand. People who probably need to sit down. Do I need to sit down simply because I'm a woman? Am I not capable of standing under my own power?

Now I'm over-reacting, they say. This poor guy was just trying to be nice and look what I'm doing to that gesture. I'm over-thinking this. Over-analyzing. Just let it *be*, they tell me.

But, of course, I can't. I can't in part because it's who I am; it's the way I've been trained to think. But I also can't because it's *who I am*. In a heavy woman's body that's between thirty and forty years old, I process this gesture differently than I did when I was younger and when I was thinner. The body I'm in, I tell them, pushes me to read this situation differently than I used to, and differently than many of them read it during our discussion. Many of the young women in my class say they have had a seat offered to them. I ask them if they've ever wondered in those moments if the person offering the seat thinks that they're an elder. They say no. Pregnant? Not usually. Do you wonder if he's hitting on you? Often. I don't: he's probably not hitting on me. Not me. Not in this body. I ask the young men if anyone has offered their seat to any of them. No. I ask them if they, themselves, would offer their seats to another man. No. To a woman? Generally, yes.

Tell me, then, that the body doesn't matter. That our reactions to it and our responses in it don't inform our thoughts and actions, our thinking about the world.

In classroom moments like these, I draw my students' attention to the fact that I have a body, one that is visually quite different from their own, *and that I make knowledge through that body*. My response to this young man on the shuttle has so much to do with my own insecurities about my particular body in this culture: gendered female, overweight, aging. Their responses to this situation might have been similar or drastically different and part of what informs those responses, I argue, is the body in which each of them moves through the world. Of course, part of that thinking comes from social constructs, from education, from past experiences, but I echo Banks when I say that I make sense of all of these things through my body. This approach also allows me and my students to interrogate those social assumptions, as Grumet argues, by revealing them in very specific and concrete ways *as* social assumptions about bodies: the way bodies are read, responded to, made meaning of, and the way that bodies, in return, read, respond, and make meaning. This example also illustrates how an embodied response—a gut reaction, a sinking feeling—can contribute to complex knowledge.

Finally, moments such as these show that multiple interpretations of the same experience are possible. In this particular story, there are a number of alternative and equally valid readings based on the experiences of different bodies as they move throughout the world. This young man was, I believe, trying to be polite. He was not attempting to enact some sort of performance of masculine superiority. Yet, it can be read that way. And it can be read as polite. At the same time. And *his* reading of this moment would probably differ markedly from my own, which does not make either of us *de facto* wrong.

Of course, embodied rhetoric and embodied pedagogy pushed too far can venture into the realm of relativism, where one stance is as valid as another. Yet, the same could be said for an inattention to the body, which has led us toward the assumption that, as Banks says, any body can stand in for any other body, thereby erasing difference and perpetuating the belief that there is simply an unmarked knowledge available for the claiming. Similarly, Bernadette Calafell, citing the influence of Cherie Moraga and Gloria Anzaldúa's "theories of the flesh," reminds us that access to such knowledge has never been equal or uncontested. Calafell explains that attention to bodies and difference has provided one way for women of color to create theory, particularly when "denied access to traditional forms of knowledge production" (105). An embodied pedagogy, then, not only makes a concerted effort to draw students' attention to how physical bodies and lived experience shape the varied constructions of knowledge, both within the classroom space and in the larger world, but also asks us to consider whose voices are often most-easily heard (or listened to or found persuasive) and what forms of knowledge are often silenced or dismissed.

As scholars such as Calafell, Moraga, and Anzaldúa illustrate, the relating of embodied experience is one way that women of color have been able to construct theory when denied access to the academy. Yet, personal and embodied experience is also one of the ways different bodies and voices are silenced. In practicing an embodied pedagogy, then, it is important to ask that students think about how their experiences speak to one another, moving in a recursive way back to the specific bodies that speak. In short, I ask that students listen for how our embodied experiences intersect, overlap, contradict, support, silence, and/or engage with other embodied experiences. For example, in the story I related, I point to how different embodied experiences generate different interpretations, and we create lists of possible interpretations of this moment (politeness; gender expectations; assumptions about age, the pregnant body, the fat body, etc.), discussing the social implications of such knowledge and the limits of interpretation. In doing so, I exemplify for students how I make knowledge through my body (and illustrate the fact that professors, too, *make* knowledge rather than simply *have* knowledge) as a way to help prepare them to recognize their bodies as sources of knowledge. I then ask them to consider the inclusion of such situated knowledge production in discussions and in written texts.

STUDENT WRITING

To that end, I turn now to a more pointed look at students' written work and, in this case, how embodied experience and embodied rhetoric function within student writing. For this assignment, I asked students to write what I called an embodied rhetorical analysis. Students analyzed pieces of writing in which authors drew on aspects of embodiment to persuade. Additionally, students analyzed how their own embodiment shaped their responses to that argument and how they were able to make sense of the text.[3] One piece students analyzed was sportswriter Tony Kornheiser's "Women Have More to Say on Everything." I chose this piece (among others) because Kornheiser makes specific reference to gendered bodies and language, arguing that women speak more often than men. He goes on to say that women are more likely to be proficient in language and men more proficient in math. I hoped that Kornheiser, known in part for his often-incendiary comments, might spark an embodied response in my students, helping them draw on their own bodies as sources of knowledge-production. Many students had just such a reaction.

In order to help students put bodies and experiences into conversation with each other, rather than seeing individual experiences as statements of fact, I asked them to read through the drafts they had brought to class and then free write for a few moments, first exploring more fully how their own gendered experiences might be affecting the meaning they were creating from these texts. One student, Miles, made the connection between his own body and the social expectations around it, writing:[4]

> I'm a guy, so I'm not supposed to like to read and I'm not supposed to talk to [sic] much. Guys are better if there [sic] the strong and silent types. My guy friends say girls talk to [sic] much and I agree because I'm suppose [sic] to but if I'm being honest I wish we would talk more. I don't think my friends that are guys are really good friends because they don't know much about me because we don't talk much. But if I told them how much I talk to a few of the girls I know, they'd say I was gay. So when I read Tony's story [sic], I know what he means because that's how my life is, but I also think that if it was okay to talk more as a guy, I would. Maybe its [sic] not about being in a body

---

3. This was an incredibly complicated assignment for students in a sophomore-level writing course, and there were varying levels of success. I have, however, continued to hone this assignment and it is now a regular activity in my upper-level undergraduate courses and my graduate courses in rhetorical theory and practice.

4. All student names are pseudonyms.

that's male, but about what people expect of you because your [sic] in that body.

Here, Miles not only meditates on cultural expectations of gender, but also on how living in a body that's coded male impacts his reading of Kornheiser. He understands Kornheiser's point because "that's how my life is"—it reflects portions of his experience as a male in this society—but he also sees other possibilities based on the way he wishes he could comfortably act, regardless of his gendered body.

This focus on personal experience, so clearly rooted in the body, can be a difficult trap to move beyond. Students are all too happy to offer their own experiences as irrefutable evidence that differing views are wrong. Instead, an embodied pedagogy asks that we push toward a fuller understanding of how experience itself is constructed, and how experience is linked to the body. Then, we must ask how an embodied experience affects all of our angles of vision, allowing us to see in particular ways but leading us to ignore other ways of being and knowing. I therefore asked that students next free write about other situations where their experiences and embodied responses made it easier or more difficult for them to really *hear* a claim or another's experience. Instead of imagining how they might *refute* a claim, as they were often doing with Kornheiser, I asked that they think about how their own embodiments might have affected their interpretation of the moment itself. Ella wrote about how growing up as a woman made it difficult for her to really hear Kornheiser:

> I want to argue with him because he's talking about me and he doesn't know what it's like to be me. As a woman I find it hard to even listen to him when he seems to be saying that all women talk too much and that's a bad thing. If I were a guy it would probably be easier for me to agree but that makes me mad, too. Because guys make these assumptions about girls and make fun of us. All girls do X. All girls talk too much. All girls are shallow. I guess now I'm making assumptions about guys which I shouldn't do if I'm going to be mad that guys do that to girls. I should try to read Tony again because maybe he's not saying its [sic] bad that girls talk too much. Maybe he wishes he could talk more. But I hear that all the time [that girls talk too much] so it makes me mad and then its [sic] hard to read the rest.

In this moment, I hear a student who is beginning to understand the way her own embodied experiences shape her encounters with a text she does not agree with. She explores the sources of that disagreement, and how living in her particular body influences her making meaning of this text. She also is starting to recognize how that experience might limit her interpretation, making it harder to imagine alternative viewpoints.

What's particularly interesting to me in this moment is how Ella imagines that Kornheiser might actually wish he were socially authorized to talk more, imagining how living in a different body might impact Kornheiser's argument and even desires.[5] Perhaps even more important, however, is this student's willingness to reread the argument, keeping in mind how her own embodied experience might have made her respond too quickly to the argument itself. This is not to say that she needed to change her mind or her response, but being aware of how her own gendered experience affects potential interpretations of any text—written, verbal, even musical or theatrical—can lead to deeper, more complex understandings.

Additionally, while drawing attention to the ways knowledge is made through the body, an embodied pedagogy makes more visible the power-dynamics swirling around those bodies. It can draw attention to how some bodies are authorized to speak and create knowledge and how others are dismissed or silenced, sometimes solely because of the bodies they inhabit. Recognition is hardly a solution, of course, but by making more evident processes that are often invisible and silent/silenced, an embodied pedagogy attempts to reach outward, body to body, knowledge to knowledge, even as we recognize that such knowing and connecting is always partial and often fraught.

I include these particular examples because they are some of the students' first attempts to grapple with how the experience of living in their own bodies affects their responses to texts. Throughout the course, I continued to encourage students to consider how being bound by their own particular bodies, their own particular skin, shaped their understandings of texts, of each other, and of the larger world. Students and I also practiced listening rhetorically and responding invitationally to texts; throughout all of these processes, I asked that students pause to recognize how seeing the world through the eyes of their particular bodies made some claims seem more immediately valid than others, or made

---

5. As a class, we also had a brief discussion on the fact that Kornheiser writes and talks for a living, something he does, in fact, mention.

some identifications easier than others. For example, when we discussed and wrote about a recent controversy on campus that involved the consistent playing of the racist and sexist song "Black Betty" at one athletic team's events,[6] students analyzed how their own embodied (racial) positionalities made certain viewpoints easier or more difficult to hear or understand, certain identifications easier or more difficult to make. In so many ways, this is what we want for and of our students—to be able to hear divergent claims and responses in complex and deeper ways. An embodied pedagogy is one way to help students achieve that goal, particularly when embodied differences might be influencing their responses.

CONCLUSION

Embodied pedagogy is, of course, only one potential approach to helping students recognize and negotiate differences.[7] Yet, embodied rhetoric takes difference as epistemologically central to knowledge construction, and therefore provides concrete strategies for feminist teacher-scholars to more explicitly make clear to students that neither experience nor knowledge are universal, that knowledge is situated and shifting, and that understanding is not something we find out there, it's something we create.

Furthermore, if one believes, as I do, that the values of feminist rhetorics can help better communicate across difference, then a pedagogy that takes those values not only as content, but also as practice, helps reinforce the importance of such cross-cultural communication, especially within the classroom. Additionally, the classroom space itself becomes a transparent site of feminist rhetorical theories and practice without (necessarily) being a class *about* feminist rhetorics, as is the case when I ask students to be self-reflexive in analyzing the impact of their own embodied positionalities. At its heart, all feminist pedagogy *is* feminist rhetoric;

---

6. See Asmar for a description of the controversy.

7. I have written elsewhere on a pedagogical approach rooted in Sonja Foss and Cindy Griffin's theory of invitational rhetoric, answering the call made by Glenn to further engage and explore this specific theory (*Unspoken* 154-57). Additionally, the contributors to the collection *Silence and Listening as Rhetorical Arts* have begun work on what Glenn calls the "tantalizing" possibilities for further considerations of Krista Ratcliffe's theory of rhetorical listening. The pedagogical turn—made first by Ratcliffe herself in *Rhetorical Listening*—within this collection points toward the interest in more explicitly connecting feminist rhetorical theories and pedagogical practices.

feminist rhetorical pedagogies, however, make more explicit the theories that inform our teaching lives.

Finally, it is important to note that, indeed, we are public figures as scholars, researchers, and authors, but we are also public figures as teachers, and, as this chapter illustrates, our teaching itself shapes the future of the field. To more purposefully reflect our rhetorical commitments within our pedagogical practices highlights the myriad impacts of feminist rhetorical theories—in communicating across difference; in uncovering the previously unseen, unheard, un(der) valued; in speaking out; in listening well; and in teaching the next generation of teacher-scholars to do the same.

Works Cited

Asmar, Melanie. "UNH's 'Black Better' bam-ba-lams its last." *Concord Monitor*, 4 Feb. 2006.

Banks, William. "Written through the Body: Disruptions and 'Personal' Writing." *College English*, vol. 66, 2003, pp. 21–40.

Bordo, Susan. *Unbearable Weight: Feminism, Western Culture, and the Body*. U of California P, 1993.

Calafell, Bernadette M. "Rhetorics of Possibility: Challenging the Textual Bias of Rhetoric through the Theory of the Flesh." *Rhetorica in Motion: Feminist Rhetorical Methods & Methodologies*, edited by Eileen E. Schell and K. J. Rawson, U of Pittsburgh P, 2010, pp. 104–17.

Glenn, Cheryl. "CCCC Chair's Address: Representing Ourselves, 2008." *College Composition and Communication*, vol. 60, no. 2, 2008, pp. 420–39.

—. *Unspoken: A Rhetoric of Silence*. Southern Illinois UP, 2004.

Grumet, Madeleine. "Afterword: My Teacher's Body." *The Teacher's Body: Embodiment, Authority, and Identity in the Academy*, edited by Diane P. Freedman and Martha Stoddard Holmes, SUNY Press, 2003, pp. 249–58.

Hindman, Jane E. "Writing an Important Body of Scholarship: A Proposal for an Embodied Rhetoric of Professional Practice." *JAC*, vol. 22, 2002, pp. 93–118. Accessed 17 Nov. 2013.

Hobson, David. "Action and Reflection: Narrative and Journaling in Teacher Research." *Teachers Doing Research: The Power of Action Through Inquiry*. 2nd ed., edited by Gail Burnaford, Joseph Fischer, and David Hobson, Lawrence Erlbaum Associates, 2001, pp. 7–27.

Kirsch, Gesa E., and Joy S. Ritchie. "Beyond the Personal: Theorizing a Politics of Location in Composition Research." *College Composition and Communication*, vol. 46, no. 1, 1995, pp. 7–29.

Knoblauch, A. Abby. "Bodies of Knowledge: Definitions, Delineations, and Implications of Embodied Writing in the Academy." *Composition Studies*, vol. 40, no. 2, 2012, pp. 50–65.

Kornheiser, Tony. "Women Have More to Say on Everything." *Dialogues: An Argument Rhetoric and Reader*. 5th ed., edited by Gary Goshgarian and Kathleen Krueger, Pearson Longman, 2006, pp. 440–42.

Loughran, John. "Teacher as Researcher: The PAVOT Project." *Learning from Teacher Research*, edited by John Loughran, Ian Mitchell, Judi Mitchell, Teachers College P, 2002.

Micciche, Laura R. "Feminist Pedagogies." *A Guide to Composition Pedagogies*. 2nd ed., edited by Gary Tate, Amy Rupiper Taggart, Kurt Schick, H. Brooke Hessler, Oxford UP, 2014, pp. 128–45.

—. "Writing as Feminist Rhetorical Theory." *Rhetorica in Motion: Feminist Rhetorical Methods and Methodologies*, edited by Eileen E. Schell and K. J. Rawson, U of Pittsburgh P, 2010, pp. 173–88.

Ratcliffe, Krista. *Rhetorical Listening: Identification, Gender, Whiteness*. Southern Illinois UP, 2005.

Ronald, Kate, and Joy Ritchie, editors. "Introduction: Asking 'So What?': Expansive Pedagogies of Experience and Action." *Teaching Rhetorica: Theory, Pedagogy, Practice*, Boynton/Cook Heinemann, 2006, pp. 1–12.

14 Teaching Interpretive Agency: Introducing Constructed Potentiality into Rhetorical Training

Sonja K. Foss and Karen A. Foss

Because rhetoric enables individuals to exert influence in the world, rhetoric and agency are seen to be inextricably linked. Conventional rhetorical training is designed to enhance students' ability to impact the world by learning to develop and present messages that reflect the best choices among available means of persuasion. Because such training is designed to give students "the confidence and power to speak out" (Steinitz and Kanter 159) and "the competence to speak or write in a way that will be recognized or heeded by others in one's community" (Campbell 3), its goal is effective participation in the public sphere.

The rhetorical agency currently taught in rhetoric courses derives from a particular paradigm or model of change. In this paradigm, which we elsewhere have labeled the *paradigm of constricted potentiality* (Foss and Foss, "Constricted" 206), the rhetor's focus is on external, material resources such as people, policies, and organizations that are fixed, tangible, and therefore constricted. Agents in this paradigm attempt to persuade those they perceive as responsible for the undesirable condition they seek to change, and effectiveness is measured by whether a change occurs in material conditions.

The introduction of feminist theory into the academy and into rhetorical studies offered us a glimpse into a paradigm of change different from the conventional one. In Cheryl Glenn's words, the theories and rhetorical practices we encountered in feminist theory seemed to shake "the conceptual foundations of rhetorical study itself" (*Rhetoric* 10). Our theorizing of invitational rhetoric (Foss and Griffin; Foss and Foss, *Inviting*), which we developed from feminist principles, suggested that alternatives to persuasion exist for generating change. Another hint of an alternative paradigm came when we wrote a book on feminist rhetorical theories (Foss, Foss, and Griffin), a project in which we encountered the work of theorists such as Sonia Johnson, Sally Miller Gearhart, Gloria Anzaldúa, Starhawk, and bell hooks. They introduced us to perspectives on change that were at odds with and not even acknowledged in the paradigm of constricted potentiality.

A few examples will suggest the kinds of challenges offered by feminist theory to the conventional change paradigm and its attendant theory of agency. Sally Miller Gearhart, for example, sees persuasion as "'a violent act'" (qtd. in Karr 22) because it violates the integrity of the audience: "When we . . . seek to change any other entity," we violate "the integrity of that person or thing and our own integrity as well" ("Womanization" 197). She offers a new definition of rhetoric as the creation or co-creation of an environment or matrix for connecting with and understanding the perspectives of others—"a mutual generation of energy for purposes of growth" ("Womanization" 198).

In contrast to the traditional assumption that if a message is well organized, well supported, and offered by a speaker with high ethos, audience members will be unable to resist the rhetor's persuasive appeal, both Gearhart and Sonia Johnson suggest that messages will be ineffective unless audience members themselves decide to change. The effort "*to change other people doesn't work*," suggests Gearhart ("Notes" 8) because only when people are ready and motivated will they choose to change. Individuals have the right to choose how to live their lives; they are the ones who get to decide when they want to change (Gearhart, "Womanpower"). Johnson sees rhetorical efforts at persuasion as disrespectful to audiences. She trusts that others are "doing the best" they can "at the moment"; all they need "from others in order to get on with their personal work" is "to be unconditionally accepted as the experts on their own lives" (*Ship* 162).

Starhawk's notion of power constitutes another difference between the traditional change paradigm in rhetoric and the new paradigm that was emerging for us as we explored feminist theory. Power is conceptualized in the paradigm of constricted potentiality as power-over, the ability to dominate, which translates into rhetors' efforts to have their perspectives prevail over others. Starhawk's constructions of power-with and power-from-within, however, suggest alternative and more complex views of power that create change by working with others and generating change from within (*Dreaming*).

The glimpses of an alternative paradigm of change suggested by these feminist theorists led us to seek out resources that might elaborate such a paradigm. We reviewed fields such as psychology, peace studies, and quantum physics; Asian, Native American, and African philosophies; various religious and spiritual traditions; and feminist theories that we hypothesized might conceptualize change and agency differently from the traditional rhetorical paradigm. We also revisited theories in the discipline of rhetoric in which the symbolic is privileged over the material, including the Sapir-Whorf hypothesis (Whorf) and social construction (i.e., Gergen; Leeds-Hurwitz; Leeds-Hurwitz and Galanes; Pearce). We labeled the alternative paradigm of change that emerged from these various literatures the *paradigm of constructed potentiality* (Foss and Foss, "Constricted").

In the paradigm of constructed potentiality, change agents focus on symbols as the resources available for their use in the change process—spoken and written words; visual rhetoric; and the thoughts, interpretations, and meanings represented by the symbols. Because of the nature of symbolicity, unlimited resources are available to rhetors in this paradigm: the ways to configure and construct symbols are limitless. Individuals always can generate new words, new metaphors, new stories, and thus new perspectives because of the "literally fabulous nature of symbol using" (Condit, *Why* 2). The potential for change in the paradigm is constructed or invented because change is continually being generated through symbolic resources.

Once we had identified the paradigm of constructed potentiality, we speculated that we might be able to offer our students a more expanded view of agency than they receive in conventional rhetorical training. In addition to knowing the traditional skills of persuasive writing and speaking, we want them to become skilled at using what we call *interpretive agency*, grounded in the paradigm of constructed potentiality. We want them to understand that they can apply a much broader and even more basic form of agency that will enable them to see how their symbolic choices can give them control over and literally change their lives.

Our intent in this chapter is to propose a unit for teaching interpretive agency in rhetoric courses. This unit can be incorporated into courses such as public speaking, composition, rhetorical theory, and rhetorical criticism and is designed to result in a greater sense of personal efficacy on the part of students. We hope that, as a result of the rhetorical training they receive in this unit, students understand how to use their interpretive power to "influence intentionally" their "life circumstances" so they "are not simply onlookers of their behavior" (Bandura 164) but are deliberate and conscious agents who determine the realities in which they live. This approach also provides students with an alternative to traditional persuasion in which domination over others and a devaluation of their perspectives are privileged (Foss and Griffin; Ede, Glenn, and Lunsford). We turn now to an explanation of our proposed unit on interpretive agency.

Course Objectives

We have six learning objectives for a unit on interpretive agency:

1. Discover the power of symbol use;
2. Explain the process of social construction or how symbols create reality;
3. Describe the paradigm of constructed potentiality that undergirds interpretive agency;
4. Identify variations in interpretive strategies across contexts;
5. Practice generating multiple options for interpretation;
6. Use symbols deliberately to create a desired reality.

Instructional Content

The primary content of the proposed unit consists of an explanation of the paradigm of constructed potentiality and the ways individuals' interpretive choices create their realities. The unit also includes a practical element: teaching students various strategies for evaluating and changing their interpretations to create the realities they desire.

Symbolic Nature of Reality

The central idea on which interpretive agency is based is that reality comes into existence through rhetoric; things and ideas are conceptualized and constructed as entities only when a rhetor interprets them and captures that interpretation in a symbol. As individuals interpret and assign meaning to the stimuli they encounter, they symbolically construct the version of the world they inhabit: "In this view, social reality is not a fact or set of facts existing prior to human activity; it is created through human interaction. We create our social world through our words and other symbols and through our behaviors" (Leeds-Hurwitz 7). In an effort to capture this notion, some physicists have described the world as "a ghost world that pops into solid existence each time one of us observes it" (Wolf 184).

INTERPRETATION AS THE KEY STRATEGY FOR CHANGE

Because individuals have choices about how to observe, interact with, and interpret entities and situations, interpretation is the basic mechanism by which individuals manifest the world. Interpretation is "the process by which an individual assigns meaning to data in light of some present concern" (Harper 193). Although individuals always are interpreting the environment around them, the application of interpretive agency involves the conscious and deliberate assignment of meaning to something or someone in order to change what is perceived to be an undesirable condition. The strategy of interpretation is used "to make another choice about what to perceive, how to interpret that perception, and how to frame that interpretation" in order to respond differently to a problematic condition (Foss and Foss, "Constricted" 214). Thus, in an interpretive model of agency, material or structural conditions are not seen as determining; rather, the interpretation of those conditions is what determines their impact on an individual. Any condition becomes a problem to be addressed only when an interpreter chooses to interpret it as something undesirable. Something seen as a problem by one person will not be seen as such by another because they have chosen different interpretations. That individuals are able to create one interpretation "is evidence that they can create another" by choosing new symbols to describe a condition (Foss, Waters, and Armada 225). Anzaldúa aptly describes the capacity individuals have to choose new interpretations: "The life you thought inevitable, unalterable, and fixed in some foundational reality is smoke, a mental construction, fabrication . . . so since it's all made up, you can compose it anew and differently" ("Shift" 558).

An interpretive choice may seem to be an inadequate response to cases of extreme danger such as torture, sexual abuse, natural disasters, or genocide. But individuals have a choice about how to interpret circumstances, even in such cases. By changing the interpretation of a condition, they can make it into something they can tolerate more easily, something that presents them with more possibilities for future action, or something they no longer regard as problematic. The Dalai Lama provides an example of such an interpretive choice concerning a very negative situation for him, his exile from Tibet:

> For example, in my own case, I lost my country. From that viewpoint, it is very tragic. . . . But if I look at the same event from another angle, I realize that as a refugee, I have another perspective. As a refugee there is no need for formalities, ceremony, protocol. If everything were status quo, if things were okay, then on a lot of occasions you merely go through the motions, you pretend. But when you are passing through desperate situations, there's no time to pretend. So from that angle, this tragic experience has been very useful to me. Also, being a refugee creates a lot of new opportunities for meeting with many people. People from different religious traditions, from different walks of life, those who I may not have met had I remained in my country. So in that sense it's been very, very useful. (Dalai Lama and Cutler 173)

Gloria Anzaldúa encapsulated the Dalai Lama's point when she notes, "You can't change the reality, but you can change your attitude toward it, your interpretation of it" ("Shift" 552). Individuals, then, can exercise their power of agency "irrespective of the conditions of their lives" because their power lies in their capacity to interpret conditions and to change their interpretation of those conditions if they choose (Fegan 264).

The adoption of interpretive agency is not a dismissal of serious problems such as genocide, nor is it a claim that changing individuals' attitudes toward genocide will makes it disappear. Rather, in the face of such an event, if rhetors understand and employ interpretative agency, they are more likely to find ways to better address genocide because they are more likely to focus on their resources for action and to feel powerful as agents who effectively can affect such a condition. Even the worst of conditions offers possibilities for new perspectives and new insights to emerge, but if individuals feel powerless in the face of such conditions, they will be unable to recognize and generate the possibilities for creative action that are present in that condition.

Self-Change as the Outcome of Change Efforts

The strategy of interpretation has a different outcome from persuasion in the conventional change paradigm. The audience for interpretation is the self rather than an external audience whom individuals are trying to change with their persuasive skills. Individuals change themselves—the only people they can change and whom they have the right to change. For Johnson, this realization came after years of trying to change, without success, legislators, members of the Supreme Court, the elders of the Mormon Church, and her own children:

> I began to remember how I had these four human beings on this planet who had come right out of my womb—I had created them . . . They were partly me, and we adored each other, we loved each other, we respected each other. . . . And I remember how I had never ever been able to make them do what I wanted from the moment they were born. They really wanted to . . . because they loved me. They tried very hard but they really couldn't do their lives the way I wanted them to. (*Living the Dream*)

Even in loving situations, such as the parent-child relationship, the parent can't change the child even if she is willing. It is the child who drives the change in herself.

Changing the self, however, does not rule out changes in material conditions because "thought forms have a certain power to bring external realities into existence" (Combs and Holland 33). Anzaldúa succinctly summarizes the relationship between self-change and external change when she asserts, "I change myself, I change the world" (*Borderlands* 70). Examples from a variety of contexts support the link between self-change and change in material conditions. Athletic mental rehearsal, for example, has been found to work as well as physical practice for improving performance (Hinshaw; Swets and Bjork). The impact of interpretation on material outcomes has been demonstrated in the area of health as well. For example, studies that show that women who believe they are at risk for heart disease are four times as likely to die from the disease as women with similar risk factors who do not hold such beliefs (Reid). Similarly, a study by Alia Crum and Ellen Langer of hotel maids, who spend their days engaged in physical activity, revealed that sixty-seven percent of the maids believed they did not get any exercise. For these women, their bodies did not seem to benefit from all of their physical activity and seemed more like the bodies of individuals who exercise very little. After the researchers explained to one group of maids the value of their work as exercise, the maids' blood pressure, weight, and waist-to-hip ratio decreased. Their bodies changed, in other words, to align with their perceptions about the amount of exercise they believed they were getting. Although self-change is the objective of change efforts in the paradigm of constructed potentiality, then, that change also can transform material conditions.

Explaining how interpretive choice functions in the paradigm of constructed potentiality provides a starting point for students to learn about and apply specific change strategies. Depending on the amount of time available, instructors can lecture on basic concepts and/or have students read articles and narratives that describe interpretive choice in action.

STRATEGIES FOR CHANGING REALITY

When rhetors decide that the reality they have created is not the one in which they want to live, their rhetorical task is to choose a new interpretation. The strategies we offer students in this unit for applying interpretive agency are reframing, appreciating, focusing on desired outcomes, and enacting.

REFRAMING

Reframing means choosing a different label for what is perceived; it is the process of shifting perspective to view a "situation from a different vantage point" (Dalai Lama and Cutler 172). As Paul Watzlawick, John Weakland, and Richard Fisch explain, reframing

> means to change the conceptual and/or emotional setting or viewpoint in relation to which a situation is experienced and to place it in another frame which fits the "facts" of the same concrete situation equally well or even better, and thereby changes its entire meaning. (95)

Individuals are always selecting interpretive frames for their experiences. In the classroom context, reframing involves students' conscious selection of a new frame to transform an unwanted set of circumstances into something benign, manageable, or palatable. Reframing a *problem* into an *opportunity*, for example, not only makes a condition not a problem but is likely to generate resources and options for action that previously were not available to the rhetor.

An example of reframing is provided by Nat Irvin II in his discussion of the "arrival of the thrivals" within the black community. He suggests that many blacks have shifted from a frame of *survival* to one of *thrival*:

> For blacks, *thrival* represents . . . a transition from seeing oneself and one's community as being the victims of history and oppression. Thrivals have moved from living in a survival mode, fighting for basic human rights, to embracing a new worldview—a renaissance where succeeding generations . . . see themselves as forces capable of *shaping* the future rather than being *shaped* by the forces of the future. (16)

Thrivals, then, are choosing a different interpretation of a history of oppression. They consider their past oppression a gift that "aids them in their drive to succeed in the future" rather than something that holds them back (Irvin 20).

Our example of the thrivals is likely to raise questions for readers and for students about the use of the strategy of reframing by groups with different degrees of privilege and resources. Reframing could be seen as a coping strategy most appropriate for use by individuals who are underresourced or who lack resources such as money and power to make changes in their lives. We suggest that it should not be considered simply a coping strategy; it can substantially improve the lives of those without material resources because such resources are not required to change an interpretation of a situation. In fact, a change of interpretation may be the only viable strategy available to them. Moreover, we do not want to suggest those with conventional resources of privilege do not need to use the strategy of reframing. Particular interpretations of situations can create unhappiness, problems, and misery for those with plenty of money as well as those without because life circumstances are not objective but are "'cognitively processed' . . . construed and framed, evaluated and interpreted, contemplated and remembered" (Lyubomirsky 240).

Appreciating

A second strategy of interpretation that we teach students is appreciating—deliberately choosing to attend to the positive aspects of a person or condition. This strategy is different from the typical conception of appreciation as an expression of gratitude after something good happens.

Instead, it involves a deliberate choice to focus proactively and before the fact on appreciating something or someone. Because every person or condition has many different aspects, finding positive aspects to appreciate is always possible. The process can be as simple as making a list of someone's positive qualities and reviewing it daily to transform an interpretation of the person as problematic into a more positive perception.

Writer Alice Walker offers an example of the transformative potential of appreciation as an interpretive strategy. In the Babema tribe of South Africa, a person whose behavior is harmful or unacceptable to the tribe is

> placed in the center of the village, alone and unfettered. . . . Then each person in the tribe speaks to the accused, one at a time, about all the good things the person in the center of the circle has done in his lifetime. . . . The tribal ceremony often lasts several days. At the end, the tribal circle is broken, a joyous celebration takes place, and the person is symbolically and literally welcomed back into the tribe. (203–04)

The community members appreciate and acknowledge the person's positive qualities rather than focusing on the undesirable qualities, facilitating a change in their perceptions of that individual. As a result, the individual may feel more connected to the community, so this may be a by-product of the strategy of appreciating, but generating such a feeling in the targeted individual is not the primary reason for the ceremony; it is designed to change the other community members' perception of the person.

Focusing on Desired Outcomes

A third strategy available to students for realizing agency is choosing to focus on desired outcomes—on what they want—rather than resisting or opposing what they do not want. Communication is generative; it produces or creates particular realities. Thus, focusing on something and talking about it—even to oppose it—manifests it as reality, so to resist something and to bestow power and energy on it through symbols create more of what is unwanted. Johnson explains, "when we identify ourselves in opposition to something we become its unwitting accomplices. By bestowing the energy of our belief upon it, by acquiescing to it, we reinforce it as reality. The very difficult truth is that WHAT WE RESIST PERSISTS" (*Going* 26–27).

Johnson uses the example of women's efforts to transform patriarchy to illustrate how resistance or opposition produces more of the unwanted condition. She imagines patriarchy as a fortress on a hill and explains what women have done to oppose it:

> Looking down the hill a short distance, I saw the women, thousands of them, a huge battering ram in their arms, crying, "We've got to get through to the men! We've got to make them stop! We've got to get them to understand that they're destroying everything!" They run at the gate with the ram. . . . . Over and over again, for five long millennia. (*Wildfire* 16–17)

Behind the gate, however, the men are reinforcing patriarchy in response to the women's actions, so the women unwittingly perpetuate the very thing they are trying to change:

> The men, drunk with adrenalin, are being spurred by the assault to incredible heights of creativity. They have invented bionic metals to reinforce the gate and walls wherever the ram reveals a weak spot, gradually making the fortress impregnable, impenetrable. . . . The assault, by forcing them to strengthen, refine, and embellish the original edifice, serves to entrench patriarchy further with every Whoom! (*Wildfire* 17)

It is the work of women ramming the gate that contributes to the reinforcement of patriarchy. Their form of resistance compounds the unwanted situation.

Choosing to focus on a desired outcome rather than resisting a problematic set of conditions may seem like denying reality or not being honest about real conditions in the world. But individuals never can focus on everything at once. They are always making choices about where to attend in terms of their symbol use. Because there is a limitless number of subjects that can be talked about, individuals necessarily select some realities and deny others every time they choose words to speak and write. As Condit notes, "Any statement about the world is necessarily incomplete. No symbol system (neither mathematics nor natural language nor symbolic logic), can re-present all of the material relations of any bit of material reality" (*How* 42). When individuals think and speak about the domestic violence a woman has endured, for example, they cannot simultaneously be focused on how resilient, accomplished, and happy she is. There is no reason why individuals must choose to focus, from all of the possibilities available, on negative conditions.

A number of well-known programs that focus on undesired behavior are often ineffective. Research has shown that these programs tend to produce more of the unwanted behavior. Scared-straight programs designed to show at-risk kids what prison is like, for example, have been shown to increase criminal activity among those in the programs an average of thirteen percent (Wilson 137); Dollar-A-Day pregnancy-prevention programs that pay teen mothers not to get pregnant result in thirty-nine percent of the participants becoming pregnant (Wilson 125); and students who complete the Drug Abuse Resistance Education (D.A.R.E) program that teaches children about the dangers of alcohol and drugs are more likely to be smoking and drinking by the eleventh grade than students who do not go through the program (Wilson 161–62). These programs are largely ineffective because they emphasize what is not wanted rather than what is. The paradigm of constructed potentiality suggests that a focus on what is desired will more likely create the conditions to bring that about.

ENACTING

Interpretive agency also can be applied using the strategy of enacting, in which students embody a chosen interpretation. Johnson captures the essence of the strategy in her admonition to "live today as you want the world to be" (*Wildfire* 251). For hooks, enacting is a "lived process of interaction" in which individuals make their ideological commitments evident to those around them through their actions (*Outlaw* 241). With the strategy of enacting, conditions do not have to change for individuals to feel differently. They act as if the changes they desire in the world already have occurred: "We *do now* what we want to be doing in the future, we *be now, feel now* how we thought we would be and feel only in some future time" (Johnson, *Wildfire* 39).

The Student Nonviolent Coordinating Committee, which sponsored sit-ins at lunch counters during the civil rights movement of the 1960s, provides an example of enacting. As black students sat at the lunch counters reserved for whites, studying and talking quietly among themselves, they enacted "*concrete* ways to throw over an entire array of deferential behavior and ideas" and claimed "the respect and dignity that segregation systematically denied them" (Hogan 23). They acted "'as if' segregation did not exist" (Hogan 3) and thus experienced a "freedom created by their own actions, freedom in that very moment. . . . It was freedom inside, freedom as an inside job" (Hogan 255).

Criteria for Evaluating Rhetorical Agency

Different criteria should be used for judging students' rhetorical efforts when using interpretive agency from those used in the paradigm of constricted potentiality. Instead of applying criteria such as the capacity to be articulate, to make a persuasive argument, or to move others to change, interpretive agency is judged by the nature of the worlds created as a result of individuals' interpretive practices. Given this perspective, students should judge the effectiveness of their rhetorical efforts by asking questions such as, "Am I creating the world in which I want to be living?" "Are the outcomes I have generated by my symbolic choices the ones I desire?" If their answers to these questions are "no," students should use different kinds of symbols to generate different interpretations that *do* have the capacity to create the worlds or realities they desire.

Teachers could also encourage students to pay attention to the interpretive choices of others around them and to observe the connections between how others engage in symbol use and the outcomes they experience. They might ask as they observe others' symbolic choices and outcomes, "What is the connection between their symbolic choices and the reality they have created for themselves?" They might notice, for example, that one friend constantly blames external conditions for everything that goes wrong in her life and that nothing changes as a result. Another friend might experience setbacks but sees them as simply minor glitches that do not derail her from creating a particular kind of life for herself. Students should ask these questions not to judge or berate others' symbolic choices but to heighten their awareness of the cause-effect relationship between symbol use and the reality experienced.

Exercises and Assignments

Many exercises can be developed for helping students practice the interpretive model of agency. We offer the following as a starting point for instructors to think about ways to teach interpretive agency in their classrooms.

ANALYSIS OF INDIVIDUALS' INTERPRETIVE CHOICES

Ask students to select characters in artifacts such as autobiographies, biographies, children's books, movies, television shows, songs, and websites. Their task is to identify and analyze the interpretive frames used by the selected characters. They might choose to analyze, for example, the character of Django in the film *Django Unchained*; his interpretive frame differs substantially from that of the character of Stephen in the same film and from the character of Solomon Northup in the film *12 Years a Slave*. Django does not accept his condition as a slave and conceptualizes himself as equal and sometimes superior to whites. As a result, even when he is in oppressive and dangerous situations, he looks for resources he can use and sees himself as responsible for securing and maintaining his own freedom.

ANALYSIS OF LARGE-SCALE HISTORICAL INTERPRETIVE CHANGES

Here, students select an historical example of a major political or social change—the fall of the Berlin Wall, the increasing acceptance of same-sex marriage, or the legalization of marijuana, for example. They compare and contrast different interpretations held by various stakeholders and explore the linguistic and other symbolic elements that shifted in the course of the evolution of the issue to produce a different interpretation and thus a new outcome. They also might investigate whether the strategies of reframing, appreciating, focusing on desired outcomes, and enacting were employed by stakeholders to help create the new reality.

ANALYSIS OF DELIBERATE CHANGE STRATEGIES

Ask students to select an instance in which a fictional character or someone they know has deliberately engaged in interpretive agency and identify the rhetorical strategies used by that individual to change an interpretation. Students should be encouraged to look for and explicate more strategies of interpretation than the four presented in the unit. The character of Ron Woodruff in the film *Dallas Buyers Club*, for example, makes use of the strategies of reframing and focusing on desired outcomes to address the AIDS epidemic and his own HIV status. The story of boxer Hurricane Carter, imprisoned for a triple homicide he did not commit, is recounted in both his book *The Sixteenth Round: From Number 1 Contender to #45472* and the film *The Hurricane*. He offers a good example of the strategy of enacting in that he refused to eat prison food or wear prison garb while incarcerated to maintain his sense of self as a free man.

Constructing a New Interpretation (Group Activity)

Divide students into small groups and ask them to share some aspect of their lives they would like to be different—for example, they would like to get a better job, find a romantic partner, have an improved relationship with a family member, or perform better academically or athletically. Together, group members identify the interpretation the student currently applies to the situation and brainstorm alternative interpretations that could be applied to create a new reality around the situation.

Constructing a New Interpretation (Individual Activity)

Ask students to select some aspect of their lives they would like to be different. Prompt them to write the story of the current condition they would like to change. In other words, they should construct the story of how their life is at the moment and their reaction to it concerning that particular issue. Students should then create a new interpretation of that issue using some or all of the following strategies, adapted from James W. Pennebaker's *Writing to Heal*:

- Adopting Other Perspectives. Ask students to write again about the same issue they did in the above exercise, this time using not the first-person style but the third-person voice—*he* or *she*. In other words, they should write about the actions and emotions of the main character in the story as though they were observing the condition from a third-person perspective. Then, ask the students to write the story one more time, this time writing from the perspective of another person involved in the situation. What is going on in that person's mind? What is she doing and feeling? How is he likely to be viewing the situation? The point of these re-writes is to encourage students to adopt multiple perspectives and thus to encourage a change in their interpretation of the condition or issue. This exercise also prompts students to become more detached from that condition or issue, which allows them to see the frame they are using to interpret it and to realize that they have other choices about their interpretation.

- Cultivating Positive Emotions. Ask students to re-read the original story they wrote. Because the story is about some aspect of their lives with which they are unhappy, it is likely to contain a relatively high number of words referencing negative emotions—words such as *sad, guilty, angry,* and *anxious.* Although acknowledging feelings around an issue is important, if students stay with the negative emotions, they are likely to overlook other interpretations and thus other choices, resources, and opportunities available to them. Prompt students to rewrite the story again, this time using as many words for positive emotions as they can while staying true to the experience—words such as *love, nice, glad, peace, proud, happy, courageous, accepting, secure,* and *calm,* for example. Ask students to reflect on any new insights they have into the condition or experience as a result of writing with more positive words.
- Finding Benefits. Ask students to re-write the story again, this time focused on finding benefits. They briefly describe the issue or condition with which they are dealing and then identify any benefits that came or will come from it or what they can find to appreciate about it. Such benefits could include a greater understanding of themselves and others or a change in the direction of their lives that led to greater happiness. Ask students to reflect on how this exercise encourages them to interpret the condition about which they have been writing in a new way.

Transforming Resistance into Creation

For this exercise, students should begin by identifying something they do not want with a statement such as, "I do not want to feel angry at my friend" or "I do not want to work at an unsatisfying job." They then turn the statement into what they do want, as in: "I want to have a good relationship with my friend" or "I want a job that I enjoy." They should write this statement at the top of a page. Their task is then to find at least ten statements that are currently true about them that match the statement they have written. The key is that the statements they write should be ones they actually believe and that are not so large of a leap that they really do not believe them. The first statements they write may be trivial and seem silly if those are the only statements they can think of that are true for them concerning that situation. Every statement should make them feel better; if they think of a statement that does not make them feel better, they should not include it. If they are doing the exercise around their job, for example, the statements they write might be things such as, "The economy is picking up, and there are more jobs available now," "I know many people who love their jobs," "I am getting clearer about what I want in a job by working at my current job," "I love doing work that is meaningful," "I have found many jobs in the past, and I can find another job again," and "I am excited about the resources I just learned about for job hunting through my university." At the end of the exercise, they should reflect on whether the exercise facilitated a new interpretation of the situation and if they feel better about that situation.

SUPPORTING THE STRATEGIES

Ask students to do research to discover what kind of support (theoretical, experimental, and anecdotal) is available for one or more of the strategies—reframing, appreciating, focusing on desired outcomes, and enacting. Timothy D. Wilson's book *Redirect*, for instance, provides examples of experimental support for the strategy of focusing on desired outcomes rather than opposing what is not wanted, while Rosamund Stone Zander and Benjamin Zander's book *The Art of Possibility* provides examples of appreciating and reframing.

WRITING THE FUTURE

In this assignment, students select an area of their lives they would like to change and identify the interpretation they typically have applied to that situation. They then identify the strategies they will use to interpret the situation differently—reframing, appreciating, focusing on desired outcomes, enacting, or others—and devise an action plan for implementing those strategies. A student might choose, for example, to employ the strategy of appreciating and make a list of twenty qualities that she genuinely appreciates about a problematic coworker. Students could then apply their chosen strategy for a specified amount of time, such as a week or a month. The student who chooses the strategy of appreciating could review her list of qualities she appreciates every day before going to work. She also could experiment with enacting, in which she acts around the coworker as though the two of them already have a cordial and effective working relationship. The student who chooses reframing would talk and act in ways to highlight the developed reframe. At the end of the time period, students analyze any shifts that have occurred as a result of their application of the strategy. Such shifts could include, in addition to changes in the actual condition on which they are working, feeling more positive emotions, falling asleep faster, feeling healthier, and drinking less alcohol (Pennebaker 53).

A Rhetorically Empowered Future for Rhetoric Students

If rhetoric instructors were to teach students both the conventional rhetorical agency that derives from the paradigm of constricted potentiality and the interpretive agency that derives from the paradigm of constructed potentiality, students would have the capacity to be effective agents in a wider variety of contexts. They would have available to them a greater variety of change strategies drawn from both paradigms, be able to make informed decisions about which kind of strategy to use in a given situation, and be more conscious of their rhetorical power. The addition of interpretive agency to students' rhetorical toolboxes, in Condit's words, would "give greater potential and vitality to their agency" (*Why* 2).

Teaching both conventional and interpretive agency has another benefit as well. It allows teachers committed to feminist principles to integrate into their courses a key commitment of feminist theory—self-determination. With the addition of an understanding of interpretive agency and its nature and function, students see that they are responsible for their own lives and for their own well-being. They are the ones in charge of interpretation; the responsibility for world creation is theirs.

The principle of self-determination that is implicit in interpretive agency also encourages students to be more respectful of the choices made by those around them. Others may not always exercise agency in the ways that students would like, but they are more likely to allow others to be different from them and to make different choices from theirs when they understand interpretive agency. They are likely to treat those around them with more civility and respect because they genuinely want others to be able to make their own decisions about their lives and the worlds they choose to create, just as they want to be able to do.

Works Cited

Anzaldúa, Gloria. *Borderlands/La Frontera: The New Mestiza*. Aunt Lute, 1987.

—. "Now Let us Shift . . . the Path of Conocimiento . . . Inner Work, Public Acts." *This Bridge We Call Home: Radical Visions for Transformation*, edited by Gloria E. Anzaldúa and AnaLouise Keating, Routledge, 2002, pp. 540–78.

Bandura, Albert. "Toward a Psychology of Human Agency." *Perspectives on Psychological Science*, vol. 1, no. 2, 2006, pp. 164–80.

Campbell, Karlyn Kohrs. "Agency: Promiscuous and Protean." *Communication and Critical/Cultural Studies*, vol. 2, no. 1, 2005, pp. 1–19.

Carter, Hurricane. *The Sixteenth Round: From Number 1 Contender to #45472I*. Lawrence Hill, 2011.

Combs, Allan, and Mark Holland. *Synchronicity*. Marlowe, 1966.

Condit, Celeste Michelle. "Why Rhetorical Training Can Expand Agency." Alliance of Rhetoric Societies, Evanston, IL. September 2003. Conference Presentation.

—. "How Metaphors About Genes Make Us Feel: Towards a Democracy of Feelings." Lingua Democratica workshop, Utrecht, The Netherlands, October 2008. Conference Presentation.

Crum, Alia J., and Ellen J. Langer. "Mind-Set Matters: Exercise and the Placebo Effect." *Psychological Science*, vol. 18, no. 2, 2007, pp. 165–71.

Dalai Lama, and Howard Cutler. *The Art of Happiness: A Handbook for Living*. Riverhead, 1998.

Ede, Lisa, Cheryl Glenn, and Andrea Lunsford. "Border Crossings: Intersections of Rhetoric and Feminism." *Rhetorica*, vol. 13, no. 4, 1995, pp. 401–41.

Fegan, Eileen V. "'Subjects' of Regulation/Resistance? Postmodern Feminism and Agency in Abortion-Decision-Making." *Feminist Legal Studies*, vol. 7, 1999, pp. 241–73.

Foss, Karen A., Sonja K. Foss, and Cindy L. Griffin. *Feminist Rhetorical Theories*. Waveland, 2006.

Foss, Sonja K., and Karen A. Foss. "Constricted and Constructed Potentiality: An Inquiry into Paradigms of Change." *Western Journal of Communication*, vol. 75, no. 2, 2011, pp. 205–38.

—. *Inviting Transformation: Presentational Speaking for a Changing World*. 3rd ed. Waveland, 2012.

Foss, Sonja K., and Cindy L. Griffin. "Beyond Persuasion: A Proposal for an Invitational Rhetoric." *Communication Monographs*, vol. 62, no. 1, 1995, pp. 2–18.

Foss, Sonja K., William J. C. Waters, and Bernard J. Armada. "Toward a Theory of Agentic Orientation: Rhetoric and Agency in *Run Lola Run*." *Communication Theory*, vol. 17, no. 3, 2007, pp. 205–30.
Gearhart, Sally Miller. "Notes From a Recovering Activist." *Sojourner: The Women's Forum*, vol. 21, 1995, pp. 8–11.
—. "Womanpower: Energy Re-Sourcement." *The Politics of Women's Spirituality: Essays on the Rise of Spiritual Power within the Feminist Movement*, edited by Charlene Spretnak, Doubleday, 1982, pp. 194–206.
Gergen, Kenneth J. *Realities and Relationships: Soundings in Social Construction*. Harvard UP, 1994.
Glenn, Cheryl. "Medieval Literacy Outside the Academy: Popular Practice and Individual Technique." *College Composition and Communication*, vol. 44, no. 4, 1993, pp. 497–508.
—. *Rhetoric Retold: Regendering the Tradition from Antiquity Through the Renaissance*. Southern Illinois UP, 1997.
Glenn, Cheryl. "2008 CCCC Chair's Address: Representing Ourselves." *College Composition and Communication*, vol. 60, no. 2, 2008, pp. 420–39.
Harper, Nancy. *Human Communication Theory: The History of a Paradigm*. Hayden, 1979.
Hinshaw, Karin E. "The Effects of Mental Practice on Motor Skill Performance: Critical Evaluation and Meta-Analysis." *Imagination, Cognition and Personality*, vol. 11, no. 1, 1991–1992, pp. 3–35.
Hogan, Wesley C. *Many Minds, One Heart: SNCC's Dream for a New America*. U of North Carolina P, 2007.
hooks, bell. *Outlaw Culture: Resisting Representation*. Routledge, 1994.
Irvin II, Nat. "The Arrival of the Thrivals." *The Futurist*, vol. 38, March/April 2004, pp. 16–23.
Johnson, Sonia. *Going Out of Our Minds: The Metaphysics of Liberation*. Crossing, 1987.
—. *Living the Dream*. Wildfire, 1990.
—. *The Ship That Sailed into the Living Room: Sex and Intimacy Reconsidered*. Wildfire, 1991.
—. *Wildfire: Igniting the She/Volution*. Wildfire, 1989.
Karr, M. A. "Sally Gearhart: Wandering—and Wondering—on Future Ground." *The Advocate*, 21 Feb. 1980, pp. 21–22.
Leeds-Hurwitz, Wendy. *Social Approaches to Communication*. Guilford, 1995.

Leeds-Hurwitz, Wendy, and Gloria J. Galanes, editors. *Socially Constructing Communication.* Hampton, 2009.

Lyubomirsky, S. "Why Are Some People Happier than Others? The Role of Cognitive and Motivational Processes in Well-Being." *American Psychologist,* vol. 56, 2001, pp. 239–49.

Pearce, W. Barnett. *Making Social Worlds: A Communication Perspective.* Blackwell, 2007.

Pennebaker, James W. *Writing to Heal: A Guided Journal for Recovering from Trauma and Emotional Upheaval.* New Harbinger, 2004.

Reid, Brian. "The Nocebo Effect: Placebo's Evil Twin." *Washington Post,* 29 April 2002, www.washingtonpost.com/archive/lifestyle/wellness/2002/04/30/the-nocebo-effect-placebos-evil-twin/6945da76-fb8e-401e-a4f2-0439d36f4c6a/?noredirect=on&utm_term=.3a360875584b. Accessed 29 February 2014.

Starhawk. *Dreaming the Dark: Magic, Sex and Politics.* Beacon, 1988.

—. *Truth or Dare: Encounters with Power, Authority, and Mystery.* Harper & Row, 1990.

Steinitz, Victoria, and Sandra Kanter. "Becoming Outspoken: Beyond Connected Education." *Women's Studies Quarterly,* vol. 19, 1991, pp. 138–53.

Swets, John A., and Robert A. Bjork. "Enhancing Human Performance: An Evaluation of 'New Age' Techniques Considered by the U. S. Army." *Psychological Science,* vol. 1, no. 2, 1990, pp. 85–96.

Walker, Alice. *We Are the Ones We Have Been Waiting For: Inner Light in a Time of Darkness.* New Press, 2006.

Watzlawick, Paul, John H. Weakland, and Richard Fisch. *Change: Principles of Problem Formation and Problem Resolution.* W. W. Norton, 1974, pp. 92–109.

Whorf, Benjamin Lee. *Language, Thought, and Reality: Selected Writings of Benjamin Lee Whorf,* edited by J. B. Carroll. MIT Press, 1956.

Wilson, Timothy D. *Redirect: The Surprising New Science of Psychological Change.* Little, Brown, 2011.

Wolf, Fred Alan. *Taking the Quantum Leap: The New Physics for Non-Scientists.* Harper & Row, 1989.

Zander, Rosamund Stone, and Benjamin Zander. *The Art of Possibility.* Harvard Business School P, 2000.

15 Re-inscribing Mentoring

Michelle Eble and Lynée Lewis Gaillet

In this chapter, we wish to extend the definition of mentoring as a "pay it forward" activity by considering the essence of synergistic, reciprocal mentoring relationships. We think that questions of how to prepare the next generation of successful teachers, scholars, and active professionals necessarily pertains to *all* scholars taking on new positions, projects, methodologies, publication venues/formats, and pedagogical platforms. Our project challenges the traditional top-down hierarchical form of mentoring. We advocate for mentoring networks that encourage building a repository of knowledgeable and expert colleagues to address a multitude of shifting/changing academic concerns. Our notion of mentoring networks embraces the positive components of traditional feminist mentoring in ways that encourage new faculty members and graduate students to join academic conversations while sustaining and enriching the research, teaching, and service of those already working in the field. Mentoring networks—unlike apprenticeship models—disrupt hierarchies, answer needs as they arise, and emphasize reciprocity.

In 2008, we co-edited *Stories of Mentoring* in an attempt to situate the status of mentoring in the field of rhetoric and composition. Our call for papers on this subject obviously touched a nerve, yielding scores of submitted abstracts in the first days following the post. Most of the submissions were multi-authored by networks of colleagues and professional friends. As we stated in the introduction:

> Contributors offer a wide array of evidence and illustrations in an effort to define the scope of this ubiquitous and ambiguous term [mentoring]. In the pages of this collection, then, the reader will find program descriptions and critiques, testimonials and personal anecdotes, copies of correspondence and e-mail

> messages, term projects and assignments, accounts of forged friendships and peer relationships (some good; some bad), both new paradigms and familiar constructs for successful mentoring, tales of pregnancy and mothering, chronicles of both administrative nightmares and dream solutions, and stories giving insight into the character of those rare individuals who embody the term "mentor." (3)

Collectively, these seventy-seven authors worked to re-inscribe the concept of *traditional mentoring*, whereby an experienced scholar advises and guides one new to the field. However, none of the contributors in 2008 offered *direct* advice for establishing comprehensive mentoring networks or webs that constitute a wide range of resources useful for establishing mutually-beneficial mentoring networks, although many chapters do discuss disrupting traditional notions of mentoring and stress the value of reciprocal mentoring. Building on our previous work in *Stories of Mentoring*, the present chapter (1) proposes new possibilities for establishing mentoring networks and (2) identifies qualities of superior practice found within one feminist organization.

In this two-part project, we describe and define mentoring networks and then illustrate how these networks operate by recounting the history of the Coalition of Feminist (formerly Women) Scholars in the History of Rhetoric and Composition, a thirty-year-old organization that fosters a large mentoring network. The mission of the Coalition was initially based on mentoring feminist scholars who would, in turn, "pay it forward" by mentoring others. However, more recently, the greater goal of the organization might be viewed as "excellence through imagination," characterized by Royster and Kirsch in *Feminist Rhetorical Practices* as "listening deeply, reflexively, and multisensibly." These two scholars contend that critical imagination "allows us to engender an ethos of humility, respect, and care—an ethos," they consider, "critical to achieving qualities of excellence" in research, teaching, and service (21). The life and future of feminist rhetorical academic practice depends upon the mutual listening that occurs among networks of mentors, including students. Furthermore, the Coalition's aims, projects, and even its essential make-up is simultaneously influenced and determined by a dynamic and synchronous exchange of ideas among all members. In our conception of a networked model—illustrated by the Coalition—mentoring is indeed a mutually beneficial, shared endeavor.

Mentoring Networks

One of our objectives herein is to examine and discuss ways that conceptions of mentoring might shift and evolve in light of how mentoring is enacted in differing contexts. Two questions guide us in this endeavor: how might established faculty members prepare themselves both to mentor and be mentored by new colleagues and graduate students, and secondly, how should emerging scholars and new faculty members position themselves within mentoring networks? In answer, we highlight in Part Two a feminist mentoring model characterized by support, knowledge, collaboration, alliances, and mutual reciprocity.

In many ways, re-inscribing "mentoring" is difficult given the term's long, confining history of referring solely to a two-person dynamic, where one party has power and knowledge and the other may not. Traditional mentoring connotes images of mentors working with their apprentices or protégés and, through this work, revealing the traditional, masculine notions of mentoring deeply embedded in our communities, cultures, and institutions. We learned in the process of editing *Stories of Mentoring* that mentoring happens in a variety of contexts; our contributors provide a series of snapshots capturing an array of ways that mentoring is enacted in the field. Nearly all chapters in that volume were collaboratively authored, and the majority of the relationships described were based on mutual benefit, debunking the traditional apprenticeship model. Given the collected rich examples that disrupt the traditional one-way/top down conception of mentoring, we concluded that collection by advocating for a complicated view of the hierarchical mentor-mentee relationship. Mentoring scholarship sometimes suggests the alternative term *reverse mentoring*, but that concept still dictates that at least one person or group is doing the mentoring, and another is receiving. The notion of reciprocity or mutuality may very well be left out in reverse mentoring. Existing mentoring terminology does not capture the complexity involved in the mentor-protégé relationship, especially for those individuals from marginalized groups who may not have opportunities to benefit from experienced faculty who share or understand the mentees' identities and backgrounds. Certainly not everyone gets mentored adequately, even in the best-laid plans.

Stories of Mentoring describes a number of complex relationships and explores the often-nuanced dynamics of the various ways that mentoring is actually negotiated. Nearly all chapters discuss the mutual respect and benefit characterizing effective mentoring relationships, regardless of participants' experiences or years working in Rhetoric and Composition—a field that has attempted to complicate the notion of mentoring by interrogating the traditional, gendered idea of the act. In "Educating Jane," for example, Jenn Fishman and Andrea Lunsford question the very term *mentor*, arguing that in many circumstances, the term mentor is "simply another word for control" (20). They prefer the connotation of *colleague*, which emphasizes "the reciprocal process of learning and teaching ourselves and others how to work most cooperatively and productively together" (31). Likewise, Wendy Sharer, Jessica Enoch, and Cheryl Glenn discuss a collaborative model for mentoring, where access to "connections" helps graduate students and new faculty "work within a mutually supportive group of professional friends and colleagues" (142).

We concluded in 2008 that "[f]uture work on mentoring should focus on fostering mentoring relations that occur across boundaries of race, ethnicity, class, gender, sexuality, and disability" (309). We would now add to that list boundaries of experience, place, space, and time. Scholarship still strives to challenge theoretical and foundational meanings of mentoring and to re-inscribe the term in ways that reflect its enactment. What can we do to perpetuate the notion of mentoring that allows more people to participate and thus mentor and be mentored, and to ensure that the activity isn't promoting a legacy of the "old-boys' (or girls') club," where only insiders or those related to certain "academic families" are invited to join? The concept of mentoring networks is one possible solution.

In our past and current positions as chairs of departments and hiring committees; directors of university programs (First-Year Writing, Writing Centers, Undergraduate and Graduate Studies); and leaders of professional organizations (the South Atlantic Modern Language Association, Coalition of Feminist Scholars, Association of Teachers of Technical Writers), we address mentoring often, as an act that is central to our work with interns, undergraduate students, graduate teaching assistants, graduate students, and new contingent and tenure-track faculty members. In many cases, universities and colleges give lip service to mentoring or assign mentors based on some arbitrary reason or pairing; universities know they have a responsibility to mentor new faculty and graduate students, but this recognition doesn't always lead to productive action. In the summer of July 2013, *Inside Higher Education* published a much-needed, five-part series on mentoring. Kerry Ann Rockquemore, in "A New Model of Mentoring," discusses a network-based model that "puts the faculty member in the driver's seat, and shifts the dynamic from a dependency model (where the mentee is at the mercy of the guru and mentoring is bestowed as a grace upon the lucky few) to empowering the new professor to build his or her own network of community and support." We think a mentoring network model like the one Rockquemore describes helps us critique the oftentimes exclusionary expert-apprentice model.

While the articles published in this series address new faculty specifically, we'd like to expand notions of mentoring networks beyond those parameters, thinking about ways to build mutually-beneficial networks of people and resources where no single mentor is responsible for the gamut of information needed by mentees, and where mentoring experiences continue throughout one's career as needs change. We also wish to expand upon the traditional one-to-one mentoring relationships that often begin in graduate school between a student and a dissertation chair or influential professor, and which may or may not continue over a career. While we know many successful relationships of this type, we are also aware that not every graduate student or assistant professor is currently involved in such a productive, individual mentoring relationship. Unquestionably, this model of hierarchical, traditional mentoring can be limiting if knowledge and advice flows in just one direction. Therefore, the networked mentoring that we envision fosters multiple relationships and connections; the relationships in a network model are multi-faceted, multi-directional, and mutually beneficial. In other words, mentoring networks depend upon relationships among many different people and connections made through varying distribution channels in the network, all which are based on specific needs and contexts.

The distributed nature of academic work and our familiarity with social networking tools contribute to the kairotic moment for thinking about mentoring in this way. Research by Clay Spinuzzi on distributed work (especially as applied to technical communication) helps us understand how mentoring networks can operate. He defines distributed work as "the coordinative work that enables sociotechnical networks to hold together and form dense interconnections among and across work activities that have traditionally been separated by temporal, spatial, or disciplinary boundaries" (268). If other types of work can be coordinated across various boundaries, then we propose that mentoring can, too. Mentoring networks (and thus, multiple mutually-beneficial relationships) can be sustained through interconnections not available even ten or twenty years ago, and they do not need to be limited to a specific time, place, program, or school. Spinuzzi asserts that the shift to distributed work values a specific set of skills: negotiation, trust, alliances, agility, persuasion, and relationship building (271–272). Focusing on these specific collaborative—and we argue, mentoring—skills highlights the possibilities inherent within a network that can lead to the synergistic and reciprocal relationships that constitute productive mentoring networks. These relationships, based on a network of people, disrupt the hierarchical nature of the traditional expert/protégé relationship that can be so exclusionary.

Mentoring networks depend upon connections with others and are sustained through an infinite number of connections when tapped by other people or nodes in the network. A network, in its simplest form, consists of at least two nodes (or points) and a connection between them. Computer networks are usually made up of a set of systems that are connected to each other, and the computers themselves are considered the nodes. The ability for the computers to share information and for someone to distribute information across all of the computers through a distribution channel makes networks powerful tools. This analogy to a computer network helps illustrate the distribution and significance of the connections that comprise a mentoring network. Distribution in a computer network is not dependent on time, place, or space, and connections make for easy distribution of information to the other nodes within the network. Updates to a network can often be pushed from one computer terminal to another, and the information is distributed across the nodes on the network and even to other networks through a shared node in the network. A computer network also connects multiple networks with one another, much as new faculty members can be quickly connected to existing mentoring networks through productive relationships with new colleagues.

Like computer workstations and servers whose networks depend on two-way connections, a mentoring network is based on connections and distribution channels among people, and these networks depend on mutual, reciprocal relationships. Having access to or, in our case, an introduction or shared research or teaching interest with someone in a mentoring network connects one with the various other nodes or people that make up the network system. Understanding the characteristics of networks, broadly defined, helps re-inscribe mentoring by building helpful connections based on goals and interests instead of merely seeking advice that is confined to one person's knowledge base, experiences, or location. This conception of mentoring is particularly beneficial for those who find themselves in a situation where they have no mentor for a specific need, such as work-life balance. A mentoring network replaces previously held notions of one knowledge-holder who passes that knowledge on to worthy protégées. Understanding the multiple ways one can organize resources (and people) to answer a multitude of questions and needs at varying points within a career provides the focal point of how a mentoring network should operate.

In our case, meaning Lynée and Michelle, we have mentored each other now for over twenty years, beginning with a traditional, top-down, teacher-student relationship. More recently, and perhaps more importantly, we have built mentoring networks based on our research interests, specific teaching and administrative experiences, and work with new colleagues. Initially, Lynée shared her mentoring network with Michelle, directing her graduate research and putting her in touch with faculty in the field who could support her work, offer employment opportunities, and help her expand into the field of professional and technical writing. From that initial and traditional act of teacher-student mentoring, we began building and enacting a network of mentoring, which the following examples illustrate:

- One summer, Lynée asked Michelle and Will Banks (one of Michelle's colleagues at East Carolina University) to serve as respondents at a Georgia State University (GSU) conference for graduate students. Some of those students engaged in follow-up email conversations with the ECU faculty.
- Nikki Caswell, a new Assistant Professor and Director of the Writing Center at ECU, shared materials and her experiences with Lynée regarding ECU's successful undergraduate peer-tutoring program as Lynée came on board as a new Writing Studio Director seeking to launch a similar program at GSU.
- Lynée has referred her students interested in technical writing to Michelle for advice.
- Wendy Sharer, Tracy Morse, and Michelle arranged for Lynée to come to ECU as a consultant for ECU's Quality Enhancement Plan (QEP). During this visit, Lynée spent time with the ECU graduate students and contingent faculty, talking about publishing issues and the realities of adjunct status.

- Lynée read and responded to a piece by Erin Frost, one of Michelle's new colleagues; the piece was subsequently published in *Peitho*.

Furthermore, we have collaborated on a textbook, *Primary Research and Writing* (2016), that addresses primary research in first-year writing classes. During our authoring of this text, we collected materials from teachers across the country (sharing our contact lists in the process), asked instructors (whom we had met separately and introduced to each other) to pilot assignments from the text in their classrooms, and corresponded with colleagues we met either through projects such as the Rhetoric Society of America/Penn State webinars that addressed archival research or at conferences regarding ways to improve the text and share assignments. We continue to help each other build mentoring networks, which provide us with resources we can access as needed. Of course, our new colleagues and graduate students at both of our universities are always a part of our mentoring networks, coalescing and diverging as they accept jobs, which ultimately creates even larger mentoring systems. Ultimately, we all benefit from the opportunities afforded by our mutual connections.

Our experience has shown us that the major difference between traditional mentoring praxis and mentoring networks has to do with disrupting the hierarchy that may exist in an individual 1:1 mentoring relationship. Mentoring networks provide students and faculty (at various levels) with a variety of resources to be accessed for specific purposes, many of which we have not always anticipated. Access to an entire network, rather than just one person's knowledge and contacts, allows the important work of mentoring to happen in different instances and among a variety of people in accordance with mutually beneficial goals and reciprocal needs. Ultimately, the core of any mentoring network should encompass a basic willingness of all parties to learn from one another and share resources.

The most successful mentoring networks also possess flattened hierarchies, so the relationships between the nodes can be traversed in either direction and allow for a fluidity that may not be possible within traditional mentoring. How we represent the relationships we have to each other and to our various networks depends first on the nodes and diverse relationships we already have in place and second on the connections we make among these variables. For example, Michelle and the late Janice Tovey became colleagues when Michelle arrived at ECU right out of graduate school, and while Michelle and Jan did not have a relationship prior to the job search, their collegial relationship provided Michelle access to Jan's Purdue network, which afforded Michelle introductions to people who would become important to her career and scholarship. Many of Jan and Michelle's early conversations dealt with the various technologies that could be used in the delivery of online courses. Michelle's awareness of possible delivery methods informed Jan's understanding of leading-edge technologies of the time (like blogs and content management systems). Over the years, while Lynée continued to advise Michelle in numerous ways, when it came to new technologies, online education, and institutional review board protocols/research ethics, Lynée turned to and referred her students to Michelle. Our willingness to learn from one another serves as an example for all of those connected to us though our mentoring networks.

If shared interests and experiences help build strong alliances and mutually beneficial relationships, then access to a mentoring network through one person assumes access to a larger network. Alliances and collaboration based on shared mentoring networks illustrate the transformative power of this network model. For example, as Michelle was contemplating mentoring networks, she and a group of colleagues from several institutions experienced the power of them first-hand at the 2013 Council for Programs in Technical and Scientific Communication (CPTSC) meeting in Cincinnati. Soon after arriving with her new colleagues Erin Frost and Matt Cox, Michelle was reacquainted with Angela Haas, whom she met years ago at a Computers and Writing conference. This time, however, Michelle and Angela quickly recognized shared connections with Erin, one of Angela's former students from Illinois State University, and Matt, a classmate of Angela's at Michigan State. These shared connections instantly created new nodes within a shared mentoring network for other colleagues, classmates, and students connected to each of us.

This example reminded us how quickly connections can be made and how shared interests can lead to productive action. By the end of the conference, and because Angela and Michelle were learning so much from some of the pre-tenure and graduate students at the conference, they began work on an edited collection, *Key Theoretical Frameworks: Teaching Technical Communication in the Twenty-First Century* (2018), which incorporates social justice methodologies and cultural studies scholarship to formulate theories for teaching technical communication.

This collection's network is quite extensive, and while a few of the connections depend on academic genealogy, the majority of the connections are based on a shared background, education, and mutually beneficial relationships that provide us all with a widespread network of people to consult. We see this sharing of knowledge and building of networks actively at play in our fields through professional organizations and conferences, but networks are not limited to place and time contexts and constraints; they can also exist through shared research interests and values, similar institutional situations and challenges, and work/life balance concerns.

We acknowledge that "academic families"—the idea that dissertation advisors as parents and the advisor of that advisor as a grandparent, for instance—have powerful mentoring capabilities, as well, but we do worry about the exclusionary possibilities inherent in them. The mentoring networks we advocate are different than genealogies like the Writing Studies Tree (writingstudiestree.org), although we like the visualization of this online project, which is a "crowd sourced database of academic genealogies within writing studies . . . for recording and mapping scholarly relationships in Composition and Rhetoric and adjacent disciplines" (http://writingstudiestree.org/about). While we have more control over which academic families we belong to than we do over our home families, we all know that familial relationships, including academic ones, can occasionally be complicated networks to navigate. Genealogies can help foster networks, but mentoring networks can exist without genealogical connections as evidenced in our experiences.

In the next section of this chapter, we use the Coalition of Feminist Scholars in the History of Rhetoric and Composition as an illustration of a mentoring network. However, it is important to note that the Coalition provides just *one* example of how integrated networking can occur. Other professional organizations and conferences that give specific time for participants to network are essential to the nurturing and sustainability of mentoring opportunities. Many major conferences now have places for graduate students to share their work, and increasingly conferences provide informal spaces for new scholars to connect and talk about their research or issues related to the disciplines. For example, the Association of Teachers of Technical Writing (ATTW) now sponsors a well-attended Women in Technical Communication networking lunch. Likewise, the Feminism(s) and Rhetoric(s) conference meetings feature a pre-conference writing workshop along with shared meals throughout the meeting, an important networking advantage for this conference. The Graduate Research Network (GRN) provides a full-day workshop for graduate students to share their research with experienced scholars during the Computers and Writing Conference, and the Research Network Forum (RNF) provides mentoring space prior to the Conference on College Composition and Communication (CCCC). Another successful long-time mentoring network, fostered by the Rhetoric Society of America under the guidance of Cheryl Geisler, specifically targets faculty working at the rank of Associate Professor who seek advancement to Full Professor. This carefully designed eighteen-month mentoring plan addresses the multitude of reasons that careers stall at the rank of Associate, including: taking on too much service, work/life balance issues, and inability to negotiate institutional terrain. Participants connect with peers and mentors from across the country to focus on promotion.

At all of these events, graduate students and colleagues at various stages of their careers learn from one another in coordinated ways. The Coalition has also been enacting this work for many years, as described below. A feminist model of networked mentoring relies on collaboration rather than control and apprenticeship, on shared knowledge rather than title or rank, and diversified rather than delegated authority. In a mentoring network, conversation and dialogue are the watchwords rather than monologue, and all participants make a commitment to provide ample support for scholars working at every rank.

MENTORING NETWORKS AT THE COALITION OF FEMINIST SCHOLARS IN THE HISTORY OF RHETORIC

The Coalition of Feminist Scholars in the History of Rhetoric and Composition originally sought to build a network of support whereby women in the field could find resources for better understanding the political nature of academic work. Formed in hotel rooms and over dinner conversations occurring at annual meetings of the CCCC, the original members wished to provide hiring support and increased opportunities for publication and promotion within rhetorical studies. The constitution, drafted by a team led by Kathleen Welch, was signed March 24, 1990, in Chicago, Illinois, by Welch (President), Marjorie Currie Woods (Vice-president), Winifred Bryan Horner (Secretary), Nan Johnson, and C. Jan Swearingen. With the signing of the constitution, these five women stepped into history by creating a nurturing, sustaining, and collegial space that fostered mentoring networks for scores of women (and men) who followed.

The Coalition's mission statement makes clear that it is:

> a learned society composed of scholars who are committed to feminist research throughout the history of rhetoric and composition. The Coalition promotes and fosters collaboration and communication among scholars in the following areas:
> 1. the advancements of research throughout the history of rhetoric and composition;
> 2. the education of women faculty and graduate students in the politics of the profession.
> 3. It aims to be a dynamic, intellectually challenging, and professionally nurturing space for teachers and scholars who are committed to defining or redefining what it means to do feminist historical work on topics and methodologies as wide ranging as pedagogical history to archival theory to embodiment in digital spaces.

From its inception, the Coalition's primary goal was mentoring, writ large. To that end, the Coalition created a welcoming space—perhaps the most well-known and certainly most visible facet of the Coalition's legacy—where initially mostly women and now an increasing array of people meet each Wednesday night of the annual CCCC to kick off the conference.

The Wednesday night gathering, advertised in the CCCC program, still serves as a reunion space for long-time friends but also as a networking venue for new scholars to form collegial acquaintances and friendships. Most importantly for this study, however, the Coalition provides a venue to distribute the best of traditional mentoring practices across a network whereby ongoing friendships and professional relationships become the basis of a web of connections including professors and subsequent generations of their students—scholars who are of the same academic generation, and alumni of particular institutions. The boughs of the family and institutional trees intertwine, circle back, and critically allow for conversations and mutual mentoring that happens when younger generations of scholars join the organization and its advisory board, serving to keep the Coalition vital in terms of mission, information delivery, and cutting-edge research practices.

Cheryl Glenn captures the feel of the Wednesday night meetings, where networking and mentoring are the key terms and activities:

> I can call on any of those women when I need help and they'll help me. It is like a sisterhood there. It's really terrific. I get so excited by meeting new scholars who have so much energy at a time in my life when I don't feel like I have enough to sustain me . . . They're in there . . . they're chewing on that material, they're getting something out of it, they've got lots of enthusiasm, and they're going to do a lot better work than I ever did considering they'll go a lot further. It's really exciting and so gratifying. (Eble and Sharer)

The spirit of Glenn's comments here pervades the events of the Coalition meetings, which historically consisted of a welcome by the officers, awarding of annual prizes (the Kathleen Ethel Welch Outstanding Journal Article, Winifred Bryan Horner Outstanding Book, Nan Johnson Outstanding Graduate Student, Lisa Ede Outstanding Mentoring Awards, along with annual Outstanding Dissertation Awards), and a roster of presentations that reflect on topical interests, suggest new research, or offer "think" pieces; the Wednesday night event is organized by the incumbent President, who often draws from across her mentoring network and from new member surveys as she designs the symposium.

The annual Wednesday night events historically conclude with roundtable mentoring tables staffed by members at various points in their careers and that address attendees' shared interests and goals. Andrea Lunsford speaks about the significance of these discussions: "[F]rom the very first, the Coalition was devoted to welcoming new women into the profession and mentoring them . . . fostering their professional growth, as well as their professional growth in their departments and in their disciplines as well as in their scholarship. So half of every session is devoted to mentoring tables . . . and sometimes they go on far, far beyond the time we had allotted for them" (Eble and Sharer). The contacts made at these tables often last years and develop into professional friendships; often too, those who originally attended the mentoring discussions go on to lead them at later annual meetings and suggest new speakers/leaders from within their mentoring networks. Kate Adams explains, "That Wednesday night thing, especially that second hour, I think is fairly unique. It's a place where people interact. Cheryl Glenn taught me how to write a grant in one of those sessions." (Eble and Sharer).

Certainly, even an organization made up primarily of collaborative women has the potential to take on characteristics of "an old boys' club" and embody traditional mentoring as the organization solidifies and gains recognition. The Coalition has faced these allegations, despite the organization's best intentions, and, yes, one advantage to the organization is the expertise and "connections" of the more experienced members. However, the Coalition has addressed these concerns to both become more inclusive and to keep the organization alive, relevant, and networked. The concept of a *mentoring network* (rather than a traditional top-down notion of mentoring) is evident in ongoing changes within the organization. For example, in the recent move toward achieving tax-exempt status, the organization realized the need to draw on its membership's expanding mentoring network for a new kind of guidance. In rewriting the by-laws, putting in place measures for assuring transparency in expanding the organization's advisory board, and actively seeking participation by graduate students and faculty members from every academic rank, the organization added new nodes to the existing mentoring schemata—drawing on the strengths of returning and new members who hold skills and connections in law and business. The rewriting and close re-examination of the bylaws resulted in drawing on existing network nodes and actively seeking new nodes—scholars who bring expertise and contacts in digital publishing, knowledge of social media platforms for expanding the organization's membership, unique approaches to research methods/methodologies, innovative conceptions of hybrid pedagogy and course delivery systems, and interesting approaches to copyright/licensing issues, among others. These new nodes within the network provide connections for the membership at large and offer opportunities for expanding the networked mentoring system at play.

For example, moving the Coalition's publication, *Peitho*, to a digital format required the expertise of a fresh editorial team—those who brought new knowledge to the mentoring network. These "connections" are comprised of members from every academic rank, creating other new connections to the mentoring system and further eroding a traditional "old girl" mentoring design. The sphere of mentoring topics has also shifted to reflect the expertise and connections of new nodes within the web. These moves create new links in the network by inviting knowledgeable graduate students and pre-tenure faculty to share their research with a group of established researchers and scholars, and to facilitate, rather than merely attend, productive conversations. A mentoring network is fluid, encouraging, moral, and ethical. Most recently the *Peitho* editorial review board has instituted a mentoring plan for shepherding manuscripts by emerging scholars deemed "revise and resubmit" through the review process.

Naturally, mentoring networks in a thirty-year-old organization happen organically, often originating and morphing from more traditional views of mentoring. The Coalition's Mentoring tables are where enduring dynamic mentoring relationships begin and expand the network. We asked past President of the Coalition Jenn Fishman and regular Wednesday night attendee Beth Godbee to explore the role academic friendships formed at the mentoring tables played in their careers. Jenn's first CCCC meeting was in 2002 in New York; the Wednesday night meeting she attended was her induction to the conference. That night, she joined a mentoring table for candidates on the job market, hosted by Lynée and Kate Adams. Jenn remembers discussing at great length the difficulties of having what might be perceived as a lit-only background in applying for rhet/comp positions. At the end of her extensive justification/explanation, she says Kate, in her cut-to-the-chase manner, said "Jenn, if I were you, I wouldn't say anything about anything until they've offered you the contract." Jenn's question and Kate's response led to fuller discussions about ongoing political splits in English departments—the tensions between literature and rhetoric/composition faculty members and how new hires might navigate these often-dicey turf wars. Years later, when Lynée became the first rhet/comp Chair of a largely literature English department, she called upon these earlier discussions for advice.

Flash forward: At the 2006 CCCC meeting in Chicago, Kate was President of the Coalition and asked Jenn to serve on the Wednesday night panel (focused on academic publishing), where she met Kris Ratcliffe for the first time. In her talk, Jenn cited Kris's new book on listening and says she "remembers only two more things: one, being up there on the dais with Carol Mattingly, Geneva Smitherman, and Sondra Perl; and two, after my talk, Kris briefly introduced herself and said something generous and complimentary about my reference to her work." In an interesting turn of events, Kris eventually hired Jenn at Marquette University.

In another beautiful strand of "the mentoring web," in 2008, Beth Godbee and Tanya Cochran—former students of Lynée—joined a mentoring table discussion led by Jenn on "Writing the Dissertation." Subsequently, both Beth and Jenn were new-hires together at Marquette where they developed and piloted a research-focused course, among many other ongoing projects. Beth shares that "[p]erhaps more than memories and initial connections with Jenn, I remember having good feelings about her and wanting to work together. So, when Kris [Ratcliffe] called and said that Jenn had already accepted an offer from Marquette, it was exciting and an easy decision to accept alongside her. (By the way, I first met Kris at a Coalition meeting, too . . . at the mentoring roundtable on WPA work)." Ask anyone who has attended the Wednesday night sessions over the years, and you will likely hear similar interconnected stories about camaraderie, serendipitous research/work intersections, and professional friendship.

But perhaps less well known than the Wednesday night sessions, Coalition members have, for nearly thirty years, rolled up their sleeves to help each other take advantage of mentoring networks to gain insights and expertise otherwise unavailable to them. These relationships provided advice and "human connections" for getting promoted, recognized, published, and aligned within the profession in overt and meaningful ways including traditional support such as writing grant and promotion/tenure letters of support; making phone calls on behalf of colleagues on the job market; and reading drafts of proposals, chapters, and manuscripts for each other. But over the years, as mentoring networks developed, the direction of mentorship also has reversed. Pre-tenure faculty members and graduate students offer advice to more experienced scholars regarding intersectional research, scholarship promotion via social media, as well as course and program (re)design.

This sense of someone having your back comes up repeatedly when members of the Coalition speak about the connections they have made by accessing the mentoring networks provided within the organization, particularly as expertise becomes more diverse in emerging areas of digital research and publishing; no longer is expertise delivered traditionally from established expert to apprentice. And for scholars working in isolation at their home institutions without faculty friends or vested dissertation directors, this sense of camaraderie is priceless. Thus, networked mentoring is put in the service of ethical action, social responsibility, and the interplay of generations of teachers and scholars that results in a view of mentoring that is not hierarchical but rather provides a system that has a life of its own—and can be accessed as members' needs arise, and shift, as illustrated in the following example.

New scholars who perhaps are initially seen as beneficiaries of a mentoring network, quickly become nodes themselves—working as colleagues within the system. For example, Letizia Guglielmo was a student of Lynée's but quickly became the conduit for publishing opportunities for the two. In a relatively short time, Letizia sought out professional development opportunities within her own/separate venues and areas of interest, bringing that knowledge to Lynée. The two have co-authored one book and edited another addressing contingent faculty issues, inviting a wide range of voices not regularly represented in traditional scholarship to join the conversation. Through this process, contributors to the collection also become nodes within the mentoring network for each other—folks who would not otherwise have become connected. The projects are published in an innovative print/online (vetted) format—one suggested by one of Lynée's current PhD students. Another of Lynée's students, working as an intern for a digital journal, arranged for an interview with Letizia and Lynée about their work with contingent faculty—an opportunity that wouldn't have come about otherwise. Letizia also introduced Lynée to her contacts within women's studies, resulting in a new trajectory for their collaborative work. Most recently, Letizia authored the Introduction to Lynée's new co-edited collection of essays, *Remembering Differently: Re-figuring Women's Rhetorical Work*, grounding the essays in a rich body of scholarship where Letizia holds expertise.

In an interview with former student and now colleague Jess Enoch, Glenn explains what it means to mentor graduate students, so they may establish their own mentoring networks for their generation of scholars:

> I try to assure students at every turn that their graduate student friends are the friends they are going to have for their lives. These are the people they are going to collaborate with and do conference presentations with. These are the people they are going to call to confide in about personal and professional issues. We have to mentor them to set up that kind of psychological and scholarly collaboration early on.

The Coalition has embodied and fostered such mentoring networks (discussed in Part I) since its inception. Horner explains how, in the early days, she and her colleagues from other universities tried to organize get-togethers at conferences for students so they could meet each other: "We also invited the well-known scholars in the field who responded with the expected grace of real scholars who are always interested in what young researchers are doing. The party was lively, and the conversation sparkled. Friendships were forged and ideas shared. It was networking at its best and mentoring at its finest" (17). And while these early meetings were more traditional in nature—whereby established scholars invited new scholars to join scholarly conversations, and young scholars actively kept others abreast of changes and new innovations within the profession—than the current mentoring network, these meetings quickly became more fluid. Nearly thirty years later, the Coalition's relationship-building work is now more accessible because of social networking technologies.

Internet communication technologies, like Facebook and Twitter, allow us to connect with other people easily in ways that didn't exist even a few years ago. The Coalition has created a social media position, greatly expanding the face and reach of the organization, keeping the organization relevant with recent blogs and threads redefining feminist activism. Specifically, the Coalition demonstrates ways an organization committed to mentoring must remain flexible to ensure the fluidity necessary for maintaining a network that both accommodates changing circumstances and is accessible to multitudes of participants. Building malleable mentoring networks can provide inclusive, collaborative mentoring experiences.

To begin constructing or recognizing a potential mentoring network, new and established members of a field first need to identify people within their own circle of advisors, students, mentors, and colleagues with whom they share similar teaching areas, research, service, and administrative interests. Then they need to trace the potential connections between these contacts. Specifically:

1. Find colleagues (students, colleagues at different career stages, administrators) interested in teaching or scholarly work, issues, or situations similar to you own.
2. Ask those you know for introductions to people doing the various kind of work you want to do or you are already doing.
3. Focus on building relationships not only with colleagues and people you know but also programs, online groups and listservs, and students/colleagues at other institutions—perhaps starting with mentoring forums sponsored by flagship organizations.
4. Use social media to connect with others across place and experience, following conference twitter feeds, social media group pages, and specific hashtags related to research or teaching interests.

5. Offer to serve as a reader for someone's work or exchange syllabi by establishing writing partnerships or groups.
6. Work with colleagues in other departments at your current institution to better learn the terrain at your school, paying close attention to college and university strategic mission statements, QEP initiatives, and internal support for your work.

As Jeff Rice explains, tracing "the connections, or relationships" with specific people in a network helps to "reveal patterns and hopefully provide insight" for your work (34). Along with the increasing digital presence and advocacy of the Coalition, other social networks like Women in Technical Communication (#womenintc), Rhetoricians of Health and Medicine (#medrhet), Digital Black Lit (Literatures & Literacies) and Composition (@DBLAC), #femrhet, #teamrhetoric, and #techcomm also provide productive digital mentoring networks where people can ask questions, make connections, and establish relationships.

Conclusion

Stories of Mentoring includes several shorter vignettes in which we briefly introduce and explore issues tangentially related to acts of mentoring networks. In "Making It Count: Mentoring as Cultural Currency," Tanya R. Cochran and Beth Godbee explain how the act of mentoring defies quantification. They suggest ways that we might move away from a banking metaphor associated with curriculum vita construction toward creating an integrated portfolio representing mentoring as a centralized, scholarly activity "that must be valued because it is valuable to the academy," not merely a service to an individual (301). We agree. The importance of establishing mentoring networks cannot be understated for both the individuals within the system and for the institutions themselves. Just as the success of the Coalition is due in great part to the organization's network-building enactment of mentoring, ongoing care for faculty is essential to the success of higher education, particularly given the rapidity of shifts in course delivery, the reduction of traditional tenure-track positions, and the abundance of strategic mission statements that downplay the role of faculty positions within commercial models of the new university. Renée Love in "A Mentoring Pedagogy" explains,

> As I think of my own mentors and life's lessons, I know that I have occupied both roles in many different forms. I realize that

> I have never had one great teacher or mentor; instead, I have been lucky to benefit from the guidance and the insights of a number of mentors, professors, and colleagues, and, at times, even strangers who passed along something of themselves to me perhaps purely for the sake of continuing the legacy of knowledge. (227)

We think Renée's experiences ring true for the majority of academics. First recognizing the concept of networked mentoring relationships and then overtly working to build and maintain such systems is vital to the happiness, success, and sustainability of faculty, students, and the academy at large.

Works Cited

Coalition of Feminist Scholars in the History of Rhetoric and Composition. http://cwshrc.org. Accessed 11 January 2017.

Cochran, Tanya H., and Beth Godbee. "Making It Count: Mentoring as Cultural Currency." *Stories of Mentoring: Theory and* Praxis, edited by Michelle F. Eble and Lynée Lewis Gaillet. Parlor, 2008, pp. 301–05.

Eble, Michelle F., and Lynée Lewis Gaillet, editors. *Stories of Mentoring: Theory and Praxis*. Parlor, 2008.

Eble, Michelle F., and Wendy Sharer, filmmakers. "In Their Own Words: The History and Influences of the Coalition." Screened at the meeting of the Coalition of Women Scholars in the History of Rhetoric and Composition. Conference on College Composition and Communication. New Orleans, LA. 2008.

Enoch, Jessica. "Feminist Rhetorical Studies—Past, Present, Future: An Interview with Cheryl Glenn." *Composition Forum*, vol. 29, Spring 2014, www.compositionforum.com/issue/29/cheryl-glenn-interview.php. Accessed 11 January 2017.

Fishman, Jenn, and Andrea Lunsford. "Educating Jane." *Stories of Mentoring: Theory and Praxis*, edited by Michelle F. Eble and Lynée Lewis Gaillet, Parlor, 2008, pp. 18–32.

Fishman, Jenn. "Coalition Mentoring Tables." Received by Lynee Lewis Gaillet, 15 Oct. 2013.

Gaillet, Lynée Lewis, and Helen Gaillet Bailey, editors. *Remembering Differently: Re-figuring Women's Rhetorical Work*. U of South Carolina P, 2019.

Gaillet, Lynée Lewis, and Michelle Eble. *Primary Research: People, Places, and Spaces*. Routledge, 2016.

Gaillet, Lynée Lewis, and Letizia Guglielmo. *Scholarly Publication in a Changing Academic Landscape: Models for Success*. Palgrave Pivot, 2014.

Gaillet, Lynee Lewis, and Letizia Guglielmo. "Professional Development off the Tenure Track." Blog post (vetted). *University of Venus: GenX Women in Higher Ed, Writing from Across the Globe*. Inside Higher Ed, 4 Aug. 2014, www.insidehighered.com/blogs/university-venus/professional-development. Accessed 5 Aug. 2014.

Godbee, Beth. "Coalition Mentoring Tables." Received by Lynée Lewis Gaillet, 15 Oct. 2013.

Guglielmo, Letizia, and Lynée Lewis Gaillet, editors. *Publishing in Community: Case Studies for Contingent Faculty Collaborations*. Palgrave Pivot. 2015.

Haas, Angela M., and Michelle F. Eble, editors. *Key Theoretical Frameworks: Teaching Technical Communication in the Twenty-First Century*. Utah State UP, 2018.

Horner, Winifred Bryan. "On Mentoring." *Stories of Mentoring: Theory and Praxis*, editors Michelle F. Eble and Lynée Lewis Gaillet, Parlor, 2008, pp. 14–17.

Lauer, Janice M. "Graduate Students As Active Members of the Profession: Some Questions for Mentoring." *Publishing in Rhetoric and Composition*, edited by Gary A. Olson and Todd W. Taylor, SUNY P, 1997, pp. 229–236.

Rice, Jeff. (2011). "Networked Assessment." *Computers and Composition*, vol. 28, pp. 28–39.

Rockquemore, Kerry Ann "A New Model of Mentoring." *Inside Higher Ed*, 15 October 2013. www.insidehighered.com/advice/2013/07/22/essay-calling-senior-faculty-embrace-new-style-mentoring.

Royster, Jacqueline Jones, and Gesa E. Kirsch. *Feminist Rhetorical Practices*. Southern Illinois UP, 2012.

Spinuzzi, Clay. "Introduction." Special Issue: Technical Communication in the Age of Distributed Work. *Technical Communication Quarterly*, vol. 16, no. 3, pp. 265–77.

Writing Studies Tree. 20 October 2013. https://www.writingstudiestree.org. Accessed 11 January 2017.

Contributors

Heather Brook Adams is Assistant Professor of English at the University of North Carolina Greensboro. Her scholarly and teaching interests include feminist rhetorics, historiography, visual rhetorics, multimodal composition, and technical writing. Her current book project explores rhetorics (and rhetorical silences) of unwed pregnancy in the United States. This project builds upon Heather's dissertation, "Secrets and Silences: Rhetorics of Unwed Pregnancy Since 1960," which won the Conference on College Composition and Communication's 2013 James Berlin Memorial Outstanding Dissertation Award.

Jean Bessette is Associate Professor of English at the University of Vermont, where her research and teaching interests include rhetoric and composition, archives and historiography, digital and multimedia, and gender and sexuality. She is the author of *Retroactivism in the Lesbian Archives: Composing Pasts and Futures*, which received the 2018 Winifred Bryan Horner Outstanding Book Award from the Coalition of Feminist Scholars in the History of Rhetoric and Composition. Her scholarship has appeared in journals including *Rhetoric Review*, *Rhetoric Society Quarterly*, *College Composition and Communication* and *Computers and Composition* as well in a number of edited collections. In addition to the Horner Book Award, she has received national awards for her work from the Conference on College Composition and Communication and the Rhetoric Society of America. Bessette holds a PhD in Critical and Cultural Studies from the University of Pittsburgh.

Michelle F. Eble is Associate Professor of rhetoric and technical communication at East Carolina University where she teaches technical and professional writing courses and research methods. She is the co-editor of *Stories on Mentoring: Theory and Praxis* (Parlor Press, 2008), co-author of *Primary Research & Writing: People, Places, Spaces* (Routledge, 2016), co-editor of *Reclaiming Accountability: Using the Work of Re/Ac-*

creditation and Large-Scale Assessment to Improve Writing Instruction and Writing Programs (Utah State UP, 2016), and co-editor of *Key Theoretical Frameworks: Teaching Technical Communication in the 21st Century* (Utah State UP, 2018). She has also published in *Computers and Composition, Technical Communication, Technical Communication Quarterly, PresentTense,* and several edited collections. She serves as Chair of ECU's Behavioral and Social Sciences Institutional Review Board, and Past President of the Association of Teachers of Technical Writing (ATTW).

Jessica Enoch is Associate Professor of English at the University of Maryland, where she teaches courses in feminist rhetoric, rhetorical theory and pedagogy, as well as first-year writing. She has published two manuscripts *Refiguring Rhetorical Education: Women Teaching African American, Native American, and Chicana/o Students, 1865–1911* (SIUP, 2008) and *Domestic Occupations: Spatial Rhetorics and Women's Work* (SIUP, 2019). With Dana Anderson, she co-edited the collection *Burke in the Archives: Using the Past to Transform the Future of Burkean Studies* (University of South Carolina Press, 2013); with David Gold, she published *Women at Work: Rhetorics of Gender and Labor* (University of Pittsburgh Press, 2019), and with Cristina D. Ramírez, she published *Mestiza Rhetorics: An Anthology of Mexicana Activism in the Spanish Language Press, 1875–1922* (SIUP, 2019). Her articles have appeared in *College English, College Composition and Communication, Rhetoric Society Quarterly, Rhetoric Review, Journal of Curriculum Studies,* and *Composition Studies*.

Rosalyn Collings Eves is Associate Professor at Southern Utah University. Her research interests include rhetorics of space in the work of nineteenth-century American women writers, particularly in the American West, as well as rhetoric and public memory. She has published in *Rhetoric Review* and *Legacy*, in addition to several edited collections. Outside of her academic work, she has published a trilogy with Knopf/Random House.

Lynée Lewis Gaillet is Professor and Chair of the English department at Georgia State University. She is author of numerous articles and book chapters addressing Scottish rhetoric, writing program administration, composition/rhetoric history and pedagogy, publishing matters, and archival research methods—and is a recipient of an NEH

Summer Research Award and ISHR Fellowship. Her book projects include: editor of *Scottish Rhetoric and It Influence* (1998); co-editor of *Stories of Mentoring* (2008), *The Present State of Scholarship in the History of Rhetoric* (2010), *Publishing in Community: Case Studies for Contingent Faculty Collaborations* (2015), and *On Archival Research* (2016). She is the co-author of *Scholarly Publication in a Changing Academic Landscape* (2014) and *Primary Research and Writing: People, Places, and Spaces* (2016). She is a past President of The Coalition of Feminist Scholars in the History of Rhetoric and Composition and Past Executive Director of the South Atlantic Modern Language Association.

Cheryl Glenn is Distinguished Professor of English and Women's Studies, Director of the Program in Writing and Rhetoric, and co-founder of Penn State's Center for Democratic Deliberation. She has earned numerous research, scholarship, teaching, and mentoring awards and has delivered lectures and workshops across North America, Europe, Asia, the Middle East, and Africa. In 2015, she received an honorary doctorate from Orebro University in Sweden for her rhetorical scholarship and influence. In 2019, she received the Conference on College Composition and Communication (CCCC) Exemplar Award. Professor Glenn's scholarly work focuses on histories of women's rhetorics and writing practices, feminist theories and practices, inclusionary rhetorical practices and theories, and contexts and processes for the teaching of writing. Her many scholarly publications include *Rhetoric Retold: Regendering the Tradition from Antiquity Through the Renaissance*; *Unspoken: A Rhetoric of Silence*; *Rhetorical Feminism and This Thing Called Hope*; *Silence and Listening as Rhetorical Arts*; *Landmark Essays on Rhetoric and Feminism*; *Rhetorical Education in America*; *The St. Martin's Guide to Teaching Writing*; *The Writer's Harbrace Handbook*; *Making Sense: A Real-World Rhetorical Reader*; *The Harbrace Guide for College Writers*; *Harbrace Essentials*; and numerous articles, chapters, and essays. She and Stephen Browne co-edit "Rhetoric and Democratic Deliberation," a Pennsylvania State University Press series. With Shirley Wilson Logan, she co-edits the Southern Illinois University Press series, "Studies in Rhetorics and Feminisms."

Karen A. Foss is a Regents Professor and professor of Communication & Journalism at the University of New Mexico. Her research and teaching interests include contemporary rhetorical theory, rhetorical criticism, feminist perspectives on communication, and social movements and social change. She is the coauthor or coeditor of *Gender Stories, Encyclopedia of Communication, Theories of Human Communication, Contemporary Perspectives on Rhetoric, Inviting Transformation, Feminist Rhetorical Theories,* and *Women Speak.* Dr. Foss's journal articles and book chapters have dealt with topics such as the Mothers of the Plaza de Mayo, feminine spectatorship in Garrison Keillor's monologues, Harvey Milk, and the birth-control debate in the Catholic Church. Her work has been recognized by various awards, including Regents Professor and Presidential Teaching Fellow at the University of New Mexico, Scholar of the Year from Humboldt State University, and the Francine Merritt Award and Robert J. Kibler Memorial Award from the National Communication Association. Dr. Foss received her Ph.D. in speech and dramatic art from the University of Iowa , her M.A. in speech from the University of Oregon, and her B.A. in Romance languages (French and Spanish) from the University of Oregon.

Sonja K. Foss is a professor in the Department of Communication at the University of Colorado Denver. Her research and teaching interests are in contemporary rhetorical theory and criticism, feminist perspectives on communication, the incorporation of marginalized voices into rhetorical theory, and visual rhetoric. She is the author or coauthor of the books *Gender Stories, Destination Dissertation, Rhetorical Criticism, Contemporary Perspectives on Rhetoric, Inviting Transformation, Feminist Rhetorical Theories,* and *Women Speak.* Her essays in communication journals have dealt with topics such as paradigms of change, invitational rhetoric, agency in the film Run Lola Run, visual argumentation, and body art. Her work has been recognized by various awards, including the Distinguished Scholar Award from the Western States Communication Association, the Francine Merritt Award and the Douglas W. Ehninger Distinguished Rhetorical Scholar Award from the National Communication Association, and the Distinguished Lifetime Achievement Award from the University of Colorado Denver. Dr. Foss earned her Ph.D. in communication studies from Northwestern University, her M.A. in speech from the University of Oregon, and her B.A. in Romance languages (French and Spanish) from the University of Oregon.

Anita Helle is Professor of English at Oregon State University, where she teaches courses in medical humanities, literacy and pedagogy, and modern American literature. She is affiliate faculty in the Program in Medical Humanities and in Women, Gender, and Sexuality Studies. Her recent research has focused on the histories and theories of archival formation and rhetorical canons of memory and on illness narrative. She is editor of *The Unraveling Archive* (University of Michigan Press, 2007) and *Theorizing Breast Cancer: Narrative, Politics, and Memory* (2013/2014) for Tulsa Studies in Women's Literature, co-edited with Mary K. DeShazer. She is co-editing a new volume of essays on Sylvia Plath, "Letters, Words, Fragments" for Bloomsbury Academic.

Jordynn Jack is Professor of English and Comparative Literature at the University of North Carolina, Chapel Hill, where she teaches courses in rhetorical theory, rhetoric of science, and women's rhetorics. She is the author of *Science on the Home Front: American Women Scientists in World War II* (University of Illinois Press, 2009) and *Autism and Gender: From Refrigerator Mothers to Computer Geeks* (University of Illinois Press, 2015), *Raveling the Brain: Toward a Transdisciplinary Neurorhetoric* (Ohio State University Press, 2019), and an edited collection, *Neurorhetorics* (Routledge, 2012). Her articles have appeared in *College English*, *College Composition and Communication*, *Rhetoric Society Quarterly*, *Rhetoric Review*, *Quarterly Journal of Speech*, and *Women's Studies in Communication*.

A. Abby Knoblauch is Associate Professor of English at Kansas State University. Her work has been published in a variety of venues, including *CCC* and *Composition Studies*. Her most recent work focuses on embodied rhetorics and fat rhetorics.

Shirley Wilson Logan is Professor Emerita in the English Department at the University of Maryland, where, prior to retirement, she taught writing, composition theory, the history of rhetoric, and women's rhetoric. Her publications include *With Pen and Voice: A Critical Anthology of Nineteenth-Century African American Women*, *We Are Coming: The Persuasive Discourse of Nineteenth-Century Black Women*, *Liberating Language: Site of Rhetorical Education in Nineteenth-Century Black America*, and essays in several collections and online. Logan is co-editor of the SIUP series Studies in Rhetorics and Feminisms, along with founding editor, Cheryl Glenn. The series has produced over fifteen volumes in the past thirteen years. She has also co-edited the collection *Academic and Professional Writing in an Age of Accountability* with Wayne Slater.

Brigitte Mral is Professor of Rhetoric, former professor of Media and Communication Studies at Örebro University/Sweden. She has published numerous books and articles concerning rhetoric in historical and contemporary situations, including: *Talande kvinnor. Kvinnliga retoriker från Aspasia till Ellen Key* (*Women Speakers. Women Rhetorics from Aspasia to Ellen Key*, 1999*),* "*We're a Peaceful Nation": War Rhetoric After September 11* (2003), *Women's Rhetoric. Argumentative Strategies of Women in Public Life: Sweden & South Africa* (2009) and *Bildens retorik i journalistiken* (*The Rhetoric of Images in Journalism,* 2011). She is currently leading a research project on "Rhetorical aspects of Crisis Communication" and head of the recently founded "Institute for Crisis Communication" at Örebro University.

Cristina D. Ramírez is Associate Professor at the University of Arizona (UA) where she teaches graduate classes in rhetorical history, theory and archival research methods. She was 2017 UA Social Behavioral Sciences Research Fellow for her latest work on barrio rhetorics and the recovery work of her grandmother, Ramona González's writings. She has published in *College English, Technical Communication Quarterly,* and her latest book, *Mestiza Rhetorics: An Anthology of Mexicana Activism in the Spanish Language Press, 1875–1922* is available through SIUP. She is Doctoral Program Director of Rhetoric, Composition, and the Teaching of English at the University of Arizona.

Krista Ratcliffe is a full professor and chair of the English Department at Arizona State University. Her research examines feminist contributions to rhetoric and composition studies as well as their intersections with critical race studies. *Anglo-American Feminist Challenges to the Rhetorical Traditions* studies how women's voices emerge in western rhetorical traditions. *Who's Having This Baby?* studies how women's voices emerge (or not) in literary and lived birthing narratives. *Rhetorical Listening* studies troubled identifications with gender and whiteness in public debates, rhetorical scholarship, and composition pedagogy; the latter won the 2006 JAC Gary Olson Book Award, the 2007 CCCC Outstanding Book Award, and the 2007 Rhetoric Society of America Book Award. Ratcliffe's research includes three co-edited collections, *Silence and Listening as Rhetorical Arts Feminisms* (with Cheryl Glenn); *Performing Feminist Administration in Rhetoric and Composition Studies* (with Rebecca Rickly); and *Rhetorics of Whiteness* (with Tammy Kennedy and Joyce Middleton), the latter being awarded the 2017 CCCC Outstanding Edited Collection Award.

Elaine Richardson is Professor of Literacy Studies, Department of Teaching and Learning. She is a graduate of the Cleveland Public Schools. She received her B.A. and M.A. from Cleveland State University, and the Ph.D. from Michigan State University. Dr. Richardson's research interests include language, literacy, and discourse practices of Afro-diasporic cultures, sociolinguistics, critical discourse studies, and the education and literacy of Afro diasporic people. Richardson belongs to a network of scholars interested in hip hop and education. Her outreach efforts include cultural literacy projects focusing on youth empowerment and mentoring. She is author of *Hiphop Literacies* (2006, Routledge), *African American Literacies* (2003, Routledge), and co-editor of *Home Girls Make Some Noise: Hip Hop Feminism Anthology* (with Dr. Gwendolyn Pough, Rachel Raimist, and Aisha Durham, Parker Publishing, 2007).

Wendy B. Sharer, Professor of English at East Carolina University, is co-editor of *Working in the Archives: Practical Research Methods for Rhetoric and Composition* (SIUP 2009), author of *Vote & Voice: Women's Organizations and Political Literacy, 1915–1930* (SIUP 2004), co-author of *1977: A Cultural Moment in Composition* (Parlor 2008), and co-editor of *Rhetorical Education in America* (Alabama 2004). Her scholarship has also appeared in the journals *Rhetoric Society Quarterly* and *Rhetoric Review* and in the anthologies *Rhetorical Bodies* (Wisconsin 1999) and *Professing Rhetoric* (Erlbaum, 2002). Currently, she is researching the teaching of writing in the camps of the Civilian Conservation Corps during the 1930s and the life of Julia Grace Wales, an early twentieth-century educator and peace activist.

Berit von Lippe is Professor in the Department of Communication, Culture and Languages at Handelshøyskolen BI (Norwegian Business School). Her research interests include semiotics, war rhetoric, critical feminist studies, mass media, and rhetoric and gender. She is author of *Reklame I Grenselaus Knoppskyting (Advertising on the Boundless Spin)*, a book of essays, *Metaforens Potens (Powerful Metaphors)*, editor and coauthor of multiple books and numerous articles such as "Surgical Warfare—Surgical Media Covering," which appeared in *Media, Politics, and Society* and "The White Woman's Burden—Feminist War Rhetoric and the Phenomenon of Cooptation" in *Nordic Journal of Feminist and Gender Research*. She teaches courses in rhetoric, gender and co-optation, post-colonial perspectives and liberal (Western) feminism, and gendered rhetorical strategies in mass media at Norwegian Business School and at outside universities.

INDEX

12 Years a Slave (film), 275

2012 Presidential election, 34, 35, 36, 37, 41, 43, 44
2016 US Presidential Election, 7, 8, 50, 51

able-bodiedness, 250, 252
abolition, 22, 29, 31
abortion, 38–40, 46
activism, 19, 25–27, 32, 118, 127, 140, 143, 165, 175, 188–189, 217, 235–236, 300
Adams, Heather, 11–12, 139, 295, 297
Afghan women, 8, 68–72, 75–82, 84–85, 87
Afghanistan, 71, 75–80, 82, 84–85, 88–90
African American female literacies (AAFL), 228, 233–234
African American Policy Forum, 231–232, 242
Akin, Todd, 40
American Anthropological Association (AAA), 150
American Historical Association (AHA), 147
American Psychological Association (APA), 150
American West, 10, 97–98, 113
Anderson, Dana, 105
Anderson, Paul V., 149

antistrephon, 59, 64
Anzaldúa, Gloria, 174, 181, 197, 255, 263, 266–268, 279, 280
Applegarth, Risa, 96–97, 113
appreciating, 269–271, 275, 278
apprenticeship model, 283, 285
Arab Spring, 27
archives, 4, 10, 11, 117–121, 123–124, 126, 129, 132–134, 171, 179, 203–204, 207, 209, 211, 213, 215, 217–218
archivettes, 118, 128–129
argumentation, 56, 216
Aristotle, 21, 95, 113, 120
artifacts, 10–11, 118–119, 123–127, 129–130, 141, 179, 210, 217, 275
Askew, Ann, 32
Aspasia, 20, 32, 55, 66
Association of Teachers of Technical Writing (ATTW), 292
auto-thanatography, 203

Banks, William P., 249–250, 254, 260, 289
Belmont Report, 146
Berlin Wall, 275
Bessette, Jean, 10, 117, 122, 134
Black Power Movement, 233
BlackGirlsUnite, 13, 234–236, 242
blogs, 51–52, 56, 208, 291, 300, 303

313

Boston, 25–26, 33, 89, 245
BRCA (gene), 204, 210–213, 219–220
breast cancer, 12, 202–218
Burke, Kenneth, 11, 14, 26, 27, 32, 49, 51, 66, 106, 110, 114, 120, 121, 134, 141, 160, 218, 219
Burke, Peter, 58
Burma, 8, 20, 28–29
burqa, 70

Calafell, Bernadette, 255, 260
Call, Caroline Healy, 8, 20, 22–23, 25, 32
Charon, Rita, 205, 219
Cheney, Dick, 45
Chihuahuita, 175–176, 178
Christianity, 32, 46, 99, 105, 185, 200
Christoph, Julie Nelson, 97, 113
civic discourse, 26
Civil Rights Movement, 233
Clark, Gregory, 96, 110–112, 114, 190, 199
class, 8, 9, 49, 55, 58, 72, 95, 96, 102, 120, 124, 132, 165, 175, 185, 196–197, 228, 235, 236–237, 248, 249–250, 253, 256, 258–259, 286
classification, 119, 120–128, 130–133, 183
Clinton, Bill, 47
Clinton, Hillary, 50
Coalition of Feminist Scholars in the History of Rhetoric and Composition, 160, 192, 198, 284, 286, 292–303
Cochran, Tanya, 297, 301–302
Coit, Eleanor, 131–132
collaboration, 12, 70, 76–77, 141, 143–144, 148–149, 151–152, 158, 184, 191, 285, 291, 293–294, 299

Collaborative Institutional Training Initiative (CITI), 140, 150, 156, 159–160
Collins, Hill, 228, 234–235, 243
Common Rule, 146–149, 154, 158
compliance, 140–153, 156, 158–159, 228, 235, 238
composition, 149, 151, 184–186, 188–189, 191, 193, 198, 200, 247, 248–249, 265, 294, 297
computer networks, 288
Computers and Writing Conference, 293
Condit, Celeste, 67, 264, 272, 279, 280
Conference on College Composition and Communication (CCCC), 34, 44, 151, 160, 260, 281, 293–294, 297
conservatives, 45–47, 49–50
constricted potentiality, 262–263, 274, 279
co-optation, 71
Council for Programs in Technical and Scientific Communication (CPTSC), 291
cultural logics, 35–36, 42–50
culture, 9, 44, 57, 65, 70, 81, 87, 100, 112, 164, 167–169, 172, 174, 176–179, 206, 207, 213, 226, 233, 235, 237, 251, 254
Cushman, Ellen, 140, 143, 160

Dalai Lama, 267, 269, 280
Dallas Buyers Club (film), 275
Daly, Mary, 197
Daughters of Bilitis, 122, 125–126, 134
Davis, Angela, 32
Davis, D. Diane, 121
Delagrange, Susan, 125, 127, 129, 134, 185–187, 190–192, 194–195, 198–199

Democrats, 34, 41, 44, 46–47, 49–51
Derr, Jill, 99–101, 109, 114
DeShazer, Mary, 12, 202, 207, 219
Dickinson, Anna, 20
differend, 49
digital publishing, 185, 190, 192, 296
Diotima, 32
disability, 9, 286
disciplinary expertise, 14
discourse analysis, 228, 238
discrimination, 20, 39, 55
disease, 120–123, 129, 202, 207, 209–210, 212–214, 218, 268
diversity, 55, 60, 78, 118, 131, 133, 158, 167, 180, 188, 209
divisio, 120, 128
division, 106, 120–121, 214
Django Unchained (film), 275
Donawerth, Jane, 6, 14
Drug Abuse Resistance Education (D.A.R.E), 273
Dussel, Enrique, 12, 14, 165, 169, 174, 176, 181

Eble, Michelle, 13, 283, 295, 302, 303
Ede, Lisa, 186, 200, 203, 219, 265, 280, 295
Ehrenreich, Barbara, 217
Einwohner, Rachel L., 155, 160
El Grito, 170, 176, 182
embodied rhetoric, 13, 208, 248–251, 254–256, 259
embodied writing, 249
enacting, 269, 273, 275–276, 278, 289, 293
enargia, 22, 25
Enculturation, 134, 191
Enoch, Jessica, 3, 11, 14–15, 32, 117, 120, 133, 134, 157, 160, 163–164, 172, 182, 203, 220, 286, 299, 302
epideictic, 24, 26, 56, 100, 102, 164, 205–206
epideictic (rhetoric), 24, 26, 56, 100, 102, 164, 205–206
epideictic rhetoric, 209
epistemologies: feminist, 144
Ethecon Blue Planet Award, 27
ethnicity, 55, 77, 96, 172, 197, 250, 286
ethos, 21, 56, 58, 73, 83, 85, 96–97, 101, 102, 104, 144, 175, 215, 263, 284
European Union (EU), 74–75, 86, 90
Eves, Rosalyn Collins, 10, 95, 114
exploitation, 22

Facebook, 56, 61, 64, 300
Faremo, Grete, 69, 83, 84, 85, 86, 89
feminist discourse, 8
feminist historiography, 3
feminist pedagogy, 236, 242, 246–247, 249, 259
feminist rhetorics, 3, 5–11, 13, 19, 20, 54, 69, 71, 87, 88, 95, 96, 141, 148, 174, 179–180, 214, 246–248, 251, 259–260, 263, 284
feminist rhetorical criticism, 54
feminist rhetorical research, 5, 7
feminist scholars, 4–6, 8, 11–12, 14, 55, 133, 142–143, 145, 150, 154–155, 180, 209, 248, 284
Field, Kate, 103
Finney, Nikky, 8, 20, 23, 24, 25, 26
Fishman, Jenn, 286, 297, 302
Flashback, 56
Fluke, Sandra, 38
Foss, Karen A., 13

316 *Index*

Foss, Sonia K., 13
Foucault, Michel, 120, 121, 134, 208, 219
Friess, Foster, 37–38, 51, 52

Gaillet, Lynée Lewis, 13, 283, 302–303
Galindo, Hermila, 170
Gandhi, Mahatma, 31
gay, 39, 118, 122, 256
Gbowee, Leymah, 8, 20–23, 25, 30, 32–33
Gearhart, Sally Miller, 263, 281
Gee, James Paul, 228, 238, 243
gender, 8–9, 34, 42–43, 45, 48, 54–55, 56, 60, 68–69, 71–75, 80, 82–87, 95–96, 98, 117–118, 120, 128, 132, 133, 165, 170, 225, –226, 230–232, 234–235, 237, 240–241, 249–250, 252, 255, 257, 286
gender equality, 8, 68–69, 71–75, 80, 83, 85–86, 231
gendered groups, 6, 57, 68, 86, 96–98, 165, 169–170, 179, 197, 203, 212–213, 227, 232–233, 240, 254, 256–258, 286
genres, 12, 60, 141, 184–192, 194–195, 197, 202–203, 205
Gilligan, Carol, 10–11
Glenn, Cheryl, 3–4, 11, 14, 27, 32, 34–36, 50–52, 55–57, 60–61, 64, 66, 70, 72, 86, 88–89, 95–96, 113–114, 117, 120, 133–134, 140, 160, 163–164, 171–173, 179–182, 184, 198–199, 203, 213, 215, 219–220, 225–226, 243, 259–260, 262, 265, 280–281, 286, 295, 299, 302; *Rhetoric Retold*, 3–5, 14, 32, 95–96, 114, 179, 181, 225, 243, 281
globalization, 69

Godbee, Beth, 297, 301–303
Goldwater, Barry, 45
GOP, 40–41
Graduate Research Network (GRN), 293
graduate students, 164, 166, 180, 183, 186, 191, 237, 283, 285–286, 289–294, 296, 298, 299
Grumet, Madeleine, 252, 254, 260
Guglielmo, Letizia, 299, 303
Gutter Letter, 131–132

Harlem Renaissance, 233
Harper, Francis, 8, 20, 29–31, 33, 219, 266, 281–282
hate speech, 65
Helle, Anita, 12, 202, 214, 219–220
hermeneutics, 9, 215, 218
Hesford, Wendy, 72, 79, 87, 89
heterosexual, 8–9, 121, 129
heuristics, 6, 9, 166
hierarchy, 58, 148, 187, 191, 290
Higginbotham, Evelyn Brooks, 20
Hindman, Jane E., 249–250, 260
historiographic methods, 4
historiography, 44, 48, 164
history of rhetoric, 3–4, 12, 55, 96, 189, 294
HIV-AIDS, 209
Hogg, Charlotte, 174, 182
Holy Land, 107, 111, 115
homosexuality, 120–122
hooks, bell, 62, 225–226, 244, 263, 273, 281
Horner, Winifred Bryan, 293, 295, 299, 303
human subjects research, 11
Hurricane, The (film), 275

identification, 26–27, 29–31, 45–47, 49, 62, 72, 78–80, 82–87, 101, 106, 110, 112, 119–123,

129–130, 132–133, 165–166, 180, 232
identity, 5, 8–10, 12, 14, 28, 43, 56, 64, 73, 95, 96–106, 109–113, 118–119, 121, 123–124, 126, 131–133, 155, 167, 169–170, 174, 176, 179–180, 194, 210–213, 226, 238, 250–251; Chicana, 9, 12, 164–166, 168–170, 172, 174, 176, 178–179, 182, 200; lesbian, 10, 117–119, 125, 127–128, 131–132, 133; queer, 127; racial, 99, 103; religious, 97, 107; sexual, 118, 121–122, 124, 126; spiritual, 104, 107, 110
identity studies, 5, 8
ideology, 71, 233, 240, 251; feminist, 72
indigenous people, 7
individualism, 45–47, 228
Ing-wen, Tsai, 7
Institutional Review Board (IRB), 11, 12, 139–141, 144–152, 154–156, 158, 159–161, 248
interpretive agency, 264–267, 269, 274–275, 279
intersectionality, 9–10, 210, 231, 247, 298
invitational rhetoric, 259, 263
Irigaray, Luce, 197
irony, 32, 36, 59, 158
Islam, 68, 87

Jack, Jordynn, 3, 15, 96, 115, 135, 221; *Science on the Home Front*, 4
Jain, S. Lochlann, 218, 220
Jewish, 9, 230
Johnson, Lyndon, 36
Johnson, Nan, 293, 295
Johnson, Sonia, 263
Joya, Malalai, 69, 75–76, 89–90

Julian of Norwich, 32, 96

kairos, 5, 72, 87, 151, 201, 209, 211–212, 287
Kairos (journal), 134, 191, 201, 220
kairotic moments, 5, 287
Karman, Tawakkol, 8, 20–21, 27–29, 33
Keller, Evelyn Fox, 10, 14
Kelly, Abby, 20, 245
Kempe, Margery, 20, 32, 114
Khan, Bacha, 31
King, Jr., Martin Luther, 28, 31
Kirsch, Gesa E., 6, 15, 143, 146, 157, 159, 161–162, 164–165, 182, 184–186, 189–190, 193, 199–204, 213, 220–221, 248, 251, 261, 284, 303
Knoblauch, A. Abby, 13, 246, 250, 261
Kolberg, Lawrence, 10
Kornheiser, Tony, 256–258, 261
Kuugongelwa, Saara, 7
Kynard, Carmen, 228, 232, 241, 244

Ladson-Billings, Gloria, 229, 244
lesbian, 9–10, 117–119, 122–134
Lesbian Herstory Archives (LHA), 10, 117–119, 123, 128, 133–134
LGBTQ issues, 7
liberals, 37
Library of Congress, 121–122, 124
Licona, Adele, 172, 182
Limbaugh, Rush, 38, 39, 52, 53
listening: rhetorical, 8, 9, 36, 50, 70, 72, 80–81, 85, 193, 205, 214, 218, 259
literacy, 11, 13, 24, 31, 141–142, 174–175, 191, 226–229, 232–235, 238, 241
location: politics of, 9, 11, 185, 248

Logan, Shirley Wilson, 5, 8, 15, 19–20, 33–34
Lyon, Phyllis, 122, 134

marginalized groups, 11, 31, 55, 165–166, 285
Martin, Del, 122, 126
Martin, Trayvon, 230
masculinist privilege, 7
maternity, 139, 154, 155
McCarthyism, 152
McDonnell, Bob, 38, 52
media, 36–38, 41–42, 45–47, 60, 61, 64, 76, 87, 90, 126, 190–191, 194, 210, 235, 300
Meeker, Martin, 146–147, 150, 161
memory studies, 4, 96
Mendoza, Juana Belén Gutiérrez de, 170
mentoring, 5, 12–14, 184, 188, 192, 234, 283–303; feminist, 13, 283, 285
mentoring networks, 13, 283–301
Merkel, Angela, 7
mestiza, 4, 164, 167, 172
metaphor, 36–37, 56, 105, 207, 249, 264, 301
methodologies, 5–6, 11, 133, 142, 145, 184–185, 195, 205, 207, 213, 248, 283, 291, 294, 296
methodology, 5–6, 11, 133, 142, 144–145, 184–185, 195, 205, 207, 213, 248, 283, 291, 294, 296
metonymy, 110
Mexican Revolution, 170, 178
Mexico, 4, 12, 115, 166–168, 170–171, 173, 175, 178
Micciche, Laura, 246–247, 261
Middleton, Joyce Irene, 34
Miller, Carolyn, 9, 15, 171, 186, 200, 211, 220, 263, 281

Miller, Elizabeth, 9, 15, 171, 186, 200, 211, 220, 263, 281
Min-ha, Trinh, 197
Mitchell, Andrea, 37, 102, 105, 107, 115, 261
moral authority, 8, 21
Mormon Church, 98–99, 100, 268
Mormons, 10, 95, 97–114, 168, 268; women, 10, 98–108, 110–112
mothers, 9, 59, 104, 109, 139–141, 148, 153–158, 237, 273
Mountford, Roxanne, 96–97, 115
Mourdock, Richard, 41, 47, 51
Mral, Brigitte, 8, 54–56, 66
My Brother's Keeper (MBK), 230

narratives, 12, 22– 23, 68, 74, 76, 104–107, 110, 165–166, 178, 197, 202, 204–207, 209, 210–213, 215–216, 218
National Assessment of Educational Progress (NAEP), 229
National Book Award, 23
National Institutes of Health (NIH), 145
National Research Act (1974), 145
nationality, 9, 132
NATO, 73, 75, 84, 88
Nestle, Joan, 117–118, 122–124, 128–130, 132–134
net hate, 8, 54, 56–57, 60–61, 63–65
Nobel Prize, 19–22, 27–29, 32–33
Norway, 8, 9, 27, 54–57, 60, 64, 66, 69, 71–88, 90
Nuremberg Code (1947), 145

Obama, Barack, 31, 37, 47, 52, 230, 244
Obama, Michelle, 37, 237
objectivity, 10
Old Testament, 25

oppression, 20, 70, 71, 165, 227, 230, 235, 241, 270
oral history, 145, 147–148, 150, 152, 154–155, 158
Oral History Association (OHA), 147
otherness, 70

pathography, 202, 206–207, 214–216, 218
patriarchy, 176, 227, 272
pay it forward, 283–284
pedagogical practices, 13, 197, 247, 259, 260
Peitho, 160, 192–193, 198, 290, 296–297
Perl, Sondra, 297
Perry, Rick, 37
persuasion, 20–21, 78, 262–263, 265, 268, 288
Phaedrus (Plato), 120, 135
Planned Parenthood, 39, 46, 51
Plato, 32, 120, 135
poetry, 25, 100, 132, 164, 168, 171, 197, 234, 237
political discourse, 8, 36–37, 41, 50, 71, 76
polygamy, 100, 102–104
pornography, 37, 121–122
Pough, Gwendolyn, 235, 241, 244
Powell, Katrina, 140, 143–144, 151, 155, 161, 184, 200
power, 7, 9–10, 13, 19, 22, 31, 43, 45–46, 48, 50, 54–55, 57–59, 64–65, 85–88, 98, 100, 102, 110, 132, 143–144, 173, 180, 185–186, 196–198, 211, 214, 228, 230, 236, 240–241, 247–253, 258, 262–268, 270–271, 285, 291; political, 74, 102; rhetorical, 32, 59, 60, 279
power dynamics, 13

power relations, 54–55, 59, 65, 247
pregnancy, 40, 47, 53, 139, 154, 273, 284
presence, 24, 68, 79, 82, 191, 216, 247, 250, 301
progymnasmata, 23
proyecto, 12, 165–166, 169, 172, 174–176, 178, 181
publishing: digital, 185, 190, 192, 296
publishing practices, 64, 82, 163, 183, 184–185, 188, 191–192, 193, 289, 297–299
Puritans, 107

queer, 118–123, 127, 133, 165, 202

race, 6, 25, 26, 72, 98–99, 103–104, 165, 167, 169, 181, 208, 227, 231–233, 237, 259
racism, 20, 47, 57, 227–228, 230, 232, 234–236
Ramírez, Cristina, 4, 12, 15, 163, 167, 173, 181–182
rape, 38, 40–41, 47, 50, 51, 53, 62, 231, 236, 240
Ratcliff, Krista, 8–9, 15, 34, 36, 42, 50, 52, 55, 66, 70, 72, 81, 90, 193, 203, 220, 259, 261, 297–298; *Rhetorical Listening*, 15, 35, 44, 52, 79, 90, 200, 202, 259, 261
Reagan, Nancy, 36
Reagan, Ronald, 36, 45
reflexivity, 144, 159, 166, 248
reframing, 71, 269–270, 275, 278
regendering, 4, 225–226, 246
Relief Society (Mormon's), 100–101, 108–109, 113, 116
religion, 9, 36–37, 47, 56, 99, 105, 112, 165
religious conservatism, 46

reproductive rights, 7, 36–39, 41, 46
Republicans, 34, 39, 41–42, 44–47, 49–52, 102
Republican National Committee, 41
Republican Party, 34, 41–42, 44, 45
research methods, 5, 10–11, 14, 158, 184, 185, 296
Research Network Forum (RNF), 293
resistance, 8, 22–23, 29, 37, 47, 54, 57, 59–61, 64–66, 70, 140, 151, 181, 205, 241, 272
Retrenchment (societies), 108
Reynolds, Nedra, 95–96, 115
rhetoric: and power, 32, 59, 60, 279; epideictic, 24, 26, 56, 77, 100, 102, 164, 205–206; history of, 3–4, 12, 55, 96, 189, 294 ; political, 34, 202
rhetoric and composition, 12, 142, 163, 164, 166, 169, 184, 187–188, 283
Rhetoric Review, 15, 114, 187, 199
rhetorical agency, 7, 85, 262, 279
rhetorical canons, 203
rhetorical criticism: feminist, 54
rhetorical education, 4, 186, 226
rhetorical history, 4, 96, 180, 225–226, 246
rhetorical listening, 8–9, 36, 50, 70, 72, 80–81, 85, 193, 205, 214, 218, 259
rhetorical situation, 8, 20–21, 43, 48, 50, 57–58, 61, 63, 84, 96, 186
rhetorical theory, 5, 13, 55, 57, 120, 180, 203, 246, 256, 265
rhetorical tradition, 96, 247

rhetorics: feminist, 246–248, 259; of the body, 3; of resistance, 54, 56; regional, 97; spatial, 4
Rice, Jeff, 301
Rice, Jenny, 97, 115, 303
Rich, Adrienne, 9–11, 15, 165, 182
risk, 63, 101, 140, 142, 146–154, 179, 191, 204, 210–211, 231, 268, 273
Ritchie, Joy, 59, 67, 165, 182, 185–186, 190, 199, 246, 248, 251, 261
Rockquemore, Kerry Ann, 286–287, 303
Rohan, Liz, 164, 182, 184, 199, 213, 220
Romney, Mitt, 37, 40, 51
Royster, Jacqueline Jones, 6, 11, 15, 70, 87, 90, 157, 162, 171, 173–174, 182, 184, 189, 193, 200, 204, 221, 227, 245, 284, 303
Rumsfeld, Donald, 45

Santorum, Rick, 37
Sapir-Whorf hypothesis, 264
Sappho, 32, 132
Saudi Arabia, 36
Schrag, Zachary, 145, 152, 154, 162
Second Great Awakening, 106
self-determination, 279
sexism, 20, 47, 56, 60, 62, 65, 227, 232, 234–236, 259
sexual abuse, 266
sexual behavior, 38–39
sexuality, 9, 36, 38, 50, 98, 120–123, 127, 226, 235, 252, 286
Sharer, Wendy B., 12, 120, 135, 164, 175, 182–184, 200, 286, 289, 295, 302
Sheriff, Stacey, 9, 15
Shome, Raka, 72, 90

signifying, 36, 196, 227
silence, 5, 8, 12, 14, 30, 34–37, 42–44, 48–50, 55, 57–60, 62–63, 65, 69–70, 72, 77, 84–86, 88, 140, 155, 179, 189, 197–198, 203, 205, 212–214, 248, 255
silencing, 5, 7–8, 57, 60, 68, 71–72, 75, 86, 88, 154, 165, 174, 184
Sirleaf, Ellen Johnson, 21–22, 33
Slave Codes of South Carolina, 24
slavery, 22, 102, 227
Smith, Joseph, 99
Snow, Eliza R., 10, 97–114, 116
social construction, 240, 264–265
social media, 57, 232, 296, 298, 300
Sontag, Susan, 204, 207, 217, 218, 221
space: physical, 112, 120
spatial narratives, 104, 105
spatial rhetorics, 4
Spinuzzi, Clay, 287–288, 303
Spivak, Gayatri, 68, 71, 81, 84, 90
Stanton, Elizabeth Cady, 20
Starhawk, 263–264, 282
status, 22, 45, 54–58, 64, 65–66, 86, 106, 172, 179, 234, 267, 275, 283, 289, 296
stereotypes, 39, 60, 112, 129, 233
Stewart, Maria, 8, 20, 25–26, 32–33
stigma, 80–81
Stories of Mentoring (Eble and Gaillet), 283–285, 301–303
Strøm-Erichsen, Anne-Grete, 69, 74–79, 81–83, 85–87
Student Nonviolent Coordinating Committee, 273
subjectivity, 11, 68, 70, 207, 213
suffrage, 7, 56
Supreme Court (US), 268

Survey of Doctoral Programs in Rhetoric and Composition, 187, 199
Suu Kyi, Aung San, 8, 20, 28, 29, 32
Swearingen, C. Jan, 293
synecdoche, 36, 119, 125, 130–133

Taft, William, 45
Takayoshi, Pamela, 140, 143–144, 151, 155, 161, 184, 200
Taliban, 19, 30, 33, 76
Tea Party, 34, 42, 47
terministic screens, 218
testaments, 214
testimony, 79–81, 147, 209
third-world women, 8
thrival, 270
Tovey, Janice, 290
trained incapacity, 11, 141, 144, 204, 218
transnationalism, 5, 7, 14, 19, 20, 29, 31, 202, 211
trolls (internet), 61, 65
tropes, 8, 35, 36, 37, 41–42, 44–48, 50, 110, 111, 119, 207
Truth, Sojourner, 20, 226, 227, 242, 244, 245, 281
Tuskegee Syphilis Study, 145

United Nations, 33, 71, 74–76, 78, 83–86, 89, 91
Uppdrag granskning (*Mission: Investigation*), 61, 67
Utah, 10, 99–116, 190, 199, 303

veils, 70, 87
victim, 79, 81, 157
victims, 39, 40, 57, 65, 69, 71, 79–81, 86, 103, 155, 231, 270
Violence Against Women Act, 39

Walker, Alice, 271, 282

Walker, David, 25
Walker, Scott, 39, 52
Walsh, Joe (Illinois congressman), 40, 52
Waples, Emily, 211–213, 216, 221
war, 8, 22, 34–52, 56, 62, 68–71, 74, 75, 81, 84–88, 170, 207; narratives, 68–69; on terror, 68, 70–71, 81, 87; rhetorics of, 68–69
war on women, 8, 34–38, 41, 45–48, 50
war-on-women debates, 34–46, 48–49, 51
war-on-women trope, 37, 42–46, 49
Weber, Max, 58
Welch, Kathleen, 293, 295
Well of Loneliness, The (Radclyffe Hall), 132
Wells, Ida B., 20, 205, 221
White House Council on Women and Girls (WHCWG), 231
Willard, Frances, 20
Williams, Fannie Barrier, 29, 30, 33, 40, 47, 53

William-White, Lisa, 195–196
Wilson, Timothy D., 278
women: Afghan, 8, 68–71, 72, 75–82, 84–85, 87; African American, 11, 20, 33, 174, 210, 226, 235; Chinese, 3; Mexican, 163–165, 166–171, 175, 176, 179–180; Native American, 3
Women in the World Summit, 22
women rhetors, 4, 54–55, 169
Woods, Marjorie Currie, 293
World War I, 175
World War II, 73, 145
Wright de Kleinhans, Laureana, 170–171, 173
Writing Studies Tree, 292, 303

Young, Brigham, 99–100, 108, 113–114
Yousafzai, Malala, 19–20, 30–33

Zander, Benjamin, 278
Zander, Rosamund Stone, 278
Zeiger, Melissa, 208, 221
Zion, 95, 98, 101, 104–112, 116

www.ingramcontent.com/pod-product-compliance
Lightning Source LLC
Chambersburg PA
CBHW021647230426
43668CB00008B/544